NO
MORE
BASHING

BUILDING A NEW

JAPAN-UNITED STATES

ECONOMIC RELATIONSHIP

NO
MORE
BASHING

BUILDING A NEW
JAPAN-UNITED STATES
ECONOMIC RELATIONSHIP

C. FRED BERGSTEN
TAKATOSHI ITO
MARCUS NOLAND

Institute for International Economics
Washington, DC
October 2001

C. Fred Bergsten has been director of the Institute since its creation in 1981. He was also chairman of the Competitiveness Policy Council, which was created by Congress, throughout its existence from 1991 to 1995 and chairman of the APEC Eminent Persons Group throughout its existence from 1993 to 1995. He was Assistant Secretary for International Affairs of the US Treasury (1977-81), Assistant for International Economic Affairs to the National Security Council (1969-71), and a senior fellow at the Brookings Institution (1972-76), the Carnegie Endowment for International Peace (1981), and the Council on Foreign Relations (1967-68). He is the author, coauthor, or editor of 28 books on a wide range of international economic issues, including Whither APEC? The Progress to Date and Agenda for the Future (1997), Global Economic Leadership and the Group of Seven (1996), The Dilemmas of the Dollar (second edition, 1996), Reconcilable Differences? United States-Japan Economic Conflict with Marcus Noland (1993), Pacific Dynamism and the International Economic System with Marcus Noland (1993), America in the World Economy: A Strategy for the 1990s (1988).

Takatoshi Ito is a professor at the Institute of Economic Research at Hitotsubashi University in Japan. From 1999 to 2001, he served as Deputy Vice Minister for International Finance in the Ministry of Finance in Japan. He was senior advisor at the research department of the International Monetary Fund from 1994 to 1997. He was professor at the University of Minnesota's economics department from 1990 to 1991; visiting professor at Harvard University's Kennedy School of Government and Department of Economics from 1992 to 1994; visiting scholar at the Bank of Japan's Institute of Monetary and Economic Studies from 1990 to 1992; and national fellow at the Hoover Institution, Stanford University, from 1984 to 1985. He has received grants from the National Science Foundation and is a research associate at the National Bureau of Economic Research. He has written extensively on international finance, macroeconomic issues, and the Japanese economy. He is the author of The Japanese Economy (MIT Press, 1992) and coauthor of A Vision for the World Economy (Brookings Institution, 1996) and Political Economy of the Bank of Japan Monetary Policy (MIT Press, forthcoming).

Marcus Noland, senior fellow at the Institute, has been senior economist for international economics at the Council of Economic Advisers as well as a visiting professor at Johns Hopkins University, the University of Southern California, Tokyo University, Saitama University, and the University of Ghana and a visiting scholar at the Korea Development Institute. He has written many articles on international economics and is the

author of Avoiding the Apocalypse: The Future of the Two Koreas (2000) and Pacific Basin Developing Countries: Prospects for the Future (1990). He is coauthor of Global Economic Effects of the Asian Currency Devaluations (1998), Reconcilable Differences? United States-Japan Economic Conflict with C. Fred Bergsten (1993), and Japan in the World Economy with Bela Balassa (1988), coeditor of Pacific Dynamism and the International Economic System (1993), and editor of Economic Integration of the Korean Peninsula (1998).

INSTITUTE FOR INTERNATIONAL ECONOMICS
1750 Massachusetts Avenue, NW
Washington, DC 20036-1903
(202) 328-9000 FAX: (202) 328-5432
http://www.iie.com

C. Fred Bergsten, Director
Brigitte Coulton, Director of Publications and Web Development
Brett Kitchen, Director of Marketing

Typesetting and printing by Automated Graphic Systems, Inc.
Cover design by Naylor Design, Inc.

Printed in the United States of America
03 02 01   5 4 3 2 1

Library of Congress Cataloging-in-Publication Data

Bergsten, C. Fred, 1941–
  No More Bashing: Building a New Japan-United States Economic Relationship / C. Fred Bergsten, Takatoshi Ito, Marc Noland.
    p. cm.
  Includes bibliographical references and index.
  ISBN 0-88132-286-5
  1. United States—Foreign economic relations—Japan. 2. Japan—Foreign economic relations—United States. I. Ito, Takatoshi, 1950– II. Noland, Marcus, 1959– III. Title.

HF1456.5.J3 B47 2001
337.73052—dc21   2001039778

Contents

Tables

Figures

Boxes

Preface

The United States and Japan are the world's two largest national economies, and economic relations between them have been a centerpiece of
the program of the Institute for International Economics throughout its
history. Virtually all of our numerous studies of the international financial
and trading systems have included a substantial component on Japan,
and Japan-United States relations, because of their centrality to global
outcomes. We have frequently addressed the Japanese economy itself,
notably in *The Yen/Dollar Agreement: Liberalizing Japanese Capital Markets*
(Frankel 1984) and *Japan in the World Economy* (Balassa and Noland 1988)
and most recently in *Restoring Japan's Economic Growth* (Posen 1998) and
Japan's Financial Crisis and Its Parallels to U.S. Experience (Mikitani and
Posen 2000).

About once a decade, we have also attempted to assess the rapidly
evolving overall Japan-United States economic relationship and to suggest
a proper policy course for it. In the wake of the buildup of unprecedented
American external deficits and Japanese external surpluses in the early
1980s, and the related onset of intense trade tensions between the two
countries, William R. Cline and I prepared *The United States-Japan Economic
Problem* (1985, revised 1987). When Japan had come to be widely viewed
as a major threat to US economic preeminence and even national prosperity, in the late 1980s and early 1990s, we commissioned and published
Laura Tyson's *Who's Bashing Whom: Trade Conflict in High-Technology
Industries* (1992), which ranged beyond Japan but extensively addressed
that country's global competitiveness, and Marcus Noland and I wrote
Reconcilable Differences? United States-Japan Economic Conflict (1993). Each of

these studies apparently had considerable impact on subsequent thinking about the issue, and policy toward it, in both countries.

This new volume assesses the Japan-United States economic relationship in the dramatically changed circumstances of the early 21st century. The United States experienced resurgent economic growth, based on a substantial rise in productivity growth, in the second half of the 1990s. Japan has been mired in stagnation for almost a decade. Europe has completed its economic integration and created the euro. China has grown dramatically. As a result of these developments, Japan's share of both the world economy and US international transactions has declined markedly. On the security side, the end of the Cold War devalued the Japan-United States relationship for a brief period but the rise of China may have revalued it by even more.

Moreover, internal changes within Japan have clearly reduced the "uniqueness" of its economic system and whatever threat it may have posed to other countries. Our analysis suggests that the myriad past US bilateral efforts to force policy change in Japan have yielded very modest results, especially in recent years. At the same time, the formation of the World Trade Organization has increased the efficacy of addressing outstanding trade issues through *multilateral* approaches.

For all these reasons, and several more that are developed in the book, we conclude that the time has come for the United States to end the uniquely Japan-specific economic policy that it has pursued for the past three decades. It should instead start treating Japan like any other major economic power, mainly within the multilateral context of overall US foreign economic policy. The arrival of new administrations in both countries appears to offer an appropriate time for such a fundamental policy reconsideration.

To conduct this study properly, we determined at the outset that it had to be coauthored by a top Japanese economist. Dr. Noland and I were thus extremely fortunate to be joined by Professor Takatoshi Ito of Hitotsubashi University, who is one of the most eminent economists in Japan and who also has long experience in the United States, having taught at both the University of Minnesota and at Harvard and having spent three years as a senior advisor at the research department of the International Monetary Fund. Professor Ito had to disengage from the project for two years, during his assignment as Deputy Vice Minister for International Finance in the Ministry of Finance from July 1999 to July 2001, but returned in time to complete the final manuscript with us.

The Institute for International Economics is a private nonprofit institution for the study and discussion of international economic policy. Its purpose is to analyze important issues in that area and to develop and communicate practical new approaches for dealing with them. The Institute is completely nonpartisan.

The Institute is funded largely by philanthropic foundations. Major institutional grants are now being received from the William M. Keck, Jr. Foundation and the Starr Foundation. A number of other foundations and private corporations contribute to the highly diversified financial resources of the Institute. About 31 percent of the Institute's resources in our latest fiscal year were provided by contributors outside the United States, including about 18 percent from Japan.

This study was supported by The Japan Foundation-Center for Global Partnership, The Freeman Foundation, the GE Fund (which provides partial support for our work on Asian issues) and the United States-Japan Foundation. Funding was also provided under our Akio Morita Studies Program, a program of studies on topics of central interest to the United States and Japan that was created in 1997 to honor our distinguished former director and honorary director, Akio Morita, the late cofounder and former CEO of Sony. That Program is funded by the Sony Corporation, The New York Community Trust-The Peter G. Peterson Fund, and Mr. David Rockefeller.

The Board of Directors bears overall responsibilities for the Institute and gives general guidance and approval to its research program, including the identification of topics that are likely to become important over the medium run (one to three years), and which should be addressed by the Institute. The Director, working closely with the staff and outside Advisory Committee, is responsible for the development of particular projects and makes the final decision to publish an individual study.

The Institute hopes that its studies and other activities will contribute to building a stronger foundation for international economic policy around the world. We invite readers of these publications to let us know how they think we can best accomplish this objective.

C. Fred Bergsten
Director
September 2001

Acknowledgments

The authors gratefully acknowledge the research assistance of Derek Bruzewicz, Erika Wada, and Scott Holladay.
We would also like to thank Richard Cooper, I.M. Destler, Wendy Dobson, Yoichi Funabashi, Ayami Hidaka, Christopher Johnstone, Edward Lincoln, Lawrence Krause, Tsunao Nakamura, Adam Posen, Jeffrey Schott, Bruce Stokes, Yoichi Takita, Daniel Tarullo, Edwin Truman, John Williamson; and seminar participants at the University of Hawaii; the Tokyo American Center; the Tokyo Foundation; the Research Institute of Economy, Trade, and Industry; and the Institute for International Affairs for helpful comments on earlier drafts of the manuscript without implicating them in any of its remaining errors.

1

The Economic and Policy Context

The United States and Japan are the two largest national economies in the world. In the century and a half since the forcible opening of Japan by Commodore Perry's Black Ships in 1854 and the conclusion of the "unequal" Treaty of Amity and Commerce in 1858, the two countries have experienced both a dramatic increase in economic integration and intermittent conflict on a range of issues from trade to finance and macroeconomic policy. In the 1940s, these tensions were a contributing factor to the outbreak of military hostilities between the two giants.

Since the conclusion of the Second World War, policymakers in both countries have built robust economic, political, and security ties, forging what has been called "the world's most important bilateral relationship bar none." They have also experienced severe economic conflicts, however. The United States has in fact maintained, during at least the quarter-century from the early 1970s to the middle 1990s, a unique Japan-specific economic policy that was quite different from its approach toward any of its other major trading partners or the world's other large economies.

This book is about the future of economic relations between Japan and the United States. That relationship turns on three key sets of variables. One, which we will argue is decisively important, is the state of each country's economy and their relative positions in the world economy. The second is the overall status of each country in the world as a whole, including its security and broader political dimensions. Third come the specifically bilateral features, both economic and political, of the relationship between the two, which are also of great salience but must be seen within the broader economic and security contexts. All three sets of determinants have changed dramatically during the past decade.

There are four potential paths for US economic policy toward Japan in the coming period. One is to maintain the unique Japan-specific approach of the past three decades, which we believe has become more and more anomalous, and should now be explicitly jettisoned. A second, at the other extreme, is to essentially ignore Japan in the years ahead—a "bypass-Japan" strategy, which some US companies have in fact adopted in devising their own policies toward Asia. A third is to pursue "deep integration" with Japan, via a free trade agreement (FTA) or even more far-reaching effort to link the two economies, in an ambitious bid to sweep aside the problems and frustrations of the past with an expansive political initiative. The fourth is a middle course, in which Japan is still important but is treated like any other major economic power or trading partner of the United States (Canada, the European Union, or Mexico), mainly through multilateral channels and institutions.

We will outline the four alternatives later in this chapter and conclude that the last of them, the treatment of Japan as a "normal country," is the best policy for the United States and for the relationship in the foreseeable future.[1] We will suggest that actual policy is already moving in this direction, but recommend that the new approach be explicitly announced as soon as possible, to clarify its adoption and to inform the myriad actors in both countries (and around the world) of the change. We will outline the four alternatives after first spelling out the context for the new policy.

A Reversal of Fortunes

As recently as the early 1990s, Japan was widely viewed as the strongest economy in the world, and there were extensive doubts about the fundamental health of the US economy. Despite the highly adverse effects of two oil shocks in the 1970s and the *endaka* (strong yen) episode of the middle 1980s, Japan had averaged almost twice as rapid growth as the United States for three decades (table 1.1). Japan's per capita income passed that of the United States in the early 1990s and was more than 40 percent higher (at market exchange rates) in 1995. Measured unemployment in Japan generally remained less than one-third the recorded US level. Japan, with less than half the population of the United States,

---

1. To clarify, we mean the phrase "normal country" in a literal, generic, or nonspecific way—not in the particular sense sometimes attached to this phrase in Japanese domestic politics. That issue—of whether, e.g., Japan should revise its Constitution to enlarge the permissible scope of military activities—will be taken up in chapter 6.

Table 1.1 GDP, per capita income, and unemployment in Japan and the United States, 1950s-2000

Measure	1950s	1960s	1970s	1980s	1990s	2000
GDP growth rate (percent)						
Japan	n.a.	9.1	4.4	3.9	1.2	1.5
United States	n.a.	4.4	3.3	2.0	3.0	4.1
GDP market exchange rate (billions of dollars)						
Japan	30	95	537	1,739	4,126	4,895
United States	395	718	1,665	4,066	7,341	9,873
Per capita income (at market exchange rate)						
Japan	324	952	4,782	14,380	30,403	38,690
United States	2,621	3,733	7,757	17,154	28,011	36,478
Per capita income (at purchasing power parity)						
Japan	n.a.	7,008	12,842	17,189	23,303	24,041
United States	n.a.	15,583	19,833	24,175	29,586	30,600
Unemployment rate (percent)						
Japan	n.a.	1.3	1.7	2.5	3.1	4.6
United States	4.5	4.8	6.2	7.3	5.8	4.0

n.a. = not available.

Sources: IMF, *International Financial Statistics*; US Department of Labor, Bureau of Labor Statistics (for unemployment data).

3

Figure 1.1   Cumulative net capital outflows, 1970-99

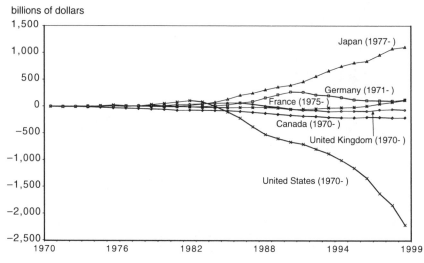

Source: IMF, *International Financial Statistics.*

achieved a total GDP (at market exchange rates) that was only 30 percent less than the total GDP of the United States as late as 1995.[2]

International indicators painted an even starker picture. By the middle 1980s, Japan had become the world's largest net capital exporter and the world's largest creditor country by a large and growing margin over runner-up Germany (figure 1.1). The United States, which had been the world's largest creditor country as recently as the early 1980s, had become the world's largest net capital importer and debtor country by a huge margin over runner-up Canada. The US share of world exports declined steadily, while Japan's share rose sharply into the middle 1980s, almost equaling that of the United States at one point (figure 1.2).[3] Japanese firms bought sizable shares of US industry and property throughout the 1980s, while US investors remained minor players in Japan. In 1990, Japan

---

2. The significance of many of these statistics can be challenged. As will be discussed in chapter 4, the data on incomes converted to a common currency at market exchange rates overstate the true comparative level of income in Japan. Similarly, differences in definitions mean that similar levels of true unemployment result in lower measured unemployment in Japan. What is indisputable, however, is that according to a variety of measures, correctly interpreted, the Japanese economy substantially outperformed the US economy during this period, and that Japan's superior performance was widely perceived by both the elites and the broader publics of both countries—and viewed as a "threat to American dominance" by many in the United States.

3. This is true even when the share of US multinational firms producing from foreign locations is taken into account.

Figure 1.2   US and Japanese shares of world exports, 1960-99

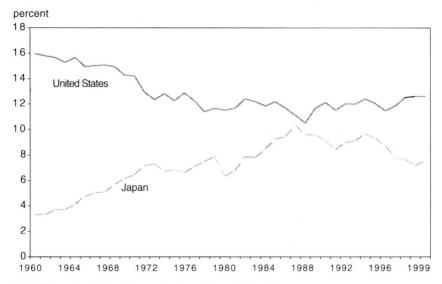

Note: Figures include only exports of goods, not of services.

Source: IMF, *International Financial Statistics.*

replaced the United States as the world's largest donor of foreign assistance, and it steadily increased its margin throughout the decade.

These macroeconomic developments were replicated, and in many observers' eyes magnified, at the industry-specific level. Japanese-based firms seized large chunks of world market share from their US (and other foreign) competitors in a host of key industries. Japanese companies produced more than 50 percent of world semiconductors as late as 1989, while US companies' share hovered below 40 percent. Similar developments had already occurred in automobiles, numerous consumer electronics products, and (in an earlier period) steel. Japanese banks appeared to dominate world finance, in 1990 accounting for the top 5 banks and 6 of the top 10.

Moreover, Japan's region was clearly the most dynamic in the world. "Asian tigers" and "the Asian miracle" became household terms, partly due to the impact of Japan's own development on its neighbors, partly due to the active engagement of Japanese companies, and partly through emulation of Japan's "economic model."[4] Latin America, the backyard of the United States, was by contrast suffering through the debt crisis and "lost decade" of the 1980s.

---

4. See World Bank (1993).

This pattern originated in the 1960s and broadly persisted throughout the 1970s and 1980s. Hence it seemed sufficiently grounded to constitute an established trend and to justify extrapolation into the future. Ezra Vogel, a leading US expert on Asia, already proclaimed *Japan as Number One* in 1979.[5] Clyde Prestowitz, an experienced trade negotiator with Japan, posited the *Trading Places* of the two countries. The so-called revisionists— Fallows, Johnson, van Wolferen, and Prestowitz—argued that the United States could recoup only by simultaneously adopting much of the Japanese system and declaring economic war on Japan itself, without regard to the likely negative impact on the security relationship between them (see especially Johnson 1982, Fallows 1989, Prestowitz 1988, and van Wolferen 1989). By the late 1980s, surveys regularly showed that far more Americans were afraid of Japan than of the Soviet Union (James 2000).

US policy responded to these perceptions and pressures. As will be detailed below, a succession of presidential administrations from that of Richard Nixon to that of Bill Clinton, under strong pressure from the Congress and large parts of the business community, adopted Japan-specific approaches that were unique to the foreign economic policy of the United States. Despite the continued centrality of the security relationship, Japan was the target of a series of sharp economic attacks from the United States, ranging from the "Nixon shocks" of 1971 (which were both economic and political) to the "managed-trade" initiatives of the middle 1980s to middle 1990s. The United States coerced Japan into a series of bilateral "dialogues," "initiatives," and "frameworks" to pursue US concerns that stood alone in the annals of global economic relationships.

The seeming verities of less than a decade ago appear surreal at the outset of the 21st century. Economic growth in the United States has been more than double that of stagnant Japan for a decade, reversing the ratio of the previous 30 years (table 1.1). After more than a decade of steady expansion, interrupted only by the brief recession of 1990-91, US domestic demand growth accelerated to 5 percent annually in the late 1990s— relative to 1 percent for Japan throughout the decade, including two recessions and perhaps a third in 2001. Consensus estimates in the two countries suggest that the sustainable trend growth is now at least 50 percent higher in the United States—3 percent a year, versus 2 percent in Japan—because US productivity growth substantially exceeds Japanese productivity growth and is widely expected to continue to do so, absent significant reform in Japan; and because the US labor force will continue to expand, whereas Japan's is already declining owing to the aging of its population and its resistance to immigration. This resurgent US economic performance was led by many of the high-technology sectors that were widely viewed, less than a decade earlier, as under intense threat from

---

5. He also, however, perceptively sensed the *Comeback* of the United States (Vogel 1979, 1985).

Japan. Even measured unemployment in the United States fell below that in Japan by the end of the decade.

Government finances exhibit similarly dramatic reversals. The government of "thrifty" Japan has now run annual budget deficits of more than $300 billion, larger in absolute terms than have ever been incurred by the United States, and the largest as a share of GDP of any country belonging to the Organization for Economic Cooperation and Development (OECD). Japan's national debt has reached $6 trillion and is still climbing, whereas US debt peaked at about $5 trillion and is now declining rapidly. In 1999, the Government of Japan replaced the United States as the largest issuer of government debt, and the OECD projects that it will undertake more than 90 percent of net OECD debt issues in the coming years.

Sectoral data naturally mirror these aggregate shifts. In contrast to a decade earlier, when Japan accounted for the world's 5 largest banks, by 2000 Japan provided only 2 of the top 10. The profitability of Japanese banks lagged behind their European and US counterparts throughout the entire 1990s. After a series of capital injections beginning in 1998, Japanese banks are still far from being strong in their balance sheets and earning power. They are still withdrawing from foreign operations. Even in the traditional manufacturing sectors, such as automobiles, US companies have improved their positions vis-à-vis most Japanese firms. Respected authors now ask *Can Japan Compete?* (Porter, M. Sakakibara, and Takeuchi 2000) and note that Japan's performance has been slipping, even in its most successful industries.

Regional developments appear to replicate these swings in national fortunes. The Asian financial crisis of 1997-98 derailed the "miracle economies," at least for a while, and exposed weaknesses in financial systems and corporate governance that undermined confidence in Japan itself and its entire "economic model." Latin America continues to have its troubles, but the creation of the North American Free Trade Agreement (NAFTA) and Mercosur have imparted new bursts of dynamism to the largest countries in the region.

To be sure, a few elements remain unchanged. Some Japanese auto and electronics firms remain at the top of their world leagues. US external deficits have continued to grow sharply, and its net foreign obligations stand far above all others', now exceeding $2 trillion (about 20 percent of its GDP). Japan's external surpluses remain the largest in the world, as does its net creditor position of about $1 trillion (about 25 percent of GDP[6]).

---

6. Paradoxically, Japan is running the largest domestic deficits of any OECD country while remaining the world's largest creditor in external terms; whereas the United States is still the world's largest international debtor, even after converting its domestic budget position into a substantial surplus.

Moreover, the United States confronts a series of vulnerabilities that are somewhat reminiscent of those faced by Japan in 1990. The most obvious in the short run are macroeconomic uncertainties due to possible further declines in the still richly valued stock market, a possible decline of real estate prices in some regions, and consequent reverberations in the banking sector; there are many who still believe that the United States is a "bubble economy" à la Japan a decade ago. The United States also faces a possible sharp change in the external value of its currency, most likely in the downward direction, whereas Japan's problems in the early 1990s were subsequently compounded by a record appreciation of the yen; a major fall in the dollar while the US economy was still near full employment could lead to a substantial rise in prices and interest rates, and hence a plunge in the financial markets, that could sharply deepen the turndown of 2000-01.

The United States also continues to face a number of more deep-seated economic problems. It is unclear whether the sharp rise in productivity growth, which fueled the dramatic rise in output in the second half of the 1990s, will turn out to be sustainable. The private savings rate is abysmally low and partly explains the country's large external deficits and dependence on foreign capital. The US primary and secondary education system, although gradually improving and clearly a high priority of national policy, remains inadequate to equip many Americans to compete effectively in a globalized, high-technology world economy. Partly as a result of these educational deficiencies, the United States has experienced a domestic backlash against globalization for almost a decade that could limit the country's ability to reap the benefits from further international-ization of its economy.

But the economic underpinnings of the Japan-United States relationship have virtually reversed during the past decade. Indeed, it is abundantly clear that Japan's economic problems of the 1990s, which continue as this book is completed, are far greater than those of the United States in the 1970s and 1980s. We leaned against the wind of "Japanaphoria" and "Ameropessimism" a decade ago (Bergsten and Noland 1993), but no one even came close to predicting either component—let alone both ends—of the turnabout of the past decade. Those who extrapolated from the past have been proven decisively wrong.

Indeed, Japan's weakness rather than its strength has become the greatest concern of the United States (and the rest of the world). Since 1998, there has been recurrent fear of a true implosion of the Japanese financial system—runs on banks, widespread failures and defaults, withdrawals of funding around the world by the world's largest creditor country, free falls of the stock market and the currency, and a renewal of financial crisis in East Asia and perhaps the entire world. This shift in the nature of "the Japan problem," and perceptions of it, dramatize the reversal of the past decade.

Japan will of course eventually overcome this crisis, as it has so many others in the past, and restore at least a modicum of economic growth. But Japan also faces important long-term problems. The most notable is an aging population that, on current trends, would lead to a halving of its total population by 2050. Hence there is reason to believe, from both the US and Japanese perspectives, that an important part of the "reversal of fortunes" of the last decade will persist.

This book is about future economic policy between the United States and Japan. Hence it is essential that we attempt to assess the future course of the two economies as one important starting point for the analysis and subsequent prescriptions. This, in turn, requires us to try to explain both the performance reversal of the past decade and its implications for future developments.

Was the shift simply a temporary phenomenon based on an inevitable US recovery from its policy errors and economic woes of the 1970s and early 1980s, and on a series of Japanese mistakes that should be avoidable in the future? Even worse, did it simply reflect a US bubble à la Japan's bubble a decade earlier that could burst at any moment and throw the United States back to slow growth or even renewed stagflation? Indeed, could Japan come back strong during the next 5 to 10 years, as the United States did after *its* earlier "decade(s) of decline"?

Or does the reversal of the 1990s represent a lasting change, with the United States seizing a permanent lead in the technology revolution of the modern era and Japan continuing to decline due to its structural rigidities and aging population? Does the answer lie somewhere in between, with the United States likely to keep doing reasonably well, if not as well as in the late 1990s, and with Japan resuming at least some of its traditional dynamism and thus creating a world where the two largest national economies are moving ahead roughly in tandem? What would be the implications for the Japan-United States economic (and overall) relationship of these very different relative economic patterns?

Chapter 2 will attempt to answer these questions for the United States, assessing both the structural changes that have transpired within the US economy and the macroeconomic record. Chapter 3 will provide a similar analysis of Japan. Our emphasis in both cases will be on the likely persistence of the radical changes of the past decade, the outlook for the future, the interaction between the two economies, and the implications of all these developments for policy. Our goal is to discern the economic foundations for the relationship that are likely to prevail for the next decade or so, recognizing the huge errors that any similar effort of 10 years ago would almost surely have made and hence the inherent uncertainty of the exercise.

Before turning to the underlying economics, however, it is essential to consider the other two dimensions of the relationship. We will thus review briefly the two countries' overall global positions and the specifically bilateral interactions between them during the past three decades.

The Global Positions

These dramatic changes in the economic performance of the two countries have of course also affected their overall global positions. The strong economic resurgence of the United States has strengthened its status and prestige, and restored luster to both "the Anglo-Saxon model" and US "soft power." Conversely, Japan's decade of stagnation or worse, along with the broader Asian crisis, have dimmed the Japanese star that shone so brightly a decade ago.

In addition, the demise of the Soviet Union and the end of the Cold War resulted in a decline in the relative importance of US security alliances, including its alliance with Japan. The revisionists and other "economic hawks," who favored a much tougher stance in US trade negotiations with Japan, argued that the United States had always deferred to Japan for security reasons but could now follow their advice. The Clinton administration indeed adopted a hard line on trade matters in its first couple of years in office and then, after a short hiatus, instituted an equally tough approach on macroeconomic and monetary issues during its second term. We will evaluate those efforts in chapter 5, but it is clear that the epochal change in the global security situation was a key enabling factor.[7]

However, this tendency has been tempered by the rise of China, which presents major challenges to both the United States and Japan in both security and economic terms. In the case of the United States, China's perceived challenge had already led to a reevaluation of security matters as early as 1995-96, leading to the Nye Report on strengthening the military alliance with Japan and contributing significantly to the reduction in US economic pressures. It was demonstrated again during the George W. Bush-Junichiro Koizumi summit in June 2001, where economic issues largely took a back seat.

For Japan, China presents a challenge to its vision of its unfettered role as the regional leader of Asia and the go-between intermediating between the developing countries of the Asia-Pacific region and the rich industrial countries of the OECD. This vision has in fact been shattered by the concomitant rise of China and the stagnation of Japan itself. Japan is still

---

7. The only period of comparably "tough" US economic policy toward Japan was 1971-73, with President Nixon's import surcharge and threat to use the Trading with the Enemy Act to bludgeon Japan into new restraints on its textile exports to the United States. That episode occurred when Japan was just emerging as a global economic power, however, and remained totally dependent on the United States for security.

far richer and more technologically advanced than China, and its trade flows and financial markets remain much larger than those of its neighbor. However, according to some estimates of national output converted at purchasing power parity equivalents, China has now exceeded Japan in terms of total GDP (and become the world's second largest economy, trailing only the United States). Moreover, China possesses considerable military assets (including nuclear weapons) and appears to have much greater confidence in asserting its influence, regionally and even globally.

Japan's relations with the rest of Asia have of course been plagued throughout the postwar period by memories of its imperialist adventures earlier in the century and its perceived failure, by contrast with Germany, to come to terms with its past. But the rise of China has, for the first time, confronted it with a real rival for regional leadership. Hence it has had to undertake major efforts to recoup its position, sometimes stumbling badly (as with the failed proposal for an Asian Monetary Fund in 1997, torpedoed by China as well as by the United States) and sometimes more successfully (as with its efforts to help the Asian countries in crisis to recover by providing them with strong financial support in 1998-99).

Neither the United States nor Japan covered itself with glory during the Asian financial crisis. Japan's huge policy errors in 1997—primarily its sharp tax hikes when the economy was still stagnating (Posen 1998), and implosion of the financial system with failures of large financial institutions (Cargill, Hutchison, and Ito 2000)—threw its economy into recession and the yen into sharp depreciation, helping trigger and then deepen the crisis (Noland et al. 1999). The partial recovery of the most heavily affected crisis countries has occurred despite the continued stagnation of Japan, however, belying the notion that Japan was essential to regional prosperity. Conversely, Japan's provision of large credits to the recovering Asian countries has been appreciated by its recipients, in contrast to their perception of a grudging and at times opportunistic response on the part of the United States.

Emerging out of this sense of disappointment with, and even abandonment by, Washington and the international financial institutions headquartered there, appears to be a serious attempt by Asia, for the first time in history, to create regional economic arrangements that would reduce its dependence on the West and the global economic institutions—especially the International Monetary Fund (IMF), but also the World Bank and even the World Trade Organization (WTO) (Bergsten 2000). The outcome of these efforts remains unclear at this time but, as with the Asian Monetary Fund debate in 1997, they may at some point force Japan to make tough choices between its Asian neighbors (seeking greater self-determination) and its US ally (wanting to preserve dominance for the "Washington consensus").

Figure 1.3 Exports and imports, 1955-2000 (as percent of GDP)

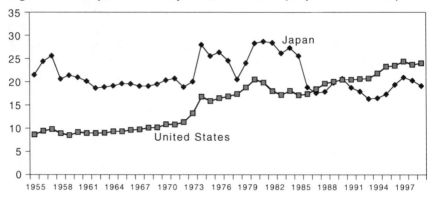

Source: IMF, International Financial Statistics.

The quest for meaningful Asian regional arrangements, even if confined to the economic domain, may ultimately turn on whether Japan and China can get together, to provide joint or at least cooperative leadership for the exercise, as Germany and France did in Europe. That issue will also pose tough choices for the United States, basically similar to those it faced when Europe began to unite seriously in the early postwar period. Would a resultant Asian bloc be a force for stability in the region, and thus less likely to require yet another US military intervention in Asia? Or would it simply be a much tougher economic competitor, whose discrimination against outsiders and possible threat to the existing institutional order would be too high a cost to accept?[8]

How the United States might react to such a development would relate to the further acceleration of globalization and the backlash against it. On the one hand, the US economy has experienced dramatic globalization during the past four decades—a near tripling of the share of external transactions in its GDP, a swing of great speed for such a mature economy (figure 1.3). As a result, the United States is now more exposed to global

8. Postwar Japan has never harbored global political aspirations. It has, however, viewed itself as the world's second leading economic power (or at least tied for that position with Germany). Japan in fact periodically campaigned to promote international use of the yen to a position at least roughly equal to that of the deutsche mark as runners up to, albeit far behind, the dollar. The amalgamation of Europe into an effectively integrated economy has clearly pushed Japan into a distant third in the world output league, however. Perhaps even more important symbolically, the creation of the euro—and the view in some quarters that it could come to rival the dollar as the world's leading currency—pushed the yen to a distant third in the currency tables. With its relative decline of course accelerated by its own economic stagnation in the 1990s, Japan has clearly dropped a notch in the global economic rankings, and there is now considerable space between it and the top two. Any future trilateral leadership of the world economy could well involve some Asian regional entity, rather than Japan itself, as perhaps anticipated by the decision of the private Trilateral Commission in 2000 to replace Japan with an East Asian regional group as one of its three "poles."

economic events than either of the other two economic superpowers—and considerably more so than Japan, whose external engagement remained essentially unchanged during the same period (except for a sharp runup in the 1970s, due to the huge rise in oil prices). We will argue in chapter 2 that this is a major reason for the sharp improvement in US economic performance in the 1990s.

On the other hand, and clearly related, a substantial backlash against globalization has arisen in the United States, mainly because of concerns that further increases in the openness of the economy will cause job dislocation and significant declines in lifetime incomes for less-skilled workers (Scheve and Slaughter 2001; Kletzer 2001). Very little of that backlash has been directed against Japan, another indicator of its declining salience to US policy; most of the concerns are aimed at countries with low wages, and with allegedly low labor standards and low environmental defenses. But much of US international economic policy—most notably trade policy, with the failure to obtain any new negotiating authority since 1994, but also policy toward international investment and to some extent toward the IMF—has been stalemated. Hence the United States has been unable to exercise its traditional leadership on these issues, either globally (as in the WTO) or at the regional level (as in the Asia Pacific Economic Cooperation forum, or APEC). This backlash developed during the period of stellar US economic performance. Any prolonged slowdown, let alone recession, could intensify the domestic politics of these issues and even push the United States in an antiglobalization direction. Hence this development could have a substantial, though indirect, impact on the Japan-United States relationship.

It is clear, however, that the 1990s were a "decade of decline" for Japan, gauged by the welfare measures of economics but even more clearly in the relative terms of political science. The completion of European integration has created a new global economic superpower that, combined with Japan's recent economic weakness, relegates it to a sharply lessened position in international economic and financial councils. The rise of China presents Japan with a real rival for the leadership of its own region, a contest it may well lose unless China itself goes off course or Japan engineers a dramatic improvement in its economic and political positions. The Asian financial crisis, in addition to weakening both the economies of the region and the luster of the "Japanese model," has triggered a push for Asian regional cooperation that will almost certainly face Japan with conflicts between the region and the United States. The further intensification of globalization strengthened the US economy, while the backlash against it raised new threats to US openness—including toward Japan.

Despite all this—or perhaps because of it?—both the United States and Japan report that their security relationship is stronger than ever. Jolted by the risks to the overall relationship engendered by the Clinton administration's tough approach to trade issues in its early years, the foreign policy leadership of the United States initiated an extensive review of security ties with Japan in the middle 1990s and emerged with a strong reiteration, and some upgrading, of that dimension of the relationship. By all indications, the Bush administration will intensify this effort. A key question for the future, and for this book, is whether a positive overall relationship can persist if there is continued conflict or even sharp tension over economic issues. Another is whether, in light of the fundamental changes in the global and regional security situations, the overall relationship is still of cardinal importance to either of the two countries. We will analyze these issues in chapter 6.

At this point, it is enough to note simply that the 1990s brought a dramatic shift in the relative positions of the United States and Japan in both the economic and security spheres. The United States became "the only superpower" in both military and economic terms, while Japan slipped at least a notch, both globally (behind the European Union) and regionally (vis-à-vis China). The end of the Cold War fundamentally altered the global security posture. As a result, the US "need for Japan" may have declined in both the economic and security dimensions. In setting the stage for our in-depth analysis of all these issues, it remains to describe the state of the bilateral economic relationship at the outset of the 21st century and the impact that these sweeping changes appear to have had to date.

The Bilateral Relationship

Japan stands alone as the only target of a persistent country-specific economic policy in the postwar history of the United States. In 1971, President Nixon imposed an import surcharge that was directed largely at Japan and threatened to apply the Trading with the Enemy Act—an enormous affront to the closest US Pacific ally, especially in light of memories of the Second World War—to force Japan to limit its textile exports to the United States.[9] In the late 1970s, Japan was a primary focus of the Carter administration's "locomotive theory," which sought expanded macroeconomic stimulus in other countries to broaden the sources of global growth and help reduce the large deficit (for that time) in the US external balance. Both of these initiatives toward Japan were

---

9. As early as 1969, one of the authors prepared a meeting of the National Security Council (NSC) to address US economic relations with Japan (which at the time emphasized Japan's export prowess and US import policy, Japan's protection against US exports, the impediments to US investment in Japan, and textiles). Despite the comprehensive coverage of US foreign policy issues by the NSC under the Nixon-Kissinger regime, no other country was singled out for such attention on the economic front.

taken within a multilateral context, however, and unique Japan-centered policies were still to come.

US concerns about Japan reached their apex from the early 1980s to the mid-1990s. During this period, the United States under administrations of all types, which were in turn under enormous pressure from the Congress and large parts of the US business community, simultaneously bludgeoned Japan to restrain its own sales to the United States and launched major initiatives aimed at opening the Japanese market. President Ronald Reagan imposed a "voluntary export restraint" agreement on Japanese autos during his first months in office, and subsequent similar arrangements on steel and machine tools; sought a sharp appreciation of the yen with his Plaza Agreement in 1985; adopted a "tough" trade policy, including widespread use of Section 301, the Unfair Foreign Trade Practices component of the 1974 US Trade Act (including against Japan) the next day; negotiated the first "managed-trade" pact on semiconductors in 1986-87; and launched the Market-Oriented Sector Specific (MOSS) effort in 1985-87. President George H.W. Bush followed with the Structural Impediments Initiative (SII) in 1989-91. President Clinton had his Framework Talks in 1993-95, which included negotiations on autos and auto parts that were the most rancorous since the textile disputes of the early 1970s. Most recently, a US-Japan Economic Partnership for Growth was announced by President Bush and Prime Minister Koizumi in June 2001.[10] All of these initiatives embodied elaborate sets of commissions, task forces, working groups, and forums through which the United States would seek to maintain pressure on Japan to alter its policies across a wide array of specific issues and policy areas.

This Japan-specific policy on the part of the United States has been justified on three mutually reinforcing grounds. First has been Japan's size as the world's second largest national economy, largest global creditor, and rival to the United States in fields such as high-technology manufacturing and finance. Second has been Japan's distinctiveness in terms of economic institutions and organization. From these two considerations flowed the conclusion that Japan's size and distinctiveness combined in

---

10. The Armitage Report on United States-Japan relations (IISS 2000), prepared and signed by a number of Japan experts, including several who subsequently became high officials in the administration of President George W. Bush—including Deputy Secretary of State Richard L. Armitage and Deputy Secretary of Defense Paul D. Wolfowitz—implied a continuation of the traditional approach. Its economic section concludes that "bilateral trade negotiations remain an essential tool," emphasizes the "mounting frustration with which successive US administrations have tried to prod Tokyo to adopt a range of invented and reinvented trade and economic policy options," stresses deregulation and further trade liberalization rather than macroeconomic measures as the keys to restoring Japanese growth, and is full of the usual "Japan must . . ." pressurizing (including on minutiae such as "the quality of Japanese economic statistics"). It is interesting that it also raises the possibility of a Japan-United States free trade area.

a way to uniquely disadvantage US firms and workers in sectors in which they competed with Japanese producers—whether in agriculture, industry, or services—to the detriment of US national interests. Third, it was felt that, mainly for geopolitical but also for economic reasons, the United States had a unique ability to affect policymaking in Japan. Moreover, the political economy of US trade policy formation created domestic support within the United States for this relatively intrusive approach. Together, these considerations provided the basis for a Japan-specific economic policy.

The first point is largely self-evident. Japan is the second largest national economy in the world. Its weight has been viewed as sufficiently great to affect global and US economic outcomes, especially because of its dynamic performance from the 1960s through the 1980s. It has also been thought of as a major determinant of economic performance in all of Asia, a region that accounts for about a third of the world economy and has been its most rapidly growing component for the past three decades, despite its recent troubles.

Second, Japan came to be viewed by many as a truly "different country" with a unique economic model. To these observers, Japan's growth and competitive success could not be explained by conventional analysis. In particular, governmental intervention and industrial policy were widely thought to be key elements in its stunning economic success.

Even more important, many Americans perceived Japan as a competitor that was not only different but also "unfair." The specific charges ranged from "closed markets" to "government-subsidized industrial policies" to "competitive undervaluation of the yen." The overall picture was one of marked cultural and societal differences that produced clever violations of the international rules and norms by which the United States and most other countries played the international economic game. Such perceptions were fed by a steady stream of "revisionist" analyses of "why Japan is different" and "unfair Japanese trade practices," such as its rejection of foreign skis that "would not work on Japanese snow" or of imported foods that were "incompatible with Japanese intestines." The policy implication was that overt US governmental counteraction was required to "fight fire with fire." Among professional economists, "strategic trade theory" provided a modicum of intellectual support for these views.

Taking all this together, Japan was viewed more and more throughout the 1970s and 1980s as a potential threat to US global economic supremacy and even to its own prosperity. As Japan's trade surpluses (and US deficits) mounted, and as Japanese industries achieved world leadership and even dominance in a number of key sectors, widespread fears of "losing the competitive race" arose in the United States. Japan was "eating our lunch" and even "had won the Cold War." Just as the United States felt compelled to launch a concerted national response to the challenge posed by the Soviet Union to US security and global political leadership, many Americans (and many friends of the United States in other countries) concluded that the United States needed to launch a concerted national response to the challenge posed by Japan to US prosperity and global economic leadership.

Further complicating the situation, the United States had major security interests in Japan—the country that, for all the conflict on economic issues, was praised again and again as the "linchpin of the Pacific" (President Nixon) and "America's unsinkable aircraft carrier" (Prime Minister Yasuhiro Nakasone). The economic disputes, if left unresolved, could both weaken the security relationship itself and undermine US political support for continued security ties ("protecting Japan"), and hence threaten a fundamental tenet of US foreign policy in a key part of the world. Explicit efforts to resolve the economic tensions were therefore required.[11]

Moreover, in part because of this security relationship, but also because of Japan's lack of other close allies and its reliance on US markets, the United States has thought it had a unique ability to pressure Japan for policy changes much more aggressively than it could pressure other countries. Reform-seeking Japanese, including Prime Minister Kiichi Miyazawa as late as 1993, encouraged this view by *asking* the United States to apply *gaiatsu* ("foreign pressure"; see box 5.5) to affect the internal policy debate in Japan. And *gaiatsu* was often effective, at least in the 1980s, because those who applied the US pressure often had domestic allies in Japan, and Japan still wanted to accommodate to the United States. It is interesting, and somewhat ironic, that this was in turn partly because of the widespread perception, in both countries, that Japan was on the ascendancy and that the United States had fallen on hard times and needed help.

But actually achieving Japanese change has turned out to be exceedingly difficult. Moreover, the United States has never even considered pushing other countries to such an extent, with the partial exception of Germany (due to similar security ties) in the earlier postwar period. Only its unique relationship with Japan even made the efforts plausible.

This tendency was reinforced by the political economy of trade policy formation in the United States. Specific US industries and other groups have taken advantage of all these factors in their perennial effort to win protection against imports or governmental support for their exports. Steel and textiles were the most important examples in the 1970s. Autos and again steel dominated the relationship in the 1980s. Semiconductors, auto parts, and telecommunications equipment were central in the 1990s, and steel arose again in 1999. The quasi-permanence of a Japan-specific policy opened the door for industries seeking help, and numerous indus-

---

11. Many believe, however, that security issues have been a "moderating" factor, rather than an "aggravating" factor, for the Japan-United States relationship. We will discuss this tension in chapter 6.

tries have been quick to push the opening wider, generating irresistible pressure (including through the Congress) even on administrations that might have been reluctant on their own to maintain the Japan-specific economic policy.

As a result of these elements, the United States has conducted a unique "Japan economic policy" during much of the period since about 1970. The substantive emphasis of that policy has shifted with great frequency, focusing variously (and sometimes simultaneously) on (1) increasing access to the Japanese market, (2) restricting Japanese access to the US market, (3) enhancing opportunities for US investment in Japan, (4) reducing opportunities for Japanese investment in the United States, (5) structurally reforming the Japanese economy, (6) fostering more expansionary Japanese macroeconomic policies, (7) pursuing a stronger exchange rate for the yen, and (8) seeking Japanese support for US multilateral trade and international financial initiatives. We turn next to an appraisal of the alternative strategies through which the United States might pursue these, and its other, economic objectives toward Japan in the early 21st century.

Policy Alternatives

There are at least four alternative strategies that the United States could adopt for its future economic relations with Japan. At one extreme, it could simply write off Japan as a significant global economy and adopt a "bypass-Japan" or "benign neglect" policy. At the other extreme, it could seek "deep economic integration" with Japan via negotiation of a bilateral free trade area or "open marketplace" agreement (Stokes 2000) and/or a monetary integration compact (McKinnon and Ohno 1997). In between, it could maintain the policy of the last three decades under which Japan is treated as the single most important economic counterpart of the United States and thus the frequent target of country-specific trade, structural, macroeconomic, and monetary demands (Lincoln 2001).

Or, as we will recommend, the United States could dismiss the premises that have underlain its policy for three decades and reorient its policy toward Japan within its global economic policy, treating Japan as "a normal country." We will argue that US national interests would be better served in the future by such a policy, which roots its relationship with Japan in the multilateral institutions rather than in a continuation of the Japan-specific policies of the past. But before making our case for this policy and elaborating the specifics of our proposals, in chapter 7, it is worthwhile to sketch out the alternative approaches.

A "Bypass-Japan" Strategy

The first policy option rests on extrapolation of the dramatic changes of the 1990s: the "decade of decline" for Japan, the resurgence of the US economy, and a series of global developments that devalue the importance of Japan—especially with respect to China and the rest of Asia. It also rests on the view that "nothing ever changes in Japan," or changes so slowly that policy efforts to expedite the process are bound to fail. Hence a realistic appraisal of the future, according to this strategy, suggests that activist attempts to change Japan are certain to produce disappointing results and that the potential benefits are not worth much anyway. The conclusion is to neglect or bypass Japan altogether.

This approach has been adopted by some US companies. These firms, instead of entering Asia via Japan, have rejected that traditional mode in favor of launching their Asian efforts elsewhere, notably in China. In terms of economic policy, the "bypass-Japan" idea implies that the United States would pay no more attention to Japan than to any other middle-sized economic power.

We believe this approach would be counterproductive to US national interests. Japan remains the world's second largest economy and trader, and its largest surplus and creditor country. Its companies remain highly competitive in a number of key sectors. It has never exercised the international economic leadership that those attributes permit, but it nevertheless must participate actively if most international economic initiatives are to succeed.

Moreover, a bypass-Japan strategy by the United States would enable Japan to evade responsibility for the success of global economic initiatives. It could even encourage Japan to pursue regional options, or to withdraw into an inward-looking approach, without paying much attention to their consistency with broader multilateral arrangements and global objectives. Some Japanese might *like* the bypass-Japan approach for these reasons—along with a broader desire to be left alone, or at least to stop being singled out for badgering by the United States (and, to some extent, by the rest of the world).

In light of its own interests, however, the United States will need to continue working closely with Japan. The United States will need to seek Japan's support for most major multilateral projects, even if it does not pursue Japan with the bilateral zeal of the past. A stated policy of benign neglect or bypassing Japan would represent a substantively counterproductive strategy and convey the wrong message to Japan itself.

"Deep Integration"

"Deep integration" implies a substantial meshing of different national economies into a more and more united whole (Lawrence 1995). The European Union is of course the prototype. In contrast to ignoring or bypassing Japan, this second policy option would involve a concerted effort at economic integration via a gargantuan leap of political will that would sweep away the structural and sector-specific impediments to the two countries' economic exchanges.

Proposals for deep integration between the United States and Japan have taken a number of forms. The most common is for a bilateral FTA that would eliminate tariffs, and perhaps all other border barriers, between the two countries.[12] Some variants would install a special dispute-settlement mechanism between them, à la Canada-United States or NAFTA (Kuroda 1989).[13] An even more ambitious concept is for a Japan-United States "open marketplace," which would also penetrate "behind the border" to address more subtle barriers to international exchange (especially in Japan).[14]

Somewhat similar proposals have been made for monetary and macroeconomic policy. One suggestion, based on the idea that Japan's periodic economic problems have been caused by an overvalued yen that in turn derives from US trade policy pressures, calls for a yen-dollar stabilization pact that would rest on the coordination of monetary policy between the two countries (McKinnon and Ohno 1997).

These proposals derive from the frustrations of attempting to resolve Japan-United States economic conflicts on the traditional issue-by-issue basis. They observe that major political initiatives, embodied in far-reaching commitments to economic integration, have overcome even the most intractable commercial problems between long-standing rivals—as with France and Germany in the European Union, but also Argentina and Brazil in Mercosur—and so should work between allies such as Japan and the United States. They emphasize the large potential benefits from deep integration in both economic and political terms. They cite the similar levels of economic development in Japan and the United States, at least as measured by per capita incomes, and the similarities of their economic structures as well; as noted, most US opponents of further globalization have excluded Japan from their list of major targets.

However, any initiative to create an FTA (or something deeper) between the United States and Japan would have severely adverse effects on the

---

12. In principle, the United States and Japan agreed to free all trade between them as part of their commitments under the Bogor Declaration of APEC in 1994 to achieve "free and open trade and investment in the Asia Pacific by 2010." In practice, there has been no progress toward realizing this goal except through the several multilateral sectoral pacts (financial services, information technology, telecommunications services) negotiated since that time through the WTO.

13. It would also be possible to create a new bilateral dispute-settlement mechanism without a free trade agreement (Greenwald 1996).

14. Stokes (2000) proposes that the two countries agree to pursue such a structure by 2010, which he calls a "more ambitious grandson of SII" (p 3), though he acknowledges they would be highly unlikely to achieve it in practice.

global trading system and thus on the overall trade policies of the two countries. Any such proposal for free trade among high-income countries, like the proposals to create a Trans atlantic Free Trade Area between North America and Europe, would raise the specter of new discrimination against the world's poorer countries and—in addition to being a substantively bad idea for that reason—would deepen North-South tensions at a time when they are among the most vexing impediments to reaching international agreement on launching a new multilateral round in the WTO and elsewhere. In addition, US espousal of such a huge regional initiative could further jeopardize the multilateral structure of the world economy just when the United States should be reemphasizing its centrality.

In financial terms, the United States and Japan are very far from constituting an "optimal currency area" that could logically move toward a monetary union. They are characterized by considerable asymmetry in the impact of external shocks on their economies, so they should respond differentially, not similarly (let alone identically), to such events. There is virtually no labor mobility between them, especially into Japan, and there are no fiscal transfers between them nor any prospects thereof. The two main adjustment devices that are required to replace currency and monetary policy changes are thus totally absent, relegating the prospects for intensive monetary cooperation to the sidelines.

Most critically, the deep integration proposals fail to acknowledge both the enormous societal differences between Japan and the United States, and the absence of any compelling security motivation that could overcome these differences. All the successful integration efforts of the past and the contemporary efforts in that direction—notably the European Union, but also Mercosur and NAFTA—have had to overcome major economic and cultural differences among their members. In all these cases, however, there was an overriding security concern that enabled courageous political leadership to overcome extensive opposition to the merger: the obsession in postwar Europe of avoiding another fratricidal conflict on the continent, the decision by Argentina and Brazil to cease their potentially deadly nuclear competition, and the recognition in the United States that its southern border could become a severe threat to domestic tranquility unless Mexico were able to achieve much greater stability in the future. The only development that could conceivably generate the political momentum in Japan and the United States to justify such a project would be the rise of an ideologically objectionable and territorially expansionist China—a distinct, though unlikely, possibility.

In an earlier study of the Japan-United States economic relationship, two of the current authors stressed the prospect for partial convergence between the economic policies and institutions of the two countries (Bergsten and Noland 1993). We believe that convergence has continued, albeit slowly, during the intervening decade. In Japan, this has been driven by a combination of ideological shifts toward greater market-orientation by some policymakers and market pressures that have made the maintenance of the status quo untenable (Porter, M. Sakakibara, and Takeuchi 2000). On the US side, some convergence has occurred through corporate adoption of Japanese management techniques.

This continuing process of convergence is another reason why we conclude that the United States should now treat Japan as a "normal country" and eschew Japan-specific economic policies. At the same time, as was noted above, vast differences between the two countries are certain to remain for the foreseeable future. It would thus be economically inappropriate, as well as politically impossible, to pursue any of the deep integration options over the 5- to 10-year time horizon of this analysis.

Business as Usual

The most plausible alternative to our "Japan as a normal country" proposal is thus a continuation of the approach of the past 30 years (Lincoln 1999, 2001). As was noted above, the Japan-specific economic policy has rested on three broad principles: that Japan was more important to the US economy than any other country and that its competitive prowess represented a compelling threat to US interests, that Japan was sufficiently different (and perhaps "unfair") to require tailored approaches, and that the United States had sufficient leverage to pursue such a policy successfully. As will be demonstrated in this book, we believe that all these elements of the traditional equation have changed substantially. As a consequence, we believe that following the traditional approach in the future would lead to even greater frustrations than in the past. Hence we recommend a modest but important shift in US policy.

The changes in all three tenets of traditional US policy toward Japan are clear. As will be detailed in chapter 4, Japan is now considerably less important to US economic interests, and its weakness rather than its strength now represents the greatest threat to the United States (and the world as a whole). The process of convergence in policy and institutions between the two (as was just noted, and as will be elaborated in chapters 4-6) has reduced at least some of the "difference" between them (and thus perceptions of Japanese "unfairness"), although significant differences in economic policies and institutions persist in some areas. The prospect for successfully conducting Japan-specific policies has been sharply reduced, especially on trade issues, by fundamental changes in Japanese attitudes and by the creation of the WTO, as will be described in chapter 5; the United States simply can no longer use, and thus can no longer credibly threaten, unilateral trade retaliation against Japan.

Hence we conclude that the business-as-usual, Japan-specific approach of the past three decades has become infeasible as well as unnecessary.

A major proponent of that option, Edward Lincoln of the Brookings Institution, throws doubt on his own proposal when he concludes that "American options in encouraging a reform process that underwrites a healthy economic recovery are actually quite limited" (Lincoln 2001, 17). He also acknowledges that "the most important result is the need to lower American expectations about what can be accomplished" (Lincoln 1999, 16).

The key practical issue is how our proposed "Japan as a normal country" strategy would differ from that long-established pattern. We turn finally to a brief explanation of our proposed strategy, including an appraisal of how the United States would pursue its remaining, very real, and very important economic objectives toward Japan under such an approach. The proposal will be elaborated in more detail in chapter 7.

Treating Japan as a "Normal Country"

Our main policy conclusion is that the Japan-specific policy of the past has become an anomaly and that the time has come for the United States to start treating Japan as a "normal" nation. Japan of course remains the world's second largest national economy and third largest economic entity (behind the European Union as well as the United States). It is by far the world's largest surplus and creditor country. It remains a formidable competitor in many sectors. It is still the third largest trading partner of the United States. Hence economic relations with Japan, across a wide spectrum of macroeconomic and trade issues, will remain important and active—on a par with US economic activities with other major players, such as Canada, the European Union, and Mexico.

But there is no longer any need for a special "Japan policy." The completion of economic integration in Europe and the rise of China have reduced Japan's relative importance to the world economy and to the United States. Japan's growth is likely to approximate that of the United States itself, or even average a bit less, rather than exceed US growth by a threatening degree. Its "economic model" is sufficiently tarnished by the record of the 1990s to obviate the fears of supercompetitiveness that it had inspired a decade ago. Its "uniqueness" and "unfairness," to whatever extent they may have existed in the past, are declining as Japan slowly converges toward world norms, and especially as it joins the trend toward reduced governmental management of the economy. Past US efforts to wring concessions on reforms from Japan, even when US leverage was much greater, were disappointing. That leverage is much less than it was a decade or two ago. The time has come for the United States to start treating Japan as a normal country rather than as a unique and unfair economic superpower that requires dedicated special attention.

A normal-Japan policy by the United States would have a number of elements. First, most US foreign economic goals toward Japan would be pursued through multilateral channels. The main tool for trade issues would be the WTO (and perhaps APEC). The chief instrumentalities for macroeconomic issues would be (a hopefully revitalized) Group of Seven (G-7) and the IMF, with a subsidiary place for the Manila Framework Group (an approximate equivalent of the APEC finance ministers). The United States would encourage more regional cooperation in Asia, including Japan, as long as it is consistent with the existing multilateral processes, à la European Union and NAFTA.

Second, the United States would make a continuing effort to elicit support from other key members of these multilateral groupings to join its initiatives toward Japan. Effective use of the multilateral institutions requires active coalition diplomacy, in which the United States would seek maximum cooperation from other countries in promoting policy changes in Japan. The most important allies would be the main European countries in the G-7, IMF, and WTO, and the major Asian countries (especially the Association of Southeast Asian Nations, Australia, China, and South Korea) both in those same organizations and in APEC and the purely Asian groupings. The United States could, in at least some cases, also pursue its efforts through these Asian countries in forums where it is not a member itself, such as any Asian Monetary Fund or subregional trade agreements that might eventuate with membership limited to Asia.

Japan should of course pursue a parallel strategy of eliciting support from other key members of the multilateral institutions to support its initiatives toward the United States. Such competition within the multilateral framework would be exceedingly healthy for each of the countries, for the relationship between them, for the organizations, and for the system as a whole. The multilateral institutions should be the focal point for addressing economic issues and disputes, especially between large countries such as Japan and the United States, and our proposed strategy would accord a central role to that approach.

Third, the United States would continue to support economic reform and economic reformers in Japan. The United States clearly has a continuing interest in further deregulation and structural reform of the Japanese economy, as well as other economies, especially to strengthen Japan and to reduce the risks that its weaknesses would carry for the rest of the world. US commercial interests are not irrelevant in this context, but they are a decidedly secondary factor in the equation and should be treated as such. If a particular US company's parochial interest becomes a paramount element in the government's initiatives, it becomes quite counterproductive to the bilateral relationship. The United States should continue to play an active role in the policy debate in Japan, however, and might even have greater success by doing so in an objective, multilateral manner rather than under the threat of punitive retaliation if Japan fails to do its bidding.[15]

Fourth, the United States should generally place its emphasis on macroeconomic, monetary, and structural issues rather than sector-specific trade problems. The criterion of salience is again central: The broader macroeconomic issues are much more likely to be of importance to the United States as a whole (as opposed to specific industries or firms) than the narrower topics. They are also more likely to find allies in Japan and hence to succeed in reaching their goals.

Fifth, the United States would reserve the right to take unilateral policy initiatives in some cases where the stakes were sufficiently significant. For example, Japan's disastrous decision to bring on a recession by sharply raising taxes in 1997 appeared likely to threaten the Asians' recovery from their financial crisis and even the world economy. Hence the United States was correct to make forceful, repeated, and public demands to Japan over the issue—though it would have been much more effective to do so preemptively in 1996 and early 1997, before the decision became embedded in Japanese politics, than after the event, when it was too late to alter the outcome (Shafer 2000). Even in such instances, however, the United States should make every effort to mobilize international support for its initiatives—including through the multilateral institutions.[16]

The United States has of course always used multilateral tools to some extent in its initiatives toward Japan, especially to pursue its macroeconomic and monetary goals. But it is curious that the United States has frequently failed to mobilize other key countries to support its efforts. The Europeans, and even the other Asians that are affected most directly, have had relatively little to say in recent years about the critical need for Japan to fundamentally reform its financial system and to stimulate its economy through expansionary fiscal and monetary policies. A conspiracy seems to be at work: The United States apparently feels that its unilateral approaches will succeed or fail on their own, whatever third countries

---

15. There is also a potential major role in this context for "track two" diplomacy, so favored in Asia in recent years, through which nongovernmental actors carry forward an issue that arouses high political sensitivities and thus counterproductive responses when conducted in official circles. Whatever tracks are followed, the United States should consistently seek allies within Japan that share its desire to promote deregulation, restructuring, and reform.

16. Such "exceptions to the rule" would not apply in such relatively mundane cases as continued Japanese cartelization of the flat glass industry or the interconnection charges levied on its customers by NTT. The changes in Japanese practice that have been pursued by the United States in such cases would clearly be beneficial for Japan and, to a lesser extent, to the United States and other countries. In the changed circumstances of the early 21st century, however, they do not justify treating Japan as a special case for unilateral attack. Very few trade cases would. As a result, individual US firms and industries would be discouraged from seeking new governmental jihads on their behalf, and the risk of "political capture" of US policy would recede substantially.

may do, and those other countries apparently believe that their involvement will not affect the outcome, so they remain largely silent and let the United States make the running, avoiding ruffling their own diplomatic relations with Japan.[17]

Emphasizing the multilateral route vis-à-vis Japan would have several positive externalities. Other countries besides Japan, notably in Europe, have structural problems, and a multilateral focus would enable the United States to address those issues simultaneously. Other countries along with Japan, of course, maintain sector-specific trade barriers, notably in agriculture, and a multilateral focus (with allies such as the Cairns Group) also would attack them. Other countries and groups along with Japan need to be actively brought into the integration of competition policy in the WTO, notably the European Union but more and more a number of developing countries as well, so multilateralism also would pay dividends there. Other countries, along with Japan, face severe problems in their financial sectors and would benefit from increased monitoring by the IMF. These issues are elaborated in chapters 4, 5, and 7. The excessive resort by the United States to bilateral approaches to Japan has inevitably shortchanged some of these other important goals, and a multilateral focus would help redress the balance.

A multilateral focus for US policy *toward* Japan would also improve the prospect for conducting at least some parts of US policy *with* Japan. Despite its weakness, Japanese agreement is essential for pursuit of key global initiatives such as a new trade round in the WTO and convincing reform of the international financial architecture. In addition, Japan's new flirtation with regionalism needs to be firmly anchored in a multilateral context (as it seems to be so far). These extremely important US goals would be served by renewed emphasis on multilateral channels in handling the economic problems between the two countries themselves.

Conclusion

The United States does not normally conduct "economic polices" toward specific countries. It generally pursues a set of global economic policy goals: support for economic growth and stability in the United States itself, maintenance of a prosperous and stable world economy, and promotion of broader US foreign policy and national security objectives. Those global

---

17. Europeans and Asians also do not join unilateral US demands on Japan because they fear that similarly strong pressures may subsequently be applied to them. Japan, Europe, and most Asian countries are in agreement on opposition to a number of US approaches, including its use of section 301 of its trade law and antidumping duties. This outcome prevails even if US demands on Japan in a particular case may have beneficial spillover effects on Europeans and Asians. Hence the proposed shift in US policy toward Japan would also have beneficial side effects on US relations with its other major economic partners.

objectives must of course be implemented through relations with specific countries at specific times, but the resulting "country policies" are usually tactical innovations to promote the broader multilateral purposes. The United States has no economic policy toward Germany or the United Kingdom, or toward Canada (its largest trading partner), despite the existence of an FTA between the two and NAFTA, or toward the European Union (the largest economic entity in the world).

Japan has been the major exception to this pattern for the past three decades. The United States has not always pursued a Japan policy during this period, and the Japan policies that it has embraced have often differed substantially across the three decades. But the presence of a Japan-specific approach has been both frequent enough and intense enough to clearly identify the existence of such an exception to the usual US global approach (and to inspire a virtual cottage industry of studies of the topic). The Clinton administration even created a "Japan team," under its newly created National Economic Council, to deal with "the Japan problem."

The United States focused primarily on restricting Japanese sales to the United States from the early 1970s through the mid-1980s, on expanding foreign access to the Japanese market from 1985 until 1995, and on macroeconomic and monetary matters during the past 5 years. Virtually every aspect of Japanese economic policy, ranging from the broadest structural and macroeconomic issues to the most detailed sector-specific trade topics, has been addressed. The United States has employed nearly every policy instrument that is available to it: multilateral, regional, bilateral, and unilateral—often in combination and sometimes with one providing a cover for the others (as when the United States forged multilateral currency agreements in 1971-73 and 1985-87, with the Group of Ten or Group of Five countries, whose chief purpose was a sharp appreciation of the yen). Table 1.2 summarizes the intersection between the objectives pursued by the United States and the tactics it has deployed, with specific examples that illustrate the different cells in the matrix. We will assess the payoff from some of these approaches in chapter 5 before recommending a new strategy in chapter 7.

For its part, Japan has still tended in some instances to display the traditional pattern of yielding marginally and grudgingly to US *gaiatsu*, most recently in the Nippon Telegraph and Telephone Corporation (NTT) interconnection case (see box 5.5). Moreover, some of the key Japanese ministries initiated ideas for a new version of the traditional Japan-specific policy that produced the Economic Partnership for Growth in June 2001. Elsewhere, however, it was making major changes in its "America policy." It joined the European Union at Seattle in December 1999 to counter US efforts to launch a new round of multilateral negotiations in the WTO that was limited to pursuing US objectives. It rejected US proposals for a new steel agreement in 1999 and instead

Table 1.2 US economic policy toward Japan

Scope	Goal or instrument				
	Security	Macroeconomic stability	Export expansion	Import protection	Foreign direct investment
Multilateral	United Nations Security Council	IMF Group of Seven	World Trade Organization	World Trade Organization	World Trade Organization/OECD
Regional	ASEAN Regional Forum	MFG AMF?	APEC SRTAs?	—	APEC
Bilateral	United States-Japan Security Treaty	Reference range Currency intervention	VIEs (Clinton) SII (Bush) MOSS (Reagan)	VERs	BIT
Unilateral	Nuclear deterrent	Currency intervention	Devaluation, Section 301	ADD Import surcharge	Exon-Florio

ADD = Antidumping duties.
AMF = Asian Monetary Fund.
APEC = Asia Pacific Economic Cooperation.
ASEAN = Association of Southeast Asian Nations.
BIT = Bilateral Investment Treaty.
IMF = International Monetary Fund.
MFG = Manila Framework Group.
MOSS = Market-Oriented Sector-Specific.
OECD = Organization for Economic Cooperation and Development.
SII = Structural Impediment Initiative.
SRTAs = Subregional trade arrangements.
VIEs = Voluntary import expansion agreements.
VERs = Voluntary export restraint agreements.

fought a series of antidumping charges on a case-by-case basis, winning victories in the WTO. It rejected US entreaties to pursue a series of sectoral liberalization initiatives, especially in agriculture, in APEC in 1998, effectively bringing that institution's trade liberalization efforts to a halt. It rejected strong US entreaties to abandon its plan to raise taxes in 1997, which threw the economy into recession (as the United States had forewarned). It stiffed the US initiatives on autos and auto parts in 1995.

More broadly, Japan has begun to reverse its postwar policy of relying solely on multilateral approaches. It has launched a series of exploratory negotiations for bilateral "free trade areas" with Mexico, Singapore, South Korea, and perhaps others. It has reinvigorated its earlier push for regional monetary arrangements, at least partly to counter US dominance of the global financial system. It was in fact starting to sign a series of bilateral "swap arrangements" with neighboring countries by the middle of 2001.

Economic policy in both the United States and Japan toward the other is thus in considerable flux. The future of each is highly uncertain. The impact on the global economic system could be profound. Both countries clearly need to review the premises on which past policy have rested.

We believe that the dramatic changes in the economic positions of the two countries, and the shifts in global developments that affect both, counsel a fresh look at the relationship and at policy in both countries. Indeed, we conclude that these changes suggest a completely new approach, particularly by the United States. We turn next to an in-depth analysis of the key issues that can provide a foundation for such a new strategy for the future.

2

The Resurgence of the American Economy

The US Economy and Japan-United States Economic Relations

The resurgence of the US economy was one of the major global events of the last years of the 20th century. Along with other contemporary developments—the end of the Cold War, the further economic integration of Europe and the creation of the euro, and Japan's "decade of decline"— it has had profound effects on the world economy. Whether the US recovery of the period turns out to be lasting or a transitory phenomenon is a critical question that will have a significant impact on the economies of other countries, including Japan.

The answer to this question will also have important consequences for the foreign economic policy of the United States, and especially for the its relationship with Japan. Continued strong performance by the US economy, and the increased self-confidence that springs from it, will reduce US concerns about the economic performance of Japan (and other countries). Hence, it will reduce the pressure that the United States places on them to alter their own economic policies (Bergsten and Noland 1993).

Indeed, the unique "Japan policy" conducted by the United States for a quarter-century, from the early 1970s through the middle 1990s (as described in chapter 1), now looks to have been largely a historical accident. The United States entered its own period of economic difficulty in the early 1970s, with a substantial decline in productivity growth and hence economic growth that led to a prolonged stagnation of real wages and incomes. The oil shocks, and the gasoline lines they produced, revealed for the first time in the postwar period the deep vulnerability of the United States to external events. Double-digit inflation and a plunging dollar heightened national anxiety in the late 1970s. Along with the rise of Japan to global economic prominence, these forces drew the United States into a policy toward that country that was unique in US experience.

The intensity of this Japan-specific US policy accelerated sharply in the middle 1980s with the crisis in overall US trade policy that then developed (Kunkel 2001). The sharp increase in US budget deficits during the first Reagan administration, coupled with the rise in interest rates that was necessary to overcome the double-digit inflation of the late 1970s, produced a dramatic rise in the value of the dollar and record increases in the US trade and current account deficits, of which the largest share by far was with Japan. The huge dollar overvaluation, especially against the yen, drastically altered the politics of US trade policy—with a sharp rise in the number of industries seeking import relief and a sharp fall in the export interests that resisted such proposals. Key members of Congress opined that "the Smoot Hawley tariff itself would have passed overwhelmingly had it come to the House floor" at that time.

Under the leadership of his new secretary of the treasury, James Baker, President Reagan reversed his foreign economic policy to head off such a risk, with both the Plaza Agreement to drive down the dollar and a "tough" new trade policy to show Congress that he could be trusted to "defend American interests." Japan—as the main surplus counterpart to the US deficits and the primary threat to US economic supremacy—was the chief target of these actions, and the unique US policy toward that country was ratcheted up further. This intensified pressure persisted for most of the next decade, through the Clinton administration's effort on autos and auto parts, until it ran aground in the middle of 1995.

Clear evidence of a new US attitude toward Japan can be observed in the second half of the 1990s. As the US economy regained its competitiveness and noninflationary growth shifted into high gear in the middle of the decade, the United States—despite rapid increases in its trade and current account deficits—relaxed its attack on Japanese trade policies and even substantially scaled back its assault on Japanese structural rigidities. The United States—motivated especially by the onset of the Asian financial crisis, and by Japan's huge fiscal and monetary policy errors—launched a renewed effort to influence Japanese macroeconomic and financial-sector policies in 1997-98, but even those initiatives waned as the decade came to a close. The new Bush administration in 2001 essentially maintained the policy toward its chief Pacific ally that it had inherited, if anything downplaying the economic issues even further relative to security concerns, indicating that the sense of renewed confidence continued despite the sharp slowdown in US economic expansion.

These changes in the US attitude were well founded. The focus of the early Clinton administration on Japanese trade policies, especially concerning such products as semiconductors and automobiles, were based on "strategic trade theory" concerns that those policies could severely harm important US industries and even the entire US economy (Tyson 1992). When it turned out that the relevant US industries were doing quite well and in fact contributing substantially to the resurgence of the overall US economy, with at best modest help from the trade policy initiatives, the salience of such initiatives waned perceptibly. Even more important, the overall US economy surged dramatically, despite the absence of much help from these initiatives—indeed, when the Japanese economy as a whole was stagnating and thus *dampening* global growth. When it also turned out that the initiatives were likely to bear little fruit (as will be analyzed in chapter 5), they were dropped precipitously after the middle of 1995.

The renewed US attention to Japanese financial and macroeconomic policies in the late 1990s reflected a new and opposite concern: that Japan's economic *weakness* could adversely affect the United States (and the world as a whole). There were widespread fears in 1997-98 that Japan's relapse into recession, compounding and compounded by the Asian crisis, could jeopardize US and global economic growth. The severe structural weakness of the Japanese banking system, in particular (as will be described in detail in chapter 3), posed a threat to regional and even global stability.

Hence the United States, with increasing force and public criticism, sought major changes in Japanese fiscal, monetary, and banking policy. But the US and world economies subsequently accelerated, to their most rapid growth in 30 years, without much improvement in Japanese performance. Most of the East Asian countries recovered from their crises, despite continued weakness in the largest economy in the region. Thus the United States was able to throttle back its concerns about Japanese weakness in the late 1990s, as it had previously throttled back its concerns about Japan's strengths in the earlier period. The world had clearly learned how to prosper despite a decade of stagnation in Japan, and US concern over Japan's prospects increased only modestly, even with the sharp slowdown in US and global growth after the middle of 2000.

The strong US economic performance of the late 1990s simultaneously muted most of the domestic political pressure in the United States to restrict US markets for Japanese products. US economic strength, coupled with the strong performance of US exports throughout the 1990s—except for the period of the Asian crisis—dampened the pressure to open Japan's market to US products even more. In particular, the steady reductions in unemployment to their lowest levels in 30 years greatly weakened the political impact of pleas for special help from the government vis-à-vis Japan.

Steel was the sole exception among major industries (see box 4.2). A series of antidumping actions were taken on steel in the late 1990s and an import quota bill for steel did pass the House of Representatives in early 1999 (but was soundly rejected by the Senate and clearly would have been vetoed by President Clinton) (Hufbauer and Wada 1999). President Bush initiated an "escape clause" case for steel in early 2001 (Hufbauer and Goodrich 2001). But no other import restrictions against Japan were seriously considered, and the intensity of the US pressure on Japan to further open its markets—even for such previously "politically sensitive" products as semiconductors and auto parts—waned appreciably.

Even the sharp slowdown in US growth, and modest increases in unemployment (with much larger increases in *manufacturing* unemployment) that began in the middle of 2000, had generated very little protectionist or mercantilist pressure against Japan by the middle of 2001. To be sure, generalized antiglobalization pressures remained strong—as they had throughout the boom years of the late 1990s. Most of those pressures, however, were aimed at "low-wage countries" such as Mexico (in the NAFTA debate) and China (in the debate over its entry to the WTO and US granting of permanent normal trade relations), and at countries with allegedly low labor and environmental standards. Japan met none of these criteria, even in the view of those most aggressively against globalization.

In addition, the combination of the US economic slowdown and record trade deficits produced a surge of concerns in the middle of 2001 by US industry, labor, and agriculture over the adverse effect on US competitiveness of the continued strength of the dollar. Even there, however, the calls for remedial action were generalized and aimed more at the euro than, as in past periods, at the yen. There was even some sympathy for the weakness of the yen in view of Japan's continued travails and its desperate need to find a vehicle to promote the recovery of its own economy.

This reduction in US pressure on Japan was particularly noteworthy in that one of the traditional sources of such pressure was increasing steadily, and in fact reached its *worst* position in history: the US trade and current account deficits, both globally and bilaterally with Japan itself (see figure 4.1). Historically, increases in US bilateral deficits have been the most accurate "leading indicator" of trade disputes with individual countries, especially Japan (Noland 1997a). The largest runups in those deficits have produced the most aggressive US attacks on Japanese economic policies in the postwar period: the import surcharge of 1971; the "locomotive" approach of the late 1970s, which sought major changes in Japanese macroeconomic policies to stimulate global growth and to reduce the US imbalance; and the reversal of Reagan policies in 1985, which produced the first "managed-trade" agreement (in semiconductors) and the infamous Section 301 authority for unilateral retaliation against countries (especially Japan) that did not open their markets to US products, along with the Plaza Agreement, which produced a 50 percent depreciation of the dollar against the yen. Yet the recent escalation of US external deficits, to annual rates of about $450 billion and 4.5 percent of GDP, coexisted with the significant *cooling* of tensions described above.

It must of course be noted that the persistence, and even the growth to record levels, of the external deficits had several *beneficial* effects on the US economy during the boom period of the late 1990s (Bergsten 2001b). The rising dollar, which was an important cause of the increasing deficits, and rising net imports themselves dampened import prices. This in turn checked prices of competitive domestic products and helped restrain inflation, perhaps by 1 percentage point a year (Rubin 2000). This reduction of inflation in turn helped restrain interest rates, perhaps by 1-2 percentage points. The net capital inflows that both caused and financed the current account deficit also further moderated interest rates and helped facilitate the sharp increases in investment that fueled the boom. The administration and the Federal Reserve could never publicly admit that they welcomed the trade deficits—though the administration did constantly extol the virtues of a "strong dollar"—but the deficits' positive contribution to the strong performance of the economy undoubtedly limited their zeal for attacking Japan's contributions to it.

Moreover, Japan's share of the US global deficit fell sharply during the 1990s. Japan consistently accounted for about half of the US worldwide imbalance before 1992 (see figure 4.1)—partially explaining why the aggressive US trade initiatives of the earlier period were aimed so clearly in its direction. But that number fell steadily to about 20 percent in 1999. Moreover, in at least some time periods, China replaced Japan as the single largest counterpart of the US deficits.[1] Japan's external surplus, though still sizable, in fact *declined* steadily in late 2000 and the first half of 2001, while the US deficit remained near record levels. Hence, another traditional source of Japan-US economic tension has moderated substantially during the past decade.

The reliability of this analysis—which suggests that the juxtaposition of US economic difficulties and strong Japanese performance explains much of the economic conflict between the two countries for a quarter-century—is complicated by the fact that there is no earlier period of comparable US economic strength after Japan had become a major global player and thus a serious competitor of the United States. The only prior period of prolonged US economic expansion in the postwar era came during the 1960s, when Japan was still regarded as a poor if rapidly developing country. Indeed, President John F. Kennedy, in seeking Congressional approval to negotiate the Kennedy Round of multilateral trade

---

1. The US data, however, clearly overstate the magnitude of its bilateral deficit with China (Lardy 1994; Hufbauer and Rosen 2000).

liberalization in 1961, cited as a rationale "the need for new markets *for Japan and the developing nations*" (italics added) (Preeg 1970). As we will see below, US industry in fact failed to recognize the rise of Japan (and Europe) by the end of that decade, and thus let its own competitiveness slip to a point that severely weakened the US economy for the next decade or so.

During the steady rise of Japan to global prominence in the 1970s and 1980s, however, the US economy was experiencing an extremely difficult period. Labor productivity growth dropped sharply, from the 3 percent annual rate of the first postwar generation to about 1.5 percent during the period 1975-95 (table 2.1), and overall economic growth declined correspondingly. Average unemployment in the United States exceeded 6 percent in the 1970s and 7 percent in the 1980s, in comparison with the 4.5-4.8 percent rates of the 1950s and 1960s and a "full-employment norm" of about 4 percent. Average real wages stagnated during this entire period, and actually declined for the lowest two quintiles of the labor force. Double-digit inflation became rampant in the late 1970s and early 1980s, and interest rates correspondingly soared above 10 percent.

This extended period of mediocre US economic performance correlates almost perfectly with the onset, and maintenance, of an extremely aggressive US foreign economic policy toward Japan—commencing with the "Nixon shocks" in the early 1970s through the Clinton Framework Talks that extended into the middle 1990s. The adoption and maintenance by the United States of a unique "Japan policy" in the economic sphere for more than two decades thus seems to have been primarily the result of an equally unique historical coincidence—an extended period of travail for the US economy, coupled with the dramatic rise to global prominence of the Japanese economy at the same time, exacerbated by the intense interaction between the two, including the very sizable aggregate imbalance in their trade positions throughout the period.

There is of course an alternative hypothesis: that it was Japan's weak economic performance in the 1990s, rather than strong US results, that primarily induced (and politically enabled) the United States to relax its pressures on Japanese policies. That weakness has been evident both at the macroeconomic level and in the failure of much of Japanese industry to exploit high value-added areas of the "new economy." This development (which will be analyzed in depth in chapter 3) is undoubtedly an element in the equation as already emphasized. Indeed (as was noted in chapter 1), a "bypass-Japan" mentality has come to influence parts of US industry, and is part of the thinking of some US authorities.

However, some of the leading firms in Japan's dynamic internationally competitive sector—its Sonys and Toyotas—have maintained or even strengthened their global positions, even as Japan's overall economy has suffered its "decade of decline." There has been very little, if any, letup

Table 2.1 The growth of US labor productivity, the labor force, GDP, and the unemployment rate, 1960-2000
(annual growth rate, percent)

Year	Productivity[a]	Labor force[b]	GDP growth	Unemployment rate
1960	1.9	0.7	2.5	5.5
1961	3.7	0.2	2.3	6.7
1962	4.6	1.6	6.0	5.5
1963	3.9	1.9	4.3	5.7
1964	4.6	2.3	5.8	5.2
1965	3.6	3.2	6.4	4.5
1966	4.1	2.3	6.6	3.8
1967	2.2	2.4	2.5	3.8
1968	3.1	1.7	4.8	3.6
1969	0.5	2.6	3.1	3.5
1970	2.0	−0.2	0.2	4.9
1971	4.4	2.4	3.1	5.9
1972	3.3	3.6	5.3	5.6
1973	3.2	3.6	5.7	4.9
1974	−1.7	−0.3	−0.3	5.6
1975	3.5	0.6	−0.3	8.5
1976	3.6	3.6	5.2	7.7
1977	1.6	4.8	4.5	7.1
1978	1.1	3.7	5.7	6.1
1979	0.0	2.4	3.4	5.8
1980	−0.3	−0.3	0.0	7.1
1981	1.9	0.0	2.5	7.6
1982	−0.4	−0.6	−1.9	9.7
1983	3.6	4.0	4.2	9.6
1984	2.8	3.1	7.3	7.5
1985	2.0	1.9	3.9	7.2
1986	3.0	2.3	3.4	7.0
1987	0.5	2.8	3.5	6.2
1988	1.2	2.0	4.2	5.5
1989	1.0	1.5	3.5	5.3
1990	1.3	0.3	1.7	5.6
1991	1.1	−0.7	−0.2	6.8
1992	3.9	1.3	3.3	7.5
1993	0.5	2.1	2.4	6.9
1994	1.3	2.7	4.0	6.1
1995	0.7	0.3	2.7	5.6
1996	2.8	2.2	3.7	5.4
1997	2.3	2.2	4.4	4.9
1998	2.7	1.4	4.3	4.5
1999	2.5	1.4	4.1	4.2
2000	3.1	1.0	4.1	4.0
Averages				
1960-74	2.9	1.9	3.9	5.0
1975-95	1.6	1.8	3.0	7.0
1996-2000	2.7	1.7	4.1	4.6

a. Labor productivity is the output per hour of all persons in the business sector.
b. Labor force is the civilian labor force, age 16 years or older.

Sources:
Productivity growth: US Department of Labor, Bureau of Labor Statistics, http://www.access.gpo.gov/usbudget/. *Labor force growth:* US Department of Labor, Bureau of Labor Statistics, http://www.access.gpo.gov/usbudget/. *GDP growth:* US Department of Commerce, Bureau of Economic Analysis, http://www.access.gpo.gov/usbudget/. *Unemployment:* US Department of Labor, Bureau of Labor Statistics, http://www.access.gpo.gov/usbudget/.

of the pressure they have brought to bear on their US competitors and the US economy. Indeed, we will suggest below that this continued pressure—along with similar pressure from other foreign competitors—has been a major positive factor inducing the rising productivity and hence strength of the US economy during this period. Moreover, unlike the earlier period of Japanese weakness and US strength during the early postwar years, Japan is now a rich country whose per capita income, depending on market exchange rates, has at times considerably exceeded that of the United States.

The most directly international measure of Japan's economic prowess—its global trade and current account surpluses—in fact rose to record highs in 1993-94 and continued to exceed $100 billion annually, even as they declined into the earliest part of the 21st century. These surpluses derived partly from Japan's economic weakness, both its stagnant domestic economy (which dampened demand for imports) and the periodic depreciations of its currency. But the surpluses also reflected the continued competitive strength of Japanese manufacturing. The persistent and growing strength of the United States provides a much more plausible explanation than Japan's weakness for most of the reduction in US pressure on Japan, though the latter was clearly a contributing factor.

Any projection of the future Japan-United States economic relationship—and especially any prescriptions for its conduct—thus must be rooted in a judgment concerning the course of the US economy for at least the next few years. (It must also be rooted in a parallel judgment concerning the Japanese economy, to which we will turn in chapter 3.) Renewed strong US performance, particularly with continued low levels of unemployment, would probably presage a continued lower level of US anxiety concerning Japan. This would not suggest a new era of "benign neglect," however, because the US external deficit will almost certainly require correction at some fairly early point, because politically sensitive and powerful US sectors will continue to face tough competition from their Japanese counterparts, and because Japanese *weakness* could cause as much (or more) trouble for the United States than Japanese strength—including for adjustment of the US deficit, because that would inevitably *add* to the pressures on the Japanese economy. Moreover, a relapse by the United States to its mediocre economic record of the 1970s and part of the 1980s, especially with rising unemployment, could trigger renewed aggressiveness toward Japan (and other parts of the world). Hence we now turn to an assessment of the outlook for the US economy.

Sources of the US Economic Resurgence

Writing in the middle of 2001, after the sharp slowdown that began in the middle of 2000 and persisted for at least a year, it is clearly premature to attempt a definitive analysis of the resurgence of the US economy in the late 1990s and its likely future course. During the second half of the decade, however, the US economy surprised most observers with the acceleration in its growth and job creation to unanticipated levels without triggering significant inflation. It has grown for almost 20 years, except for a very short recession in 1990-91, and for more than 10 years without interruption (despite the sharp slowdown from mid-2000 to at least mid-2001). There is a rising consensus on the causes of, and the future prospects for, this remarkable record—but nothing that could yet be called "conventional wisdom."

In addition, it is worth remembering that no one foresaw the strength and sustainability of this US expansion. Even discounting the doomsayers and "American declinists," some of whom saw Japan as dominating the world economy by now, there was no contemplation of anything like the magnitude and duration of the US rebound. It must also be noted that the United States, during all this progress, was still viewed by some as a "bubble economy" that could burst at any time, as Japan did a decade ago—and that the precipitate decline in the NASDAQ, along with the lesser but substantial declines in the broader market indices, provide at least modest support for that view. In addition, the large and growing external deficit suggests that, at some point, the dollar could fall sharply and cause substantial disruption, as it has on three previous occasions during the postwar period.

Even if no such immediate problems eventuate, it is also clear that the United States continues to face daunting economic and related social problems—such as low private savings, an inadequate primary and secondary education system, substantial income inequality, and an extended period of wage stagnation that only began to disappear in the later stages of the boom of the 1990s. Any temptation toward US triumphalism must thus be tempered by the shortcomings that could disrupt future progress in both the short and long runs. Nevertheless, the recent record is impressive, and we turn to a necessarily tentative analysis of its sources as a basis for attempting to judge the likely future course of the economy—with its significant, perhaps decisive, impact on US economic relations with Japan.

Three factors seem to account for most of the US resurgence. The first is the sharp pickup in labor productivity growth, from less than 1.5 percent annually during the period 1975-95 to about 2.5 percent in the second half of the 1990s, which in turn seems to derive largely from the commercialization of the new information technologies and the competitive pressures of globalization. The second major change is the structural shift of the federal budget from large deficit to large surplus, which produced part of the needed boost in national savings, enabling real interest rates to decline substantially and thus to promote private investment. There are cyclical elements in both these shifts: productivity always picks up during an expansion, the expansion itself helps to strengthen the fiscal position, and both have faltered during the slowdown of 2000-01. Both productivity and the budget have clearly experienced substantial underlying improvement, however, even when all short-term factors are taken into account.

The third key element in the economy's improvement is the superb conduct of monetary policy during the past two decades by the Federal Reserve under the leadership of Paul Volcker and Alan Greenspan, which has quelled rapid inflation and then permitted the expansion to proceed without premature tightening of monetary policy. One additional result of these sea changes in fiscal and monetary policy has been the restoration of a high degree of flexibility for the future; monetary and/or fiscal stimulation can now be deployed to counter almost any significant deterioration in economic prospects or any abrupt crises, and thus is available to keep the expansion going even if it should be hit by negative shocks. Both types of stimulation were of course used promptly in 2001, with precisely this goal in mind.[2]

Increased Productivity Growth

Sustainable growth of course rests on increases in productivity of the economy (see box 2.1 for the relevant definitions and concepts). The underlying cause of the slow growth of the US economy from the early 1970s to the middle 1990s was the sharp slowdown in the growth of labor productivity to less than 1.5 percent a year from about 3 percent annually throughout the first postwar generation (table 2.1). With labor force growth at 1 to 1.5 percent a year, economic growth thus averaged only 3 percent. Such growth was adequate to bring unemployment below 6 percent for only 4 of those 20 years, and it averaged close to 7 percent during the two decades—far higher than in the previous quarter-century. Indeed, many economists believed as late as the middle 1990s that the US growth potential had dropped to annual rates of 2 to 2.5 percent.

Starting in about 1996, however, labor productivity increases rose sharply, to an average of 2.7 percent a year (table 2.1). Total factor productivity growth—the best single measure of the underlying efficiency of the economy—rose even more sharply (especially if the special computer sector is excluded) (CEA 2001). Economic growth thus rose sharply, to an average of 4.1 percent in the second half of the 1990s (table 2.1). Domestic demand growth averaged almost 5 percent annually during

---

2. Lindsey (2000) instead attributes "America's 17-year boom" to deregulation, cuts in marginal tax rates, "supply-side" management of capital and labor, and a "revolution" in capital markets. These factors, especially deregulation, have undoubtedly contributed to the rise in productivity growth, but the elements cited in the text appear to be more important.

Box 2.1 Productivity concepts and definitions

Economists typically use two primary concepts of productivity: labor productivity and total factor productivity (TFP). Labor productivity equals real output per hour of work or per employee. It thus incorporates all contributions to output except for the quantity of labor itself. The three main components of labor productivity growth are capital deepening (i.e., increased investment), changes in labor quality (as firms substitute toward workers with more skills) and TFP—which includes everything else.

The growth of labor productivity plus the growth of the labor force equals output growth, at least during prolonged periods. At the same time, the increase in labor productivity equals the growth of real wages (and approximates the growth of per capita income). There is also a considerable negative correlation between growth in labor productivity and inflation. Hence changes in labor productivity are central to an economy's performance.

But we obviously want to know more about the underlying sources of growth in labor productivity, and this is where TFP becomes important. TFP is defined as real output per unit of all inputs and is essentially the amount of output growth not explained by the measured growth of capital and labor. It is frequently interpreted as a proxy for technology, which is important and certainly included, but TFP also picks up such phenomena as increasing returns to scale, reallocation from low- to high-productivity activities, and improvements in organizational structures and management techniques. It is thus the best aggregate measure of the total efficiency of an economy and must play a central role in any assessment of a country's underlying strength and improvement, especially during a period of rapid technological and management change (including due to globalization), such as that experienced by the United States in the late 1990s. (This description draws heavily on Steindel and Stiroh [2001]. See their excellent paper for more details.)

1997-99, and productivity growth accelerated *after* a half-decade of growth for the first time in the postwar period. About 16 million jobs were created in the 1990s. Unemployment declined steadily, to just above 4 percent by early 1999, and remained there until early 2001.

The comparison between productivity growth in the United States and in other countries in recent years is noteworthy (table 2.2). During the 1980s and the first half of the 1990s, labor productivity growth was slower in the United States than in every other G-7 country except Canada—and was about one half that of Japan. In the latter half of the 1990s, labor productivity growth was higher in the United States than in all other G-7 countries—especially including Japan (Gust and Marquez 2000).

The crucial questions, of course, are why productivity growth accelerated so sharply and whether that acceleration is likely to prove sustainable. Expert analyses diverge at this point. Gordon has argued that virtually all of the pickup occurred in durable manufacturing, including in the information technology sector itself, and that very little impact of the "new economy" could be seen "in the remaining 88 percent of the economy" (Gordon 2000, 50). Conversely, Jorgensen and Stiroh find that total factor

Table 2.2 Average growth rate of productivity in Group of Seven countries, 1981-99

Country, region, and productivity estimate	1981-89	1990-98	1990-95	1996-98	1996-99
Australia					
Labor productivity	1.45	2.37	1.79	3.52	3.12
Capital deepening	0.45	0.82	0.64	1.16	1.06
TFP	1.01	1.57	1.15	2.41	2.11
Canada					
Labor productivity	1.42	1.26	1.34	1.10	0.92
Capital deepening	1.31	0.96	1.08	0.73	0.67
TFP	0.14	0.31	0.26	0.69	0.27
France					
Labor productivity	3.41	2.12	2.26	1.86	1.61
Capital deepening	1.10	1.09	1.35	0.57	0.05
TFP	2.26	1.03	0.89	1.31	1.12
Germany					
Labor productivity	n.a.	2.13	2.26	1.96	2.14
Capital deepening	n.a.	1.09	1.22	0.91	1.06
TFP	n.a.	1.03	1.02	1.04	1.07
Italy					
Labor productivity	2.33	2.09	2.72	0.81	0.67
Capital deepening	0.87	1.18	1.36	0.82	0.82
TFP	1.45	0.88	1.32	−0.01	−0.14
Japan					
Labor productivity	3.12	2.48	2.89	1.64	2.07
Capital deepening	1.15	1.44	1.56	1.21	1.23
TFP	2.00	1.03	1.31	0.46	0.85
United Kingdom					
Labor productivity	3.37	1.72	1.78	1.60	1.47
Capital deepening	0.42	0.53	0.57	0.44	0.54
TFP	2.90	1.20	1.21	1.18	0.95
United States					
Labor productivity	1.59	1.78	1.47	2.42	2.57
Capital deepening	0.73	0.77	0.68	0.96	1.11
TFP	0.86	1.01	0.79	1.46	1.47
Of which, labor quality	0.34	0.39	0.42	0.32	0.31
OECD					
Labor productivity	1.31	1.43	1.02	2.26	2.30
Capital deepening	0.25	0.24	0.16	0.40	0.54
TFP	1.09	1.20	0.85	1.91	1.80

n.a. = not available.
OECD = Organization for Economic Cooperation and Development.
TFP = total factor productivity.

Note: The sum of capital deepening growth and MFP growth does not always add up to labor productivity growth because of rounding errors. Measures of labor productivity, capital deepening, and MFP are those in Oliner and Sichel (2000), plus their estimated growth of labor quality.

Source: Gust and Marquez (2000).

productivity growth has tripled and that capital deepening has increased substantially as well. They reject Gordon's view and conclude instead that productivity growth has extended beyond information-technology-producing industries, which "could be interpreted as evidence of a new economy," and that the US economy "has undergone a remarkable transformation" and "may be recuperating from the anemic productivity growth of the past two decades" (Jorgensen and Stiroh 2000, 152, 160, 129).

Moreover, the US Council of Economic Advisers found through a series of industry analyses that "the spread of information technology throughout the economy has been a major factor in the acceleration of productivity" (CEA 2001, 33). Its studies showed "striking evidence of improvement" in wholesale and retail trade, financial institutions as a group, and some other components of the services sector. It concludes that "improved business practices and more-productive use of information technology have played an important role in the acceleration of productivity" (CEA 2001, 31).

An even more optimistic analysis has been offered by Greenspan (2000). Noting the "serendipitous emergence of a once- or twice-in-a-century surge in technology" and "the virtually unprecedented surge in innovation that we have experienced over the most recent half decade," he concludes that "capital deepening has surged during the past seven years and innovations, synergies, and networking effects have boosted significantly the growth of multifactor productivity." He rejects Gordon's view that the productivity increase has been narrowly based, arguing instead that "virtually every part of our economic structure is, to a greater or lesser extent, affected by the new innovations" and that "there is, with few exceptions, little of a truly old economy left."

Related to, but even more important than, the resolution of this debate over the breadth of the productivity pickup is its future outlook: whether it has largely been completed or, to the contrary, might still be at an early stage. The latter view has been espoused by Greenspan, who has stressed "the continuing acceleration of productivity" and that "credible evidence that the rate of structural productivity growth has stopped increasing is still lacking." Virtually all industries, in services as well as manufacturing, are now deeply into the process of applying the new technologies to their endeavors. Historically, it has taken surprisingly long periods to commercialize the new technologies of the day—which would explain the delayed payoff to the US economy and suggest that more, perhaps considerably more, might still be ahead.

Conversely, the official projection of the Council of Economic Advisers in early 2000 saw labor productivity falling from its pace of nearly 3 percent in the previous years (as then estimated) to an average of 2 percent for 2000-10 and slightly less toward the end of the decade (CEA 2000, 85). Gordon believes that the cyclical effect accounts for half a percentage point of the productivity pickup and that further gains from computer investment are unlikely; indeed, he concludes that "the greatest benefits of computers lies a decade or more in the past, not in the future" (2000, 50).

But several careful analyses of the productivity pickup, some even taking account of the sharp economic (and thus productivity) slowdown of mid-2000 to mid-2001, conclude that there was very little cyclical contribution to the dramatic rise of 1995-2000 (Baily 2001; Basu, Fernald, and Shapiro 2001; CEA 2001). Even Gordon has acknowledged that "only a few years ago the consensus was that potential GDP was growing at a 2¼ percent annual rate (whereas) now the debate is whether that rate is 3½ or 3¾ percent . . ." (BPEA 2000; Baily 2001, table 2, summarizes and compares the remarkably similar conclusions of the major studies on this topic). Jorgensen and Stiroh, while noting that the sustainability of recent growth trends "hinges to a great degree on the prospects for continuing progress, especially in the production of semiconductors," conclude that "upward revisions of growth projections seem a reasonable response as evidence accumulates of a possible break in trend productivity growth" (Jorgensen and Stiroh 2000, 184-85).

Gordon's own suggestion that only half a percentage point of the recent growth upturn was cyclical leaves room for a significant upward revision of the potential growth rate. Even the earlier and lower CEA and other estimates of early 2000 would still see the economy growing at 3 percent annually. The chief author of the CEA analysis, taking into account the stellar productivity performance in 2000 as well as the downturn after mid-2000, and acknowledging that some of the pickup in productivity growth may have been temporary rather than structural, more recently has projected a sustainable economic growth rate of 3-3.5 percent (Baily 2001, 12). It thus seems likely that US growth has moved to a considerably higher plane and will provide a much stronger foundation for the country's foreign economic policy, most notably toward Japan.

Globalization

The prospect for continued solid US expansion is strengthened by the even greater likelihood that globalization, the second major spur to the pickup in productivity growth, is still at an early stage. Most of this increased globalization of the US economy has of course resulted from the technological revolutions in transportation, communications, and the rest of the global infrastructure, although steady reductions in trade barriers have also been an important factor. Globalization plays an important, if often underappreciated, role in the US economic resurgence because its rapid onset in the United States has been a major spur to the competitive improvement of the private sector, by far the leading source of the productivity surge (Richardson and Lewis 2001).

The United States has in fact globalized extremely rapidly. The share of external trade in US GDP has almost tripled since 1960, increasing US openness to a level that approximates that of the European Union (as a group) and exceeds Japan (see figure 1.3). As a result, US firms realize that they are now competing in a truly global economy. Complacency permeated US industry after the extended economic expansion of the 1960s, the only postwar parallel to the present experience, because it still viewed itself as operating in a largely self-contained continental economy. Such complacency is of course nowhere to be seen at present. Indeed, US firms—whether in the tradable or nontradable sectors—continued to make constant efforts to expand their efficiency throughout the domestic boom of the late 1990s.[3]

The competitive pressures of globalization have clearly improved the labor productivity of US firms. In addition, the antiinflationary impact of globalization—both its short-run effect through the stronger dollar and trade deficit, cited above, and its permanent impact through greater openness for the economy—accounts for part of the pickup of economic growth.

Most of this source of improved US growth is structural and likely to continue. It could even accelerate, because globalization is still at an early stage. Studies show that national borders still matter a great deal in determining international commerce, even between Canada and the United States—with their close geographic proximity, linguistic and cultural similarity, and free trade area for more than a decade (Helliwell 1998). Additional countries are participating effectively in international trade and finance. Competitive pressures from globalization are likely to increase rather than diminish.

The main risk to the outlook in this area is the political backlash against globalization. This has been especially manifest in the United States, blocking most further reduction of its own trade barriers (and therefore any serious multilateral liberalization) since 1994, despite the strength of the US economy. The Congressional split over the issue mirrors a fundamental split in public opinion, which is based largely on a deep division along educational lines between more- and less-skilled workers (Scheve and Slaughter 2001). A small but significant number of workers do in fact suffer substantial lifetime earnings losses from job dislocation in trade-intensive sectors (Kletzer 2001), and others fear that "there but for the grace of God go I." Hence the backlash could escalate if unemployment were to rise, especially with the trade deficit at such sizable levels, and impede the continued expansion of globalization, which is otherwise quite likely and which has been so beneficial.

---

3. Baily notes that "intense global competitive pressure helps companies looking for ways to cut costs and raise productivity" (2001, 33).

Figure 2.1 Investment as a share of US GDP, 1960-99

percent of GDP

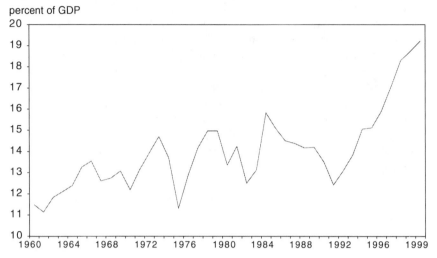

Note: The figure represents gross private domestic investment as a share of GDP.

Source: US Department of Commerce, Bureau of Economic Analysis.

Savings and Investment

As noted above, capital deepening has been an important component of the sharp pickup in US productivity growth. Economic expansion requires increased investment, as well as more efficient investment, and US investment as a share of the economy rose substantially during the 1990s (figure 2.1). Indeed, real business outlays for equipment and software grew at double-digit rates for an unprecedented period of almost 10 years (figure 2.2).

Many of the competitiveness studies of the 1980s and early 1990s called for major changes in US tax and other policies to induce more investment (Competitiveness Policy Council 1992). The main change that actually occurred was the dramatic reversal in the budget posture of the US government, which took considerable pressure off the financial markets and left US interest rates considerably lower than they otherwise would have been. This presumably spurred a great deal of the pickup in private investment that has now been recorded.

The budget reversal, the second major source of the economic resurgence of the 1990s, is perhaps as remarkable as the pickup in productivity growth. The federal deficit reached almost $300 billion (4.7 percent of GDP) as recently as fiscal 1992. It was transformed into a surplus of almost $240 billion (almost 2.5 percent of GDP) in fiscal 2000. Hence the budget improved by an average of 1 percent of GDP a year for 7 years—a pattern of achievement in the United States that we will be proposing for adoption

Figure 2.2 US investment in nonresidential equipment and software, first quarter of 1960 through second quarter of 2001 (percent change from four quarters earlier)

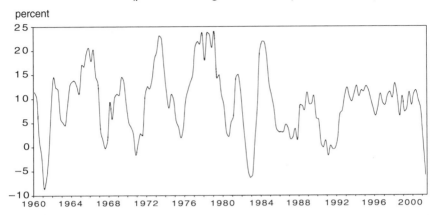

percent

Note: The data for nonresidential equipment and software were calculated by multiplying chain-type quantity and price.

Source: Department of Commerce, Bureau of Economic Analysis.

by Japan in chapter 3. The latest projections for the next decade cumulated to a unified surplus of more than $4 trillion before the tax cut of early 2001, about half linked to Social Security and the other half outside that context. The outgoing Clinton administration in fact projected a total elimination of the national debt (still close to $3.5 trillion) by 2012, although the tax cut has now eliminated that possibility, and many experienced observers doubted that such a cumulation of budget surpluses would ever take place in any event.

The direct impact of this swing in the federal budget position is of course to increase total national savings. During the same period, however, personal savings dropped considerably—from 8.7 percent of GDP in 1992 to 2.4 percent in 1999.[4] Some of this decline presumably reflects the sharp rise in asset prices during the same period, notably for equities and real estate, and does not indicate as much of a "real" decline as the official figures suggest. But national savings, as recorded in the national income accounts, have risen very modestly (about 2 percentage points of GDP) during a period when national investment has climbed sharply,

---

4. There has traditionally been an inverse relationship between public and private savings in the United States, with surprisingly small changes in their sum (net national savings). That relationship broke down in the 1980s, however, when both public and private savings declined. There had thus been some expectation that a reduction in public dissavings would *not* be offset by lower private savings but, at least to date, that has not occurred (at least in the recorded numbers).

requiring a large increase in net capital inflows from abroad. These two phenomena—low private (and hence national) savings and a rapid buildup of obligations to foreigners—are among the underlying problems that could threaten continued good US performance. They do not detract, however, from the major contribution that budget correction made to the record of the 1990s—and they in fact suggest that such a record might never have been compiled in the absence of such extensive fiscal improvement.

Monetary Policy

A third key contribution to the US economy in the 1990s was stable and effective monetary policy. The Federal Reserve took virtually sole responsibility for eliminating the inflationary excesses of the 1970s—needing in fact to counter the huge budget deficits of the 1980s, as well as the legacy of the oil shocks and excessively easy monetary policy in earlier periods—and had achieved most or all of its goal of restoring stable price expectations by the early 1990s. It remained vigilant on that front, however, tightening policy in 1994 and again in 1999-2000, when it feared that demand pressures were again outrunning supply and raising a threat to the low-inflation environment it had created so successfully.

The Fed's other major contribution to the US economic success of the 1990s was its willingness, for most of the decade, to let unemployment decline to a steady succession of new 30-year lows without taking restrictive countermeasures. Few US economists, as recently as 5 years ago, believed that price stability could be retained if unemployment fell below 5.5 or even 6 percent.[5] Most central banks, including most previous Feds, and most monetary economists would probably have tightened money far sooner than the Greenspan Fed. Chairman Greenspan had enormous faith in the productivity revolution that was taking place, however, as described above. He in fact believed that the official productivity data substantially underestimated actual developments (Davis and Wessel 1998), and thus pursued an approach that succeeded spectacularly in achieving both lower unemployment and continued price stability.

Future Risks

The US economic resurgence of the past decade thus rested on a sharp acceleration of productivity growth, driven primarily by the commercialization of new technological innovations and fundamental improvements

---

5. The most notable exception was the late Robert Eisner. Robert Solow also envisaged "experimentation" to see how low unemployment could fall without igniting price pressures.

in fiscal and monetary policy. However, the economy slowed sharply from the middle of 2000 to at least the middle of 2001; GDP growth dropped from 5-6 percent to about 1 percent. Hence new uncertainties arose about the outlook. Moreover, we know that the United States faces important risks and weaknesses, in both the short run and more structurally, with two particular vulnerabilities: the level of the stock market, even after the declines from the highs of early 2000, and the exchange rate of the dollar.

This book is of course about the medium-term to long-term economic relationship between Japan and the United States. Thus we are concerned about short-term swings in the two economies only to the extent that they alter our analysis of the underlying situation and hence the outlook over a longer horizon. The main lessons from the US turndown of 2000-01 for our purposes seem to be twofold: that both the rate of change and composition of the downshift closely resemble the typical US slowdown throughout the earlier postwar period, and that most of the causes of the slowdown seem to have been largely or wholly (or even more than wholly) reversed by the middle of 2001. Hence the evidence at the time of this writing in the middle of 2001 provides no reason for us to amend our basic optimism about the underlying strength of the US economy, even if future growth turns out to be less robust than the remarkable performance of 1997-99, and thus about the presence of a strong foundation for the US side of the Japan-United States economic relationship in the foreseeable future.

The United States typically experiences V-shaped cycles, with sharp declines in growth followed by rapid recoveries back to (or at least toward) the pre-slowdown rate (figures 2.3 and 2.4). In the latest case, growth dropped from an annual rate of 5.3 percent in the four quarters ending in June 2000 to 1.2 percent in the four succeeding quarters. This decline of 4 percentage points ranked near the middle of the 10 significant slowdowns experienced by the US economy during the postwar period.[6]

Likewise, the composition of the latest slowdown looks quite typical. The "contribution" of private consumption and equipment investment was quite similar to their "contribution" in the nine previous downturns. Inventory declines and falling government spending played a substantially larger role, partially offset by stronger than usual other investment (Baily 2001, table 8). All in all, there is no reason to believe that recent events carry any unusual implications for the long run.

This conclusion is reinforced when the causes of the slowdown are disaggregated. There were four key factors, each of which subtracted

---

6. Baily (2001, table 7). All but one of these other declines produced negative growth in at least two consecutive quarters, and hence a recession as conventionally described. The latest fall did not do so because the starting base was so high, higher in fact than in all but one of the earlier periods.

Figure 2.3   Annual growth of US GDP, 1960-2000

percent

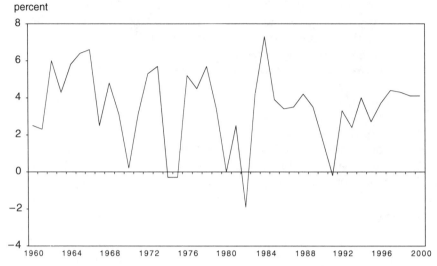

Note: Real GDP annual growth rate.

Source: US Department of Commerce, Bureau of Economic Analysis.

Figure 2.4   Quarterly growth of US real GDP, first quarter of 1960 through second quarter of 2001

percent

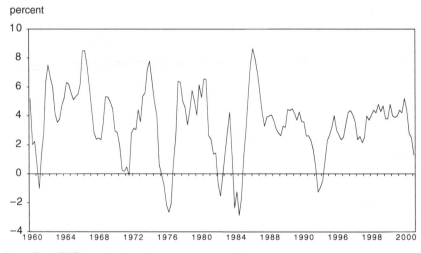

Note: Real GDP growth, from the same quarter of the previous year.

Source: US Department of Commerce, Bureau of Economic Analysis.

roughly 1 percentage point from growth: the rise in world energy prices in 1999, the increase of 150 basis points in short-term interest rates by the Federal Reserve in late 1999 and early 2000, the wealth effects generated by the fall in the stock market, and the timing impact—positive for growth in 1999, negative in 2000—of the Y2K phenomenon. Each of those elements had changed substantially by the middle of 2001: world energy prices had dropped back to their long-run trend level, the Fed had *reduced* interest rates by 275 basis points and thus far more than offset the previous hikes, the broad equity indices (though not the NASDAQ) had recovered to within 10 percent or so of their historic highs, and the Y2K effect had dissipated. These causes of the slowdown were quite traditional and suggest that it is likely to follow the traditional US cyclical pattern, including a fairly early and reasonably solid recovery. This likelihood is reinforced by the income tax cut legislation of early 2001, which is projected to inject another 1 percent of GDP at an annual rate into the economy in the second half of the year and some continuing stimulus thereafter on an ongoing basis.

The Pessimistic View

There is, however, an alternative view of the slowdown of 2000-01 that has more worrisome implications for the long run (Makin 2001). This view emphasizes two interrelated phenomena: the possibility of continued reduced levels of private investment, especially in the high-technology sector, and the risk of a sharp fall in consumption stemming from the negative wealth effect caused by the sharp decline in the equity markets and the historically high level of consumer debt. Roach puts the view succinctly: an "American-style L" will produce growth of only 1.5-2 percent during 2001-03 as "the earnings recession deepens and labor cost-cutting intensifies . . . (so) the noose will slowly tighten on the saving-short, overly-indebted, and wealth-depleted American consumer" (2001).

The fundamental fear of this school of thought is that the exuberant investment boom of the late 1990s, which accounted for one-third of total US growth as opposed to its typical share of one-sixth (Makin 2001), left the US economy with substantial overcapacity. Hence investment will remain depressed for several years, both dampening economic growth in the short run and dropping productivity growth well below its late-1990s rates.

Such a sustained fall in investment would have two additional effects. One would be continued downward pressure on profits and hence on equity prices, reducing the prospects for an early rebound to their previous levels and possibly presaging further substantial declines. The other is upward pressure on unit labor costs, as output falls while unemployment levels remain relatively unchanged at first, but which shortly produces layoffs and higher unemployment.

In turn, these forces coalesce to trim consumer demand, the main bulwark of the economy throughout the first four quarters of the 2000-01 slowdown. Rising unemployment translates into slower growth of incomes. Stagnant or lower equity prices would sustain or worsen the wealth loss. The historically high levels of consumer debt would become more salient. Consumption weakness would join investment weakness in slowing the economy, perhaps through an extended period of stagnation (or even stagflation), if not outright recession.

There are of course responses to all these concerns. As noted above, the fall in investment during the 2000-01 slowdown was about the same as in the typical postwar recession—which usually ended in a sharp V-shaped rebound. It is true that household equity wealth fell by $5 trillion from its peak in early 2000 to early 2001—but this came on the heels of a rise from $8 trillion to $18 trillion from 1995 to 2000, a huge gain whose impact is likely to swamp that of the partial retrenchment.[7] Despite the rise in unemployment in early 2001, housing sales hit record levels, and automobile sales remained strong. The interest rate and tax cuts were of course intended to stimulate and reinforce precisely such effects.

Key Uncertainties

Whatever one's view of the short-run prospects for the US economy, there clearly remain several key uncertainties. Most important, it is unclear at this juncture whether productivity growth will rebound to the 2.5 percent level, or even anything close to it, when overall economic growth picks up again. The sharp rise of 1996-2000 could turn out to have been a one-shot jump in the *level* of productivity, rather than a lasting increase in its *rate*. We simply will not know until the slowdown that began in the middle of 2000 has run its course and the short-term negatives cited above have disappeared.

Likewise we must acknowledge that many observers, especially outside the country, continue to view the United States as something of a "bubble economy"—even after the substantial correction in the equity markets that took place in 2000 and early 2001. To be sure, stock market valuations—especially for the high-technology NASDAQ, but even for the Dow Jones Industrial Average and the broader indices—reached very high levels by historical standards by early 2000, with price-earnings ratios that were roughly double their historical averages. There was thus widespread concern that a sharp correction, as in Japan in the early 1990s, could create a sharply negative wealth effect that would slow the economy sharply

---

7. Lettau, Ludvigson, and Barczi find that "unsustainable, or transitory, changes in wealth have little influence on consumer spending" and that even *permanent* movements in wealth mainly act contemporaneously and "bear little relation to *future* consumer spending" (2001, 19; italics in original).

Figure 2.5   US major stock indices, January 1990-June 2001

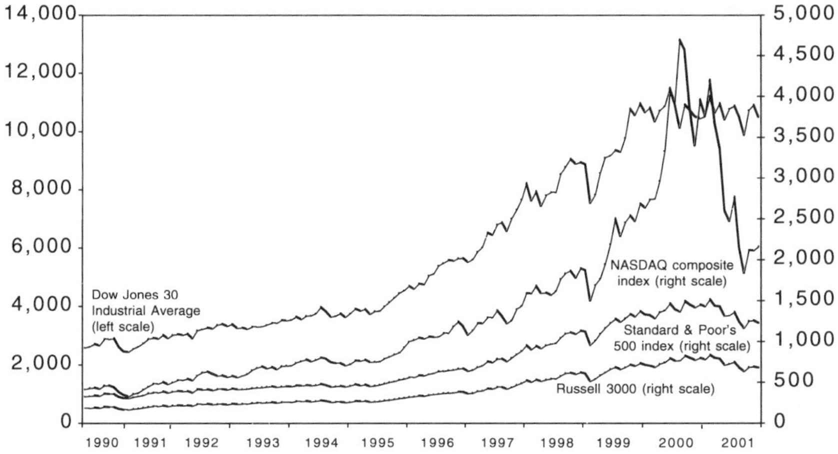

Note: Monthly data.

Source: http://finance.yahoo.com/m1?u.

or even push it into prolonged recession—and many of those concerns have lingered even after the more subdued effects of the market declines of 2000-01.

The stock market, particularly the high-flying "Internet stocks," had certainly corrected substantially by early 2001 (figure 2.5). The broad averages had dropped by 10-20 percent from their peaks, and the NASDAQ had fallen by 60 percent. Moreover, it could be argued that higher-than-historic stock valuations are justified by several factors: the lower inflation of the past half-decade; the reduced volatility of US economic performance, with only two quarters of recession during the past 19 years; the sharp reduction in the risk premium as half the population, and many of its most conservative institutions, have now become equity investors; the reduction in capital gains taxes to their lowest levels since 1941; and the sharp drop in the costs of buying (but also selling) stocks.

We have no intention of trying to predict the future course of the US stock market, especially writing at a time when the short-term outlooks for both the economy and the market itself are so unclear. Most important for our purposes in this book, however, even a renewed sharp decline in the stock market would not be likely to derail the US economy. The substantial improvement in productivity growth, even if it is not fully sustained, clearly suggests that the United States is *not* a bubble economy. The US financial system exhibits few of the weaknesses that translated market declines into economic declines in Japan (as will be described in chapter 3). Any bubble is clearly limited to the equity markets, with few counterparts in the real estate and other markets that have exacerbated equity declines elsewhere. Even the sharp market decline in 1987, when the Dow Jones Industrial Average fell by 22 percent in one day—more than it fell in the full year after reaching its all-time peak in early 2000—did not weaken the economy substantially.

Econometric models suggest that changes in household wealth, from either equity or housing sources, produce changes only 3-6 percent as great in personal consumption expenditures (Ludvigson and Steindel 1999; Davis and Palumbo 2001). Moreover, housing wealth exceeded equity wealth in the aggregate portfolios of households as recently as 1995, and its continued steady growth has offset a considerable portion of the recent decline in equity values.[8] The consumption effect of the sharp fall in equity prices took over a full percentage point off GDP growth at annual rates in the first half of 2001, but the continued increase in housing wealth offset about half that impact ("Why Consumption Holds Up," *Macroeconomic Advisers' Economic Outlook*, 15 May 2001). Moreover, monetary policy à la 1987 and 2001 could be and has been deployed to counter the effects of such a shock on the economy—in contradistinction to the monetary policy conducted by the Bank of Japan during Japan's slump (as will be discussed in chapter 3).

One crucial difference between the United States in 2000-01 and Japan in 1990, in terms of possible stock market overvaluation, is structural and works to the advantage of the United States. The US market is supported by institutional investors, including pension funds and mutual funds, and by the personal savings of wealthy individuals. By contrast (as will be described in chapter 3), the Japanese market was largely supported by money borrowed from the banking system, either directly or through real estate projects. When the stock-land bubble burst in Japan, the banks were left with nonperforming loans to companies that had invested in real estate. The stock price declines thus hit Japanese banks directly by depreciating their own stock portfolios. Because the unrealized capital gains of banks counted as tier II capital in meeting their Basel capital-adequacy ratios, the stock price declines destroyed much of their capitalization. This would not happen in the United States in the early 2000s, even if the stock market crashes, in light of its stronger banking system; the absence of any significant real estate bubble; and the lesser overvalu-

---

8. Both equity and housing wealth equaled about $8 trillion in 1995. Stock market wealth soared to $18 trillion in 1999, after which it dropped to $13 trillion in early 2001, while housing wealth climbed to $11 trillion during that same period. Virtually all of the swing in equity wealth effects on consumption from early 2000 to early 2001 were accounted for by swings in the NASDAQ, but there is no evidence that these swings have a disproportionate impact on the economy ("Why Consumption Holds Up," *Macroeconomic Advisers' Economic Outlook*, 15 May 2001).

ation of the equity markets themselves, especially after the corrections that have already occurred.

As was noted above, another potential threat to sustained and substantial US recovery is the possibility that private investment will remain depressed for a prolonged period because of the excessive capital spending and resultant overcapacity in the telecommunications sector, and perhaps the information technology sector more broadly, during the exuberant boom of the late 1990s. It is certainly true that such overcapacity exists and that new capital spending in these sectors is likely to be subdued for a while. It is also true that the sizzling pace of investment in them was a major factor in the rapid growth of the late 1990s, explaining much of the rise in the rate of expansion above the long-term sustainable norm of perhaps 3 to 3.5 percent.

However, telecoms account for a very small share of the total US economy. Information technology as a whole, depending on how broadly it is defined, accounts for a minor percentage as well. The "old economy" continues to represent the great bulk of the overall picture. Moreover, as was noted above, it is the increased *utilization* of the new technologies by traditional sectors that seems to have provided much of the pickup in productivity growth and hence overall expansion of the economy. Depressed telecoms and/or information technology sectors could slow US growth during the next few years, and could certainly keep it from resuming the peak rates of the late 1990s, but need not block a reasonably rapid recovery. They also should of course bounce back in the medium run and resume making a positive contribution to the broader economy.

Yet another potential depressant for economic activity is the low level of personal savings, and associated high level of household debt, that has come to pervade the economy. It has been argued that these patterns will inevitably be reversed, as households seek to restore their balance sheets and reduce their debt, and a modest turn in this direction in fact occurred in early 2001. This would be good for the economy in the long run, for it would enhance total national savings and reduce the country's reliance on foreign capital (and hence the current account deficit). In the short run, however, it would presage a fall—perhaps a sharp one—in consumer spending that could weaken the single most important component of the entire economy and thus produce slower growth. If the net savings balance of the private sector were to revert to its historical mean during the next 3 years, annual GDP growth could be limited to about 1 percent through 2006; even a fall of half in the private-sector deficit would hold growth to about 2 percent a year during that period (Godley and Izurieta 2001).

Such fears have of course been expressed for many years, because personal savings has dropped steadily since the early 1990s, but consumer spending has remained extremely robust, even since the downturn that began in the middle of 2000. Most observers believe the chief reason is the sharp and, until recently, steady growth in household wealth generated by the dramatic rise in equity values and the steady, substantial increase in housing values. These wealth increases, which are not counted as "savings" in the national income accounts, have swamped the declines in household savings out of current income throughout the past two decades.

Including capital gains in income, the imputed "personal savings rate" has exceeded 10 percent of disposable income throughout the past two decades; exceeded 20 percent for most of that period; and reached 44 percent at the height of the bull market in 1999 (before of course turning sharply negative in 2000) (Lusardi, Skinner, and Venti 2001). Simply including *realized* capital gains produces an "adjusted personal savings rate" of 9-12 percent throughout the 1980s and 1990s, with considerably less volatility (Peach and Steindel 2000). These increases in household *assets* have been greater than the simultaneous rises in household liabilities (debt), so the hypothesized "need to restore balance sheets" is much less compelling.

Moreover, total national savings have risen as the decline in government dissavings via the federal budget has been greater than the fall in private savings. Hence the situation is sustainable *unless* there were to be a substantial and lasting decline in equity prices and/or home values. The possible risk to the economy then reverts primarily to the earlier question of whether a further substantial decline in the equity market is likely.[9]

The other chief risk is that the large shortfall in the capacity of US domestic savings to finance total national investment could be shocked from the other side of the equation, its external dimension. It is this shortfall that requires the United States to import capital from the rest of the world, currently at the rate of almost $4 billion every working day (to finance the United States' own large capital outflows as well as the current account deficit). The *net* capital inflow of about $2 billion daily in turn defines the level of the current account deficit, which has risen to about $450 billion.

The final threat to sustained US expansion in the future is thus the exchange rate of the dollar. The US external deficit is already well above 4 percent of US GDP. It rose at an annual rate of about 50 percent for the 3 years 1998-2000 before leveling off with the slowdown in the economy (and hence the demand for imports). US net foreign obligations approximate $2 trillion, which is only 20 percent of GDP, but has been rising at 20-25 percent a year. The external deficit has reached levels that have proved to be unsustainable in other OECD countries—and in the United States itself in earlier periods (Mann 1999, forthcoming 2002).

---

9. Peach and Steindel note that "a truly massive decline in the market value of household assets would be required to bring the ratio of aggregate debt to financial assets back up to levels associated with the economic downturns of the early 1980s and early 1990s" (2000, 4).

If foreign investors become unwilling to fund this US need for foreign capital at current prices, the most likely result will be a substantial depreciation of the dollar. A dollar fall of 20-25 percent could cut the external deficit roughly in half and return it to sustainable levels, for at least a while, at about 2-2.5 percent of GDP. Such a dollar decline would tend to take place primarily against the euro and against the yen, which are severely undervalued against all currencies as of this writing (Wren-Lewis and Driver 1998, updated 2000).

Because markets tend to overshoot, there could be a temporary dollar depreciation in excess of the "needed amount." Even a decline of 20-25 percent, however, would tend to increase the price level by 2 percentage points or so, because every fall of 10 percent in the trade-weighted dollar pushes up prices by about 1 percent. Such a depreciation would increase nominal interest rates by at least as much, and probably considerably more, as investors insisted on higher real rates to offset their fears of further depreciation of the currency and as the Fed raised rates to limit the inflationary risks from additional depreciation itself. These two developments would also tend to drive the stock market down. Moreover, this "triple hit" on the economy could not be countered by an easing of monetary policy without risking even further currency depreciation. These adverse effects would of course be more certain if they occurred while the US economy were still near full employment.

The concerns about the future of the US economy thus come full circle. The boom of the late 1990s, and at least some of the dramatic jump in productivity growth that was its most encouraging feature, relied heavily on sharp increases in private investment and relatively low levels of inflation and interest rates. Those crucial elements of the US economic resurgence were greatly facilitated by the strong dollar and the rising external deficit which, for all the problems they were building up for the longer run, played a central role in the success story.

It is quite possible that the economy could resume substantial growth, in the 3 to 3.5 percent annual range, without such dollar strength, because the slowdown of 2000-01 brought interest rates to much lower levels and further dampened the risk of inflation. Likewise, domestic savings could (and, in the long run, certainly should) replace foreign capital in supporting a substantially larger share of US private investment (though the lower level of domestic spending that would result would slow growth for at least a transition period). But the external imbalances could greatly complicate the adjustment to a new equilibrium, and even leave the economy with less long-run growth than now seems likely.

A substantial fall in the dollar is inevitable unless all economic history is repealed. But a "soft landing" for both it and the US economy, which would spread the depreciation over an extended period of time and thus minimize its adverse impact on the economy, is quite possible, for three reasons. One is the underlying strength of the economy and its likely continued growth, if at somewhat reduced rates, as was described above—which is presumably the chief reason that the dollar remained so strong after the middle of 2000 despite the fall in US growth, interest rates, and equity prices. This strength should attract continuing sizable investments into dollar assets and prevent any free fall of the currency. Second, neither Europe nor, especially, Japan (as will be discussed in chapter 3) is likely to exhibit a highly dynamic recovery that would suddenly attract a flood of investment inflows away from the dollar.

The third mitigating probability is concerted sterilized intervention by the Group of Three (G-3) if necessary to slow the pace, and perhaps even to moderate the extent, of the inevitable slide in the dollar.[10] In light of their own economic circumstances, neither Europe nor Japan would want a sharp appreciation of its currency, any more than the United States would want a free fall of the dollar. Hence this would be one of those relatively rare cases where the national interests of the G-3 are likely to coincide and thus pave the way for effective cooperative action. It is of course still possible that the authorities could fail to act in a timely manner, or that they could be overwhelmed by the markets even if they tried. But both the economics and politics point toward a gradual adjustment of the dollar—which would still have substantial, but considerably lesser, costs for the United States—rather than a crisis collapse and a substantial disruption of US economic growth.

Conclusion

Despite the slowdown that began in the middle of 2000 and the uncertainties about the future that have resulted, the United States enters the 21st century with an economy in its best shape since the Second World War. Economic expansion has continued almost uninterrupted for almost 20 years. More than 33 million new jobs have been created during this period. Domestic demand grew at almost 5 percent annually for the last 3 years of the 1990s. Both productivity growth and investment have been unprecedentedly strong for prolonged periods. The unemployment rate has approximated 4 percent, a 30-year low, since early 1999. Core inflation remains little above 2 percent.

This performance rests on firm foundations. Labor productivity growth rose sharply during the second half of the 1990s, to about 2.5 percent a year and, with the labor force rising at least 1 percent annually, would

---

10. Frankel and Dominguez (1993) and Catte, Galli, and Rebecchini (1994) make the case that sterilized intervention can be effective if conducted skillfully. That view is supported by the three G-7 interventions of the past 6 years: to weaken the yen in 1995, to strengthen the yen in 1998, and (less clearly) to strengthen the euro in 2000.

if resumed support steady economic expansion of about 3.5 percent a year (with the usual cyclical fluctuations around trend).[11] The private sector is continuously strengthening its performance, driven by the information technology revolution—especially the broadening and deepening application of this technology throughout the old economy—and the competitive pressures of globalization. Hence a faster rate of productivity growth is likely to continue, even if it turns out to be not quite as rapid as in 1996-2000.

In addition, the prospects for economic policy are strongly supportive of future expansion. There is scope for further monetary easing if the economy were to require it. The continuing surpluses in the federal budget, even after the tax cut of 2001, suggest that further tax cuts or other fiscal stimulants are available if needed.

To be sure, there are important risks. The stock market could experience another substantial correction. Private savings could rise, perhaps in response to an equity fall, and dampen consumer spending for an extended period. Investment could remain depressed, at least in the high-technology sectors. The exchange rate of the dollar could depreciate sharply and substantially. Most important, the acceleration of productivity growth in the late 1990s could turn out to be unsustainable, or even a one-shot episode. Any of these developments, or especially several coming in tandem, could dampen growth by 1-2 percentage points for 1-2 years, or even for the long run. They are unlikely to derail the prospects of steady, sustained growth for the foreseeable future, however, if at a lesser rate than in the recent boom period.

This optimistic outlook does not imply, by any means, that the United States has overcome all its economic (and related social) problems. During the two decades before the middle 1990s, the real incomes of large parts of the US population had stagnated or even declined, and income inequality had increased substantially. These trends had begun to be corrected in the late 1990s, but we cannot be sure that the reversals will continue or how far they will go. Moreover, as was noted, private savings have fallen to very low levels, and presumably will increase at some point—with a corresponding slowing of consumer demand. Despite some progress and much effort, the primary and secondary education systems remain inadequate to prepare many Americans to compete in a global economy. Partly as a result, there exists a substantial backlash against globalization, which could make it difficult for the United States to expand further (or even maintain) the openness to the world economy that has been so important to its success—especially if the inevitable temporary

---

11. In its May 2001 projections for the US economy during the coming 10 years, the Congressional Budget Office—which estimates its numbers on the conservative side due to its focus on drawing implications for the government budget outlook—assumes expansion of 2.4 percent in 2001, 3.4 percent in 2002, and 3.1 percent during the next 8 years (CBO 2001).

slowdowns in growth produce substantial increases in unemployment while the trade deficit remains large.

Our conclusion, however, is that the US economy is likely to maintain much of its renewed strength for the period of time that is relevant for the topic of this book—the next 5 to 10 years. It is not a bubble economy that is likely to implode, even if the stock market and/or the dollar exchange rate were to experience the substantial declines that are quite possible for both. It continues to face several severe underlying problems, but they have not impeded the recent revival and most are en route to improvement. Indeed, US performance could strengthen further if the information technology revolution itself, the commercialization of the new technologies, and globalization—three of the key factors in fostering the sharp increase in US productivity growth—turn out, as was suggested above, to be in their early stages. US policy will of course need to remain supportive for such continued progress to eventuate, particularly at the macroeconomic level of fiscal and monetary affairs, but also to maintain open markets and continue down the path of globalization more generally.

This optimistic prognosis for the US economy augurs well for its economic relationship with Japan. US economic troubles during the 1970s and 1980s, coupled with Japan's dramatic economic successes, were a key factor in the development of widespread concerns (and even paranoia) in the United States about the "threat from Japan." These concerns in turn provided much of the basis for decisions by a series of administrations and Congresses to develop, and attempt to implement, a unique "Japan policy" that would reduce the perceived threat and contribute positively to US recovery.

As was traced earlier in this chapter, the propensity to pursue this anomalous Japan-specific policy may have been largely a historical accident born of the coincidental juxtaposition of prolonged but temporary US economic weakness and Japanese ascendancy. The US concerns and resultant Japan policy then waned sharply, as the US economic resurgence gathered strength in the late 1990s (and as Japan weakened). Continued US economic strength should provide a firm foundation for a more normal, and more healthy, Japan-United States relationship in the years ahead.

In chapter 7, we will attempt to draw out in some detail the implications for Japan-United States economic policy of this outlook for the United States. Before doing so, however, it is necessary both to take a similarly close look at Japanese economic prospects and to appraise recent economic relations between the two countries. We turn next to these issues.

3

The Japanese Economic Malaise

Japan's macroeconomic performance affects its relative standing in the world and its bilateral relationship with the United States in a variety of ways. Domestic demand-led growth and a strong yen encourage imports, strengthening the economies of Japan's neighbors in Asia and contributing to a reduction in the politically sensitive bilateral trade imbalance with the United States. A growing economy makes Japan a more attractive destination for investment as well.

Beyond these direct trade and investment linkages (which will be discussed in detail in chapter 4), a prosperous, self-confident Japan is more likely to work in partnership with the United States to address pressing global issues. In contrast, for both economic and political reasons, a Japan mired in the malaise of continued poor performance is unlikely to play a constructive role in world affairs. Already, the implications of Japan's "lost decade" are beginning to be felt in the development and security spheres, as Japan cuts its budget for development assistance and considers reducing financial support for US military bases on its soil.

Some in the United States would regard Japan's relative weakness during the past decade as a desirable development. As a consequence of its superior economic performance, the United States has enhanced its status relative to Japan, and Japan's comparatively weak performance has undercut the ideological appeal of the "Japan model." Although such sentiments are understandable, and although the (at least temporary) interruption of Japan's increase in its relative economic prominence has helped to ease tensions with the United States, the advantages of a strong, stable Japan overwhelm such considerations.

Figure 3.1   Real GDP growth in Japan, 1955-2000 (percent)

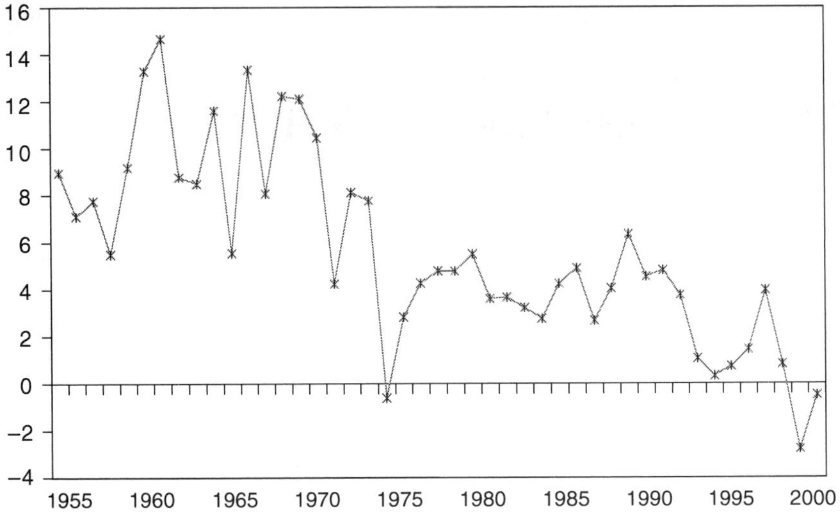

Source: IMF, *International Financial Statistics.*

In this chapter, we examine the recent macroeconomic performance of the Japanese economy, focusing on three key issues: the condition of the financial system, and the conduct of both monetary and fiscal policy. (Some of the discussions of structural issues are deferred to chapter 4.) The chapter concludes with policy recommendations to spur improvement in Japan's macroeconomic performance.

The Lost Decade

The growth of the Japanese economy during the past decade has been the slowest 10-year performance of any large industrial country in the postwar period, averaging about 1 percent a year, in dramatic contrast with its previous performance (figure 3.1). Between 1992 and 2000 (except 1996), the growth rate each year has been less than 2 percent, and the growth rate in 1998 was − 2.5 percent (later revised to − 1.1 percent when the price deflators used to calculated the national accounts were rebased), the worst in the postwar history of Japan. And not just the growth rate was low; the financial system weakened as well. Three of the top 20 banks failed in 1997-98, and there was genuine concern about a possible financial system implosion in 1998. The prolonged recession, with only tentative, short-lived recoveries, gradually raised unemployment, and by the end of the 1990s, the unemployment rate had become higher in Japan than the United States—which would have been unthinkable just several years earlier. In Japan, the 1990s are now known as the lost decade.

The core problem of the slow growth in the 1990s was nonperforming loans (NPLs) in the financial sector. As stock and land prices fell, the construction and real estate sectors were caught with overvalued inventory of land and structures. As real estate failed to produce profits, developers suspended payments to banks. Banks' provisioning for NPLs had lagged behind the pace of rising NPLs. It was widely believed that banks often lent more so that companies could appear to pay interest (a practice called evergreening). As the banks failed to produce profits, they started to restrict lending.

In an attempt to lift the economy from recession and deflation, 11 economic stimulus packages were put together and implemented between 1992 and 2000. However, much of the touted stimulation proved to be illusory: some of the claimed spending simply amounted to asset transfers, and in other cases the fiscal stimulus was offset by tax or fee increases or cuts in spending elsewhere in the budget. Indeed, Japanese fiscal policy was so opaque as to require a small cottage industry of private-sector analysts in Tokyo trying to divine what the government's fiscal policy stance actually was. Moreover, to the extent that additional spending was undertaken, project selection was atrocious, and the multiplier effect on these projects was low (see box 3.1).

Because of shortfalls in tax revenues from the negative growth in 1998 and large discretionary fiscal expenditures from 1998 to 2000, Japan's debt-GDP ratio has increased sharply. The IMF projects that its gross debt-GDP ratio will to rise to 150 percent by 2005. This will be the highest level—surpassing Italy—among the Group of Seven (G-7) countries. The challenge of fiscal policy is to keep the level sustainable, which requires substantial consolidation—in total, 10 percent of GDP—in the next 10 years, but without triggering a recession.

Monetary policy during the period 1989-91 was tightened aggressively in an attempt to stop asset price inflation and burst the bubble. After the economy turned precariously weak in 1992, monetary policy was eased to support an economic recovery. However, in 1993-94, the economy did not recover as it normally would have after a recession. The rate of growth remained relatively low, and rather than accelerating as the economy picked up, the rate of inflation continued to decline, eventually turning into deflation. Although by 1999 monetary policy loosened with the introduction of the so-called zero interest rate policy, real interest rates (the difference between the nominal rate and the rate of inflation) remained high due to deflation. Japan was caught in a liquidity trap—a situation not observed in an industrial country since John Maynard Keynes first diagnosed the syndrome during the Great Depression.

Box 3.1 The road to nowhere

The construction industry is the single largest source of Japanese political campaign funds. The industry in effect acts as an intermediary, recycling public tax revenues and postal savings funds to politicians for private use through excess profits generated through bid rigging (*dango*).

Perhaps nothing better illustrates the political ties that bind the Liberal Democratic Party and the construction industry than Japan's virtual obsession with pouring concrete. Although, as Mulgan (2000) observes, the ratio of paved to unpaved roads in Japan is higher than in the United States, the Japanese government perennially invests almost 30 percent of its public works budget in pavement. Despite the government's rhetorical nods to information technology infrastructure and quality-of-life programs in public investment, these initiatives are dwarfed by traditional road building.

The gasoline tax is earmarked for constructing roads, regardless of efficiency. Unless this linkage is severed, road construction is automatic. In 2001, the Koizumi cabinet made ending this practice one of its highest reform priorities.

Bridges are another favorite. In a famous case, the government spent more than $7 billion on a gigantic suspension bridge linking the islands of Honshu and Shikoku, despite the fact that the existing ferry service was used by only a few hundred cars daily. And in addition to the ferry service, two other bridges already connect Honshu and Shikoku. The decision to build three bridges was made in the 1970s at the strong urging of politicians from Shikoku and never reversed.

Ports and harbors provide yet another opportunity for pork-barrel largesse. For some fishing ports, expenditures on port improvements exceed the value of 10 years' worth of catches from the harbor.

For inland locations, bullet trains are a preferred vehicle for public spending. While Yoshiro Mori was secretary-general of the LDP, he secured funding for a new bullet train line that would cruise his bucolic home region of Hokuriku. Price tag: $19 billion. Passenger projections: unavailable.

(box continues next page)

In sum, easy monetary and fiscal policies have been applied, without lasting effects on growth. By the end of the decade, government debt had become very high, and it constrained additional fiscal stimulation. Structural reforms in the financial sector may put additional downward pressure on economic activities, as the resolution of bank NPLs leads to more corporate bankruptcies and unemployment. The policy debate has moved to whether fiscal deficits can be reduced without too much of a negative impact on the economy, rather than providing further stimulation, and whether "unconventional" monetary policy may be needed if deflation continues.

Only 10 years ago, the Japanese economy was hailed, and often feared, for its strength. High economic growth, excellent manufacturing companies, large current account surpluses, and large, strong banks seemed to dominate the world. After 10 years, some manufacturing sectors are still strong, and current account surpluses are still large, but the banking sector has crumbled, and economic growth has slowed to a crawl.

Box 3.1 *(continued)*

The problem, of course, is that these white elephants generate operating deficits in addition to their initial costs. In 2000, the Ministry of Finance estimated that it would have to inject about $47 billion in taxpayer money to cover the hidden losses associated with these investment projects. For example, later that same year, it was reported that the MOF had to inject more than $7 billion into the Shikoku bridge project, for which interest payments are double the meager toll collections. The Hokuriku bullet train line is also expected to end up on the public dole, despite the privatization of the railroads. The government has already absorbed more than $20 billion in theoretically privatized railroad debt (Tadaaki Ito 1996).

Unfortunately, questionable spending is not confined to physical infrastructure. In October 1998, the government began extending emergency loan guarantees to small and medium-sized enterprises (including construction companies) that have been plagued by high default rates. Central and local governments have also invested $32 billion in nearly 10,000 so-called third-sector public-private partnership companies. The best known of these, the Sea Gaia luxury resort in Miyazaki, collapsed in 2001 with ¥326 billion in liabilities.

Faced with this mounting tab, the public is beginning to revolt. Public opinion polls indicate that the opposition to wasteful public spending is coming not only from urban voters, but even bedrock rural LDP constituencies. In January 2000, the population of Tokushima, a small southern city, voted a resounding "no" in a nonbinding referendum on the central government's plan to provide the region with yet another billion-dollar dam. The local governments are saying no to these projects because they have to shoulder some of the costs, typically 10-30 percent. This means that local governments, businesses, and residents—the principal beneficiaries—assess the prospective benefits of the projects at less than 10-30 percent of costs. This is remarkable testimony to how truly wasteful some of these projects are. Indeed, the political popularity of Prime Minister Koizumi can be interpreted as a more general, though possibly transitory, revolt against the status quo.

Economic Developments and Policy Reactions

It is hard to argue that the growth slowdown was produced by changes in fundamental economic factors, such as technological change and changes in factor (labor and capital) accumulation. Investment still has been high relative to that in other countries and, although Japan's labor force will soon decline, this cannot explain past performance.[1] However, it could be argued that in about 1990 Japan reached a technological turning point associated with a natural slowing of growth. Its very high economic growth during the 1950s and 1960s, and moderately high growth—much better than that of other G-7 countries—in the 1970s and 1980s, are often explained by a natural "catching-up" process to the most advanced coun-

---

1. The Japanese fertility rate has fallen to 1.4, and this, combined with a demographic bulge, will soon lead to a decline in the workforce and eventually the population in about 10 years. This will have macroeconomic consequences, unless the female labor participation rate is raised or more immigration is allowed. See Kasa (1997), Matsunaga (1997), Dekle (2000), Faruqee and Mühleisen (2001), and Seike (2001) for further discussion.

Figure 3.2   Real GDP growth in Japan and the United States, 1980-2000 (percent)

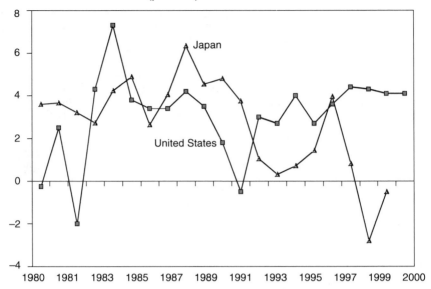

Source: IMF, International Financial Statistics.

tries in technology (especially in the 1950s and 1960s) and in per capita income, and by Japan's own innovative efforts in manufacturing processes (especially in the 1970s and 1980s) (cf. Eaton and Kortum 1997). According to this explanation, once the Japanese economy fully caught up with the Western countries in technology, say by the mid-1980s, its slower growth rates were inevitable, because "easy" opportunities for technological progress had been exhausted.

The difficulty with this explanation is that the United States, the putative technological leader, grew much faster than Japan during the 1990s. In fact, the United States enjoyed its longest peacetime boom in the 1990s, leaving Japan and the European countries behind. As was seen in chapter 2, one explanation for this growth is the advent of the "new economy."[2] However, Japan's economic troubles appear to have started earlier than the United States' information technology-induced productivity spurt (1995-2000) (figure 3.2). Many economists estimated Japan's potential

---

2. The contrast between Japanese dominance in manufacturing and financial sectors in the 1980s and US dominance in the 1990s is remarkable. As was demonstrated in chapter 2, the strong performance of the US economy in the 1990s was in part due to the success of the new economy—sectors that are related to information technology and its application to "old" industries. In Japan, reallocation of resources from the old economy to the new economy did not proceed well, due to capital-market inefficiencies and regulatory problems. The Japanese economy failed to exploit the opportunity of the information technology

growth rate in the 1990s at 2.5 percent a year (about the average among the G-7), so the difference between this potential rate and the roughly 1 percent actually achieved remains a puzzle.

There is little reason to believe that the potential growth of Japan suddenly became lower in the 1990s. The reasons for the lost decade, and its cures, must be found elsewhere. The slow growth of the 1990s can be attributed to a series of negative shocks to the economy, most conspicuously in the financial sector; inappropriate or insufficient policy responses to these shocks; and structural rigidities, which prevented the economy from achieving its full potential.

The Bubble Economy

The recession of the early 1990s was an inevitable retreat from the speculative boom of the late 1980s. (By the late 1980s, the Tokyo stock market had become the largest in the world, and the land under the Imperial Palace in Tokyo was worth as much as all the land in California, or all the land in Canada, or all the land, houses, and factories in Australia!) Firms leveraged these apparent gains to finance an investment boom. In retrospect, some of this investment was ill-advised.

Land and stock prices, which had risen three- and fourfold between 1985 and 1990, subsequently plunged by as much as 50-60 percent in a few years. The gains in stocks and land between 1985 and 1990 were completely wiped out between 1990 and 2000. Official National Accounts statistics indicate that Japanese households lost approximately ¥500 trillion (more than 100 percent of GDP) of their net wealth between 1990 and 2000.

At the beginning of the 1990s, it was thought that it would be necessary to treat the overheated economy of the late 1980s with a cold shower. From the end of 1989 to the beginning of 1990, stopping the ever-rising land prices took the center stage of policy. The burst bubble was partly a natural reaction to excessively high prices and partly due to policy measures—such as a series of official discount rate hikes (from 2.5 to 6.0 percent in 15 months in 1989-90) and the regulatory measures on bank lending to real estate sectors (introduced in March 1990).[3] When land

revolution in the 1990s—the Internet, personal computers, and information technology industries. Without a remedy for its structural barriers to information-based industries—more labor mobility, merit-based pay, as well as competition in the communications and broadcasting industries—the Japanese economy will continue to lag behind the US economy. The potential growth rate of Japan will never come close to the US rate unless regulatory and legal reforms unleash the full potential of information technology industries (Murakami 1998).

3. Rising land prices were regarded as an enemy of public policy to provide affordable housing. Several policy measures were taken to stop land prices from rising, some constructive (raising the interest rate; changing tax provisions, which impeded the conversion of agricultural land in urban areas to other uses; and imposing a ceiling on banks' lending)

prices started to fall after the fall of stock prices in 1990-91, there was a sense of relief among the policymakers. As a result of price declines, housing became more affordable for first-time buyers by the end of the 1990s.

However, as asset prices declined, the economy went into a self-reinforcing downward spiral. Stock and real estate holdings had been used extensively as loan collateral in the bank-centered Japanese financial system; and, as asset prices plunged, bank lending was squeezed.[4] The economy weakened, but monetary policy remained inappropriately tight and, with the benefit of hindsight, amounted to overkill.[5] Monetary easing was behind the curve in 1992 and 1993, aggregate demand for consumption and private fixed investment collapsed, and a full-blown recession developed.

Sasaki-Smith describes the "self-righteous jubilation of the entire nation that falling asset prices would rectify the disparity between the haves and have-nots of land which was caused by the asset price inflation of the 1980s" (1999, 17). Virtually unnoticed amid the celebration, however, was the fact that the hard landing had put many construction and real estate firms into de facto bankruptcy. Banks threatened to repossess the collateral, although large borrowers could threaten to bring banks with them, if they were driven to bankruptcy.[6] However, it turned out to be very costly to repossess the collateral of bankrupt borrowers; and, in a kind of truce, banks began evergreening loans in the hope that land prices would rise.[7]

---

and some questionable (suspension of auctions of government land and an approval system for land and housing sale prices).

4. Shimizu (2000) presents evidence indicating that the fall in land prices had a much bigger impact on the volume of bank lending than did the decline in stock prices. See also Ueda (1996) and Kwon (1998). However, as Fukao (1998) points out, the banks' enormous holdings of stocks and bonds in effect represent off-balance-sheet lending and a potential concentration of lending risk. He gives the example of Sanwa, Tokai, and Sakura banks, whose holdings of Toyota stock in 1997 respectively represented 37, 79, and 40 percent of their capital.

5. Jinushi, Kuroki, and Miyao (2000) provide a sophisticated econometric demonstration of the Bank of Japan's (BOJ's) tardy reactions. The peak of the boom, officially dated by the Economic Planning Agency, was February 1991. However, monetary policy was not loosened until July 1991, when the official discount rate was reduced from 6.0 to 5.5 percent. The BOJ was too preoccupied with making sure that stock and land prices would not go up again. Unfortunately, commercial banks and real estate companies were behaving as though land prices would stop declining. The land holding companies kept hoarding land, so that the land prices declined only gradually.

6. Under the accounting and bankruptcy rules in effect at the time, NPLs had to meet rigorous criteria to be declared tax-free write-offs. At the same time, under the bankruptcy code, restructuring could not proceed without the approval of the principal creditors, and hence the banks exercised considerable influence over the timing of bankruptcy applications. Reputational concerns encouraged evergreening to forestall bankruptcy (Shikano 2001).

7. There are three issues. Consider the case of a single parcel of land used to secure six equally valued loans from six banks. Suppose the property falls to one-sixth of its original

There was no winner in this silent war of attrition that produced large macroeconomic costs. Provisioning and business as usual, paying dividends by realizing large but dwindling latent capital gains, continued in the meantime. The capital bases of banks were seriously damaged by draining resources that could have been used more productively to get rid of NPLs.

There could have been possibly two ways to manage the macroeconomy during the period 1992-95, after the bubble burst. Monetary policy could have been more accommodating to support stock and land prices.[8] The aggressive easing of interest rates by the US Federal Reserve after the US technology bubble burst in 2000-01 suggests that it learned from the Bank of Japan's (BOJ's) mistakes. In addition, if land prices had been judged as absolutely overpriced, real estate companies and banks could have been forced to dispose of nonperforming loans right away, forcing distressed companies to sell some unused land (which became commonplace only after 1998). Even if land prices had plummeted due to rapid sales, it would have been better in the long run. Realizing potential losses in, say, 1995 would have been much better than the gradual squeezing of remaining assets in the following years. Neither route was chosen. The health of financial institutions and the macroeconomy sank gradually.

Financial-Sector Problems

Almost immediately after the bubble burst, problem loans to the real estate sector and illegal lending activities began surfacing.[9] The first institutional failures were among local credit cooperatives, and in 1991 the deposit insurance fund was tapped for the first time since its establishment in 1971. The following year, the government established a Credit Cooperative

---

value. If the owner is forced into bankruptcy and the land sold, under Japanese law only the first lender would be repaid. Any decision to foreclose, however, requires the assent of a majority of the creditors. The result is gridlock. Second, it is difficult under Japanese tenant law to evict tenants from a building that is being sold or repossessed. Third, many of these properties had been occupied by *yakuza* (gangsters), impeding sales or conversion to new uses. See Wanner (1998a) and Lincoln (2001) for further details. Gillian Tett and Fiona Graham, *Financial Times*, 6 June 1998, give specific examples.

8. Unfortunately, part of the slowness of the BOJ to react could be blamed on the poor quality of Japanese consumer price statistics. The statistics were constructed by a government agency from observations taken from Japan's traditional rigid-price retailers and missed the major shift in spending toward new discounters in the late 1980s and early 1990s. When the BOJ did its own survey in 1995, it found that deflation was running at more than 3 percent a year (Makin 1996).

9. In 1991, executives of the Fuji, Tokai, and Kyowa Saitama banks were arrested for fraud. The most spectacular case involved the Industrial Bank of Japan, which participated in lending a reputedly gangster-connected Osaka restaurant owner more than $2 billion on the basis of forged documents.

Purchasing Company to buy their dud loans. In a decade-long recurring pattern, the government either underestimated or simply refused to acknowledge the magnitude of the problem (Packer 1999). A turning point came in December 1994, when the two credit cooperatives (*shinyo kumiai*)—Tokyo Kyowa Credit Union and Anzen Credit Union—in Tokyo were found to be in trouble.[10] During the period of rapid growth, failure among Japan's highly regulated financial institutions had been relatively rare, and the ones that occurred had been more or less successfully handled by merging distressed institutions into healthier ones.[11] The supervisory framework was built on the assumption that no institution would fail in the traditional environment of heavy regulation. However, financial liberalization had been proceeding since the mid-1980s, and the regulatory framework was outdated.[12]

The handling of these cases was further complicated by two factors. First, the primary responsibility for supervising credit cooperatives was vested in the prefectural government, the Tokyo metropolitan government in this case. However, the prefectural government possessed even less institutional capacity than the Ministry of Finance (MOF) to deal with the situation. Second, the effective owners of these two institutions were heavily involved in connected lending and political corruption.[13] Indeed, it was later revealed that MOF officials had been wined and dined and even flown to Hong Kong on a private jet by one of the key figures in the collapse of the two credit cooperatives (Hartcher 1998; see box 3.2).

When the MOF and the Tokyo metropolitan government arranged a plan to take over assets of the two institutions and to use "public money" to create a new financial institution, the Tokyo Kyodo Bank, the plan was met with strong opposition from a public that regarded it as a bailout for crooked bankers. In early 1995, the Tokyo metropolitan assembly

---

10. O. Ito (n.d.), and Cargill, Hutchison, and Ito (1997, chap. 6) provide a detailed account of the credit cooperative failures.

11. Four assisted mergers occurred between 1991 and 1993. Regulations on branching made the going-concern values higher than otherwise. The network of branches in a particular area was valued highly by institutions that wanted to expand operations in that area, sometimes an institution in the same area and sometimes an institution from another area. See Hutchison (1997).

12. No other institutions were interested in merging with these institutions, and losses that were estimated in these institutions exceeded what the deposit insurance corporation could inject to help a merger. Conversely, there was little formal regulatory power (other than *gyosei shido*—administrative guidance or jawboning) in the Ministry of Finance to supervise effectively or to force an institution to shut down.

13. Fukao (1998) argues that the frequent presence of *sokaiya*, or corporate racketeers, in financial-industry scandals indicates the need for improved internal and external accounting and auditing standards backed up by enforcement either through improved supervisory regulation and/or shareholder lawsuits.

Box 3.2 Corruption, accountability, and credibility

The Japanese government has been dogged by a series of financial corruption scandals since the Recruit shares-for-influence affair of the late 1980s that brought down the Noboru Takeshita cabinet. In 1997, the formerly untouchable Ministry of Finance was ensnared.

Beginning in March 1997 a probe by the Tokyo Prosecutor's Office found that the Big Four brokerage houses (Nomura, Daiwa, Nikko, and Yamaichi) and the Dai-ichi Kangyo Bank had paid more than $100 million to racketeer Ryuichi Koike in an attempt to prevent the disclosure of embarrassing information. The scandal eventually spread beyond the financial sector to involve Mitsubishi, Toshiba, Hitachi, and other corporate giants.

As the Prosecutor's Office continued its investigation, it found evidence of collusion between the financial firms and their putative regulators at the MOF, including coverups of illegal financial activities by Japanese firms in the United States, such as in the case of the 1995 Daiwa bond-trading scandal. On 18 January 1998, two Nomura Securities executives and the finance director of the Japan Highway Public Corporation (a former MOF bureau chief) were arrested on charges that Nomura had expended nearly $3 million on bribes and entertainment to win business. A week later, for the first time in 50 years, the MOF was raided by 100 prosecutors, and two relatively low-ranking officials were arrested.

The scandal would go on to involve additional financial institutions, the resignations of the minister of finance and two MOF mandarins, the suicides of one sitting MOF employee and a former MOF official (at that time a member of the Diet), and tawdry revelations. In the end, 44 officials received "severe" reprimands for their wrongdoing, with 17 forced to take pay cuts. Eisuke Sakakibara—the vice minister for international affairs and the MOF's face to the world—and 13 others received warnings. (Sakakibara voluntarily accepted a temporary cut in pay.) Fifty-eight other officials received lighter reprimands. See Hartcher (1998) for a critical look at the light punishments.

Beyond providing fodder for the tabloids, the MOF prosecutions arguably had two important effects on policy. First, the scandals sent the ministry reeling and inhibited its ability to deal proactively with domestic and international issues, such as the brewing commercial banking crisis and Asian financial crisis.

(box continues next page)

rejected the funding for public money to the resolution plan, and new Governor Yukio Aoshima was elected on the platform that no financial assistance be provided to these institutions. The Tokyo Kyodo Bank was then established with Deposit Insurance Corporation and BOJ capital subscription, and without money from the Tokyo metropolitan government. This case established the precedent that, in the absence of genuine reform, it would be very difficult to use public money. It also encouraged other local governments to oppose central-government initiatives.

A second sign of financial trouble came later in 1995, when private-sector nonbank institutions that were supposed to have specialized in housing loans, known by their Japanese language acronym as "*jusen*," became a focus of concern (see box 3.3). The *jusen* sector had accumulated large nonperforming loans from lending to real estate developers. Rehabilitation plans from 1992-93, which had assumed a recovery in land prices,

Box 3.2 Corruption, accountability, and credibility
(continued)

Second, the scandals made vividly clear to the public that, in the clubby world of Japanese finance, regulatory forbearance ruled—encouraged by corruption, close *amakudari* (golden parachute) relationships between the regulators and the firms that were under their supervision, and a reluctance to recognize losses and admit, implicitly, to bungling. By comparison, during the US savings and loan debacle, the US government obtained 1,850 indictments, eventually securing 1,600 criminal convictions. During Japan's massively larger crisis, there have been roughly 100 indictments.

The apparent inability or unwillingness of the MOF to seriously regulate the financial sector directly led to the establishment of an independent financial regulatory agency, the Financial Services Agency (FSA). This body got off to a good start under its reformist leader, Hakuo Yanagisawa. However, after Yanagisawa was removed in a cabinet reshuffle, the agency rapidly frittered away its credibility. One of Yanagisawa's successors (he had five) was forced to resign in a bribery scandal (unrelated to his role at the FSA); another was forced to quit after being taped telling bankers that they should come to see him if faced with an unduly harsh inspection and implying that additional capital injections would be available, no strings attached; and a third formally proposed that credit cooperatives, where much of the rot lies, be held to lower standards than the large banks. After a 14-month absence, Yanagisawa was brought back for a second tour of duty in July 2000.

This track record raises basic questions about the credibility of Japanese prudential supervision, both internally and internationally, and the extent to which the political elite comprehend this credibility problem. As *The Economist* editorialized in 1997, "For eight years, the financial authorities have lied, dissembled, and fudged in the hope that they could muddle their way out . . . but confidence has been sapped by dissembling" (29 November 1997). We would add that nothing has fundamentally changed with the shift in supervisory responsibility from the MOF to the FSA. The politicization of the regulatory function remains undiminished. One avenue for improvement would be to establish the legal independence of the agency, and to replace its politician chairman with a respected technocrat, along the lines of the US Securities and Exchange Commission.

had collapsed by 1994. By 1995, the *jusen* were thought to account for one-third of the banking sector's NPLs, which amounted to ¥8 trillion (about 1.5 percent of GDP). Because some banks and agricultural cooperatives had established these *jusen* companies and/or lent to *jusen*, problems were cascading through the financial system, and there were systemic risks if the *jusen* failed outright.

The burden-sharing rule was unclear, and it took several months to find a compromise solution among stakeholders. After acrimonious negotiations, an accord was reached, under which banks were asked to surrender their claims and fill the balance-sheet holes, while the politically well-connected agricultural cooperatives and their prefectural organizations got back most of their lending, and the public supplied the rest. This established a precedent that the major nonbank institutions would be

Box 3.3   The *jusen* problem

The seven *jusen* companies, financed and largely staffed by large commercial banks, life insurance companies, and securities firms—with former MOF officials in high-ranking *amakudari* positions—were established in the 1970s to provide individual housing loans, while the commercial banks concentrated on lending to large corporations. When demand for commercial loans declined, the commercial banks entered the housing loan business, squeezing the *jusen*. In the second half of the 1980s, the *jusen* started to lend to riskier customers, namely, real estate developers. When the land price bubble collapsed, the real estate developers stopped servicing debts, and the *jusen* were hard hit.

Commercial banks that founded the *jusen* were major lenders to the *jusen*, as were agricultural cooperatives. When the time came to write off the debts and close down the *jusen*, the Ministry of Finance and the banking community insisted on proportional burden sharing, whereas the Ministry of Agriculture, Forestry, and Fisheries and agricultural cooperatives insisted that the coops should not bear any losses. The final resolution was closer to the agricultural cooperatives' position: The coops lent ¥5.5 trillion to seven jusen companies, and shouldered the burden of only ¥0.53 trillion, while the banks lent ¥1.45 trillion and took losses of ¥1.17 trillion. During the debate, it was revealed that the director general of the Banking Bureau of the Ministry of Finance had sent a memorandum during the negotiation of the first rehabilitation plan of 1992-93 to a counterpart in the Ministry of Agriculture, Forestry, and Fisheries indicating that the coops would not be held responsible in any future *jusen* resolution. This memo was crucial in getting the coops off the hook. (See Takatoshi Ito 2000 and Cargill, Hutchison, and Ito 1997 for more details; Saeki 1997 provides the agriculture sector's view.)

treated more leniently than the big banks.[14] The banks were outraged—having been encouraged into the *jusen* venture, they felt forsaken by the MOF. The injection of public funds (¥685 billion) was small relative to either total *jusen* losses or the amount that would have to be injected into the commercial banking system 3 years later. Nevertheless, as in the earlier case of the credit cooperatives, the public was outraged that taxpayers' money had been used to clean up a mess associated with shady characters and their extravagant lifestyles.

The *jusen* imbroglio clearly showed that the Ministry of Finance was not prepared for situations that required closing financial institutions. The existing legal framework was inadequate; the MOF lacked the political clout to engineer a fair resolution; and the MOF itself was compromised by cozy regulator-regulated relationships through *amakudari*, the practice of bureaucrats retiring to positions in institutions that their ministry regulated.

The MOF, the overseer of the apparently mighty Japanese banks, did not have a strategy or political power to restructure financial system. In the markets, this apparent inability to resolve the financial sector's troubles

---

14. See Cargill, Hutchison, and Ito (1997, table 6.2) for the exact burden sharing.

Box 3.4 The Daiwa scandal

Problematic Japanese financial-market regulation spilled onto the front pages of US newspapers in the autumn of 1995. In September, it was revealed that during a period of 11 years, Toshihide Iguchi, then the head of Daiwa Bank's New York operations, had engaged in 30,000 fraudulent trades, losing the firm $1.1 billion in the process. The following month, the former car salesman pleaded guilty to numerous criminal charges totaling up to 90 years in prison and implicated a number of his superiors in an illegal coverup. US regulators closed Daiwa's US operations, and federal prosecutors would eventually obtain criminal convictions against another Daiwa executive and fines of $340 million against the firm after it pleaded guilty to 16 criminal charges associated with the coverup.

The real bombshell came in October, when it was revealed that MOF officials had known about Daiwa's illegal activities for more than a month before Daiwa officials informed US regulators of the problem. During this period, Daiwa was permitted to raise money in capital markets on more favorable terms than it would have otherwise gotten if the truth had come out. The former director general of the Banking Bureau, Yoshimasa Nishimura, reports without apology in his memoir that, when first notified by the Daiwa Bank, he was unaware of the international agreement (known as the Basel Protocol) that stipulates prompt reporting of any irregularities to the relevant foreign authorities (Nishimura 1999). According to Nishimura, the Daiwa Bank was to give him a detailed report, and there is no evidence that he consulted other MOF officials on this matter before the Daiwa Bank reported back several weeks later.

Western press sources reported that Ministry officials requested that Daiwa officials continue their coverup. However, the gap in notifying the US authorities is less evidence of conspiracy than of the sheer incompetence of the MOF's Banking Bureau at the time. Either way, the result was to increase the "Japan premium" (see the text for a definition of this term), as doubts deepened about the state of Japanese banking.

MOF officials lamely explained that their failure to alert the US bank supervisors to criminal activities being perpetrated on US soil was due to "cultural differences." This led a well-known commentator to write that "the persisting illusion has been that somehow Japan can engineer international engagements entirely on its own terms" (Samuelson 1995). Another longtime observer commented that "the MOF does not appreciate the enormity of its blunder in its handling of the Daiwa bank scandal . . . Financial systems are based on confidence . . . Such trust comes from personal contact, and being told the unvarnished truth. When the Japanese rely on studied ambiguity so that they can avoid making real disclosures, they undermine this process" (Krause 1995). See Mizuno (1996) for further details on how the MOF manipulated the Japanese press while infuriating Western policymakers.

contributed to a growing awareness of the possibility of a financial crisis. Skepticism regarding the MOF's ability to prevent financial crisis was reinforced by its mishandling of the 1995 Daiwa Bank scandal that touched the United States (see box 3.4).

After seeing public resistance to injecting fiscal money into troubled financial institutions, even a debate on considering the use of government money to clean up the financial sector was sealed. A comprehensive framework to deal with contingencies was badly needed. As early as

1995, a clearly desired policy response would have been to establish a framework to shut down weakening institutions before they became insolvent, and to devise a least costly way to liquidate or rehabilitate the financial institutions. This policy failure of not establishing a financial-supervision framework early enough—even with strong signs of need—cost the Japanese economy dearly. By not taking forward-looking actions in 1995, when the weakness was obvious, Japan wasted at least 3 years in dealing with weak financial institutions.[15] Hutchison and McDill (1998) estimate that the temporizing cost Japan approximately 1 percent of GDP annually. In effect, Japan had engaged in regulatory triage, first allowing credit cooperatives to fail, then small banks (Spiegel and Yamori 2000). Large banks would be next.

Failures of major financial institutions occurred in November 1997. Yamaichi Securities, one of the Big Four securities houses, and Hokkaido Takushoku Bank, one of the 20 big banks, failed in that month. The failure of Yamaichi, with its revelation of large previously undisclosed losses, generated a spike in the "Japan premium"—the higher interest rate that Japanese banks had to pay on their interbank eurodollar and euroyen borrowing relative to their US and European counterparts.[16]

At the time, these were by far the largest financial-institution failures of the postwar period. Moreover, the failures were accompanied by disclosure of incompetent or duplicitous behavior on the part of the regulators and criminal behavior by the financial institutions. Yamaichi was forced to admit that it had engaged in *tobashi* (the illegal concealment of losses through the use of multiple offshore accounts and accounting periods) and made large payments to *sokaiya*, or corporate racketeers.[17] Fukao (1998) reports that at the time of its bankruptcy, the brokerage was carrying ¥260 billion in losses on securities investments—more than half of its capital—that neither MOF nor BOJ examinations had uncovered. It emerged that the authorities knew of Yamaichi's imminent collapse for 10 days before revealing the information publicly. It was alleged that company insiders sold the firm's stock during this period.

The fear of financial fragility shook consumers' confidence as well as institutional investors' and, although all deposits were guaranteed by the government, business sentiment turned sharply negative. Financial institutions became skeptical of each other about their counterparts' viabil-

---

15. See Cargill, Hutchison, and Ito (2000, chap. 3) for more details.

16. Peek and Rosengren (1999) find that financial-market disruptions, government policy actions, and changes in financial-market conditions had an impact on the Japan premium. Government announcements not backed by concrete actions had little impact. The revelation of previously undisclosed losses, as in the Yamaichi case, had a major impact.

17. Similarly, the earlier collapse of Sanyo Securities, Japan's 7th largest broker, had been accompanied by the losses in 14 previously unknown affiliate companies not listed in the company's financial statements.

ity after the collapse of formerly reputable institutions. Japanese financial institutions were squeezed out of international lending by the Japan premium and withering credit lines.

From December 1997 to March 1998, the financial markets remained weak and credit remained tight. The government pushed through necessary legislation for a ¥30 trillion coffer for bank recapitalization, and at the end of March all 18 major banks (together with 3 regional banks) received ¥2.1 trillion in public money for a capital increase (in the form of subordinated loans and preferred stocks). The government abandoned any pretense of realistic accounting when it permitted the banks to value their landholdings at their relatively high market valuations while valuing their stocks at their relatively high book values. The chairwoman of the committee handling the banks' applications later admitted that she had not looked at their balance sheets. Managements were left intact—in stark contrast to the experiences of South Korea and the United States during similar banking crises. The fiscal injection was met with howls of public criticism.[18]

This package was widely regarded as insufficient to resolve the NPL problem, and did not stem the deterioration in business sentiment and consumers' confidence. Aggregate demand fell, and the crisis deepened in 1998. The public was further outraged by the revelations of bribery scandals in the banking sector, involving public officials, and resisted additional injections of public funds. Prices were falling, and a deflationary implosion became a realistic possibility. Norio Ohga, the chairman and chief executive officer of Sony, publicly compared Prime Minister Ryutaro Hashimoto to Herbert Hoover.[19]

The Japanese financial system was on the verge of collapse. In the spring of 1998, it was widely rumored that the Long-Term Credit Bank of Japan (LTCB), a large, publicly financed institution, would fail, despite the fact that the government had reported that its capital-adequacy ratio was more than 10 percent at the end of March.[20] It seems that the market

---

18. Resistance to the bailouts was understandable. The government had to budget ¥685 billion for the resolution of *jusen*. In return, the banks merely pledged to try to increase profits and tax payments. Supervision was weak, so it was unclear that a limit to injection was not guaranteed; disclosure of true states of nonperforming loans was inadequate; and incompetent bank executives were not held accountable.

19. According to Ohga, "If you look at what Hoover was saying at the start of the Great Depression and what Mr. Hashimoto is saying at this moment, they are very similar" (Paul Abrahams, Michiyo Nakamoto, and Gillian Tett, *Financial Times*, 3 April 1998).

20. Shimizu (2000) argues persuasively that the long-term credit banks (of which LTCB was the most prominent) had occupied a privileged position in the "convoy system" of financial regulation of the postwar period, and as such had been disproportionately disadvantaged by the gradual financial liberalization of the 1980s. LTCB's reputation had been tarnished by its involvement with the failures of the Tokyo Kyowa and Anzen credit coops and the associated improprieties.

had correctly determined what the government auditors had missed: the LTCB's subsidiaries had huge hidden losses. The bank's stock price collapsed, falling below the psychological barrier of 100 yen on 19 June, and deposits (in the form of bank debenture) were withdrawn. The LTCB announced that it would merge with the Sumitomo Trust, but this did not materialize, because the Sumitomo Trust insisted on full disclosure of the subsidiaries' balance sheets. There was real uncertainty as to how this case and others would be resolved. Seiroku Kajiyama, a prominent LDP politician and government advisor, declared that weak banks "should be crushed," while the MOF's Eisuke Sakakibara averred that Japan "can't allow failures."[21]

The Diet (Japanese legislature) debated through the summer how to reform financial supervision and deposit insurance, with an immediate application to the LTCB in mind. In early June, the cabinet resolved to pass two pieces of special legislation. One hived off the regulatory functions from the MOF, establishing the independent Financial Supervisory Authority (later renamed the Financial Services Agency, or FSA), and specified a "prompt corrective action" procedure. The second piece of legislation provided for a second capital injection.

In October, after a long debate in the Diet, two new laws were enacted, one to reform the deposit insurance corporations and one to establish a recapitalization fund. A total of ¥60 trillion was pledged to protect depositors from failed institutions, fill the losses in failed institutions, and help recapitalize banks. The LTCB applied for nationalization under the new law on 23 October.

Failures in the financial sector were not limited to banks and other deposit-taking institutions. Life insurance companies began failing as well.[22] The pessimism about the Japanese economy hit the bottom in the fourth quarter of 1998.[23] GDP growth had turned negative, and the economy was shrinking. In December, the Nippon Credit Bank (Nippon Saiken

---

21. Peter Landers, *Far Eastern Economic Review*, 8 January 1998. Sakakibara's statements were meant to indicate that LTCB had extensive international dealings so that a sudden collapse could set off a chain reaction internationally. A compromise was nationalization and reorganization rather than a precipitous closure.

22. Nissan Life failed in April 1997, and Toho Life failed in June 1997. The root problem for life insurers was the low return for their portfolio relative to their promised payouts. The companies had promised a guaranteed minimum rate for long-term life insurance policies with a savings feature (a universal-life type). The guaranteed rate for policies written at the beginning of the decade was 4 percent, whereas the current return is less than 2 percent. The bad fundamentals encouraged further bad investment—a familiar moral hazard in the financial sector. Life insurance policy holders had to accept lower benefits for their existing policies.

23. Stock prices slumped, as did the yen. On 9 October, the Nikkei 225 (stock price index) went below ¥13,000 for the first time in about 13 years. On 16 November, Moody's downgraded Japanese government bonds from Aaa to Aa1.

Shinyo Ginko, or NCB) was suddenly declared insolvent by the FSA.[24] This action was viewed as a signal of the FSA's independence, inasmuch as the bank's survival had generally been regarded as politically determined.

During the first quarter of 1999, a battle ensued to put the financial system back on track, starting with the "zero interest rate policy" introduced in February. Because the short-term interest rate cannot become lower than zero (otherwise, people will use and hoard cash), many consider the zero interest rate as the limit to which the Bank of Japan can extend its loose monetary policy. In addition, on 16 February, the MOF reversed an earlier decision to stop buying the long-term bonds that had riled the market. These steps lowered the long-term interest rate.

Recapitalization of major banks was done at the end of March. A total of 15 banks received ¥7.46 trillion in public money.[25] Unlike the year earlier, the March 1999 action was enough to convince the markets that the financial crisis was over. In April, the Japan premium that plagued Japanese banks virtually disappeared, and the prices of Japanese bank stocks rose sharply.

An obvious question is why the authorities could not have carried out a correct capital injection—massive capital infusions, with strict rehabilitation plans varying from one bank to another—back in 1998. Japan had wasted another year.

Rehabilitation of the Banking Sector

One result of the collapse of real estate prices in the early 1990s was the de facto bankruptcy of many Japanese firms, especially in the real estate sector. However, Japanese accounting rules and bankruptcy procedures gave banks an incentive to engage in evergreening, which they did with enthusiasm (Shikano 2001). A combination of recession, deflation, and a revision of the bankruptcy law in April 2000 significantly reduced the incentive to evergreen, and as might be expected the number of bankruptcies and bad loans has increased.

Considerable uncertainty remains as to the magnitude of the bad loan problem in Japan. The FSA puts loans into four categories: healthy; in

---

24. The reputation of the FSA received a further boost when it declared in December 1998 that Nippon Credit Bank (NCB) was undercapitalized and nationalized it, under the new power the FSA acquired. According to the FSA, problem loans accounted for nearly half of NCB's lending. Japanese newspapers reported that the unreported dud loans had been parked in affiliates through *tobashi* deals (*The Economist*, 19 December 1998). Because the NCB had earlier received a capital injection from the Bank of Japan and other banks that had been arranged by the Ministry of Finance, it would have been difficult to take strong action if the FSA had not been created.

25. This time, Bank of Tokyo-Mitsubishi did not apply for the capital injection, citing its healthier balance sheet.

need of attention (interest payments have been in default for more than 3 months); in danger of bankruptcy; and, finally, loans to bankrupt companies. No provisions are necessary for healthy loans; provisions must be made for the other three categories on a sliding scale. As of the summer of 2001, total loans outstanding are estimated to be ¥455 trillion. Of these, the FSA estimates that on a gross basis ¥151 trillion fall into categories two, three, and four, or ¥80 trillion net of any collectible collateral. (Category-three and -four loans combined are ¥34 trillion.) The FSA vehemently disputes the notion that the ¥151 trillion figure should be regarded as "bad loans," because it does not include collectable collateral, and in any event, not all category-two loans will turn bad. Indeed, the FSA argues that Japanese banks have already adequately provisioned for the category-two loans (at a rate of 15 percent). Five largely nontradable sectors—construction; wholesale trade; retail trade; finance, insurance, and real estate; and other services—account for 85 percent of the bad debt.

Outside observers are considerably less sanguine. The Democratic Party, the largest opposition party in the Diet, puts the number of category-three and -four loans at ¥150 trillion (in comparison with the FSA's ¥34 trillion), whereas other unofficial estimates typically have been in the range of ¥40-80 trillion.[26] One can point to several pieces of evidence that suggest the higher unofficial estimates are probably more accurate.

In June 2001, the *Nikkei* carried a report on the prior categorization of loans for 605 firms that had filed for bankruptcy in the previous 6 months. They found that, 1 year before bankruptcy, 70 percent of the loans carried by these firms were classified as either category one (healthy, 7 percent) or category two (needing attention, 64 percent), implying that the existing FSA categorization was a poor indicator of reality. For example, when the retailer Sogo went bankrupt, it was discovered that loans extended to Sogo by LTCB and NCB, two nationalized banks that in principle had been stripped of bad loans, were classified as category two ("loans to be watched closely") and, as a consequence, were underprovisioned.

To cite another case, in March 2000, Sumitomo Bank reported only ¥265 billion of questionable loans to the construction industry, less than its total exposure to Kumagai Gumi, a troubled builder. A few months later, when Kumagai Gumi requested that Sumitomo and three other banks restructure its debts, Sumitomo was forced to write off ¥260 billion in an effort to avert Kumagai Gumi's bankruptcy.

Similarly, it has been reported that when Fuji, Dai-ichi Kangyo, and the Industrial Bank of Japan merged to form Mizuho Holdings, their internal evaluations of borrowers were disparate, with lenders with little at stake more likely to place a loan in the problem categories three and four. Likewise, in a number of instances, banks have continued to catego-

---

26. Gillian Tett, *Financial Times*, 20 April 2001; Nakamae (2001).

rize loans to certain firms, such as Mycal and Daiei, as "healthy" or "needs attention" when debt issued by these firms is trading at a huge discount in the capital markets. This would also be consistent with the valuations of distressed assets in the secondary market, where they trade at fractions of their face value.

Finally, econometric modeling by Shimizu (2000) suggests that the volume of bank lending, especially to small and medium-sized enterprises, remains high relative to the level of asset prices (collateral), implying that more bad loans have yet to be recognized. In light of this sort of evidence, the BOJ has reportedly urged the FSA to develop better methods of measuring questionable loans.[27]

The following month, Goldman Sachs issued a report putting the total level of risky loans at ¥237 trillion, or about 50 percent of GDP, with category-three loans—those to virtually bankrupt firms—at ¥170 trillion. The FSA, in contrast, puts this figure at ¥24 trillion.[28] The government's reaction was to shoot the messenger. FSA Minister Hakuo Yanagisawa was quoted as saying, "It is unfortunate that someone should throw doubt on the government's numbers. This situation should never arise."[29] The FSA then let it be known that it was scrutinizing the research reports of foreign bank analysts and subsequently penalized ING-Barings over an unflattering report about Daiwa Bank that contained several factual errors.[30] In August 2001, the IMF's annual review of Japan cited the higher estimates of NPLs produced by private-sector analysts, and the FSA again complained, with Commissioner Shoji Mori stating, "It is irresponsible of an international organization of authority to use what market analysts said."[31]

---

27. Moreover, as Fukao (1998) observes, private-sector accountants and auditors have a financial incentive to turn a blind eye to window dressing to get work.

28. David Atkinson, the author of the Goldman Sachs report, argues that the FSA is ignoring deflation. In particular, with interest rates virtually zero, the ability to make interest payments is not a useful indicator of borrowers' ability to repay principal. Instead, he argues that the ability to repay principal out of operating profits should be the relevant criterion. On this basis, he obtains the much higher bad loan figures. Of course, operating profits are not the only means of repaying principal—presumably, these loans are at least partly backed by collateral.

29. Gillian Tett, *Financial Times*, 27 July 2001.

30. In May 2001, ING-Barings sent to clients a report with a "sell" recommendation for Daiwa Bank. The report contained a misprinted capital ratio of 4.79 percent, whereas the actual ratio was 7.49 percent. After protest from Daiwa Bank, ING-Barings subsequently took out full-page ads apologizing for the mistake.

31. Japan Economic Newswire, 20 August 2001. The substance of the dispute is that private-sector analysts attach a higher likelihood of failure to category-two ("needs attention") loans than does the FSA, which (following international practice) counts only categories three and four as nonperforming. This, of course, begs the question of how the loans are classified in the first place.

The obvious implication of the higher figures produced outside the FSA is that Japanese banks may be grossly underprovisioned.[32] Despite writing off ¥60 trillion in bad loans since the burst of the bubble—a figure greater than the sizes of the Canadian, South Korean, or combined Belgian and Dutch economies—the outstanding amount of nonperforming loans has not markedly declined. Indeed, new "bad loans" are appearing at roughly the rate at which banks are writing them off. For example, with the banks generating profits of about ¥2.5 trillion a year, it would take them 3-4 years to write off existing "official" bad loans out of earnings, or perhaps 10 years if the commonly reported ¥40-60 trillion figure is accepted. If the actual level of bad loans is much higher than the official numbers indicate, abrupt provisioning could push banks below their Bank for International Settlements (BIS) capital-adequacy guidelines or into outright insolvency, or make them unable to make dividend payments on preferred shares owned by the government (from the previous capital injection)—triggering their effective nationalization (through the conversion of preferred to voting shares).

With this background, on 6 April 2001 the Yoshiro Mori government announced an emergency economic package sometimes called the Yanagisawa Plan (after FSA Minister Hakuo Yanagisawa), an emergency measure to strengthen the financial sector, in particular the banks. The plan has two pillars:

1. Removing nonperforming loans from the balance sheets. Existing nonperforming loans should be removed from the banks' balance sheets within 2 years, and new NPLs should be dealt with within 3 years.

2. Equities on the balance sheets of banks should be reduced, and the Banks' Shareholding Acquisition Corporation will be established to purchase equities from banks.

For the first pillar, "final disposal" is an official code word for removal of NPLs from bank balance sheets. It reflects official recognition that having sufficient provisioning (on the asset side) is not enough to prepare for losses from NPLs.[33] Banks are expected aggressively to remove NPLs

---

32. This suspicion was amplified when the Tokyo-Mitsubishi Bank Group sharply increased provisioning for the period ending March 2001. In August 2001, Mizuho, Daiwa, Asahi, and Chuo Mitsui increased their provisioning by 25-60 percent in an effort to regain investor confidence.

33. There have been three kinds of problems with the just-provisioning strategy. First, provisioning is for possible losses that are supposed to be the difference between the size of loans and collateral recovery values. However, as land prices have continued to decline, possible recovery values have declined continuously. Past provisioning thus becomes insufficient. This problem could have been (and can be) avoided if loans were (or are) foreclosed and sold to the market. Second, even if provisioning is sufficient, having both provisioning and bad assets on the balance sheets will be a drag on bank management, because it lowers

from their balance sheets by arranging debt-equity swaps with some haircuts (for viable companies), forgiving debts, or foreclosing loans with sales of collateral assets (for nonviable companies). Banks have hesitated on these actions, partly due to political and social repercussions. The new policy may provide them with the political cover to act.

As for the second pillar, Japanese banks' equity holdings have become risky assets. Until the beginning of the 1990s, banks' equities were a source of confidence. Banks had purchased those equities for cross-shareholding (*keiretsu*) purposes in the 1950s and 1960s. By the end of the 1980s, their market value was much higher than their book value. A portion (45 percent) of the latent capital gains was allowed to be counted toward tier II capital in the Basel capital-ratio calculation. When stock prices plummeted from 1990 to 1992, however, Japanese banks had to issue subordinated debts to make up losses in tier II capital by declining latent capital gains. Latent capital gains further declined in the second half of the 1990s. Due to further declines in stock prices, banks increased book values by realizing remaining latent capital gains to cover losses.

By March 2001, almost all latent capital gains had been wiped out among major banks. There are variations among the banks, so that some have latent capital losses and some gains. Those banks with losses must deduct the losses from tier I capital. Moreover, mark-to-market accounting has been introduced (as of 1 April 2001, with the first semiannual reporting at the end of September). Therefore, at this point in time and with this level of stock prices, any risk models would tell the banks to get rid of equities. Stock prices are extremely volatile, and the downside risk is enormous. When stock prices decline further, the damage to the balance sheet as well as to the risk ratio will be large. If one bank is smart enough to sell all its equities between March and September 2001, the bank may be able to clean up its balance sheet without too much damage. However, if banks sell these equities simultaneously, then it would be a large disruption to the equity market. This is a coordination failure. On that ground, public intervention can be justified. The question is, what kind of public intervention?

The operational details of the Yanagisawa Plan remain unclear. With respect to the disposal of NPLs, banks may not follow the wishes of the FSA. The standard answer is that the FSA will monitor progress, and with a threat of nationalization (by converting preferred shares to common shares), the FSA can influence commercial banks' behavior.[34] If banks were hesitant in the past to deal with NPLs squarely (e.g., pushing compa-

---

the risk-based capital ratio. Having got rid of both assets and liability of the same size will improve the capital ratio and the return on capital. Third, loan classification has been too optimistic.

34. This "threat" is rapidly becoming an empty one as the FSA chooses not to exercise its right to nationalize banks that have not achieved their rehabilitation plans.

nies into bankruptcy to resolve the case) due to a fear of social and political repercussion, the 6 April decree gave the banks political cover. However, in the absence of obvious carrots and sticks, we are not confident that the banks will proceed to deal with nonperforming loans just because of the 6 April announcement.

Details on the second pillar can also be questioned. Will the Banks' Shareholding Acquisition Corporation be established with private (bank) financing only? As of the summer of 2001, the plan is that only private-sector capital will be used to purchase equities from the banks. If this is the case, the banks' risk exposure will not change on the consolidated basis. If not, then the government has to put up some capital to take some risks from price volatility—but, after the two previous capital injections, bailing out banks is politically unpopular.

Another issue is whether all or part of the shares (if partly, who decides which shares and at what prices?) should be removed from balance sheets. According to the current plan, banks are supposed to be banned from holding equities altogether or up to the amount of bank capital. If only part of portfolios is sold to the corporation, there is a problem of adverse selection—banks sell only bad stocks with bleak futures, with their better knowledge of borrowers. Therefore it is only fair to purchase all banks' holding of stocks, yet this would require funding so large as to strain credulity. Rather, this appears to be yet another ill-conceived "price-keeping operation" measure designed to prop up the banks by buying their stock holdings. As such, it amounts to a transfer from the taxpayer to the stockholders of the banks.

The more fundamental problem of the existence of too many banks is not addressed. Even if banks do not follow the guideline of disposing of their NPLs within 2 years, there will not be a penalty. For the disposal of bad loans, the FSA should take examination seriously, and make sure that provisioning is sufficient. If collateral values decline or are even expected to decline, then additional provisioning should be required. If banks are discovered to have hesitated to classify particular loans to be less serious so as to avoid provisioning, the FSA should force the appropriate provisioning or write-offs. If the FSA allows banks to "waive" or forgive loans, as has been mooted, this will amount to a cost-free transfer from the taxpayer to these failing firms. This maintenance of capital-eating zombie firms will adversely impact their otherwise viable competitors, and retard the efficient reallocation of capital. The amount of NPLs among the largest 16 banks has been constant, at about ¥19 trillion from 1999 to 2001. This is despite increasing provisioning and writing off.[35] Clean bank

---

35. E.g., for the semiannual accounting period ending March 2001, losses from NPLs (provisioning and removal from balance sheets) amounted to ¥4.4 trillion for the 16 banks. Conversely, the operating profits of these banks are ¥3.6 trillion. Those loans newly classified as nonperforming amounted to ¥3.4 trillion. Because more loans become nonperforming

balance sheets, with capital injection if necessary, will be the key to a vital economy.[36]

The banking sector in Japan is too crowded for all existing banks to flourish in the future. A revival of the Japan premium could act as a permanent drag on the competitiveness of Japanese banks until questions about the stability of the Japanese financial system are resolved (Spiegel 2001). Indeed, it is virtually certain that the sector as a whole will shrink. Posen (2001) recommends that the FSA close or merge half the banks. Megamergers—such as those between Tokyo-Mitsubishi Bank, Mitsubishi Trust and Banking, and Nippon Trust Bank; or between Dai-ichi Kangyo, Fuji Bank, and the Industrial Bank of Japan; or those to come in the future—may perversely be creating institutions that politically are too big to fail. As Kashyap (2000) observes, throughout the 1990s, Japanese banks were simultaneously among the largest banks in the world and the least profitable—surely an unsustainable state of affairs. Moreover, the mergers appear to have done little to achieve cost savings or efficiency improvements. The banks seem to have learnt their lesson: "survival of the fattest."

Unfortunately for the banks, a slim-down is on the way. More businesses have moved to the capital markets, where larger companies can obtain necessary funding through corporate bond issues and equity issues. Even smaller companies are now able to do initial public offerings at fairly early stages. Banks are left with less creditworthy borrowers. The deposit-loan spread remains too narrow for banks to earn healthy profits. Several major banks are withdrawing from overseas operations, and domestic markets are getting more crowded. A major reduction in the number of banks, branches, and employees is in the offing.

To stop the cycle of debt deflation and nonperforming loans, what is needed is a package of demand-stimulation policies and supply-reform policies. A once-and-for-all removal of NPL assets from banks' balance sheets would obviously be good for the long-term revival of the banking sector, and in turn for the expansion of loans for investment on the supply side. But final resolution of NPLs will have a negative short-term impact on the demand side.

---

as more loans are written off, the outstanding amount of NPLs appears to be constant. The past trend of ever-increasing NPLs cannot be ignored.

36. If final disposal does not proceed as expected, a more drastic measure should be considered. The Asset Collection Agency (ACA) can be established with a government equity injection, and nonperforming assets should be bought from banks with discounts. The ACA can be operated as is the Housing Loans Collection Agency, which was established after the *jusen* industry debacle. The ACA can sell assets to the market or to any investors willing to pay a fair price. When weaker banks are nationalized due to poor performance and declining capital, then bad assets can be separated and moved to the ACA, and a good bank (without nonperforming loans) should be sold with a premium. Due diligence is a key.

The bottom line is that the measures announced on 6 April 2001 are inadequate. History suggests that the government has erred on the side of regulatory forbearance, and there is no convincing reason to believe that this will not continue. The initiation of mark-to-market accounting will be a shock to the banking sector, and may provide an entry point for more drastic action. We will return to this in chapter 7, in our policy recommendations.

Monetary Policy

Having missed its cue, Japanese monetary policy returned to center stage toward the end of the 1990s. In response to declining output and signs of a credit crunch in 1998, the BOJ relaxed monetary policy.[37] Traditional open market operations provided liquidity to the banking system, but banks were reluctant to lend to corporations, and instead fattened cash reserves to keep capital-adequacy ratios high in the wake of failures of large financial institutions. Indeed, as Morsink and Bayoumi (2000) observe, the fact that the impairment of the banks hampered the transmission of monetary policy reinforces the urgency of addressing the financial questions discussed in the previous section. Moreover, as noted above, Japan had entered into deflation.

Table 3.1 shows the major macroeconomic statistics from 1996 to 2000. The GDP growth rates are shown in two series, an old System of National Accounts (SNA) based on 1990 prices and a new SNA based on 1995 prices. Because the new SNA became available only in December 2000,[38] policy judgments during this period were based on the old statistics available at the time. The new SNA includes new methods in measuring

37. On 9 September 1998, the Bank of Japan lowered the operating interest rate target (overnight call rate) from about 0.45-0.50 percent to 0.25 percent, while the official discount rate was kept at 0.5 percent. On 13 November 1998, the BOJ added new instruments, such as commercial paper (CP) and corporate bonds (CBs), to the list of eligible securities for market operations. These corporate securities held at commercial banks were discounted at the BOJ. This helped provide liquidity to corporations that had difficulties in issuing, or rolling over, these CPs and CBs at favorable rates, or borrowing from banks.

38. As observed by the IMF (1999), the methods used to compile Japanese government economic data are rather opaque. Some analysts have attributed the volatility of Japanese quarterly GDP data to improper deseasonalization of the data. The 1996 and 2000 first-quarter figures were clearly affected by the extra day in the leap year. However, most of the quarterly fluctuations are due to the volatility of some of the underlying supply-side data series, and in this regard Japan is quite different from other countries. Annual figures are compiled from value-added data, similar to the procedures in other countries. In 2000, the method of calculating GDP was brought more closely into line with international standards to treat, e.g., investment in software as an investment rather than an expenditure. In addition, the base year for the price deflator was changed from 1990 to 1995. These changes resulted in a significant revision of the GDP series.

Table 3.1 Macroeconomic data for Japan by quarter, 1996-2000

Year, quarter	GDP growth rate (68 SNA, 1990 prices)	GDP growth rate (1995 prices)	Inflation rate (percent)	Yen/dollar exchange rate	Short-term interest rate (call rate) (percent)	Long-term interest rate (percent)	Stock prices (Nikkei 225) (yen)
1996, 1	2.6	1.0	0.0	105.8	0.46	3.32	20,516.7
1996, 2	0.5	0.8	0.2	107.6	0.48	3.35	21,928.3
1996, 3	0.4	-0.4	0.2	108.9	0.46	3.08	21,084.2
1996, 4	1.6	1.5	0.3	112.8	0.48	2.69	20,768.0
1997, 1	1.3	2.9	0.4	121.2	0.50	2.55	18,290.0
1997, 2	-2.0	-3.2	0.2	119.6	0.50	2.66	19,576.5
1997, 3	0.9	0.4	0.4	117.9	0.49	2.27	19,162.4
1997, 4	-0.6	0.7	0.5	125.2	0.45	1.95	16,431.8
1998, 1	-1.2	-0.6	0.1	128.1	0.43	1.95	16,522.6
1998, 2	-0.2	0.1	0.1	135.9	0.44	1.67	15,562.3
1998, 3	-1.2	-1.1	-0.2	140.1	0.39	1.26	15,251.6
1998, 4	-0.5	0.1	-0.3	119.8	0.23	1.41	14,102.9
1999, 1	1.5	0.5	-0.1	116.7	0.15	1.92	14,476.7
1999, 2	1.0	1.5	-0.1	120.9	0.03	1.58	16,772.9
1999, 3	-1.0	-0.1	0.0	113.7	0.03	1.77	17,728.3
1999, 4	-1.6	-1.5	-0.2	104.5	0.02	1.77	18,176.1
2000, 1	2.5	2.4	-0.2	107.1	0.02	1.76	19,487.3
2000, 2	1.1	0.2	-0.3	106.6	0.02	1.70	17,842.3
2000, 3	-1.2	-0.6	-0.4	107.6	0.14	1.79	16,486.0
2000, 4	-0.3	0.8	-0.5	109.8	0.25	1.69	14,827.4

SNA = System of National Accounts.

Source: IMF, International Financial Statistics.

some commodities and services. The GDP growth rate is measured quarter to quarter, whereas the inflation rate is measured by the change in consumer prices (excluding fresh food) from the same quarter of the previous year. The inflation rate from the second quarter of 1997 to the first quarter of 1998 is lowered by 1.80 percentage points to eliminate the effect of the consumption tax rate increase (from 3 to 5 percent).[39]

On the basis of a very fragile financial system and weak demand in 1998, a large supplementary budget was introduced in the fall of 1998.[40] In February 1999, the Bank of Japan lowered the call rate to zero, and then announced that its zero interest rate policy would continue "until the deflationary fear is dispelled." This contributed to flattening the yield curve.

The negative growth rate in 1998 and the BOJ's responses in 1999 attracted attention from economists inside and outside Japan (e.g., Krugman 1998; Hoshi and Nagaoka 2000; Bank of Japan 2001). Paul Krugman (1998) argued for "unconventional" monetary policy—purchase of long-term bonds—aiming at an inflation rate of 4 percent for 15 years. Because the nominal interest rate is bounded from below at zero, deflation means high real interest rates. Many economists debated what would be appropriate economic policies to get out of deflation at a zero interest rate—or out of a liquidity trap.

In 1999, the first-half growth was again positive, reflecting a large fiscal package and a special credit guarantee program for small and medium-sized companies. The effects from the zero interest rate policy also were taking effect. However, the second half of 1999 was weak, recording negative growth rates. Deflation continued. In September 1999, there was an expectation that the monetary stance would be further relaxed—"quantitative easing" became a topic of debate. However, the Bank of Japan did not adopt this approach. Instead, BOJ Governor Masaru Hayami indicated that he was disposed toward *raising* the interest rate.[41]

In 2000, the growth rate was again very high (2.4 percent) in the first quarter. The Nikkei 225 stock index rose from ¥13,000 in January 1999 to ¥20,000 in April 2000, spurred by a worldwide boom in the information technology sector.[42] The second-quarter growth rate was moderate (0.2

---

39. The reason that the adjustment is not 2 percentage points but 1.8 points is incomplete pass-through. The continuity of the rate changes appears to suggest that 1.8 points may be a good number. No sophisticated modeling was done to infer the adjustment amount.

40. The magnitude of negative growth in 1998 was first thought to be 3 percent (in 1999), and then revised to be 2.5 percent. When the new SNA became available, the growth rate of 1998 was −1.1 percent. (Compare the old SNA and new SNA in table 3.1). The severity of the 1998 downturn was thought to be extremely serious at the time.

41. News conference on 21 December 1999.

42. However, the drop in the NASDAQ from April to December 2000 also brought down the Nikkei index. The composition of the Nikkei index was changed in April 1999. A direct comparison therefore is not appropriate.

percent). However, it was thought to be 1 percent at the time. It was said at the time that the supply side was bright but the demand side was sluggish. Optimists believed that the supply-side indicators were acting as leading indicators, so that the economic situation would continuously improve.

With this information, the BOJ raised the interest rate, with a 7-2 vote in its Monetary Policy Committee on 11 August, stating that the economy was recovering and deflationary fear was dispelled.[43] Other interest rates, including the commercial lending rate and the 3-month repurchase rate, moderately increased after the August move.[44]

Economic activity in the second half of 2000 was at best sluggish. The external environment also had deteriorated. The US economy was weakening, and exporters that rely on US markets were becoming more cautious on production and investment. The magnitude of deflation was becoming larger. With this added information, the BOJ again eased monetary policy on three decision dates in February and March 2001. The BOJ has effectively gone back to the zero interest rate policy, and declared that the policy will remain in force until the inflation rate becomes positive. This is a significant policy change, as will be discussed below.

However, the point at this juncture is that, by raising the interest rate in August 2000, the Bank of Japan did not support economic recovery. Its refusal of quantitative easing in 1999-2000, and its decision instead to raise the interest rate in 2000, are regarded by many as assertions of its independence rather than sound monetary policymaking. Although the interest rate was brought down to zero again in March 2001, monetary stimulus was not in its full thrust between August 2000 and March 2001, and deflation worsened.

The Liquidity Trap

At the beginning of 2001, Japan was faced with a difficult macroeconomic environment. Its recovery from the recession of 1998 had been very weak.

---

43. The government opposed the decision to raise the interest rate. According to the April 1998 BOJ law, the government submitted a motion to delay the voting on raising the interest rate, but it was voted down in the Monetary Policy Committee. Some observers regard the interest rate increase at the earliest opportunity as a political act aimed at demonstrating the BOJ's "independence" under the new law.

44. Those who advocated the increase in the interest rate in August 2000 cited the following reasons: (1) the zero interest rate policy is an extreme measure aimed at an extremely weak economic condition; (2) the economy is on the way to recovery and deflation fear is dispelled; (3) the zero interest rate might induce moral hazard, i.e., undisciplined fiscal deficits and irresponsible bank lending; and (4) raising the interest rate by 0.25 percent is by no means tightening. (See Posen 2000, 205, for quotes from Governor Hayami to the effect that raising the interest rate would encourage structural reform by the private sector.) On the contrary, those who opposed lifting the interest rate argued that (1) with the large GDP gap, a little

Its annual GDP growth rate was less than 1.5 percent, with no sign of acceleration. Its output gap was estimated to be anywhere between 4 and 6 percent of GDP.[45] Prices—measured by any of the indices—have been declining in the past 3 years. The unemployment rate has risen to near 5 percent, a record high for the Japanese economy, with no sign of declining. Moreover, after two capital injections, banks' balance sheets are still plagued by NPLs, and the resolution of the banking crisis has become a highly politicized issue.

In normal circumstances, these conditions would call for stimulative monetary and fiscal policies, namely, lowering the interest rate and increasing government expenditures. However, Japan's room to maneuver is limited on both fronts. Five big fiscal packages have been introduced since the tax increase of 1997, so that the debt-GDP ratio has reached about 120 percent, and is rising. If current levels of budget deficits (6 percent of GDP) continue, the debt will eventually become unsustainable (see box 3.5). The interest rate has been virtually zero since the spring of 1999. At the zero interest rate, Japan is in a liquidity trap, where the conventional channels of monetary transmission do not work.

The nominal interest rate cannot be negative. Otherwise, people will keep assets in the form of cash rather than deposits.[46] Therefore, there is an absolute lower bound at zero on the nominal interest rate. As deflation continues, the real interest rate (the nominal interest rate minus the inflation rate) increases. Rising real interest rates discourage investment (including in consumer durables) and dampen aggregate demand. The fall in demand encourages further price cutting, setting off a self-reinforcing deflationary spiral.

Similarly, declining asset prices, and expectations of further decline, will impede consumption and investment through negative wealth effects. As goods and asset prices go down together, the real debt increases. That is, the real burden on borrowers (holders of nominal contracts, e.g., borrowers with a fixed nominal interest rate) will increase. The increase in the real debt burden discourages consumption and investment. This is called debt deflation.

Successful macroeconomic management requires the avoidance of deflationary spirals and debt deflation. This, in turn, becomes a question

---

bit of economic recovery would not cause inflation; and (2) there is no rush to raise the rate when a full recovery is doubtful.

45. Some think that the GDP gap is much larger. An estimate depends on an assumption of the potential GDP and a judgment as to how unused capacity might disappear rather than accumulate for a GDP gap; see Bayoumi (2000b).

46. To enforce a negative interest rate without causing a massive shift to currency holdings, some effective way to "tax" cash holdings would have to be devised. One way for such a tax is that currency (e.g., 10,000 yen notes) would have to be approved for circulation with stamps every, say, 6 months. Because such taxation on cash would be a complicated and costly operation, it is regarded as unrealistic.

Box 3.5   Sorting out Japan's government finances

Japan's public finances are a source of considerable controversy and potential importance to the world economy. The controversy emerges from the complex, some would say opaque, nature of Japan's government accounting. Japan's gross government debt-GDP ratio stood at roughly 120 percent in 2001, with the IMF predicting that it would rise to 150 percent by 2005. This makes Japan's situation the worst in the OECD, and puts it in the same league with Italy and other countries that have experienced debt crises.

However, Japan's debt, net of government assets, is claimed to be far lower—about 100 percent of GDP excluding its social security system, and about 50 percent of GDP if social security is included (IMF 2000). However, because the social security assets are more than offset by pension liabilities, the IMF argues that social security assets should be excluded when assessing Japan's situation. The Bank for International Settlements believes that "the net government debt/GDP ratio is on an unsustainable upward path, even if its level is still modest by international standards" (BIS 2000, 20). Technically, unsustainability arises when interest payments to existing bonds have to be financed by new issues of bonds and the level of taxes cannot be raised for economic and political reasons. However, it could become an issue earlier when investors, in anticipation of a crisis, demand higher interest rates to refinance the debt.

Moreover, there are reasons to believe that these net debt figures overvalue government assets, and hence understate the severity of the problem. For one thing, Japan maintains an extensive network of public corporations and public-private partnerships (e.g., the Japan Highway Public Corporation and the Honshu-Shikoku Bridge Authority; see box 3.1). As the OECD observes, "the economic value of financial assets in public corporations is partly supported by future payment of subsidies by the government which should be registered as liabilities and offset against assets" (OECD 2000b, 65).

(box continues next page)

of whether there is a policy instrument to generate inflation when the interest rate is at zero. Because this situation had not been observed in an industrial country since the 1930s, this used to be an academic question asked only in the classroom. But now it is one of the most relevant policy questions in Japan.

Inflation Targeting

Under a policy of inflation targeting, a central bank announces a target (range or point) for the inflation rate and commits to use its policy instruments to achieve that target. In the 1990s, many central banks—including those of New Zealand (1990), Canada (1991), the United Kingdom (1992), Sweden (1993), and Australia (1993)—adopted inflation targeting, typically as a means of providing a policy mandate to newly independent central banks in countries with histories of inflation. Experiences with inflation targeting have been generally favorable, in that the central bank managed to reduce the inflation rate to the target range within a few years.

Box 3.5 *(continued)*

In addition, both gross and net debt become larger if implicit liabilities—such as social welfare expenditures and civil servant pensions (for which the government has no reserves)—are included. According to the OECD (2000b), these alone would increase Japan's gross and net debt figures by 150 percent of GDP, although, as the IMF observes, recent pension reforms have reduced future liabilities by perhaps 20 percent of GDP. Contingent liabilities (e.g., government guarantees on private financing of public and parastatal corporations, and private small and medium-sized enterprises) could also be large, as demonstrated in the Japan National Railway Settlement Corporation case. Tadaaki Ito (1996) extensively discusses these "hidden losses" and their use to minimize current apparent liabilities through "financial manipulation."

The ¥64 trillion question is if and when this will begin to bite. Views are mixed. One analysis is colorfully titled "Could Japan's Financial Mount Fuji Blow Its Top?" Answer: Yes (Asher and Dugger 2000). Ninety-five percent of Japanese government debt is held by Japanese residents, and they have shown no indication of shifting out of it. This could change if there were a revival in the stock market prompting a portfolio shift from bonds to stocks, or if investors began to flee yen-denominated assets more generally. This uncertainty has led the ratings agencies, initially Moody's, followed by Fitch-IBCA and Standard and Poor's, to downgrade Japanese sovereign debt from AAA to something on a par with Spain's.

The real economic implications of a stock market rally and capital flight are quite different. A market rally might signal a revived Japanese economy and increased tax revenues that would permit Japan to grow its way out of its debt, absorbing the increased interest-servicing costs associated with higher interest rates on Japanese government bonds. Capital flight would be a different story, however. A precipitous shift out of yen-denominated assets could cause the yen to crash and disrupt financial and trade ties with the rest of the world, especially with the United States. A yen crash would also create inflation in Japan. This would be one way of ending the country's deflation, though not the way the authorities had in mind.

In principle, inflation targeting would also be one way of getting out of a deflationary spiral.[47] Advocates of inflation targeting in Japan typically list four major reasons for adoption. First, the intention and objective of the Bank of Japan will become clearer, independence from political pressure will be strengthened, and accountability will be enhanced. With an explicit policy of inflation targeting, the BOJ can fend off "pressures" from politicians by citing that it has committed to produce price stability. In return, the BOJ will be accountable for achieving this target.

Second, monetary policy may become more flexible and forward looking, because inflation targeting gives a clear policy objective and communication with the market will be easier with the announced target. Third,

---

47. For the case in favor of inflation targeting, see Takatoshi Ito (1999); Posen (1998); Bernanke et al. (1999); and Cargill, Hutchison, and Ito (2000, chap. 5). See Okina (1999), and Fujiki, Okina, and Shiratsuka (2001) for a contrary view.

the BOJ can clearly define and enhance instrument independence—its freedom to choose its policy instruments. Fourth, the inflation target provides an anchor for expectations. Indeed, by announcing that it will target a range of positive inflation rate, say 1-3 percent in 2 years, the BOJ may raise the expected inflation rate, a step toward getting out of a deflationary cycle (e.g., by encouraging the purchase of consumer durables). The benefit of inflation targeting may be realized even before all the right policy measures take effect through the real side of the economy.

Skeptics counter, first, that the mere announcement of adopting inflation targeting may not lift expectations out of a negative inflation rate. Second, there is no obvious tool to inflate the economy, once the interest rate is zero. They argue that the interest rate is the only channel of monetary policy, and once it reaches the lower bound of zero, monetary policy is completely ineffective. Moreover, by announcing something that it may not be able to achieve, the BOJ may actually lose credibility. Third, there is no perfect measure of the price index, and it is difficult to determine the correct range for the target.

Fourth, once inflation starts (i.e., the economy successfully gets out of deflation), it is difficult to stop it. Sooner rather than later, the inflation rate will become too high. Governor Hayami stated that setting a target for inflation was a dangerous policy that "could cause uncontrollable inflation" (quoted in Posen 2000, 200). Finance Minister Masajuro Shiokawa, a former BOJ official, said that inflation targeting would "cause runaway inflation and send the economy spinning out of control" (David Ibison, *Financial Times*, 22 August 2001). Even Prime Minister Koizumi got into the act, claiming that "this policy [inflation targeting] is difficult, as we could not control it" (Caroline Batt, *The Daily Telegraph*, 24 August 2001). Fifth, there is no precedent for inflation targeting being introduced to increase the inflation rate. All recent cases of inflation targeting involve an operation to reduce inflation—not to reverse deflation.

This skepticism can be rebutted as follows. First, the experience of the United Kingdom shows that the introduction of inflation targeting and the independence of the Bank of England have resulted in a significant drop in inflation expectations. Second, there are ways to cause inflation even if the interest rate is zero. Quantitative easing (further increasing the monetary base at the zero interest rate) would encourage economic activity directly, or at least encourage activity indirectly though an increase in prices.[48] Theoretically speaking, if people's holdings of money

---

48. Operationally, this could be achieved in a variety of ways. Quantitative easing through increasing purchase of long-term bonds would likely lower the full spectrum of interest rates. That would encourage bondholders to purchase riskier assets (e.g., asset-backed securities, equities, and foreign-currency-denominated bonds). Increased demand for asset-backed securities would help to increase real estate investment. Increased demand for equities would tend to increase equity prices, and result in wealth effects to stimulate aggregate demand. An increased demand for foreign-currency-denominated bonds implies

double, they will spend it, at least partly, to increase consumption. That would stimulate economic activity (if the economy is under capacity) or increase prices (if the economy is over capacity). Either one would contribute to extricating the economy from its deflationary spiral. Of course, whether such an unconventional step is needed or not depends on output and price developments.

Third, the issue of imperfections in price indices is well understood, and not a serious hindrance to the implementation of a successful inflation-targeting policy.[49] Fourth, it is inconceivable that the inflation rate would jump precipitously without time for a policy reaction in an economy such as Japan's. Indeed, the upper bound of the inflation target would act as a natural restraint on policymakers. In any event, it is strange to worry about too much inflation when deflation is at issue.

Fifth, inflation targeting is as effective in increasing the rate of inflation as in reducing it. The experience of price targeting in Sweden in the 1930s is credited with having prevented deflation in the wake of large depreciation resulting from a collapse of the gold standard (Berg and Jonung 1999). Even in more recent experiences of inflation targeting in Canada and New Zealand, the inflation rate did go below the floor of the target and policy was adopted to move back up to the target range. Having a target must have helped inflation expectations not to be too low in the stage of a declining actual inflation rate.

The Bank of Japan law was revised and the new law became effective in April 1998. There were two major changes, among others, that the BOJ had long wanted (Cargill, Hutchison, and Ito 2000, chap. 4). First, legal independence from the Ministry of Finance was established. Earlier, the governor could have been dismissed at any time, but under the new law, the governor's tenure is guaranteed. Second, price stability was established as a primary BOJ objective. Earlier, the BOJ was to help the economy achieve its maximum strength (a very vague concept), whereas Article 2 of the new law gives price stability as the BOJ's objective.

One may be skeptical of the additional benefit of announcing a numerical target, given that Article 2 sets price stability is the objective. However,

---

yen depreciation. That would help export industries. Although exact channels cannot be known beforehand, quantitative easing, even at the zero interest rate, would have positive effects on the economy.

49. One technical question in practicing an inflation target is which price index should be adopted, and what range should be specified. Many countries use the consumer price index (CPI) as the price index, for its widespread use and familiarity among consumers and corporations. Target ranges are different from one country to another, but they are quite similar. The Bank of England targets 2.5 percent (with a tolerance range of 1 percent), whereas the Bank of Canada targets the 1-3 percent range. It is well known that price index contains an upward bias, due to the fixed base-year weights and inadequate adjustment to quality improvements, and an inflation rate of 1.0-1.5 percent corresponds to true price stability. Although there is no perfect index to represent inflation, the CPI inflation rate is an acceptable indicator, if the upward bias is taken into account when the target is determined.

it was clear that when the BOJ tolerated deflation (a sustained negative CPI inflation rate), which started just after the new law became effective, it had no coherent notion of price stability. Governor Hayami and other members of the bank's Policy Committee argued that price declines may not necessarily be a bad thing (after all, price declines resulting from innovations in computer technology or in the distribution system may be regarded as good), confusing relative price changes with a disastrous fall in the absolute price level.[50] Numerically defining a target of inflation, say 1-3 percent, might have prompted the BOJ to ease earlier and to do so more aggressively. For example, the short-term interest rate might have approached zero earlier than February 1999. With independence should come accountability.

One might question a narrow focus on targeting the inflation rate. However, inflation targeting does not mean only targeting the inflation rate of the near future. Policies should be formulated to maintain price stability for a long time. If the inflation rate is increasing, one must predict and prevent the rate from going above the target range. Because it takes time for monetary policy to take effect on the economy, it must be conducted in a forward-looking manner, that is, to predict the future inflation rate with currently available information. Obviously, the GDP growth rate, GDP gap, and the exchange rate, among others, should be taken into account in formulating monetary policy. The bottom line is that there are and were credible alternatives to the policy that the Bank of Japan has followed.

Has the Bank of Japan Embraced Inflation Targeting?

In three meetings in February and March 2001, the Bank of Japan took measures to ease monetary policy.[51] In the third meeting, on 19 March, the bank moved again to ease its monetary stance. The decision consisted of three items: (1) The monetary instrument was changed from the call rate to reserves (balance of the current accounts) at the BOJ, with the reserve target being ¥5 trillion. (2) If there is any difficulty in providing liquidity, the amount of purchases of long-term government bonds will be increased. (3) The policy stance will be maintained until inflation—

---

50. See Posen (2000) for specific quotes. It is natural that prices of goods and services that benefit from innovation and productivity increases will fall relative to other goods. Monetary policy would be neutral to such relative price movement. However, inflation or deflation is a phenomenon of average price movements, and this is a result of monetary policy.

51. The BOJ also issued a statement that acknowledged deflationary pressure, reflecting weak demand. This was new. BOJ officials previously had insisted that some of the deflationary force was prompted by supply-side conditions, e.g., innovations in the distribution system. The BOJ also emphasized the importance of structurally reforming the financial system.

measured by the current consumer price index (excluding fresh food-stuffs) in comparison with that 12 months ago—becomes stable above zero.[52] Moreover, the decision was accompanied by a statement that the BOJ "strongly hopes" that structural reforms, including addressing the NPL problem, would be advanced by leadership of the government.

Among the decisions made on 19 March, the most important item is the commitment to maintain relaxed monetary policy until the inflation rate becomes positive (item 3 above). This could be interpreted as a shift by the BOJ toward embracing inflation targeting. However, proponents of this view were disheartened when Governor Hayami, answering questions, denied this.[53]

However, the new policy does have an element of inflation targeting. It would be preferable to set the floor inflation rate at 1 percent instead of zero, and it is better to have a ceiling as well as a floor. Moreover, by denying that it is inflation targeting, the BOJ is not reaping the benefits of expectation effects.

We strongly recommend that inflation targeting be adopted, so that monetary policy can become transparent and so that the Bank of Japan can adopt an aggressive policy, if necessary. The present zero interest rate policy, although an improvement over the policy undertaken between

---

52. The change in the instrument from the interest rate to the reserve at the BOJ, with a target of ¥5 trillion (item 1) simply means that the zero interest rate policy is reintroduced because the required reserve is about ¥4 trillion, and a ¥1 trillion excess reserve is only possible with the call rate being driven down to zero. Therefore, in essence, item (1) means that monetary conditions will revert to the position that was in effect prior to the lifting of the zero interest rate policy in August 2000. One may conclude that, in this sense, calling it a change in the monetary instrument is rather a red herring. However, one may see the change in instrument is significant, because it might mean that the amount of reserves can be flexibly changed if an environment becomes weak, e.g., deflation becomes worse.

Some economists argued that monetary easing that would go beyond zero interest rate policy was needed to combat deflationary forces and to lift economic activities. The most frequently proposed measure was to increase the amount of government long-term bond purchases. Item (2) means that, in case the BOJ finds it difficult to achieve a ¥5 trillion reserve by purchasing treasury bills from financial institutions, it would purchase long-term bonds in the secondary market. This seems to have some common thread with an earlier argument, although there is a proviso. Putting items (1) and (2) together, the BOJ seems to have opened a possibility that it has made clear how it might use the monetary tool in the near future. However, this is still only one possible interpretation of items (1) and (2), and not a sufficiently concrete one.

53. Nevertheless, the commitment is much better than a previous promise, "the zero interest rate policy until the deflationary fear would be dispelled." Previously, the BOJ was reluctant to choose a particular price index and to set a numerical target. Worse still, it tended to argue that there could be good deflation. Therefore, this is a major shift in the commitment to combat deflation with a transparent target. E.g., with this commitment, lifting of the de facto zero interest rate would not happen while the CPI inflation rate is still negative. That is to say that the August 2000 interest rate increase could not have happened if item (3) had been in force.

August 2000 and March 2001, is a decidedly poor substitute for an explicit policy of inflation targeting. Monetary instrument independence should be respected, with an accountability of the results placed on the BOJ. Inflation targeting is a good framework for achieving this balance.

Fiscal Policy

Fiscal policy, especially fiscal spending with new issues of government bonds, is a traditional discretionary, countercyclical tool that can be used to lessen the magnitude of an economic downturn. Japan used this tool frequently in the 1980s and 1990s, with uncertain results. Some question the effectiveness of fiscal policy by citing a prolonged recession despite repeated fiscal policy packages. Yet other critics argue that the fiscal tightening in April 1997 was at least partly to blame for the severe recession in 1998.

Although the official dating of the trough of the business cycle was October 1993, the economy hardly recovered from the fall of 1993 onward. In response to the sagging economy, the government introduced a series of economic stimulus packages. The packages of August 1992 and April 1993 were significant, their combined size being ¥26 trillion (5 percent of GDP). However, only ¥10 trillion (2 percent of GDP) was net incremental expenditures, the true stimulus or the so-called *mamizu* portion (Posen 1998, table 2.4).[54] The announced "size of the package" is usually deceptive, because the Japanese government, trying to impress the public with "announcement effects," puts in items that had been already budgeted or had no budget consequences. This is to say that the estimated real additions to spending in 1992 and 1993 were only 40 percent of their advertised value. As the Japanese government replayed this tactic time and time again from the mid-1980s on, its credibility eroded like that of the boy who cried "wolf." Indeed, McKibbin (1997) argues that these exaggerated announcements actually had a perverse effect: by contributing to yen appreciation and long-term interest rate increases without delivering additional demand, they actually depressed real GDP.

With these gentle fiscal nudges, the economy started a recovery, albeit slowly, in 1993-94. Additional stimulus came through the special income tax reduction introduced in 1995 (with a precommitment of reversing it and of increasing the consumption tax rate in 2 years). The size of the total package of April 1995 was ¥4.8 trillion, whereas the net incremental expenditures (*mamizu*) share was higher than previous packages at 56 percent, amounting to 0.6 percent of GDP. With the strong performance of the economy in 1996, the precommitment to a tax increase was carried out in April 1997.

---

54. See also Mühleisen (2000) for further discussion of Japanese fiscal policy.

Tax increases in April 1997 pulled back the economy: The consumption (value-added) tax rate was raised from 3 to 5 percent, a special income tax cut made a few years earlier was repealed, and contribution rates to social security were increased. The tax burden (including the social security contribution) increased by about ¥9 trillion (nearly 2 percent of GDP). As one long-time observer of Japan declared, "in retrospect the Japanese government made its worst macroeconomic mistake in fifty years when it decided in early 1997 to give top priority to budget deficit reduction and shifted from an expansionary fiscal policy to a strongly restrictive fiscal policy (Patrick, 2001, 22). Another observed, "The result was disastrous for Japan. It also contributed to the Asian financial crisis later that year, when Japanese imports collapsed and distressed Japanese banks withdrew loans to other Asian countries" (Shafer 2000, 211). In anticipation of the consumption tax increases, consumers shifted their timing of consumer durable purchases forward to the fourth quarter of 1996 and the first quarter of 1997. The result was a temporary boom in 1996 and a sudden decline in consumption in the second quarter of 1997.[55]

Did the tax increase cause a recession in 1998? It was certainly a contributing factor. Given the falling asset prices and the weakness of the financial sector, the ¥9 trillion withdrawal at once was too much. The long-run need for fiscal consolidation was and remains understandable, but under the circumstances this fiscal contraction was too much and premature.

Owing to the large fiscal stimulus packages in the second half of the 1990s, Japan's debt-GDP ratio has rapidly risen to a level that is the worst among G-7 countries (tables 3.2 and 3.3). Unless its budget deficits are contained soon, the country's fiscal debt will become unsustainable. A quick withdrawal might be detrimental to the economic recovery that is needed to get it out of the deflation cycle. However, gradually withdrawing deficit spending would not have too much of a negative impact. It is necessary to avoid the catastrophic collapse of the government bond market down the road. (Such an apocalyptic scenario was the theme of a popular best-selling novel, Ma-in Koda's *Nihon Kokusai*, or *Japanese Government Bonds*.) The withdrawal should be carried out with a careful medium-term strategy, with a waiver clause—in case of a severe negative shock, fiscal tightening can be shelved.

One way to achieve gradual fiscal tightening without much withdrawal of support is to design a cutback in fiscal spending in the areas that do not affect other activities—namely, bridges and tunnels to nowhere. In fiscal 2000, the government deficit (on the SNA base) was about 6 percent of GDP. Having deficits means that the fiscal stance is supportive. But the magnitude of the deficits has to be lessened gradually. We propose

---

55. To see consumption shifting due to the consumption tax increase, quarterly GDP growth rates can be examined. The quarter-to-quarter growth rates were negative in the second quarter of 1996 (1996:2Q) and 1996:3Q, but turned to 4.4 percent (annualized rate) in 1996:4Q and 8.4 percent in 1997:1Q. The growth rate plunged to −6.4 percent in 1997:2Q. Consumption started to recover in 1997:3Q. A predicted pattern of the effect of the consumption tax increase is evident in the data. What was unexpected was that the consumption sank again in 1997:4Q.

Table 3.2 Government deficits (SNA-based, central and local government consolidated), **as a ratio of GDP**

Country	1992	1993	1994	1995	1996	1997	1998	1999	2000	2001
Japan	−2.0	−4.8	−5.1	−6.4	−6.9	−5.9	−7.1	−8.8	−7.8	−7.7
Japan[a]	1.5	−1.6	−2.3	−3.6	−4.2	−3.3	−5.0	−7.0	−6.0	−6.0
United States	−6.7	−5.7	−4.5	−3.9	−3.1	−2.0	−0.9	−0.4	0.8	1.0
United States[a]	−5.9	−5.0	−3.6	−3.1	−2.2	−0.9	0.3	1.0	2.3	2.6
United Kingdom	−6.5	−8.0	−6.8	−5.8	−4.4	−2.0	0.4	1.3	2.7	2.2
Germany	−2.5	−3.1	−2.4	−3.3	−3.4	−2.7	−2.1	−1.4	1.4	−1.7
France	−4.2	−6.0	−5.5	−5.6	−4.1	−3.0	−2.7	−1.8	−1.4	−0.1
Italy	−9.5	−9.4	−9.1	−7.6	−7.1	−2.7	−2.8	−1.9	0.1	−1.0
Canada	−9.2	−8.7	−6.7	−5.4	−2.8	0.2	0.2	2.2	2.5	2.1

a. With social security accounts.

SNA = System of National Accounts.

Source: Organization for Economic Cooperation and Development, *Economic Outlook,* December 2000.

Table 3.3 Government debt (SNA-based, central and local government consolidated), **as a ratio of GDP**

Country	1992	1993	1994	1995	1996	1997	1998	1999	2000	2001
Japan	59.3	63.7	68.8	76.2	80.5	84.6	97.4	105.3	112.3	118.6
United States	74.1	75.8	75.0	74.5	73.9	71.4	68.4	65.3	59.5	54.6
United Kingdom	49.4	58.4	56.1	61.1	60.6	60.9	62.0	57.0	53.5	50.7
Germany	41.8	47.4	47.9	57.1	60.3	61.7	63.0	60.6	59.6	57.8
France	44.7	51.6	55.3	59.3	62.3	64.7	65.2	65.0	64.6	63.6
Italy	116.1	117.9	124.0	123.1	121.8	119.8	117.7	116.6	112.0	108.3
Canada	110.3	116.9	117.5	120.6	120.9	117.4	116.2	111.6	105.9	100.5

SNA = System of National Accounts.

Source: Organization for Economic Cooperation and Development, *Economic Outlook,* December 2000.

a medium-term strategy to lower the deficit-GDP ratio by 1 percentage point every year (so that the deficit-GDP ratio will be lowered to 5 percent in 2001, 4 percent in 2002, etc.), with a waiver in the case of unforeseen negative shocks. The primary balance will be restored by 2006 or 2007. The debt-GDP ratio will be at about 160 percent by then.

The Koizumi government has made a promise to keep a cap on new government bond issues at ¥30 trillion for fiscal 2002 (April 2002-March 2003). If no reforms are made, new issues are expected to be ¥33.3 trillion. Therefore, the government pledge of ¥30 trillion can be translated as a 10 percent cutback in government bond issues. The withdrawal is about 0.7 percent of GDP, and well in line with a medium-term strategy of a 0.5-1.0 percentage-point withdrawal each year, which is roughly what the United States accomplished in fiscal 1993-2000.

Ideally, the government should develop a comprehensive medium-term plan, including a cap on borrowing and spending by local governments. A cutback on government-affiliated corporations should be considered, in addition to the cap on the central government's bond issues. However, the ¥30 trillion cap on government bond issues may be simple enough to send the message to the public, and is a constructive first step.

The dampening effect of the reduction in fiscal spending could be offset by shifting spending from low- to high-multiplier projects. Three to 4 percentage points of this decrease may be achieved by cutting back public works budgets that were added in the fiscal stimulus packages in 1998, 1999, and 2000. Public works composition should be drastically shifted from traditional projects (highways, bridges, tunnels, agricultural roads, dams, concrete riverbeds, etc.) to urban infrastructure (making roads wider, better city planning, expanding fiber-optic cable networks and cable television networks, etc.) where higher multiplier effects are expected. Also, tax rules, deregulation of housing, and other policy measures can complement public spending.

We believe that building larger, more comfortable houses in urban areas (close to work) will lead to more private consumption (i.e., a higher multiplier) than construction of bridges and tunnels that almost no one will use. The impact on the construction industry (which politicians worry about) is minimal if houses are built instead of bridges.

However, if the cutback in public spending is delayed, this would have large long-term costs. Currently, the high debt-GDP ratio is a concern, although it is not yet reflected in the level of the long-term bond rate. It would be costly to adjust the fiscal situation once the interest rate started to rise due to the unsustainability concern.

In sum, we recommend gradually withdrawing fiscal support by reducing deficit spending, starting now. A 0.5-1.0 percentage-point improvement in fiscal deficits (SNA base, central and local government consolidated) every year for the next 7 to 8 years should be kept on track, with an escape clause that deficit reduction may be shelved if the growth rate is expected to become negative due to external negative shocks. A natural way of doing this would be to define the fiscal targets in terms of the full-employment budget position.

Trade Conflict and Yen Appreciation

During the 1990s, the yen-dollar exchange rate fluctuated between 80 and 150. The yen appreciated from 140 yen per dollar in 1991 to 80 yen per dollar in April 1995, and then depreciated to the weakest point of the decade, 147, in August 1998, before turning around to start an appreciation phase. The yen reached near the 100 mark again in January 2000, before easing back to the 120s.

In the 1980s, movements in Japanese and US current account balances mirrored each other. Increases in the Japanese current account surplus were accompanied by increases in the US current account deficit from 1980 to 1987. This development was partly caused by the dollar's appreciation from 1980 to February 1985, and was partly due to increasing fiscal deficits in the United States. The dollar's depreciation in 1985-87 resulted in some, but not all, correction of the external imbalance.[56]

The inauguration of the Clinton US presidential administration in January 1993 ushered in a particularly contentious period of trade relations between Japan and the United States (as will be discussed in greater detail in chapter 4). The failure to reach an agreement on trade issues during the February 1994 summit between President Clinton and Prime Minister Morihiro Hosokawa was unprecedented in postwar history. Hosokawa's refusal to accede to US demands (which will be described in more detail in chapter 5) was widely supported in Japan. The US administration subsequently ratcheted up the pressure on Hosokawa's immediate successors, culminating in a confrontation over automobiles in the spring of 1995. As the Japanese economy went into a recession, the yen appreciated from 125 in January 1993 to about 105 in the summer of 1993 (figure 3.3).

It was rumored in the market that the United States would talk the yen up to put pressure on Japan, especially in regard to the auto dispute (E.

---

56. The external imbalance in the two countries increased again in the first half of the 1990s. But in the second half of the 1990s, the movements of the Japanese and US current accounts were somewhat delinked. Japanese current account surpluses decreased sharply in 1996, from a $110 billion surplus in 1995 to a $66 billion one in 1996. The level of the surplus in Japan increased to $110-120 billion in 1998-2000, but this is less than the record surpluses of $130 billion in 1993-94. However, US deficits increased sharply, from $109 billion in 1995 to $435 billion in 2000. In other words, for this increase in US current account deficits in the second half of the 1990s, the contribution of the Japan-United States bilateral imbalance was negligible.

Figure 3.3   Yen-dollar exchange rate, 1990-2001

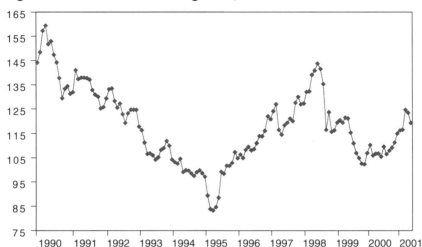

Source: IMF, *International Financial Statistics*.

Sakakibara 2000), although in fact it never did so.[57] It would be very difficult to explain, on the basis of economic fundamentals, the yen's appreciation from 100 yen per dollar in January to 80 yen per dollar in April 1995.[58] This rapid appreciation by 20 percent caused a sense of panic among exporters and their suppliers.

Japanese monetary authorities clearly viewed any yen value higher than the level of 100 yen per dollar as misaligned, under the macroeconomic circumstances of the time.[59] On a number of occasions, US and Japanese

---

57. Former Clinton administration officials deny that there was any such policy, and point to the fact that the United States did not make such public statements. The media interpreted the yen's appreciation as being in response to large trade imbalances, and US officials did not dispute these interpretations. The yen's appreciation might then be regarded as a tacit or implicit stick to increase pressure on the Japanese government in the auto dispute.

58. Both interest rates and growth rates were changing in ways to encourage the yen's depreciation: The interest rate in Japan was lowered much faster than in the United States, so that the Japan-United States interest rate differential was increasing, and the growth rate had been declining in Japan from 3 percent in 1991 to 1 percent in 1995, while it had been increasing in the United States. However, the current account surplus movements may have explained the yen-dollar movements: The Japanese surpluses grew from $68 billion in 1991 to $131 billion in 1994, while the US current accounts went from a $4 billion surplus in 1991 to a deficit of $121 billion in 1994.

59. The official discount rate was lowered from 1.75 to 1.00 percent on 14 April 1995, the first move in 2.5 years. The Ministry of Finance and the BOJ intervened massively from January to April 1995, but in vain. The market turned around in April, after hitting the record high of 79.75 yen per dollar after the United States joined the Japanese authorities in a joint intervention. The intervention continued until August 1995 to push back the yen over the 100 level. The official discount rate was again lowered, from 1.00 to 0.50 percent,

Figure 3.4   The Japanese current account balance (t) and real exchange rate (t-1), 1980-2000

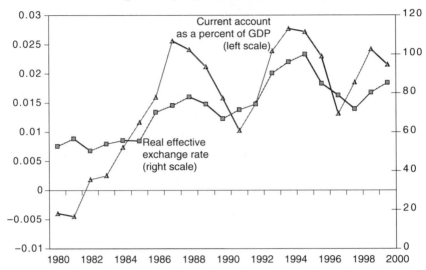

Source: IMF, *International Financial Statistics.*

monetary authorities conducted joint market interventions in 1994 and 1995.[60] Both interventions and lowering of the interest rate were instrumental in firming the trend of yen depreciation from the fall of 1995.

The lagged impact of exchange rate movements on trade balances is well understood, although the relationship between the exchange rate and other macroeconomic aggregates in the United States and Japan is at best uncertain (Noland 1989a, 1989b). As an illustration, in figure 3.4, real exchange rate appreciation tends to lower current account surpluses in the following year, especially in the 1980s.[61]

Indeed, some even make the extreme claim that Japan's poor macroeconomic performance can be attributed entirely to the secular appreciation

---

on 8 September 1995. This was in response to weak economic news due to the strong yen, and in accordance with a massive intervention in August.

60. The US monetary authorities intervened jointly with the Japanese authorities in the yen-dollar market 5 days in 1994 and 8 days in 1995. The Japanese authorities intervened unilaterally 50 days in 1994 and 32 days between February and November 1995.

61. After the Plaza Agreement in 1985, Japanese multinational firms began moving substantial portions of their production offshore. E.g., automakers such as Toyota shifted production facilities to North America to avoid trade restrictions, and consumer electronics producers such as Sony shifted production to compete with rival producers. As a result, the sensitivity of profits (on a globally consolidated basis) to exchange rate fluctuations declined. Once Japanese exporters saw that it was possible that the yen could go to the 80 level, they hesitated to increase production capacity at home. Repeated episodes of yen appreciation in the 1980s and 1990s accelerated foreign direct investment, which contributed to the diversification of production locations.

of the yen due to trade friction (cf. McKinnon and Ohno 1997, 1998; McKinnon 1998). Yet, although trade tensions and yen appreciation may have played a bit part in Japan's macroeconomic tragedy, it strains credulity to give them top billing over the financial, monetary, and fiscal mishaps reviewed above.

As will be discussed in chapter 4, trade plays a relatively small role in the Japanese economy, and trade with the United States a smaller role still. For bilateral trade relations to determine macroeconomic outcomes in Japan, the tail would truly have to wag the dog. Bayoumi (2000a) confirms that it does not. Second, as is shown in figure 3.3, the yen has not appreciated secularly—it has gone through intermittent periods of appreciation and depreciation. Nor, for that matter, do surveys of market participants indicate that they always expect the yen to appreciate (whether these expectations are fulfilled or not).

Third, the existing econometric evidence generally rejects the hypothesis of unidirectional causality between the Japanese exchange rate and other relevant macroeconomic variables (Noland 1989b). Indeed, a sophisticated econometric analysis of the 1991-93 recession found that most of the yen's appreciation during this period was predictable on standard macroeconomic grounds, and although unpredictable movements in the exchange rates accentuated the downturn, the impact of the exchange rate was small relative to other forces, such as the collapse of investment following a period of excessive capital accumulation and decline of asset prices (Brunner and Kamin 1996). Ramaswamy and Rendu (2000) similarly find that a fall in investment due to overaccumulation of capital was the predominant cause of Japan's slowdown in the 1990s, and that the external sector had no impact, despite the yen's appreciation. The bottom line is that (as will be detailed in chapter 5) trade tensions cooled noticeably after 1995—but the deterioration of the Japanese economy did not.

Structural Reforms

In Japan's period of high growth, it was fashionable to ascribe its superior economic performance to the unique institutional characteristics of the Japanese economy, such as the *keiretsu* system, the bonus payment system, the main-bank system of corporate governance, and the system of lifetime employment (see box 3.6). Now that Japan is having economic difficulties, it has become fashionable to claim that these institutions are impediments to growth. If anything, these institutions were weakening in the 1990s, and if they are a source of the problem, the growth rate should have accelerated.[62]

---

62. These institutions appear to be a relatively recent (i.e., postwar) phenomenon (T. Okazaki 1993; Noguchi 1995). Japanese institutions are not immutable—they have changed in the past and undoubtedly will change in the future.

Box 3.6 *Keiretsu*

Keiretsu are networks of affiliated firms that typically have long-standing financial, managerial, and product market interlinkages. A *keiretsu* might consist of a group of large core firms (including financial firms) linked across markets, together with their vertically linked input suppliers, and possibly a captive distribution network. *Keiretsu* are a multifaceted phenomenon, but two aspects of this form of industrial organization can be distinguished in this context: so-called vertical *keiretsu*, which involve vertical supply relationships in product markets; and horizontal *keiretsu*, which involve many firms in different sectors. The former are sometimes called distribution *keiretsu*, and the latter financial *keiretsu*. However, as Matsushita (1997) observes, the term is rather vague and does not necessarily involve contractual relationships between the affiliated firms. Instead, these may be de facto relationships based on repeated transactions.

Vertical *keiretsu* may involve considerable cross-ownership, as well as product market linkages. Sheard (1997) notes that Toyota owns 25 percent of the stock shares of its top suppliers, which in turn sell 43 percent of their output to Toyota; likewise, at one time Nissan owned 30 percent of its suppliers' stock, and they sold 55 percent of their output to Nissan (Dodwell Marketing Consultants 1997). However, foreign penetration (notably Renault's takeover of Nissan) indicates that vehicle assemblers are encouraging their suppliers to diversify their customer bases, and the introduction of an online automobile parts exchange are expected to weaken these links in the auto sector even further. In the electronics sector, Matsushita owns 54 percent of the stock of its primary suppliers, which sell 51 percent of their output to Matsushita; and Hitachi owns 50 percent of the stock of its principal suppliers, which sell 30 percent of their output to Hitachi.

According to the IMF (1998), these cross-holdings are "pervasive" and higher than those observed in other industrial countries. According to the Nomura Research Institute, the ratio of shares reciprocally held by listed Japanese companies declined throughout the 1990s, reaching 11 percent in March 2000. Since then, distress sales have probably reduced this figure further. The anticipated sales of stocks held by banks spurred by changes in accounting rules effective in April 2001 will in all likelihood contribute to additional erosion in horizontal cross-holdings. Bank sales of equity holdings were given another push by the emergency measures announced in April 2001.

Although there may have been some unwinding of horizontal cross-holding due to bank consolidation or distress sales, the decline of the Japanese stock market in the 1990s has actually afforded large, better capitalized firms the opportunity to tighten their control over suppliers, suggesting that vertical integration may actually be increasing.

Evolving Institutions

Lifetime employment means that jobs for "core employees" (regular workers, excluding part-time workers) are almost guaranteed, unless the company experiences extreme hardship such as a bankruptcy or takeover (e.g., the Long-Term Credit Bank and Nissan). This makes labor a quasi-fixed factor of production. Moreover, to the extent that remuneration is determined by tenure and seniority, this provides an incentive against employees changing jobs and contributes to rigidity in the labor market.[63]

At the same time, however, lifetime employment encourages firms to invest in the development of their employees' human capital, because they are confident that they will be able to capture the return on that investment—rather than watching their investment depart for greener pastures. Discretion in job assignments, including assignment to subsidiaries and affiliated companies, and flexible net pay (including bonuses) and overtime hours by management, accompany the implicit commitment of lifetime employment. Flexibility in pay and hours as well as job assignments well serve large companies with many divisions and diversified products. Deferred payments in the form of severance pay at retirement (prevalent among all types of Japanese firms) and nonportable pension schemes also well serve companies that are expanding their businesses. The commitment to lifetime employment was not too large a burden for companies in a growing economy.

The reason that these institutions (lifetime employment, large deferred payments, flexible hours and job assignments) became a problem is twofold: They are problematic when growth slows and internal opportunities are no longer expanding; and they do not suit the new economy, where innovation rather than skill accumulation is essential.

On the capital-market side, the new technology rewards investors that accept high risks for high returns. Equity financing fits well. However, the strength of the Japanese financial markets was patient, relationship-based banking, and not (NASDAQ-like) equity financing, much less venture capital operations.

Similarly, *keiretsu* may be good or bad in the new century, depending on the rationale for the institution and the changes in the environment. Vertical *keiretsu*—parts to assembler, and manufacturing to retail distribution—may survive in the new economy, although exclusive parts suppliers and exclusive dealerships are fading away. Moreover, with the Internet revolution, channels of parts procurement and retail distribution are becoming shorter and more competitive. Some vertical *keiretsu* will have to transform significantly.[64] These issues can largely be addressed through rational decision making in the private sector.

---

63. The Miyauchi Committee, chaired by Orix head Yoshihiko Miyauchi and coordinated by subsequent Koizumi cabinet Economy Minister Heizo Takenaka, concluded that "[the] lifetime employment and the seniority-based wage system, which have played a key role in building a stable employment relationship, undermine corporate profitability and competitiveness. They also hinder labor market fluidity and prevent the appropriate transfer of human resources into growth fields, while being an obstacle to workers' displaying their ambitions and capabilities" (JERI 2001, 4-5).

64. With regard to vertical *keiretsu*, the Miyauchi Committee observed that they "were effective in reducing business risk and promoting the stable expansion of business, but in an increasing number of cases, such entrenched ties have been a hindrance when a company

Horizontal *keiretsu* are much more endangered. Because latent capital gains from equity holdings by banks have disappeared (as explained above, as a result of realizing gains for offsetting losses from nonperforming loans and preparing to introduce mark-to-market accounting), banks have been selling equities from cross-share holdings in the past few years and are expected to continue doing so in the coming years. Although stocks from horizontal *keiretsu* companies may be the last to be sold, the attraction of horizontal *keiretsu* is diminishing. As the banks are at the center of horizontal *keiretsu*, dissolving cross-share holding from banks will imply less of whatever power (benefits or costs) there was in keeping horizontal *keiretsu* together. Enterprise groups among the manufacturing groups may remain strong, but relationships with banks will be weakened. Some (e.g., the Miyauchi Committee) believe that the net effect of the dissolution of these ties will be to improve the efficiency of capital allocation. As Fukao (1998) observes, the dissolution of these ties and their replacement by more performance-oriented capital markets will encourage the abandonment of lifetime employment practices as well, as has occurred in continental Europe.

We agree that these institutions are problematic in the new century. However, just destroying old institutions may not serve the economy at large. Japan's institutions per se may not be the source of the problem of low growth, except that traditional labor relations—including lifetime employment, the seniority wage system, and the like—may not be suitable for the new economy. It is important to create new opportunities not bound by old conventions.

Chronic Housing Problems

One of the most unsatisfactory aspects of the lifestyle of a typical Japanese citizen is the size, quality, and cost of housing. Floor space for a typical Japanese house, controlling for income level of households and commuting distance, is smaller than European counterparts, not to mention US counterparts. Poor durability has become a concern. Misguided regulations encourage extremely inefficient land use and urban sprawl. Employees face lengthy commutes, and despite the enormous geographical dispersion of Japanese cities, parks and other public green spaces are in short supply—per capita municipal park space in Tokyo is one-fifth that of Paris, one-fifteenth that of London, and one-twentieth that of Washington. These long-standing problems are well recognized in Japan, and, for example, were highlighted by an important official panel on economic

---

attempts to slash costs under global competition. The recent growth of e-commerce on the back of the Internet and other areas of IT innovation is giving even greater momentum to this trend" (JERI 2001, 4). Also see Hoetker (2001) for a discussion of this phenomenon in the notebook computer industry.

reform, the Maekawa Commission, which in 1987 called for "a revolutionary improvement in the quality of life."

Although housing and related land-use issues are primarily microeconomic, they have macroeconomic implications. Household consumption could increase if floor space became larger, because space would be provided to install consumer durables. Women's labor participation rates could increase if labor-saving appliances or a nanny could be accommodated in a house. If all family members could have their own rooms, that would allow more productive activities at home, including home offices with computers with Internet connections. If the relative price of housing could be reduced, the accumulation of savings to finance housing purchases would fall, possibly reducing excess household savings as well (Balassa and Noland 1988).

To put an end to deflation, it is essential to have consumption growth. After all, 60 percent of GDP is household consumption. Consumption has long been stagnant, even when there was some glimpse of high growth in investment. The best bet for increasing consumption is in the area of housing.

Problems in the housing market stem from several sources. First-time visitors to Japan are typically stunned to find small agricultural plots under cultivation in the inner suburbs of urban areas. This pattern of land use has been encouraged by policies such as trade protection, which artificially boost the rate of return in agriculture, whereas property and inheritance tax policies discourage the conversion of agricultural land to alternative uses. Changes in the tax law introduced in the early 1990s were supposed to resolve this problem and encourage the conversion of urban agricultural land to more efficient uses, but little conversion actually has taken place.[65]

A second source of problems in the housing market are zoning regulations—including "sunshine laws"—that ostensibly were enacted to ensure access to sunlight for homeowners, which effectively limit the height of buildings in many urban neighborhoods to a few stories.[66] These

---

65. Traditionally, a greatly reduced real estate rate on agricultural lands was applied to these agricultural patches. Once converted to residential lands, they were subject to high capital-gains taxes. The law was revised to equalize the rate of taxation on agricultural and nonagricultural lands, and to provide relief from the capital-gains tax at the time of conversion. However, the law contained a grandfather provision: If the owner elects to keep the agricultural land for the rest of his or her life, and the heir also will keep it as agricultural land, the reduced rate still applies. These lands thus were "locked in" for agriculture. Otherwise, the higher rate will apply (and presumably the land will be converted to residential land, sooner or later). Although it was a smart idea to attempt to tax agricultural land in the residential area, the options made things worse by locking away some agricultural lands forever.

66. The height of detached houses (as well as high-rise condominiums) is regulated. The size of floor space of a detached house is regulated in the multiple of square meters of land

regulations represent a highly inefficient way of handling what, in economics terminology, is an externality—that is, when the welfare of one agent is dependent on the activities of another and private costs do not reflect this dependency. In the case at hand, the construction of a new high-rise would adversely affect the welfare of existing homeowners by reducing their access to sunlight, increasing congestion and so on. If current homeowners are able to prevent new construction, through legal obstacles, however, a less than socially optimal quantity of housing will be built. This is what has happened in Japan. Yet if developers are not required to compensate current homeowners, then too much housing will be constructed because the losses of existing owners are not properly taken into account. The task is to devise a system of incentives that yields the socially optimal amount of housing.

Two standard ways of dealing with externalities are internalization and compensation. A variety of solutions are imaginable. For example, residents on a block could jointly decide to accept taller houses, recognizing that though sunlight might be limited on the lower floors, the existing access to sunlight could be preserved on upper floors.[67] Voluntary initiatives of this sort by local districts should be encouraged to reform restrictions on houses. Another approach would be to formally revise existing regulations. The sunshine laws could be repealed, and a law modeled after those in other countries could be enacted that requires developers to purchase additional surrounding tracts on a per-unit basis, and to convert a specified percentage of the land into public parks and playgrounds. Instead of buying a single plot and building a single high-rise amid smaller homes, developers would be required to purchase additional plots and develop a residential complex, thereby internalizing the true social cost of development.

Alternatively, one could revise the sunshine laws to permit new construction, but require developers to compensate those adversely affected. A simple rule might require developers to compensate affected homeowners for the value of their structures (but not of their land). Land and structures are contracted for separately in Japan, so it would be relatively easy to assess the value of the structure. Current homeowners would be

---

lot (the cubic restriction). Even within this constraint of the cubic restriction, the shape of the house has to be configured, subject to other restrictions, not to cast shadows onto neighboring plots.

67. Alternatively, one may go underground. The proportion of houses with a basement is not very high in Japan (relative to the United States, where land prices are comparatively low). The high land prices and height restrictions should encourage building basements. Of course, construction costs of basements are about 50 percent higher than those of aboveground buildings—even if a basement is counted as a part of floor space for real estate tax purposes and the cubic restrictions. However, given the scarcity of land in Japan, basements should be encouraged by tax incentives and a relaxed cubic restriction.

free to remain and suffer the discomfort of reduced sunshine, or to sell their land and relocate.

These considerations relate to the quantity of housing. Other aspects of public policy contribute to the poor quality of the housing stock in Japan. Houses are valued at about half of market value for inheritance tax purposes, whereas liability (mortgages) are fully deducted. Financial assets are assessed at their market values for inheritance. Hence, the elderly with large assets have an incentive to acquire houses (owner occupied, second houses, and rental properties) in planning to pass assets down to heirs. Houses that are most suitable for this strategy are apartment buildings with wooden structures (and fast depreciation) with lots of tenants (and lower valuations as rental properties). To minimize financial assets and to maximize rental properties and associated mortgages is a valid inheritance-tax-saving strategy. This has contributed to the building of poor-quality rental properties.

Existing tenant laws also discourage the construction of high-quality housing. The traditional tenant (land and structures) law in Japan gives strong rights to tenants. Even when a lease expires, a landlord cannot terminate a lease unless the tenant agrees to move out or the landlord has a reason to demand termination of the lease; "a reason" is interpreted by a court that the landlord has no other place to go but to reclaim the place for his or her own living space. There have been cases of professors subletting their houses to go abroad for a year who could not move back in. Naturally, landlords of apartments do not build first-rate structures, fearing that their tenants may not move if they need to reclaim the unit or the whole building.

The new tenant law was introduced in 1993, and contracts written under it now can be terminated without "a reason." However, the old tenant law remains in force, and all existing contracts under it are grandfathered. The penetration of contracts under the new law is not widespread.

Yet another tax distortion exists for company and government housing. Employees' housing can be built at the company's expense, whereas subsidized rents in company housing are not taxable as income. Employees of large corporations are offered corporate housing, and government employees are offered their housing. Corporate and government housing is justified on the ground that employees are frequently moved around for jobs and assignments. However, the quality of this housing is not high. If firms offered first-class housing, then they would be criticized for extravagance, so subsidies in fact contribute to the proliferation of poorly constructed housing. The irony is that the company housing subsidy (a nontaxable pecuniary perquisite) is contributing to smaller than optimal, substandard housing (typically 4- to 10-story buildings with tens of small family units) all over Japan.

In addition to zoning changes, tax changes can also be undertaken to stimulate the housing sector. The consumption tax can be eliminated on new structures. The size ceiling (currently 240 square meters) on existing tax relief measures (e.g., reduced real estate tax rates and real estate registration taxes) could be raised or eliminated completely. The existing income ceiling for those who claim the tax credit for owner-occupied housing could be raised or eliminated as well.

In summary, land use and housing are the source of deep-seated problems in Japan, relating primarily to a variety of tax and zoning issues. And despite their microeconomic nature, problems in the housing market have macroeconomic implications. (Indeed, they were even the subject of bilateral discussion between Japan and the United States during the Structural Impediments Initiative of 1990-91; and they were the subject of an expert group under the Enhanced Initiative of 1997, which was disbanded in 2001, "given the progress made in addressing housing issues.") As we have indicated, a number of reforms could be adopted to address these issues that could improve both the macroeconomic performance of the Japanese economy and the quality of life in Japan.

Assessment

After the lost decade of the 1990s, the weaknesses of the Japanese economy are obvious. The first problem is mounting nonperforming loans in the financial sector. The profit base of banks is thin, and new nonperforming loans emerge as soon as old ones are provisioned for. A second problem is deflation, and although there is no guaranteed cure for deflation, the Bank of Japan seems to be unwilling to use all the weapons in its arsenal. The third problem is fiscal—at 140 percent of GDP, government debt is the highest among the G-7 countries. Although net debt is estimated to be much lower than gross debt (50 percent of GDP, comparable to that of European countries), the quality and reliability of net debt estimates are highly doubtful.

The growth prospects for the Japanese economy in the next few decades are mixed. Its traditional strength has been its high household savings rate, highly educated and motivated workforce, and well-managed manufacturing sector. Excellent corporations such as Toyota and Sony are as strong and innovative as ever, and relatively new industries, such as mobile phone services and computer hardware makers, are thriving. Renault's rehabilitation of Nissan suggests yet another avenue for industrial resurgence. Although the Internet has been slow to be develop in Japan, it is changing quickly as Internet technology expands through cable television and optic fibers, as well as via faster connections through telephone lines, and wireless technology quickly penetrates urban areas.

Reviving growth potential through changes in tax structures, regulations, and other aspects of social policy is necessary. Economic recovery and the revival of growth are not impossible, but the road to recovery is narrow, and driving down it must be done carefully.

Aggregate demand must be stimulated in an environment where the nominal interest rate is already zero and fiscal stimulation is not possible without raising further concerns about debt sustainability. In short, it is important to stimulate private-sector aggregate demand—household consumption, fixed investment, and housing investment. However, to enable short-run recovery, a medium-run policy commitment needs to be laid out now. A credible medium-term vision—how to reduce fiscal deficits and how to get out of deflation—is needed to generate optimistic expectations, because confidence in medium-run policy success is important to stimulate aggregate demand in the short run.

In the medium run, supply-side policy is critical, especially because the rate of growth must be increased to "grow out of debt," but also because demographic changes, specifically a shrinking labor force, will tend to depress Japan's growth potential. Monetary policy must be based on a principle that price stability—no inflation and no deflation—needs to be maintained in the medium run. In the medium run, financial policy—including bank and insurance company supervision—needs to be strengthened, and Japanese financial institutions, with a tremendous home-court advantage with their large deposit base, should regain strength. Microeconomic policy needs to be employed to promote productivity and growth. More effective use of female labor is desirable, and an increased role for immigrants or "guest workers" also may become important. Labor relations and the pension system need to be reformed, so that workers can move from low-productivity firms to growing ones. Workers need to be flexibly trained in marketable skills in the education system, so that they can use their skills in any organization, not just in a particular firm.

During the next few years, Japan must achieve several intermediate objectives to put its economy back on the potential growth path: (1) Stop deflation. (2) Restore fiscal sustainability. (3) Solve the financial-sector fragility problem. (4) Implement structural reforms in sectors such as telecommunications, housing, and agriculture. These objectives should be adopted as a package, because policies under (2), (3), and some aspects of (4) tend to be contractionary, whereas those under (1) and other aspects of (4) may be stimulating, offsetting the other effects.

This is not simply a matter of interest to Japan. The financial turmoil described in this chapter has had a direct impact on real economic activity in the United States (Peek and Rosengren 1997, 2000), and continued malaise in Japan will affect its capacity and willingness to address broader global responsibilities. It is to these issues that we now turn.

4

The Economics of Japan-United States Trade and Investment

The economic relationship between Japan and the United States is not defined solely by the macroeconomic issues discussed in the previous two chapters. An important part of the story involves the volume and composition of trade—the products and services each country exports and imports to and from the other—and ultimately the impact of this trade on economic welfare in each society.

The commodity composition of international trade is determined by the interaction of two broad forces. One consists of economic fundamentals, such as technology, the quantity and quality of factors of production, and institutional organization embodied by the economy. The other is public policy. Government actions shape economic life in a variety of ways that have intended (and unintended) effects on the market outcomes that we observe. The form and content of these public-policy interventions reflect a complex interaction of economic goals, domestic politics, bilateral pressures, and the constraints that the global environment imposes on both firms and governments.

This chapter and chapter 5 analyze the impact of these two broad forces, economic fundamentals and economic policy, on the bilateral trade relationship of Japan and the United States. Historically, this relationship has been shaped by the two countries' complementary patterns of specialization in products such as agriculture and manufactures, and their rivalry in the high-technology sphere. These patterns of interaction continue to play an important role.

In the past decade, however, as the interaction of technological advance and policy reform has led to an expansion of cross-border investment and international trade in services, issues of investment and services have increased in prominence relative to more traditional issues of trade in primary products and manufactures. Although the focus in the past has been on US complaints about access to the market for manufactured goods in Japan and the intensifying rivalry between the two countries in high-technology sectors, the focus is shifting toward trade in services. The bilateral relationship could become more difficult, owing to Japan's lagging competitiveness in some parts of this more and more important component of economic life. The implication is that the regulatory and competition policy issues that are central to investment and trade in services will be even more important in the coming decade than they have been in the past.

Understandably, during the past 50 years, success in constructing a rules-based multilateral trade regime has been greatest in the traditional areas of merchandise trade. As a consequence, the issues of increasing salience to the bilateral relationship are also those for which relatively little international progress has been achieved and that have the greatest potential for progress.

If one conceptually regards these developments as describing the *substantive* issues, then the *procedural* context for dispute resolution is changing as well. The formation of the WTO has, in certain respects, fundamentally altered the resolution of trade disputes between the two countries. The impact of the WTO has been felt primarily through its constraint on the US recourse to unilateral measures, but also through its limitation of Japanese policy, most notably in agriculture. More generally, the strengthening of the WTO has encouraged the attainment of national objectives through multilateral channels. This is to say that both the bilateral agenda and the resolution of bilateral disputes are more and more conditioned by the functioning of the international system.

This chapter begins with a review of the trade and investment relations between Japan and the United States, and then discusses how these are affected by each country's policies. Chapter 5 then goes on to analyze dispute resolution in the 1980s and 1990s, and make recommendations for more constructive relations in the future.

The Economic Context

According to US Department of Commerce figures, total bilateral merchandise trade between Japan and the United States reached $212 billion in 2000, its highest level ever, with Japan running a record surplus of $81 billion (figure 4.1). Yet despite the historically unprecedented magnitude of trade between these partners, the two countries occupy positions of differing importance in each other's global trade and investment relations (figure 4.2). The United States is Japan's largest trade partner, and in

Figure 4.1 Global and bilateral trade balance in goods for Japan and the United States, 1986-2000 (billions of dollars)

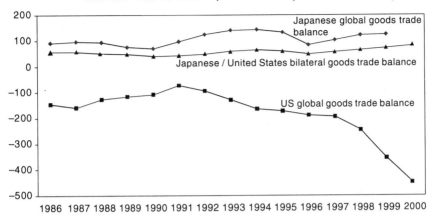

Sources: IMF, *International Financial Statistics*; StatsCanada, 1980-97 (CD-ROM).

Figure 4.2 Bilateral imports and exports as shares of total imports and exports for the United States and Japan, 1980-1999 (percent)

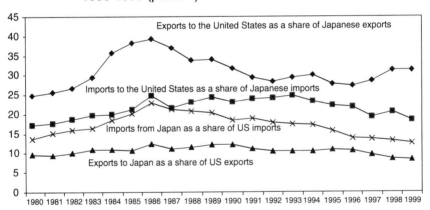

Sources: StatsCanada, 1980-97 (CD-ROM); Department of Commerce, Bureau of Economic Affairs; Ministry of Finance, Japan.

recent years, trade with the United States has accounted for about a quarter of total Japanese trade (imports plus exports). In contrast, Japan is the third or fourth largest US trade partner (depending on whether or not the EU member states are treated as a single entity), accounting for less than 10 percent of US trade in recent years. As figure 4.2 shows, if anything there has been a declining trend in the importance of each country in the other's trade. Both countries' trade has increased more rapidly with faster-growing regions such as the rest of Asia (abstracting from the temporary impact of the financial crisis in 1998), and trade between the United States and its immediate neighbors has expanded quickly as a result of regional integration through NAFTA.

The aggregate figures, however, do not tell the whole story. Table 4.1 reports sectoral trade shares for the United States and Japan globally and bilaterally according to broad categories of the Standard International Trade Classification (SITC) system. Both globally and bilaterally, US trade pattern exhibits less specialization across categories, as befits a large continental economy endowed with a variety of natural resources. Although 84 percent of US merchandise exports are manufactures (SITC categories 5-8) (about half of US exports consist of machinery and transportation equipment), the United States also exports large amounts of other agricultural products and other natural-resource-based goods. Within manufactures, the United States has specialized in knowledge- and human-capital-intensive high technology.

In contrast, Japan exhibits a "spikier" pattern of specialization. Merchandise exports are entirely concentrated in manufactures, with almost three-quarters of global exports consisting of machinery and transport equipment alone, whereas food and fuels account for 30 percent of imports. Within manufacturing, Japan (like the United States) has more and more specialized in human-capital-intensive high-technology products (Noland 1996a).

The product composition of bilateral trade largely conforms to the pattern of each country's global trade—the United States exports a diverse basket of goods to Japan, with nonmanufactures, notably food, somewhat more prominent, and machinery and transport equipment somewhat less prominent in comparison with the worldwide pattern of US exports. At this broad level of aggregation, the sectoral composition of Japanese exports to the United States is quite similar to that of Japanese exports worldwide.

The relative endowments of the two countries also influence the bilateral pattern of their trade. Japan's relative resource scarcity means that it tends to run a net deficit in such products as oil or food. For any given level of its global imbalance, Japan will tend to run net deficits with oil exporters such as Saudi Arabia, and tend to run surpluses with importers of manufactures, either in the form of intermediate inputs (e.g., with South Korea in capital goods), or in the form of consumer products (as happens with the United States).

That said, one would still expect Japan to import some manufactures. One of the most notable characteristics of the postwar global trade boom has been the rise of intraindustry trade in differentiated manufactured

Table 4.1 Composition of Japanese and US trade globally and bilaterally, 1999 (percent)

	Japan				United States			
Total by SITC classification	Global exports	Global imports	Bilateral exports	Bilateral imports	Global exports	Global imports	Bilateral exports	Bilateral imports
	100	100	100	100	100	100	100	100
0—Food and live animals	1	14	0	15	6	3	15	0
1—Beverages and tobacco	0	1	0	4	1	1	4	0
2—Crude materials, inedible, except fuels	0	7	0	6	3	2	6	0
3—Mineral fuels, lubricants, and related materials	0	16	0	1	1	7	1	0
4—Animal and vegetable oils, fats, and waxes	0	0	0	0	0	0	0	0
5—Chemicals and related products n.e.s.	7	7	5	10	10	6	10	5
6—Manufactured goods	8	13	6	5	9	11	5	6
7—Machinery and transport equipment	73	31	76	42	53	47	42	76
8—Miscellaneous manufactured articles	11	11	10	14	12	17	14	10
9—Commodities and transactions n.e.s.	0	0	3	2	4	5	2	3

n.e.s. = not elsewhere specified.
SITC = Standard International Trade Classification.

Sources: US and bilateral trade data, http://dataweb.usitc.gov; Japanese trade data, http://www.mof.go.jp/english/trade-st/199928ce.htm.

Table 4.2 Selected trade indicators for five industrial countries

Indicator	Japan	United States	Germany[a]	United Kingdom[a]	South Korea
Intraindustry trade index					
1990	0.26	0.55	0.56	0.59	0.28
1997	0.36	0.62	0.50	0.59	0.43
Import share of domestic consumption of manufactures, 1995 (percent)	7.00	19.90	10.30	19.40	25.90

a. Intra-European Union trade has been eliminated from intraindustry trade index calculations. Intraindustry trade index calculations have also been adjusted for trade imbalances.

Sources: StatsCanada 1990-97 CD-ROM; Global Trade Analysis Project, Purdue University, Web site database, http://www.agecon.purdue.edu/gtap/data.htm.

goods among the high-income industrial economies, and Japan appears to exhibit unusually low intraindustry trade relative to other industrial countries (table 4.2). It is less clear whether this reflects extraordinary Japanese competitiveness in manufacturing, distinctively strong preferences for home goods among Japanese purchasers, or a relatively closed market.[1] In any event, intraindustry trade in Japan increased in the 1990s, because of increases in imports of traditional export products (not exports of traditional import goods), both globally and bilaterally, though it still remains below that of comparable countries.[2] Likewise, the import share of domestic consumption in manufactures in Japan is lower than in other large industrial economies, although (as in the case of intraindustry trade) this figure has risen slightly over time, eroding Japan's distinctiveness.[3]

The discussion thus far has concerned merchandise trade. One of the notable trends in recent years has been the growing global importance of trade in services—financial, communications, engineering, transportation, educational, and professional services—as well as in tourism. The service sectors have assumed a more prominent role in the external trade of both

1. See Lincoln (1990, 1999) for the latter interpretation. Unlike the figures reported in table 4.2, Lincoln does not adjust his calculations for Japan's trade imbalance. As a consequence, his indices provide a downwardly biased indication of Japan's intraindustry trade. Similarly, Lincoln's figures on intraindustry trade (and on the share of imports in apparent consumption) apparently do not exclude intra-European Union trade. This omission tends to exaggerate Japan's distinctiveness.

2. See Menon (1997).

3. There is econometric evidence that the income and price elasticities of Japanese manufactured imports have been increasing since the 1980s, and that there has been a secular increase in imports since 1985 (Arize and Walker 1992; Ceglowski 1997). The pattern of change by end-use category suggests that these increases are related to the ongoing integration of the Japanese economy with those of its Asian neighbors (Ceglowski 1996).

Figure 4.3   Ratio of services trade to goods trade, globally and bilaterally, for Japan and the United States, 1986-2000

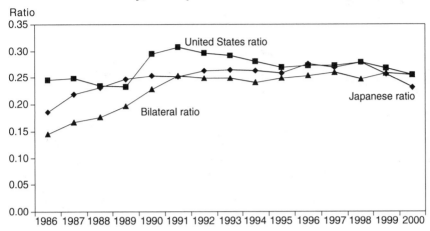

Sources: IMF, *International Financial Statistics* CD-ROM; StatsCanada, 1980-97, CD-ROM; US Department of Commerce, Bureau of Economic Affairs, http://www.bea.doc.gov/bea/ai/ 1099srv/intlserv.htm; US International Trade Commission, http://dataweb.usitc.gov.

Japan and the United States, and in their bilateral relationship (figure 4.3). In a reversal of the merchandise-trade situation, Japan runs a global deficit, and the United States a surplus, both globally and bilaterally with Japan (figure 4.4). Indeed, since 1992, US service exports to Japan have been more than half the level of its total merchandise exports. The primary drivers of Japan's growing service deficits have been travel and tourism expenditures, as well as the education category. In both cases, these results reflect a complex legacy of regulation and associated vested interests, which contribute to a lack of competitive pressure and the relative inefficiency of heavily regulated industries in Japan.[4]

The asymmetrical relative prominence of Japan and the United States in each other's trade relations also holds for investment. Historically, far more investment has flowed out of Japan than into Japan, and Japan maintains the world's largest net stock of foreign direct investment (FDI). In comparison, the stock of inward FDI is comparatively low, reflecting scant flows until recently. According to Fukao and Ito (2000), the ratio of inward investment stock to GDP is less than 1 percent, whereas the

---

4. The IMF (1998) observes that the nonmanufacturing sector of the Japanese economy is regulated far more heavily than manufacturing, and that productivity is far lower. For a specific example, Lincoln (1999) provides an informative discussion of the declining competitiveness of Japanese airlines. The possible impact of deregulation in general, and in the civil aviation sector in particular, is taken up below.

Figure 4.4 Global and bilateral services trade balances for Japan and the United States, 1986-2000 (billions of dollars)

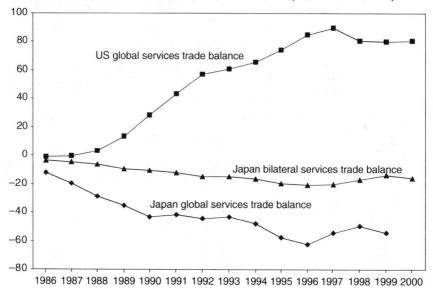

Sources: IMF, *International Financial Statistics* (CD-ROM); US Department of Commerce, Bureau of Economic Affairs, http://www.bea.doc.gov/bea/ai/1099srv/intlserv.htm.

equivalent figures are 16 percent for the United States, 21 percent for the United Kingdom, and 26 percent for France.

This is important, inasmuch as direct investment is an important modality of economic exchange, especially in knowledge-intensive sectors where information asymmetries between potential buyers and sellers make arm's-length transactions suboptimal. (E.g., it may be difficult for a firm to convince a potential licensee of a proprietary technology of its worth without revealing trade secrets. It may be preferable for that firm to simply establish operations in the target market itself.) Also for this reason, US firms have historically preferred to hold majority stakes in their foreign subsidiaries. At the same time, Krueger and Ito (2000) caution that FDI statistics are generally among the least reliable economics data, and quantitative comparisons such as these should be evaluated with a critical eye.[5]

The lion's share of sales by US firms' affiliates in Japan are to the local market. However, FDI is complementary to exports (i.e., US investment

---

5. Fukao and Ito (2000) argue that Japanese inward FDI flows are seriously underreported in commonly cited statistics. The Ministry of Finance figures understate actual inward FDI flows because they are based only on voluntary reporting of cross-border capital flows, excluding any reinvestment from retained earnings and investment through capital borrowed in Japan. See also Fukao (2001).

and exports are positively correlated; Noland 1996b), and one would expect intrafirm trade to play an important role in international trade, especially in high-technology products.[6] However, recent data from the US Commerce Department indicate that trade with affiliates accounts for a falling share of US exports to Japan (less than half in 1997, the most recent year for which data are available), whereas intrafirm trade accounts for a rising share of US imports from Japan (more than 80 percent in 1997). Moreover, in Japan the share of US assets accounted for by majority-owned subsidiaries (67 percent) remains below the global average for all US investment (86 percent).

That last comparison may reflect the historical legacy of Japanese policies that discouraged foreign investment in general, and majority ownership in particular.[7] However, the flow of FDI into Japan has been rising rapidly in recent years, more than quadrupling between FY1997 and FY2000 (according to Ministry of Finance figures) to more than $25 billion at exchange rates prevailing in FY2000. (As a point of comparison, the annual flow of FDI into the United States tripled during the same period to more than $300 billion.) Even with this rapid increase, outward investment still exceeds inward investment by more than 3 to 1, and Japan still is the destination for only about 5 percent of US outbound FDI, despite accounting for more than twice that share of world output (excluding the United States, and measured at prices adjusted for purchasing power).

The increase in investment into Japan is due in part to distress sales of failing Japanese firms.[8] (Abegglen [2001] goes so far as to praise foreign investors for graciously assuming Japanese firms' underfunded pension liabilities.) According to Stokes (2000), in 1998-99 four-fifths of merger and acquisition (M&A) deals in Japan involved distressed firms. And although M&A activity in Japan was up in 1999, it fell the following year, with cross-border activity involving acquirers outside Japan declining by almost half. M&A activity still accounts for only 7 percent of stock market capitalization in Japan, in comparison with 14 percent in the United States, and 10 percent in the European Union. Even at its peak, the number of mergers and acquisitions was less than a tenth of that in the United States. Eighty-six percent of these deals are purely intra-Japanese, and the number of Japanese takeovers of foreign firms exceeded the converse

---

6. The positive correlation between trade and foreign investment has been documented for Japan as well, starting with Kojima (1978). See also Kawai and Urata (1995) and Bayoumi and Lipworth (1998).

7. See Encarnation (1992), Mason (1992), and WTO (1995) for historical descriptions of Japanese FDI policies.

8. To cite some well-known examples: Long-Term Credit Bank was bankrupt and had been nationalized before it was sold to Ripplewood Holdings, and Japan Leasing (bought by GE Capital) was bankrupt, as was Yamaichi Securities (its retail operations were acquired by Merrill Lynch).

by 50 percent. No hostile domestic bid has ever succeeded, although in 2000 Boehringer Ingelheim, a German pharmaceutical maker, took over SSP, a Japanese drug company.[9] That said, the share of stock trading accounted for by foreigners more than tripled during the 1990s, and foreigners now own perhaps 40 percent of the freely floating shares. The issue of whether these figures reflect fundamental capital market imperfections that impede the existence of a genuine market for corporate control will be taken up in the next section.

The United States is usually the largest single destination for outbound Japanese FDI, typically accounting for 25-40 percent of the total (though in 1999 it was exceeded by the EU member countries in the aggregate). Indeed, despite increased Japanese interest in the rest of Asia, investment in the United States is typically two to three times that of Japanese investment in the region. Japanese firms face the same organizational, locational, and internalization incentives to invest in the United States as US firms do with respect to Japan (Alexander 1997a; Blonigen 1997; McKenzie 1998).

US trade policy may further encourage Japanese investment, as confirmed by the survey responses reported by Urata (1998). Voluntary export restraints on autos in the 1980s encouraged "tariff-jumping" investment by Japanese auto assemblers in the United States, and today, antidumping cases in the United States, discussed in the following section, are having the same effect.[10] In most years, the United States is also the largest foreign investor in Japan, and in 1999 invested just over $2 billion in Japan, according to Ministry of Finance (MOF) data.[11]

In contrast, Japan is either the third or sixth largest investor in the United States, again depending on whether the EU member countries are counted individually or in the aggregate. Although Japanese investment in the United States increased substantially in 1999 to $8 billion, this figure was still less than half the previous peak of $20 billion in 1990. Moreover, during the post-bubble period, Japan's investment in the United States

---

9. Paper bids are subject to two-thirds majority votes by the shareholders of both sides, in effect requiring that hostile bids be for cash.

10. A good example of this would be Fuji Film's construction of a state-of-the-art photographic facility in Greenwood, South Carolina, in 1995 after an antidumping case filed by Kodak. Blonigen and Feenstra (1997) find that Japanese investments in the United States at a detailed sectoral level of disagreggation are correlated with antidumping cases. Barrell and Pain (1999) find that Japanese FDI flows into the United States and European Union are correlated with antidumping actions in each of the two regions. Blonigen (2000) finds that antidumping cases encourage Japanese multinationals to invest in the United States, though he describes the quantitative impact of this effect as "modest." See also Blonigen and Feenstra (1997).

11. In 1999, however, the United States was topped by France due to Renault's takeover of Nissan, and was even surpassed by the Cayman Islands. The DaimlerChrysler takeover of Mitsubishi Motors caused the United States to lag behind the European Union in 2000 as well.

has been of the same magnitude as Switzerland's. Nevertheless, Japanese investment in the United States is a multiple of US investment in Japan.

During the late 1980s, Japanese purchases of "trophy properties" such as Rockefeller Center, the Pebble Beach golf course, and the Columbia Pictures movie studio made the headlines, and the scale of Japanese investment raised concerns among some Americans, and even became a topic of popular culture (e.g., Michael Crichton's novel *Rising Sun*). However, with the end of the bubble and the onset of financial retrenchment in Japan, many of these investors were forced to sell their acquisitions, sometimes at a profit and in other cases with large losses. These aggregate figures suggest that the United States remains central to Japan's global trade and investment relations, whereas Japan, at least in the post-bubble period, occupies a less important position from the perspective of the United States.

The performance of Japanese investment in the United States is generally poor, exhibiting lower returns than comparable US investments, or Japanese investments elsewhere in the world. Urata (1998) ascribes this to the inability of Japanese manufacturers to transfer the *keiretsu* system to the United States; to their misguided attempts to apply inappropriate Japanese human resource management practices in a very different environment; and to poor preproject evaluation, owing to the rushed nature of some investments (as a response to anticipated trade restrictions in the US market).

As a result of Japan's recurrent trade surpluses, its comparative advantage in manufactures, and its relatively low level of inward FDI, foreign firms generally have a smaller role in the Japanese economy than elsewhere. Official figures compiled by the MOF indicate that the foreign-firm share of sales in Japan was less than 2 percent, relative to double-digit shares in other major industrial countries, although the MOF figures undoubtedly understate actual FDI.[12] An issue is to what extent this distinctiveness is determined by economic fundamentals, and to what extent it is a product of government policy, anticompetitive practices of Japanese firms, or the distinct private preferences of Japanese consumers.

Government Policies

A variety of government policies affect trade and investment flows. Border measures such as tariffs and quotas have a direct impact on international

---

12. The MOF figures refer to 1995. Presumably, this figure has risen in the intervening years due to increased FDI and the takeovers of Nissan and Mitsubishi Motors by foreign firms. Weinstein (1997) argues that MOF methodology leads to an underestimate of the presence of foreign firms in the Japanese economy, and that the actual level of sales accounted for by foreign firms may be as much as twice as high as the official figures indicate. Even so, this would still leave Japan far below the levels observed in other large industrial countries (Bergsten and Noland 1993, table 3.3).

trade and are subject to bilateral, regional, and multilateral agreements. Internal support policies, which can have significant indirect effects on trade, also are subject to multilateral constraints, most obviously in agriculture.

However, as border protection has been removed and the two countries have become more integrated (in absolute, if not relative, terms), more traditionally domestic regulatory issues have come to the fore. As cross-border investment and international trade in services have grown, regulatory issues have become more important, insomuch as it is primarily regulation, not traditional internal or external measures, that impede this exchange. Moreover, regulation can act as a facilitating device for anticompetitive behavior undertaken by private parties, which has been a source of considerable tension in the bilateral relationship.

Border Measures

Countries typically use international trade policy to protect those sectors that are least competitive internationally. (Analytically, they protect factors of production that are "scarce" in terms of international trade, i.e., which will be adversely affected if international trade is liberalized.)[13] In densely populated, land-scarce Japan, historically this has meant intervening in markets to protect its relatively inefficient natural-resource-based industries, in particular agriculture.[14] In contrast, the United States— which has accumulated a large stock of capital and is well endowed with natural resources, but in global terms is scarce in labor—has protected its labor-intensive low- or medium-technology manufacturing sectors. Other forces (e.g., the degree of producer concentration, the extent of unionization, and the political power of specific politicians or pressure groups) further shape actual outcomes with regard to particular sectors.

The complementary pattern of specialization between Japan and the United States has meant that trade is beneficial to both countries. However, it has also meant that trade has been accompanied by painful adjustments in each country's import-competing sectors. For understandable political reasons, both governments intervene to forestall or cushion these internal adjustments. Predictably, these policy interventions, which run counter to the interests of the other country's most productive sectors, become a source of bilateral tension.[15]

---

13. See Lee and Swagel (1997).

14. Under foreign pressure, Japan has undertaken some "affirmative action"-like policies to boost imports (e.g., providing subsidized office space in Tokyo to foreign small and medium-sized enterprises that are potential exporters), though like Greaney (2000b) we are skeptical about their impact.

15. See MITI (2000) and USTR (2000) for the views of the Japanese and US governments, respectively.

Table 4.3 Average weighted tariffs, 1999 (percent)

Country or group	Total	Primary products	Manufactured goods
European Union	3.2	3.3	3.2
Japan	2.5	4.5	2.0
South Korea	7.4	9.0	7.0
United States	2.5	3.1	2.4

Source: World Bank, *World Development Indicators 2000*, http://www.worldbank.org/data/wdi2000/pdfs/tab6_6.pdf.

In examining the pattern of intervention, the simplest and conventional place to start is with tariffs. Table 4.3 reports average tariff levels for Japan and the United States (weighted by imports)—and, for comparison's sake, the European Union and South Korea. Two points are immediately obvious. Successive rounds of international trade negotiations have resulted in a situation in which, on average, tariffs are low (though they remain high in certain sectors).[16] The remaining tariffs, in general, conform to the notion that Japan protects its natural resource sectors and the United States protects manufacturing.

Tariffs are not the whole story, however, even with respect to official border measures. Both countries continue to apply nontariff protection, which in sensitive sectors dwarfs the impact of ad valorem tariffs.[17] Some progress on nontariff barriers was achieved in the Uruguay Round, which banned VERs, and established a phaseout of the highly discriminatory Multifiber Arrangement (MFA) on textile and apparel trade. In Japan, nontariff border protection is basically limited to some highly protective tariff-quota schemes in agriculture (e.g., rice), in which Japan historically maintained an import embargo, and even now permits only minuscule imports.[18] In the United States, the Uruguay Round agreement effectively eliminates recourse to quantitative protection in manufactures, so that WTO-consistent antidumping cases have become the protection instrument of choice.

Antidumping actions are the bête noire of trade policy instruments. Although antidumping laws may appeal to a certain sense of fairness

---

16. E.g., in the case of the United States, its tariff on light trucks (25 percent)—a legacy of the 1963 "chicken war" between the United States and the European Community—is of particular concern to Japan. Japanese tariffs tend to escalate by degree of processing, according higher effective protection on finished products than industrial intermediates, though this has largely been a concern of developing countries, not the United States. Unweighted average tarriffs (which would give a larger weight to highly restricted sectors) would be higher than those reported in table 4.3.

17. See Sazanami, Urata, and Kawai (1996) and US ITC (1999) for informative discussions of nontariff barriers in Japan and the United States, respectively.

18. See Kako, Gemma, and Ito (1997) for an econometric analysis of the rice tariff-quota scheme. Phytosanitary regulations have also been used to impede imports; see Calvin and Krissoff (1998) for an example.

and economic rationality—firms should not be subject to predation—they are fundamentally flawed from a national welfare perspective. In competitive markets, firms may choose to price below marginal cost in the initial stages of production, in the expectation that costs will eventually fall; indeed, Texas Instruments, a US firm, pioneered "forward pricing" in the semiconductor industry.[19]

Moreover, competitive firms may temporarily price below costs if production or distribution is characterized by quasi-irreversibilities or hysteresis. This may occur in a floating exchange rate system as a function of transitory overshoots. Dumping rules include provisions for exchange rate fluctuations, but not misalignments. For these reasons, it is clear that firms vary their exchange rate "pass-through" behavior in response to antidumping actions (Blonigen and Hayes 1999).

Dumping may arise even under competitive market conditions because of market segmentation, transport costs, or other trade impediments.[20] In addition, there are severe problems with the cost-based methods used to implement the law in the United States. Finally, because of understandable public concerns about fairness and predation, antidumping cases enable protection-seeking firms to wrap themselves in the flag.[21]

Perhaps most important, however, antidumping actions effectively create a price-floor policy, making the imposing country a high-cost production location when antidumping duties are imposed on imported inputs. During any cyclical weakening of demand, foreign firms will be tempted to cut their home prices, because their ability to compete in foreign markets is restricted by the antidumping action. The result is that downstream users of the product (e.g., manufacturers of computers or telecommunications products in the case of semiconductors, or automobile assemblers in the case of steel) in net importing regions will be put at a competitive disadvantage. This was demonstrated vividly by the US experience in the first United States-Japan Semiconductor Trade Agreement (1986), which had the effect of creating a price floor for semiconductors in the United States and damaging computer and telecoms production.[22]

Indeed, the United States is the world leader when it comes to antidumping actions, with 300 such measures in place as of mid-2000 (though

---

19. See Dick (1991, 1994) for analyses of dynamic pricing strategies.

20. This is the "reciprocal dumping" model. See Brander and Krugman (1983) and Weinstein (1992).

21. Messerlin (2000) contains a number of recommendations to address these issues in the context of the WTO.

22. Some go so far as to argue that Japanese behavior was aimed at strangling the South Korean semiconductor industry in the cradle. The Semiconductor Trade Agreement contained a provision forbidding dumping in third markets, and the South Korean industry eventually grew into the world's largest.

Table 4.4 Use of antidumping measures by four major trading bodies

Body and measures	1997	1998	1999[a]
European Union			
Number of measures in force, 31 December	137	161	183
Investigations to which domestic exporters are subject	59	42	20
Japan			
Number of measures in force, 31 December	2	1	1
Investigations to which domestic exporters are subject	12	10	11
South Korea			
Number of measures in force, 31 December	20	28	28
Investigations to which domestic exporters are subject	16	20	18
United States			
Number of measures in force, 31 December	302	326	336
Investigations to which domestic exporters are subject	15	15	7

a. Figures are for January-June.

Source: World Trade Organization, Annual Report, 1998, 1999, 2000.

the European Union actually initiated more cases in 1999). The popularity of this instrument is presumably due to the relative ease of filing cases, and the elastic definitions of cost that the US Commerce Department's International Trade Administration uses in calculating dumping margins (table 4.4).[23]

Galloway, Blonigen, and Flynn (1999), using a computable general equilibrium (CGE) model calibrated to 1993, found that antidumping cases generate a net welfare loss to the US economy of $4 billion annually. This is probably an underestimate of the current impact of such actions, for two reasons. First, the number of antidumping cases has increased since 1993. Second, Galloway, Blonigen, and Flynn only examine the impact of cases in which the US government reaches an affirmative decision and duties are applied. An extensive literature demonstrates that the mere filing on antidumping cases has a demonstrable effect on product pricing and trade flows (Staiger and Wolak 1994). That is, domestic producers can often intimidate foreign producers—which want to avoid costly legal action in the United States—into raising prices and restraining exports merely by filing a case that may be later withdrawn. With the negotiated phaseout of the MFA restrictions on textile and apparel trade, antidumping is the single most pernicious trade restriction employed by the United States, exceeding in impact the Jones Act maritime restrictions or the sugar or dairy quotas.

---

23. The United States has lost challenges mounted by Japan, the European Union, and others to its antidumping practices in the WTO. In fact, the exporting country has won every WTO case to date. See Prusa (1997) for an overview of US antidumping practices.

Box 4.1 Supercomputers

The supercomputer industry is a classic oligopoly, dominated by government and public agency purchases (Bergsten and Noland 1993). It is unsurprising that sales in this market are highly politicized, and there is evidence that both governments have acted to channel sales to their respective domestic producers. In a 1996 episode, the US Department of Commerce leaked a "pre-decision memorandum" estimating dumping margins of 163-260 percent on Japanese-made supercomputers to the National Science Foundation in an apparent attempt to steer business to Cray Research (now a division of Silicon Graphics).

The following year, the Commerce Department announced dumping margins of 173-454 percent on Japanese supercomputers, including those produced by Hitachi, which had not actually sold any in the US market. This action effectively banned Japanese supercomputers from the US market and set off years of ultimately unsuccessful litigation by NEC, one of the Japanese producers.

The US action rebounded on its 1990 agreement with Japan on supercomputer procurement. According to Southwick, "In supercomputers, for a few years, Japan made sure to purchase at least a few Cray and other US machines, but its interest in this agreement has diminished since the US government intervened, unfairly in Japan's view, against NEC in its bid for a US government supercomputer in 1996" (Southwick 1998, 7). In May 2001, the Commerce Department announced that the 454 percent dumping penalty was lifted upon an agreement between Cray and NEC. Under the deal, Cray became the sole original equipment manufacturer and distributor of NEC supercomputers and received a capital injection from NEC of up to $25 million.

Japan has been a major target of these actions, accounting for 18 percent of US antidumping cases filed between 1979 and 1999 and 17 percent of the affirmative outcomes. As of December 1999, 99 cases had been initiated against Japan, 56 with affirmative outcomes. (This 60 percent affirmative determination rate is the highest for any trade partner.) If one simply allocates the Galloway, Blonigen, and Flynn (1999) welfare loss proportionately, antidumping cases against Japan reduce US economic welfare by approximately $800 million annually.

The impact on Japanese exporters contains some ambiguity. Although the antidumping cases restrain exports, Japanese exporters are disproportionately multinational corporations operating in oligopolistic markets. Antidumping cases may act as facilitating mechanisms for them and their US counterparts to raise prices, and the firm-specific nature of this instrument encourages highly strategic uses by US firms. For example, in 1992, at the same time that it was accusing Mazda of dumping minivans, Ford was producing sport utility vehicles for its partner.

The extraordinary dumping margins that the US Department of Commerce assesses in these cases can have the effect of effectively cutting off trade (see box 4.1). For example, in 1993, the Department of Commerce imposed dumping margins of more than 300 percent on Fuji and Konica products, encouraging them to raise prices and cut sales to the US market, and in the case of Fuji, accelerate its investment in the United States. Steel continues to be a focal point. Antidumping rules have been used to restrict imports from Japan and other countries, although US practices are under fire more and more in the WTO (see box 4.2).

Internal Measures

In addition to these border measures, both countries use a variety of policies to promote domestic industry. In the case of agriculture, the extent and impact of these policies are reasonably well understood. As part of the Uruguay Round agreement, signatories committed themselves to specified reductions in aggregate measures of support, defined as all domestic support to agriculture that does not qualify for certain specified exemptions (including, e.g., research and development expenditures, production-decoupled income payments, and direct payments to farmers under environmental protection programs).

As is shown in table 4.5, domestic support to Japanese farmers is lavish, greater as a share of output or in per capita terms than that provided to farmers in a similarly rich entity (the European Union) or a similarly situated one (South Korea). Similar results are obtained with respect to a broader measure of support, the producer support equivalent measure. Moreover, while the US producer support measure fell from 30 percent in 1990 to 22 percent in 1998 as a consequence of its market-oriented agriculture reforms, the decline for Japan was far smaller—from 68 percent in 1990 to 63 percent in 1998. Indeed, farm incomes in Japan exceed the national average (OECD 2000a). This comes at a real cost to Japanese consumers—as Lincoln (2001) observes, Japanese people spend 23 percent of their income on food, in comparison with 14 percent for Americans, despite the fact that Americans eat out twice as much as Japanese people.

The averages, however, obscure the highly uneven incidence of protection of agriculture in Japan, which is, after all, the world's largest food importer, and exhibits the world's highest imported calorie equivalence (though it has declared its intention to decrease this dependency). Much of its protection is concentrated on a few products, most conspicuously rice. This protection has not promoted productivity increases, and the budget for agricultural support remains high despite the sector's declining economic significance.

Nevertheless, as Lincoln (1999) observes, Japanese protection of agriculture is a "rearguard action." In the immediate future, Japan's internal support should continue to decline because of its acceptance of the developed-country commitment in the Uruguay Round to a 20 percent reduction in its aggregate measure of support between 1995 and 2001. In the more distant future, internal support could be expected to fall even further as additional multilateral agreements are concluded, Japan's dwindling

Box 4.2 Steel

Steel is *not* primarily a bilateral issue, although Japan figures prominently. Globally, the industry is characterized by excess capacity owing to ubiquitous national promotion policies, including tolerance of cartels. This problem is not new: In 1968, legislation was introduced in the US Congress to impose import quotas, and the United States negotiated VERs with Japan and the European Community that went into effect the following year. In the decades since, the industry has periodically been afforded special protection in the United States. Indeed, during the past 20 years, the US industry has responded by adding 20 million tons of capacity, while the European Union, for example, was reducing capacity by 50 million tons. Even while domestic production has increased, however, employment in the steel industry has fallen steadily, owing to the adoption of efficiency-enhancing technological improvements.

In 1998, the United States experienced a surge of imports—mostly from Brazil, Japan, Russia, and South Korea—as a result of the booming US economy, the slump in Asia, exchange rate movements, and a reorientation by Russian producers toward foreign markets. US output declined, and a number of producers were driven out of business. By the end of the year, capacity utilization rates in the US steel industry had fallen below 75 percent. The industry filed antidumping cases, and the US Commerce Department announced penalty duties ranging from 67 percent on imports coming from Japan to 2,000 percent on those originating in Russia.

Conditions improved in 1999. Shipments increased, and by early 2000, capacity utilization exceeded 90 percent. Despite the increase in output, however, employment in steel continued its secular decline, as technological improvements steadily raised labor productivity in the sector.

In 1999, after the worst had passed and conditions were improving, the industry sought special protection, abjuring conventional "escape clause" relief. The steel quota bill failed, but the industry continued its political campaign. In 2000, US Senator Robert Byrd successfully inserted into an agricultural bill a rider that would give US steel producers, rather than the US government, the roughly $40 million in proceeds from antidumping duties. The agriculture bill, including the Byrd amendment, was signed into law in October 2000.

Japan, the European Union, and others immediately challenged this law in the WTO, as they had other aspects of US antidumping practices. In earlier cases, the WTO had ruled against mostly procedural aspects of US practices. The adverse WTO rulings have not, however, gutted the antidumping law, and both it and the steel controversy are likely to be around for a long time.

Rather than engaging in legislative chicanery, a more constructive approach would combine broadly based income-maintenance and worker-retraining programs to deal with the problem of displaced workers (whether the source of displacement be technological change, international trade, or something else), while attempting to strengthen the trade regime multilaterally, and engaging our trade partners bilaterally. Hufbauer and Goodrich (2001) make specific recommendations with respect to both the wage insurance and multilateral trade negotiation aspects of the problem.

With respect to Japan, the bilateral aspects of such a policy could include consultations to ensure that regulatory barriers do not impede imports into Japan, that competition policies are applied to support a competitive internal market for steel, that the 1999 Industrial Revitalization Law is used to promote restructuring as intended and does not become a backdoor means of subsidizing the Japanese industry, and similarly monitoring the lending practices of the Development Bank of Japan, the principal public-sector lender to the Japanese industry. Until these actions are undertaken, US producers will use antidumping measures for protection.

Table 4.5 Aggregate measures of support (AMS)

Measure	European Union	Japan	South Korea	United States
AMS (millions of dollars), 1997	56,748	26,042	2,032	6,238
AMS as a percentage of total agricultural output, 1997	23.0	32.3	8.0	3.1
AMS per capita (US dollars), 1997	152	207	44	23
Producer support equivalent (PSE), 1998	45.6	63.2	58.9	22.2
PSE per farmer (thousands of US dollars) average, 1996-98	17	23	23	14

Sources: AMS and agricultural output figures from WTO notifications of member countries, http://www.wto.org. PSE data from US Department of Agriculture, Economic Research Service. Other data from World Bank, *World Development Indicators* (CD-ROM), 1999.

farm population is losing political clout, and the Japanese budget comes under pressure from rising social welfare expenditures due to the aging of the population.

Our understanding of the impact of agricultural policies is far more complete and less controversial than that of manufactures trade. During the postwar period, Japan pursued an active industrial policy, and commentators as diverse as Johnson (1982), Shinohara (1982), and Tyson (1992) have ascribed a central role to industrial policy in Japan's postwar economic development. Analytically, these policies could be justified as an infant industry promotion strategy undertaken by a technological follower playing catch-up (Iwata 1997). Export or other external performance targets could be used to measure success and discipline the moral hazard associated with the exploitation of a captive domestic market (Ito 1992).

Domestic support policies have included direct subsidies, preferential trade treatment, preferential access to credit, government procurement preferences, the establishment of producer cartels, and public subsidization of research and development (R&D) consortia. These policies were facilitated by the existence of a network of public-sector financial institutions. Programs such as the postal saving and insurance systems acted as deposit or payment-taking institutions. These funds were then intermediated by the MOF-controlled Fiscal Investment and Loan Program (FILP) through public-sector lending institutions such as the Japan Development Bank, providing the government a mechanism by which to channel capital to preferred users or industries. External policies have included trade protection, limitations on inward direct investment, and control over high-technology trade. It is clear from studies by Noland (1993) and Beason and Weinstein (1996) that these policies had a demonstrable impact on the country's composition of output and trade, although the notion that they were welfare-enhancing was not supported. Similarly, Sakakibara and Porter (2001) found that domestic rivalry—not collusion or a sheltered home market—has induced dynamic improvements in international competitiveness.[24]

The US government also has undertaken a variety of policy interventions that collectively might be regarded as an industrial policy, although it was never articulated as such. These measures have included special tax policies, input subsidies, preferences in government procurement, public subsidies to R&D and its dissemination in the agricultural sector, and large-scale government purchases that have effectively created markets (e.g., in avionics, ground-tracking stations for satellites) often associated with defense procurement.

In both Japan and the United States, however, the impact of these policies may have waned over time, for a variety of reasons. In the United States, and to a lesser extent Japan, there has been an ideological shift away from the interventionist model. This has coincided with a drying up of public funding—in the United States due to the constraints on aggregate government spending through legislated restrictions on federal spending starting in the late 1980s, and in Japan due to the competing demands for social welfare spending due to the rapidly aging population. Moreover, in Japan, the public-sector financial infrastructure—in the form of the postal saving system, the FILP, and public-sector financial institutions—is undergoing transformations, which in principle are to make it less amenable to capital channeling in the future than it was in the past (as will be discussed in detail below). Last, the Uruguay Round agreement constrains both countries' ability to implement industrial policy through such things as input subsidies and preferential government procurement.

Structural Barriers

The picture becomes even cloudier when it comes to "structural" access barriers. It has often been argued that foreign firms seeking to enter the Japanese market through either exporting or investing have encountered other forms of nontraditional access barriers, at least in comparison with what similarly situated firms might encounter in the United States. There is a certain immediate plausibility to this assessment: the United States is an immigrant society, and the need to foster and maintain social stability has led to the development of a political system and policymaking apparatus that emphasizes inclusion, access, and procedural transparency. US firms have been technological leaders for an extended period of time, and

---

24. Ryan (1997) found that market power among manufacturers in Japan was declining, which could be interpreted as consistent with Sakakibara and Porter's analysis. However, he also found that the declining market power was associated with slowing total factor productivity (TFP) growth, though it is unclear whether this correlation was actually causal or simply reflected the contemporaneous secular decline in TFP growth due to dwindling opportunities for catch-up (Eaton and Kortum 1997).

the US role in the Cold War lent itself to ideological, strategic, and economic justifications for openness.

Japan has a very different culture and history, and it is unremarkable that policymaking in Japan is not characterized by the same degree of access or transparency. Indeed, it would be surprising if it were. In Japan—a large, relative latecomer to industrialization—the arguments for and practice of infant-industry protection were adopted quite naturally. The issue is how to disentangle access impediments, created by Japanese firms exploiting rent-seeking opportunities opened up by Japan's bureaucratically driven policymaking, from the "natural" impediment created by geographical distance from other major industrial countries or by "cultural" distance—as might be inferred from the fact that, until recently, Japan was the only OECD member whose written national language did not use an alphabet.

Bergsten and Noland (1993) identified four possible structural impediments to international economic exchange through either trade or investment: the lack of intellectual property protection, restrictions on inward investment, product liability and regulation, and industrial structure and competition policy. With respect to the first, legal changes in Japan, bilateral agreements, and the Uruguay Round agreement appear to have resolved the major disputes, though new ones will surely arise in the future as information technology and the "new economy" create issues not adequately covered under existing agreements. Changes in Japanese patent law have, for example, shifted the burden of proof from the plaintiff to defendant; introduced third-party assessment to facilitate proof of damages; widened judges' discretion in the finding of damages; and ended the practice of granting patents in Japan for inventions or innovations that are publicly used or part of public knowledge outside Japan.[25] Bergsten and Noland (1993) recommended that the United States and Japan learn from European practices in this area, including US adoption of the near-universal first-to-file patent system and Japanese speeding up of the patent-approval process and discontinuation of the practice of allowing pregrant patent challenges. According to the American Chamber of Commerce in Japan (ACCJ 2000), the government of Japan has indeed implemented the 1994 bilateral agreement that restricted pregrant challenges and speeded up the approvals process.

Likewise, it is hard to identify policies aimed at actively discouraging FDI today in Japan. For nearly a decade, surveys done by the ACCJ have found that most of their respondents believe that the situation with regard to FDI has been improving. The impediments to investment, as ranked by the respondents, were the high cost of doing business; difficulties in locating and hiring qualified personnel; general complexities; a multi-

---

25. See Koyanagi (2001) for more detail on Japanese patent law changes.

tiered distribution system (including anticompetitive practices and distribution *keiretsu*); interlocking business ownership (*keiretsu*); and lack of transparent ministry guidelines. A survey of 2,656 foreign firms conducted by the Ministry of International Trade and Industry (MITI) obtained similar results.[26] Neither survey had government policies at the top of the list.

To the extent that there is scope for policy to facilitate inward FDI, it appears to be more in the form of generic policies to improve the functioning of land and labor markets and the quality of corporate governance rather than specific policies to stimulate FDI. As the IMF (1998) observes, impediments in the form of labor and pension regulations constrain the efficient operation of Japanese labor markets. Similarly, the ACCJ, for example, recommends that to stimulate FDI "the US government should press Japan to adopt policies to improve corporate governance; increase pension portability; encourage the growth of capital markets and venture capital transactions; and increase the liquidity of Japan's land and labor markets" (ACCJ 2000, 107). To the extent that there are serious impediments to FDI beyond the generic difficulties of securing land or hiring labor in Japan, they appear to take the form of "private" barriers that may remain (as discussed below). Indeed, the government of Japan has undertaken a number of affirmative-action-like programs to encourage inward investment (especially by small and medium-sized enterprises)—although, like Lincoln (1999), we believe that their ultimate impact is likely to be small. Nevertheless, it is difficult to argue today that the government of Japan is actively trying to hamper inward FDI. If anything, the opposite is true.

Regulatory Issues

The Japanese Economic Planning Agency (EPA) has estimated that regulation restricts 40 percent of the Japanese economy. It is no surprise that regulatory issues remain at the center of the bilateral agenda, because of the direct impediment to trade and investment that they can pose, but also because of their potential role as facilitating mechanisms for anticompetitive private behavior. As the Miyauchi Commission observed, "In the non-manufacturing industries in particular, government regulations protected the vested interests of specific groups, and prevented the proper distribution of resources" (JERI 2001, 5). These regulatory issues are especially pertinent in the services area, in which government fiat—rather than the market—may be the primary determinant of market entry

---

26. In a 2001 governmental reorganization, the Ministry of International Trade and Industry became the Ministry of Economics, Trade, and Industry (METI).

and the terms under which competition occurs.[27] Regulations designed explicitly to control domestic competition also have had the effect of limiting foreign entry.

In Japan, one source of trouble relates to the array of state-owned firms or quasi-public entities, or where privatization has been incomplete (as in the case of Nippon Telephone and Telegraph, or NTT). In fairness to Japan, one can point to Deutsche Telecom or Air France as enterprises that have as much or more state involvement than their Japanese counterparts. Indeed, a partly state-owned firm, Renault, which earned rents from the import quotas imposed on Japanese cars, was permitted to take over a Japanese private competitor, Nissan. From a global, rather than bilateral, perspective, the United States may be the outlier in this regard, though even it is not immune from criticism.[28]

Another source of trouble has been in the institutional mechanisms used to ensure product safety. Rather than seeking to achieve this and other social goals through a liability law and the court system (or other "ground-up" systems), Japan traditionally used the detailed specification of regulations.[29] Not surprisingly, the Japanese government bureaucracy does not have the capability to perform this task in a complex modern economy (no bureaucracy would), so the actual specification of standards and other regulations is often devolved to quasi-official industry councils (*shingikai*) that consist of representatives of private firms or industry groups. The fast-changing nature of information technology industries has made this consensus-style decision making completely obsolete.

Furthermore, it is clear that such councils have the scope and incentives to perform their role in ways that protect the interests of incumbent producers at the expense of new entrants (foreign or domestic) and consumers.[30] The interest of Japanese officials in securing postretirement (*amakudari*) positions with these firms and organizations potentially reinforces these tendencies, and a wave of financial scandals in 1997-98 exposed the

---

27. As Alexander observes, "Many industries in which American businesses are trailblazers, such as retailing, finance, telecommunications, entertainment, and Internet products (among others), have been regulated in Japan, and local rivals consequently suffer from high costs and low levels of innovation. That offers enormous opportunities for American firms. However, the very factors that have kept these industries uncompetitive in Japan also restrict the entry of newcomers, foreign or domestic, that have new products and services" (Alexander 1997b, 3).

28. For example, the OECD has pointed out that the practice of implementing professional certification at the state—rather than the federal—level increases the costs of market entry for both foreign and domestic potential service providers.

29. Japan passed a new product liability law in 1995, moving it marginally closer to the US model. See Hamada (1996) for a comparative analysis of the US and Japanese systems.

30. See Schaede (1999). Balassa and Noland (1988) and Lincoln (1990) provide some particularly vivid examples.

coziness between the regulators and their charges, as well as their outright corruption.[31] The OECD (1999b) concluded that "lack of transparency in regulatory and administrative processes is a major weakness of Japan's domestic regulatory system. Non-transparency affects all potential entrants and competitors . . . but has disproportionate costs on foreign parties." Indeed, in a fascinating paper, Yano (2001) shows that acquiescence in anticompetitive practices in the nontraded sector of a large, trade-surplus economy can act as a "beggar-thy-neighbor" policy, shifting real income to itself from its trade-deficit partner.

Not surprisingly, regulatory issues are a topic of intense discussion internally within Japan; bilaterally, with the US government requesting both systemic and industry-specific changes; and multilaterally, through the OECD.[32] Starting in the early 1990s, the government of Japan initiated a process of reform of its regulatory practices, both systemically and with regard to particular priority sectors.[33]

So in 1999, for example, as an administrative measure, Japan introduced a public comment process on draft regulations, including administrative guidance issued to multiple parties, and passed an information disclosure law effective April 2001.[34] In principle, these changes should greatly improve the ability of individuals and firms to track the formulation and implementation of public policy. At the same time, the government of Japan has made the strategic decision to move to a regulatory system based on retroactive supervision rather than prior intervention.

Sectoral Issues

The government of Japan has designated a number of sectors as high priority, including (to name a few) finance, telecommunications, power generation and distribution, and health care. In telecommunications, restrictions on the sale of cellular phones were lifted in April 1994 as part

---

31. See Wanner (1998a, 1998b) and Lincoln (2001) for more on these points.

32. The OECD now publishes surveys of the regulatory practices of its members, and has undertaken the promulgation of "best practices" in a number of areas such as corporate governance. USTR (2000) contains an informative description of the bilateral deregulation agenda from the US government perspective. Sectorally, the United States has made deregulation of telecommunications, medical equipment, financial services, power-generating equipment, housing, and retail distribution its priorities. These are sectors in which the US government believes its producers are competitive, and there is some support for reform domestically in Japan.

33. In part, the government of Japan responded in a piecemeal fashion, issuing lists of hundreds of regulations that had been abolished, though a quick perusal of one of these lists might lead one to doubt the economic impact of the deregulation undertaken. See IMF (1998) and Lincoln (1999) for contrasting assessments of these actions.

34. See Marcus (2001) for discussion.

of a bilateral agreement with the United States, and the price-setting system was shifted from an approval to a registration system in December 1996. The result has been an explosion of cellular phone use in Japan— from 2.1 million users in 1993, before deregulation, to 50 million in 1999 (Lincoln 2001).[35] Telephone access fees (the non-NTT phone companies' access to the connection point for the "last mile") were further reduced as part of another bilateral agreement concluded with the United States in July 2000. Other telecoms reforms have included relaxing restrictions on foreign ownership of domestic systems and restructuring the giant NTT group.[36]

Nevertheless, reformers were disappointed by the April 2001 legislative proposals of the Mori cabinet, which fell far short of the reform recommendations made by a government advisory panel. Japan remains the only industrial major country without an independent telecoms regulatory body.[37] Japan's competition policy watchdog, the Japan Fair Trade Commission (JFTC), has played a passive role on telecoms issues, and the Ministry of Posts and Telecommunications has not solicited its advice. Indeed, the Ministry of Economics, Trade, and Industry (METI) went so far as to make the need for further reform in the telecommunications sector the centerpiece of its 2001 White Paper—which came out after the resolution of the interconnection dispute with the United States (METI 2001). (See box 5.5.)

The retail distribution sector has been another area of interest. The most prominent example has been the progressive relaxation of the Large-Scale Retail Store Law (*Daiten-Ho*) and its eventual repeal at the national level in April 1999. These changes have resulted in a sharp increase in large-scale retail store openings (and in the lengthening of operating hours for existing enterprises), and the entry of such foreign chains as Toys 'R Us, now the largest toy retailer in Japan, and Carrefour, a French supermarket firm.[38] In many small and medium-sized cities, a shopping district located

---

35. See Bergsten and Noland (1993) for background on the cellular phone case. Ironically, spurred by foreign pressure for deregulation, wireless communication and wireless interface with the Internet have emerged as leading Japanese sectors of competitiveness in the information technology revolution.

36. US restrictions on foreign ownership are now tighter than those in Japan. Telecom firms competing against NTT in Japan have significant foreign ownership, and the majority owner of Japan Telecom, a competitor of NTT, will be the British firm Vodafone when it completes its purchase of shares owned by British Telecom.

37. The European Union threatened Japan with a WTO complaint if it did not commit to the establishment of an independent regulatory body. To be clear, the establishment of such a regulator would in all likelihood be an improvement over the status quo, but would be no panacea.

38. See Asano (1997, 1998) for overviews of the distribution sector, and Bergsten and Noland (1993) for more on the Toys 'R Us case. Mitsugi, Takamoto, and Yamazaki (1998) contains an interesting discussion of how technological progress and telecoms reform has enabled

in front of the commuter train station or in the center of the city is giving way to large discount shops with ample parking on the periphery of town.

In the transportation field, the government announced a phased relaxation of entry restrictions and fare-setting regulations for taxis, railways, buses, ships, and aviation. A new civil aviation pact was concluded with the United States (see box 4.3). The January 1998 agreement expanded the number of airlines that have unlimited access to unspecified routes between the two countries, and for incumbent carriers, increased flights permitted between the United States and Japan, though the pact fell far short of the "open skies" agreement that the United States had sought.

In the energy sector, retail price setting for electricity and gas was liberalized in January 1996, contributing to modest declines in retail prices.[39] New entry into the electrical power generation industry was liberalized in December 1995. However, California's experience with rolling blackouts in 2000-01 after deregulation of the electricity market there has begun to knock the wind out of the reform sails in Japan.

In the petroleum sector, prices began falling in 1994 after the government began liberalizing rules on the importation of oil and gasoline. At the retail level, prices have fallen rapidly since restrictions on self-service gas stations were removed in April 1997, beginning a process of consolidation at the retail level. Japan was the only G-7 country in which the oil price increase of 2000 did not generate significant political or social reactions, because major declines in gasoline prices had occurred in preceding years.[40] Prices in Japan are now similar to those in Europe, and taxes explain most of the price differences vis-à-vis the United States.

Health care is another key area of deregulation, owing to its growing importance in the Japanese economy and the government's heavy involvement. Because of inefficiencies in delivery and Japan's rapidly aging population, health care expenditures have been rising 4 percent a year—reaching 8 percent in 2000, double its share of GDP in 1970. In the absence of reform, the government expects this share to again more than double to 19 percent of GDP by 2025. (It is about 15 percent in the United States.)

Unlike the United States, Japan provides for universal health care coverage through a combination of private employer-provided insurance and a national insurance system for those outside the employer-provided

---

"Seven-Eleven Japan" to radically increase the efficiency of retail distribution in Japan through the application of information technology.

39. See Suzuki (1997) for an informative discussion of liberalization of electrical generation and distribution.

40. Between 1998 and 2000, the typical gas price at the pump dropped from 120 yen per liter to 98 yen per liter, and the price hike during the autumn of 2000 raised the price to only 104 yen per liter. At the same time, the aggregate number of retail sales outlets declined as many relatively inefficient incumbent sellers exited the market. See Nagaoka and Kimura (1999) for a rigorous econometric study of the Japanese gasoline market.

Box 4.3 Aviation

In the 1950s, airliners could not fly between the United States and mainland Asia without refueling, so US negotiators secured for three US carriers the right to stop in Japan before proceeding to other destinations, such as Hong Kong. These "beyond rights" were at the center of a contentious renegotiation of the bilateral pact that was concluded in January 1998. The US side was interested in preserving the existing arrangement, insofar as it gave United, Northwest, and FedEx access to the rapidly expanding Asian market, whereas the Japanese carriers were much less interested in beyond rights to Latin America.

The original 1952 bilateral agreement might be described as "unfair and liberal"—it embodied both a more one-sided and a more open, competitive arrangement than Japan's Ministry of Transportation would have preferred, given the relative inefficiency of Japanese carriers. (Japanese airlines are considerably less efficient than their US competitors; private-sector analysts estimate that their costs per seat-mile are more than 50 to 70 percent higher than the US carriers, and in fact, liberalization of the market has been accompanied by restructuring at both Japan Airlines and All Nippon.) As two observers of the renegotiation described it, "It was apparent that Japan's overriding negotiating objective was to restrict US competition with Japanese airlines" (Jaggi and Morgan 1996, 169). Or, as one US official observed in 1993, although the Japanese were opposed to numerical targets in goods trade, they were in favor of quantitative limits on airline travel.

At the same time, this was not a purely United States-versus-Japan affair: There were significant differences in interests in both countries between the dominant incumbent firms (Northwest, United, FedEx, and Japan Airlines) and the latecomers (All Nippon, Continental, Delta, and American). On the US side, the newcomers were willing to sacrifice the beyond rights of the incumbents in return for expanded access to Japan. On the Japanese side, it might be more accurate to describe the government's position as one of protecting Japan Airlines, rather than promoting Japanese interests per se (which officials admitted privately). For its part, United, one of the incumbents, funded a study by the consulting firm Booz, Allen & Hamilton, which concluded that the loss of the beyond rights would reduce the US surplus in passenger traffic by as much as $7.6 billion by 2015.

(box continues next page)

---

ambit. Growing demand is swamping the capacity of the private insurance market and imposing an increasing burden on the national budget. Japan faces the need to both improve the efficiency of service delivery and expand the capacity of the system to deliver home care. The government undertook a number of reforms in the late 1990s, but most observers believe that these will not be sufficient to address the problems (Suzuki 1997; Takahashi 2001). In particular, more competition will have to be introduced into the system to encourage cost reductions by sheltered providers. One aspect of this will be to increase the degree of international competition, at least in the provision of medical equipment and pharmaceuticals, an area of longstanding interest to the United States.

With respect to factor markets, restrictions on the range of occupations where private placement firms could operate was relaxed in April 1997.

Box 4.3 Aviation *(continued)*

The issue of beyond rights was not the only one on the agenda. Japan has fewer international flights than other OECD countries—indeed, fewer than its Asian neighbors. The main Japanese airport at Narita outside Tokyo is highly congested and inefficient: With two terminals and a single runway, Narita was handling only 360 takeoff and landing slots, ranking it 153rd in the world. With a single runway, but less surrounding space, London's Gatwick Airport handles up to 810 takeoffs and landings a day. New rights would mean little, if the US carriers could not obtain landing slots. Ironically, British advisors were brought to Narita by the Japanese government to increase the number of available slots. However, the pact concluded with the United States contained a "fix" that infuriated the Europeans: To square the interests of the incumbent US carriers with the new entrants, it allowed FedEx to sell some of its unused slots to American, Continental, and Delta (at a tidy profit), which violated the "use it or lose it rule" and angered other carriers that were in the queue for the coveted slots.

In the end, the new agreement preserved the beyond rights of the incumbents while expanding access to the newcomers. Although the agreement fell short of the "open skies" liberalization that the United States had sought, the gains for both Japanese and US citizens would appear to be nonnegligible.

Findlay, Hufbauer, and Jaggi (1996) attempted to estimate the impact of barriers to trade in civil aviation by estimating (from cross-national data) the cost differentials created by regulation and then applying the potential cost reduction to expected future demand. They estimate that the annual cost savings to Japan from civil air deregulation would be $9.4 billion by 2010. It should be noted that this is not an estimate of the pure efficiency gain (the welfare triangle). Much of this figure presumably represents transfers from Japanese airlines and associated firms to Japanese consumers as enhanced competition erodes their regulatory-generated rents. US officials claimed that over 4 years the pact would generate an additional $4 billion in revenue for US carriers and save $300 million for US passengers. No estimates of expanded international trade in aviation products or services were provided, though one might expect that, given the relative efficiency of US aviation product and service providers, US firms also would benefit from the expanded opportunities afforded by deregulation. Indeed, the potential spillover effects in such sectors as tourism could swamp the direct impact of increased efficiency in civil aviation. (See Yamauchi and Ito 1996, Greaney 1997, and Lincoln 1999 for more detailed analyses.)

Also that year, the 40-hour work week was made mandatory, and the (male-female) equal employment law was strengthened. As was noted in chapter 3, restrictions on land use and real estate transactions were also relaxed in 1997. These included simplification of the process by which land could be converted from agriculture to other uses, easing of restrictions on the ratio of floor space to plot size, and requirements of prior notification of land purchases.

It is fair to say, however, that the centerpiece of the Japanese deregulation campaign has been in the financial and corporate-governance sphere. Historically, Japan has maintained a repressed, fragmented, bank-centered financial system (Meerschwam 1991; Hoshi and Kashyap, n.d.). Some argue that in the immediate postwar period this was a rational response, allowing the concentration of scarce human capital in a few key institutions. Others argue that the bank-centered financial system contributed to careful monitoring and "patient" capital (Aoki 1984, 1988).[41] Of course, as Kang and Stulz (1997) point out, causality could run the other direction as well: borrowing firms could be adversely affected when their main bank encountered difficulty. Indeed, Aoki's argument is a purely theoretical one, and it is not at all clear that the main banks actually played any uniquely effective monitoring function.[42]

However true these notions might have been in the past, by the 1980s and 1990s, corporate governance had grown lax and rates of return on capital had fallen. As the IMF observed, "the ability of the banks to discipline the corporate sector eroded considerably" (IMF 1998, 149). Capital-market discipline was hampered by "pervasive" cross-shareholding, which reduced the role of noncorporate shareholders in corporate governance. According to Stokes, "only one-quarter of Japanese public firms have an outside director, and even these generally represent the interests of the company's main bank or an affiliated firm" (Stokes 2000, 63).[43]

Furthermore, the lack of M&A activity "further reduced pressure to achieve satisfactory rates of return" (IMF 1998, 150). This was compounded by "weaknesses in accounting and disclosure standards" that "adversely affected governance" (IMF 1998, 150); Stokes adds that "even the statutory auditor, nominally independent, is usually a former employee" (Stokes 2000, 64).

Nontransparency and the absence of strong institutional mechanisms for disciplining managers have impeded foreign investment and facilitated both corruption of the state and penetration of business by organized criminal groups.[44] *Sokaiya* (corporate extortionists) often in concert with *yakuza* (gangsters) prey on corporate managers by extorting money in exchange for not revealing publicly embarrassing information. (See Box 3.2.)

Finally, the IMF observed that inadequate "bankruptcy laws have not helped enforce corporate discipline in Japan, and have discouraged

---

41. In reality, the evidence does not appear to support the notion that Japanese managers are any more patient than their counterparts in the United States (Hall and Weinstein 1996). Indeed, in one case of Japanese and American managers working in an environment embodying almost precisely the same incentives—professional baseball—the Japanese managers appear to operate with the time preferences of heroin addicts!

42. Kang and Shivadasani (1999) show that "independent" firms, without main-bank affiliation, exhibited substantially better operating performance than did their main-bank-affiliated counterparts, and document the existence of alternative institutions to monitor management. See also Scher (1997) on the ineffectiveness of main-bank monitoring.

43. See Wanner (1998b) for an overview of Japanese corporate governance issues, and Scher (1999) on the role of cross-holding.

44. Lack of transparency is said to be a major impediment to foreign investment. See Alexandra Harney, *Financial Times*, 17 November 2000, for examples.

restructuring" (IMF 1998, 150-51). These weaknesses were largely ignored when the economy was expanding rapidly and most firms' equity values were appreciating.

These problems have been exacerbated by an expansion of the public-sector financial system driven by the economy's poor macroeconomic performance during the 1990s, and the political system's unwillingness to countenance transparent restructuring of the magnitude implied by private-sector market outcomes. As the IMF observes, outstanding loans by public-sector financial institutions grew from just over 10 percent of GDP in 1977 to nearly 30 percent of GDP two decades later. Ironically, despite the "Big Bang" financial reforms described in the previous chapter, in the short run (1998-2000) at least, the Japanese government's direct lending influence has actually increased as a result of greatly expanded loans to small and medium-sized enterprises and nationalization of failed banks.[45] Indeed, the FILP has grown as the postal saving share of deposits has increased, as have receipts from the postal life insurance program. As of 2001, this picture may change, because the Ministry of Public Management, Home Affairs, Posts, and Telecommunications is no longer required to invest these funds in the FILP.

Nevertheless, the Big Bang reforms are encouraging a transformation of the Japanese financial sector. The structure of the financial system is changing; bank deposits account for a falling share of household portfolios as savers diversify into new instruments. Access by foreign service providers is improving in parallel. Foreign brokers now manage more than a third of the volume on the Tokyo Stock Exchange. Foreign fund managers continue to increase their share of the pension management business. However, foreign management of mutual funds appears to have peaked and is back at its 1991 share, as Japanese banks enter this increasingly crowded market.

Changes in the structure and operation of financial markets have been accompanied by changes in corporate governance. Bans on holding companies have been lifted, though some restrictions remain. It is hoped that this will encourage the restructuring of Japanese firms by facilitating the divestiture of subsidiaries and the concentration of activities in areas of core competence as well as the entry into new ventures. The April 2000 Corporate Rehabilitation Law should further contribute to corporate restructuring. Driven partly by the government and partly by the demands

---

45. Stokes provides the following example: "In early 2000, nationalist opposition in the Diet blocked the sale of Nippon Credit Bank to the U.S.-based Cerebrus Group, leading to the purchase by a consortium lead by Japan's Softbank. This xenophobia cost Japan's taxpayers $540 million, the difference between Softbank's purchase price and Cerebrus' offer" (Stokes 2000, 66). Friedman (2000) contrasts the secretive (and apparently politicized) actions of Japan's Financial Recovery Commission with the more transparent auction procedures used by the Resolution Trust Corporation in the United States. See also Lincoln (2000).

of foreign investors, revisions of accounting laws have been undertaken to introduce consolidated financial statements and recognize pension liabilities, though the mandatory adoption of these practices has been postponed.[46] In recent years, shareholders have successfully sued such corporations as Nomura Securities, Daiwa Bank, Dai-Ichi Kangyo Bank, and Kobe Steel for malfeasance.

Assessment

The record of the Japanese deregulation program is mixed. Observers universally hail progress in the financial sector and on corporate governance issues, although more remains to be done, and some recent postponements of scheduled actions give pause.[47] An expanded unemployment insurance system could facilitate labor shedding and restructuring. Although the implementation of these changes will certainly not be without controversy (see USTR 2000 for a US government perspective), as the OECD observes, "it seems fair to say that within a few years Japan's regulatory landscape may well have been radically transformed" OECD (1999b, 25).

Outside the financial sector, progress has been more uneven. As the IMF (1998) observes, the tendency has been to relax rather than abolish regulations.[48] It cites the example of the Diet considering raising the limit on bar exam passers from 700 to 1000 and queries why any restrictions are needed at all. Similarly, in the case of the abolition of the Large-Scale Retail Store Law, local and prefectural governments were encouraged to formulate their own laws on the basis of environmental and traffic considerations. It is not surprising that incumbent retailers have exploited these new local procedures to stifle competitors.[49] In the transportation field, the revision of the 1952 bilateral agreement has resulted in some additional flights, but air travel between Japan and the United States

---

46. See Hashimoto (1999), Shinn (1999), and Shikano (2001) for more on Japanese accounting practices.

47. For example, the introduction of limits on bank deposit insurance and the introduction of new accounting rules on banks' derivative positions have been postponed.

48. Lake (1998) observes that the term *kisei kanwa*, frequently translated into English as "deregulation," would more accurately be translated as "relaxation of regulation" and that the Japanese equivalent of "deregulation," *kisei teppai*, is not often used. He concludes that Japanese government leaders "are not really interested in a comprehensive elimination of regulation that would fundamentally change the role of government in Japanese society" (Lake 1998, 13).

49. Stokes (2000), for example, cites such cases in Yokohama and Sendai. At the same time, it should be noted that Japanese authorities are not alone in imposing such restrictions to aid incumbent retailers. Some local governments in the United States act similarly, and such restrictions are ubiquitous in Europe.

remains restricted (in part due to capacity constraints at Tokyo's Narita Airport) and costly.[50] In the energy sector, Lincoln observes that despite the legalization of self-service gasoline stations, "the combination of stiff regulations and collusion have not encouraged many stations to experiment with this new form of service" (Lincoln 2000, 95), although prices at the pump did come down following the liberalization of gasoline imports.

All this suggests that considerable scope for deregulation remains. The main beneficiaries of that process are likely to be Japanese consumers. Indeed, on these issues, when one takes into account Europe as well as Japan, the real global outlier may be the United States. The potential impact of additional deregulation on the US and Japanese economies is taken up below.

Private Barriers

The regulatory agenda is critical for another reason, as well. The historic lack of transparency at the public level has a counterpart in the organization of Japan's private firms, and has been accompanied by allegations of anticompetitive behavior of Japanese firms, either through industry cartels or *keiretsu* networks of affiliated firms (see box 3.5, "*Keiretsu*").[51] The case of the former is relatively straightforward: legally sanctioned "recession" or "rationalization" cartels, as in the soda ash industry, or illegal cartels, as in the construction sector, have acted to block imports or foreign firm activity in Japan.

However, horizontal agreements among competitors—including price fixing, cartels or market allocation schemes, and bid rigging—are all mechanisms for exploiting market power that contain the seeds of their own destruction. If prices are artificially raised, then new entrants (foreign or domestic) will enter the market attracted by supernormal profits, undermining the arrangement. In the obverse case of predation, prices may be lowered to drive competitors out of the market. However, when the incumbent firm raises prices, new entrants will reenter the market. Similarly, successful bid rigging requires some mechanism for restraining entry to sustain the arrangement, and without such a device, cartels may not be sustainable, even if legal (Warner 1996). Typically, some kind of government regulation is needed to sustain horizontally collusive behavior.

Take, for example, the construction industry, where anticompetitive problems are large and ongoing. Restrictions on entry into the construction

---

50. As in the case of retailing, similar restrictions and high prices are also encountered in Europe, with air travel between the United States and the United Kingdom being a prime example.

51. See Kotabe and Wheiler (1996) for a bilaterally oriented survey.

business (especially for foreign firms), together with the designated-bidder system in public works tendering and the practice of fragmenting major public works projects into smaller components, have contributed to cartelization. The associated rents are allocated through the practice of *dango*, a form of bid rigging in which firms negotiate with each other as to which firms will participate in bidding on a given project and at what prices. McMillan (1991) estimates that excess profits from collusion in public works projects typically amount to 16-33 percent of the price. Evidence from the few cases that have been prosecuted supports this range of estimates, the most famous case being the 1989 episode in which the US Department of Justice reached an out-of-court settlement with 99 Japanese construction firms for bid rigging at the Yokosuka Naval Base; fines levied in that case amounted to $32.4 million, or 24 percent of the billed costs.[52] Former Diet member and now Tokyo mayor Shintaro Ishihara once put the implicit cost at 40 percent. The Japanese business newspaper *Nihon Keizai Shimbun* once observed that public works cost on average 20-30 percent more than comparable private-sector projects, and estimated that ¥8-12 trillion of the public works budget was wasted. The OECD (2000b) guesses that elimination of *dango* could reduce the overall public works budget by 15 percent. As was noted in box 3.1, the construction industry is the largest source of political contributions to Japanese campaigns.

These problems are not a thing of the past. Data from FY1997 on 1,676 multiple-round, open-bidding contracts for work worth at least ¥100 million let by 34 prefectures revealed bidding patterns consistent with widespread bid rigging. In 97.9 percent of the cases, the firm that bid the lowest in the first round was never underbid. Moreover, although the bids of other firms shifted in value during subsequent rounds, the winning bidder never altered its bid, which averaged 99.2 percent of the local government's maximum acceptable cost projection (Choy 1998).

In May 2000, the JFTC issued a cease-and-desist order against bid rigging by 203 construction and 94 engineering survey companies on agricultural projects handled by the Hokkaido prefectural government (OECD 2000b). The most stunning thing about the case is that the Agricultural Department of Hokkaido actually participated in the process, establishing annual procurement targets for each firm, and suggesting pre-

---

52. McMillan (1991) discusses this and three additional cases in which excess profits due to collusion were estimated to have ranged from 9 to 31 percent. The US Justice Department subsequently settled a case against 11 Japanese electronics firms for rigging bids at the US Air Force base at Yokota. The firms agreed to pay $36.7 million in fines, or nearly 36 percent of the value of the $103 million in contracts. Ultimately, the licensing restrictions to entry facilitate these practices, and these regulations impeding entry, especially the entry of foreign firms, have become the object of comment by the United States, the European Union, Canada, and Australia (MITI 1996, 365-66, 372).

ferred winners on individual projects! According to the OECD, the amount of business received by individual firms was a function of the number of former bureaucrats that they employed. The JFTC, although it could act against the firms, is powerless to act against the prefectural government.[53] Unfortunately, this kind of collusion is not limited to construction but appears to extend to other aspects of public procurement as well.[54] The JFTC has launched multiple investigations of bid rigging and issued warnings to firms, most recently in 2000.

The role of horizontally or vertically integrated *keiretsu* is more controversial. These organizations are inherently exclusionary—the issue is whether there are efficiency gains that justify their exclusivity. Indeed, to the extent that rival vertically integrated groups compete against each other, the rents from exclusiveness may be quite limited. Although it has been claimed that members of horizontal *keiretsu* would refuse to purchase imports due to cross-industry affiliation, most US trade complaints involve vertical *keiretsu*, regarding either the refusal to purchase imported intermediate products or the use of captive distribution networks to impede the penetration of imported final products to consumers. Refusal to use higher-quality or lower-price foreign parts should weaken Japanese manufacturers in global competition. By and large, this does not appear to be the case. As a consequence, much of the international attention has focused on the institutional characteristics of the Japanese market that facilitate market segmentation between a protected home "bastion" or "sanctuary" market and a more contested foreign market.

The issue of vertical *keiretsu* has been particularly controversial for several reasons. First, at the conceptual level, there is little intellectual consensus about the optimality or desirability of differing forms of organization. Typical vertical restraints include resale price maintenance, exclusive dealing or distribution, tied sales, reciprocity agreements, territorial restrictions on dealers or distributors, refusals to deal, or vertical mergers. One line of argumentation, starting with Bork (1966, 1978), has held that the traditional competition policy approach of discouraging these practices was misguided in that these vertical arrangements enhanced efficiency—in the sense of reducing transaction and search costs, removing downstream (retail) price distortions, and encouraging optimal levels of investment in production and distribution. However, subsequent research pointed to potential divergences between private and social welfare asso-

---

53. The OECD argues that in general, local governments have not sought to eliminate *dango* because of their commitment to maintaining employment in small and medium-sized enterprises (OECD 2000b).

54. In 1995, the JFTC fined 37 domestic trading companies and department stores for bid-rigging equipment and materials contracts linked to foreign aid projects. The investigation concluded that the firms had colluded on some 631 projects worth approximately $170 million.

ciated with these practices. Salop and Scheffman (1983, 1987) explored the possibility that dominant firms might be able to induce rivals to exit or deter their entry or simply put rivals at a disadvantage by raising their costs through the application of these techniques. Hart and Tirole (1990) subsequently identified situations in which vertical integration has the effect of foreclosing the market and is the optimal strategy for the firms involved.[55] From a policy perspective, these opposing effects present a conundrum. Given the apparent difficulty of vertical foreclosure and the possible efficiency enhancements associated with vertical integration, regulatory authorities typically have taken a less decisive stance with regard to vertical agreements, in comparison with the horizontal agreements discussed above.[56]

Second, at the level of empirical analysis, *keiretsu* is a slippery concept. There are different kinds of *keiretsu*. They can be identified according to differing criteria, and as a consequence, one must be careful in assessing empirical evidence on their presence and impact.

According to the WTO, vertical supplier *keiretsu* (*seisan-keiretsu*) "may create an entry barrier to outsiders. Firstly, a *keiretsu* relationship may induce apparent anti-competitive practices such as vertical boycotting and exclusive dealing . . . long-term relationships cultivated through a *keiretsu* may push up 'switching costs' and make it more costly for *keiretsu* participants to change their business partners" (WTO 1995, 92).[57] At the same time, there are theoretical arguments that even such practices could enhance efficiency (Spencer and Qiu 2000).

A second potential impediment to trade and investment is vertical restraints within the distribution system.[58] This occurs in both consumer and capital goods. Vertically integrated firms refuse to carry the products of competitors, and product return and rebate systems are used to tilt retailer incentives toward domestically produced products. According to the WTO, vertical distribution affiliation *keiretsu* (*ryutsu-keiretsu*)

> usually set up by manufacturers, tie wholesalers and retailers together through various links including special agent contracts, extension of technical and financial

---

55. As in the case of horizontal agreements, foreclosure is difficult without some regulatory mechanism to facilitate blocking competitors' counterstrategies of parallel vertical integration or establishment of distribution networks.

56. See Dobson and Waterson (1996) for an overview of these issues. Drysdale (1995) and McMillan (1996) provide Japan-focused commentaries.

57. It is unclear whether these practices should be considered illegal or not. According to the WTO, group boycotts and refusal to deal violate the Anti-Monopoly Law (AML); however, Matsushita (1997) argues that "as long as there is strong interbrand competition, including price competition, between *keiretsu* systems, such systems are considered lawful under the AML" (p. 79). See Morici (2000) for further commentary on this point.

58. See Flath (1989) for a description of vertical restraints in Japan.

assistance, exchange of personnel and cross-shareholding. Some Japanese business practices—such as the suggested retail and wholesale price system (*tatene*), a complex rebate system, and provisions for return of unsold goods—are important aspects of such relationships.

Distribution *keiretsu* are not found equally in all sectors; they are concentrated in specific sectors, such as cosmetics, electrical appliances, and automobiles, all of which are characterized by product differentiation, specialty goods, or occasional purchases, and important market segmentation.[59] Outside the automobile sector, where the affiliation ratio is exceptionally high, *keiretsu* distributors cover at most about half of the total market (50 percent in the cosmetic sector and 40 percent in the electrical appliance sector). Although manufacturers cannot legally prevent affiliated dealers from dealing in competing products, such deals are likely to be discouraged by additional burdens on after-sale servicing and sales-promoting activities, as well as by other advantages extended or pressures exerted by *keiretsu* manufacturers (WTO 1995, 92-93).[60]

This is confirmed by the sophisticated econometric research of Ariga, Ohkusa, and Namikawa (1991), which points to administered prices in sectors where there are strong vertical relationships or *keiretsu*, suggesting that control of the distribution system acts as an effective barrier to entry.[61] Indeed, the presence of horizontal and vertical *keiretsu* is associated with lower than expected sectoral imports (Noland 1997d), and higher prices (Noland 1995b). Nishimura (1993) finds that, relative to the United States, excessive distribution cost markups are predominant in consumer goods, as distinct from capital goods or export products.

The discussion thus far has largely concerned trade in goods. Capital-market imperfections may facilitate the imposition of impediments to trade in goods (by enabling the maintenance of captive distribution systems, as was alleged in the Kodak-Fuji photographic film case) or by impeding inward FDI. Specifically, informal obstacles to M&A activity (including cross-holding and tactical impediments to acquisition) may impede the primary channel of FDI in industrial-country markets. Due

---

59. At the same time, it could be argued that in the automobile sector, Japanese part suppliers-assemblers vertical restraints are similar to and perhaps actually looser than the in-house supplier model of the US industry.

60. Although these practices may indeed restrict foreign firms' sales through existing dealer networks, it is unclear (beyond high sunk costs) how these practices deter new entrants from establishing their own dealer networks. Indeed, the Japanese competition authorities have stated that exclusive purchase agreements would violate the AML, but that JFTC investigations have failed to reveal any such violations. Legally sanctioned resale price maintenance schemes have been gradually abolished in all areas except publishing and music.

61. To cite two examples, in 1996 the JFTC raided Häagen-Dazs, and in 2000 it raided Matsushita, in both cases on suspicion of price fixing. Both companies had allegedly forced retailers to charge specified prices or face punishments for noncooperation, including withholding product shipments.

to cross-holdings, for example, in Japan only 30-40 percent of shares are actually traded, effectively precluding a market for corporate control.[62]

It has been argued that stable shareholding or large institutional shareholders provide better monitoring of managers than more diffuse patterns of ownership, contributing to superior economic performance. In the case of Japan, Nakatani (1984) found that bank-affiliated firms had *lower*, though more stable, profits. He interprets bank or *keiretsu* affiliation as acting as an insurance scheme. This conclusion is reinforced by research by Kawai, Hashimoto, and Izumida (1996), which found that distressed firms with main-bank connections pay significantly lower interest rate premiums than do firms without main banks. From this perspective, therefore, bank or *keiretsu* affiliation could be seen as a stabilizing force on the economy.

However, Lichtenberg and Pushner (1992) found that a high degree of intercorporate stock ownership in Japan was associated with lower productivity, profitability, and growth. They interpreted this as indicating managerial shirking, facilitated by protection from takeover. Gower and Kalirajan (1998) similarly found that the main-bank affiliation was not associated with improved technical efficiency in nonmanufacturing firms. Weinstein and Yafeh (1995) argue that the corporate finance incentives faced by *keiretsu* member firms encourage overexpansion, and this is the explanation for their apparently low profitability, and the difficulties new entrants face in breaking into markets dominated by *keiretsu*. For better or worse, horizontal *keiretsu* appear to be heading the way of the dinosaur: The introduction of mark-to-market accounting rules and the financial weaknesses of the banks are forcing them to liquidate their holdings of affiliated firms' stocks—although, as Lincoln (2001) points out, they are apparently dumping non-*keiretsu* holdings first. The degree of internal competition within Japan appears to be rising.

What Is at Stake?

The preceding discussion has established the fact that both the Japanese and US governments act in intentional (and possibly unintentional) ways to frustrate economic exchange. From a public-policy perspective, the issue is whether the impact of these interventions is sufficiently large to justify the expenditure of political capital needed to eliminate them. One can appeal to two sorts of evidence to answer this question: evidence derived from the quantity (volume) of trade or investment and evidence derived from prices and their behavior.

---

62. See box 3.5 on *keiretsu*. This is not to say that this phenomenon is unique to Japan— see Noland (1997b) for similar examples from continental Europe.

There is now a large literature that attempts to answer the question from the quantity side.[63] The immediate problem is how to specify the counterfactual: In other words, although we might observe low volumes of trade in a particular sector, this may reflect a myriad of influences other than public policies or private anticompetitive behavior. A typical approach in this literature is to specify a formal cross-national model of international trade, estimate it econometrically, and then interpret the residuals from the regression as indicative of the impact of trade impediments broadly defined. Because the magnitude of these effects is calibrated implicitly, model specification is critically important. Noland (1997d) nested a number of models within a general econometric framework and found some evidence that Japan exhibited unusually low imports in the aggregate, controlling for relative factor endowments and cross-national differences in factor productivity. At a sectoral level, the divergence between predicted and observed trade was explained by trade-policy variables, including tariffs, quotas, tariff quotas, sanitary and phytosanitary regulations, subsidies, VERs (both those imposed by Japan and those imposed against Japanese exports), and the presence of horizontal and vertical *keiretsu*.[64] Similarly, Weinstein (1996) and Noland (1997b) obtained weak evidence that the presence of *keiretsu* was negatively correlated with sectoral inward FDI.

The quantity evidence is nevertheless problematic because it depends so heavily on the specification of the counterfactual used to derive the implicit evidence of trade impediments. An alternative approach would be to examine prices directly. The price data could be subjected to two sorts of scrutiny: first to see if prices embody relative price distortions associated with trade barriers, and second to see if the temporal pattern of price change signals the maintenance of market power by local producers.

It is a well-known fact that the overall price level in Japan is relatively high. Attempts to compare prices cross-nationally—either as part of academic research (e.g., Summers and Heston 1991) or by private firms such as the Union Bank of Switzerland or the Economist Intelligence Unit attempting to calibrate executive compensation packages (Union Bank of Switzerland 1991)—found that the price level in Japan was unusually high relative to that in other industrial countries.

Beginning in the late 1980s as part of the Structural Impediments Initiative, Japan's MITI and the US Department of Commerce conducted two joint price comparison surveys of more than 100 products and services (US Department of Commerce 1989, 1991). The Japanese Economic Planning

---

63. See Noland (1997d) and the references cited therein.

64. The one paper that uses microdata on *keiretsu* and obtains the opposite conclusion, Ueda and Sasaki (1998), suffers from specification problems, as noted by Noland (1997d) in his more general treatment.

Agency (1989) also began conducting its own annual surveys comparing prices in major Japanese cities and cities in the United States and Europe. It is not surprising that these surveys have consistently found that prices in Japan tended to be higher than prices elsewhere. In the second Japan-United States price survey, for example, two-thirds of the prices in Japan were higher than in the United States, and on average, prices in Japan were 37 percent higher than in the United States.[65] Noland (1995b) found that tariff and nontariff barriers, as well as the presence of *keiretsu*, contributed to the differences in relative prices between Japan and the United States. Maki (1998), working from EPA data, ascribed the relatively high prices in Japan to regulation.

No one expects that the law of one price will hold everywhere and at all times. Because these initial price surveys were conducted during or after periods of yen appreciation, it could be argued that they reflected a transitory phenomenon. However, these price differences have not been eliminated in the past decade, and indeed, research on exchange rate pass-through suggests that such price differentials can persist for extended periods.[66] A 1999 MITI survey found that the average price for industrial goods (including manufactured goods and services used in industrial activities) was 67 percent higher in Japan than in the United States, 57 percent higher than in Germany, and more than 200 percent higher than in South Korea (MITI 1999b). The product-specific breakdown suggested that the prices for manufactured goods were roughly the same in Japan as elsewhere, but there were large differences in the prices of energy and services—two areas in which government regulation is ubiquitous.[67]

At present, the most comprehensive ongoing analysis of price differentials is done by the OECD. Lincoln (2001) reports that their results indicate that, at the end of 1997, prices in Japan were 74 percent higher than in the United States; the next most expensive country (Norway) was only 32 percent higher. The OECD's estimate of the purchasing power parity (PPP) of the exchange rate could be interpreted as a summary indication of the magnitude of high prices in Japan. As shown in figure 4.5, there has been some narrowing of the differential between the OECD's PPP

---

65. In the case of the United States-Japan surveys, it should be noted that the products included were not selected randomly, and might not be representative of prices in the industrial sector overall.

66. See Goldberg and Knetter (1996).

67. Again, as in the case of the United States-Japan price surveys, it is possible that the surveys done by the EPA and MITI are subject to similar selection biases. At a minimum, however, this would seem to suggest that it was not difficult for the statisticians in the Japanese government to design surveys in which their own domestic prices would appear high. Lincoln (1999) contains an entertaining discussion of differences in the prices of refrigerators and pacemakers in the United States and Japan.

Figure 4.5 Nominal versus PPP-adjusted yen-dollar exchange rates, 1990-2000

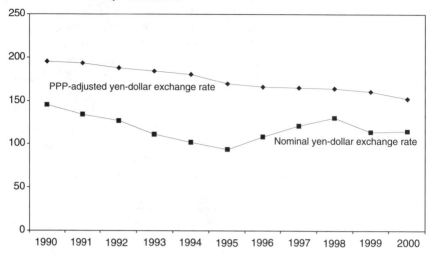

PPP = purchasing power parity.

Sources: IMF, *International Financial Statistics* (CD-ROM); World Bank, *World Development Indicators* (CD-ROM).

estimate and the actual nominal exchange rate, although the difference remains substantial.

These differences do not constitute prima facie evidence of "closedness." In addition to the obvious price wedge created by border measures such as tariffs or quotas, a variety of other factors can contribute to observed price differences: producers may price the same goods differently for various destinations (pricing-to-market), international transportation costs may be large for some goods, or domestic transportation or distribution costs within the importing country may be high for a host of reasons.[68]

With these caveats in mind, a number of studies have attempted to estimate how Japan's trade might change if the border, regulatory, and private barriers to trade and investment were eliminated. Noland (1995b), working from the 1989 and 1991 MITI-Department of Commerce price surveys, estimates that if border and *keiretsu*-related impediments to trade were eliminated, Japanese imports might increase by 28 percent, with most of this increase accounted for by the *keiretsu* variables. Elimination

---

68. Other explanations for these price differences included the price of land and inefficiencies in the Japanese distribution system (Lawrence 1991; Ito and Maruyama 1991; Itoh 1991) or dumping by *keiretsu* affiliates contributing to high prices in Japan and low prices abroad (Cheng and Kreinin 1996).

of border impediments alone might increase imports by 7 percent. If we take the US share of Japanese imports as 20 percent, and apply this to a base of roughly $300 billion, these figures suggest that the first-round, partial-equilibrium impact of eliminating all border impediments would be to increase US exports to Japan by about $4 billion. Elimination of all regulatory and private barriers could yield perhaps another $13 billion, for a total of $17 billion. Presumably, this is an overestimate of the situation today, inasmuch as the Uruguay Round agreement has reduced border measures, and cross-national price differentials have narrowed somewhat since the underlying price surveys were conducted. Moreover, the elimination of these impediments and the increase in imports would lead to a weakening of the yen, thus partly or even completely erasing any impact on Japan's global or bilateral balance.

Sazanami, Urata, and Kawai (1995) take another approach. They estimate price differentials for 47 selected merchandise categories (excluding services) thought to be accorded significant protection in Japan, and ascribe these differentials to trade impediments. As with Noland's research (1995b), these price differentials are calculated from the pre-Uruguay Round period.[69] They estimate that the elimination of barriers would double import volume in affected sectors (¥7.3 trillion or $53 billion), which would have amounted to a 20 percent increase in base-year imports—in the same ballpark as Noland (1995b). And like that other study, the Sazanami, Urata, and Kawai (1995) estimate could be regarded as a ceiling—some of the barriers implicit in the price data in 1989 have been reduced or eliminated in the intervening years. It is also a partial-equilibrium estimate—yen depreciation would offset some of these effects if the trade impediments were removed, and the general-equilibrium effects associated with the increase and redistribution of income would mean that the incidence of increased imports might differ from the specific sectoral values that they obtain.

Yet another approach was adopted by Knetter (1997). He used time-series data on exports to Japan by 37 German industries to distinguish between the competing hypotheses that high retail prices in Japan were caused by discriminatory practices against imports, or high distribution costs associated with getting goods to the point of final sale. For the vast majority of industries examined, the data were consistent with the existence of import impediments. A similar inference was drawn by Dekle (1996), who found that employment in Japan's export industries was more sensitive to variation in the value of the yen than was employment in

---

69. Sazanami, Urata, and Kawai (1995) estimate that trade barriers imposed ¥10-15 trillion in unnecessary costs on Japanese consumers in 1989 ($75-100 billion at the existing yen-dollar rate of 138). Producers got ¥7-9.6 trillion ($50-70 billion), and the government collected ¥0.3 trillion ($2 billion) in tariff revenue. The net cost to the economy was ¥1.1-2.4 trillion ($8-17 billion).

import-competing sectors. Burgess and Knetter (1998) examine cross-national evidence on the employment response in manufacturing to real exchange rate shocks and obtain results consistent with the perception that "Japanese markets are less open to trade" (161).

In the case of the United States, Hufbauer and Elliott (1994) used partial-equilibrium models to examine cases of high protection and concluded that the pure efficiency to the elimination of all tariffs and quantitative restrictions in 1990 would be about $10 billion. The US International Trade Commission (US ITC 1999) looked at the same issue using a more sophisticated, though possibly less robust, general-equilibrium model and reached a remarkably similar conclusion: in 1996, border measures imposed a deadweight efficiency loss on the US economy of $11 billion. Both studies found that most US tariff and quota protection was concentrated in the textile and apparel sector and hence would be of little direct relevance to Japan.

These studies examined merchandise trade. Estimates of the impact of barriers to trade in services are fragmentary. The US ITC (1999) discusses US barriers to services trade in the transportation, telecommunications, and financial industries, but with the exception of restrictions on maritime transport services discussed below, does not attempt any quantitative analyses. As was shown in box 4.3, potential efficiency gains in civil aviation appear quite substantial, with important spillover effects in other sectors.

Some of these gains are already in the pipeline. Since the entry of two new airlines into heavily traveled domestic routes in 1999, and the complete deregulation of fares the following year, airfares in Japan have been falling. As occurred in the United States two decades ago, Japanese airlines are quickly learning to differentiate customers with low price elasticities (typically business travelers on company accounts) from those with high price elasticities (mostly pleasure travelers with flexible schedules). The cheapest ticket on a long-distance route (limited availability with respect to travel dates and capacity) is about a fifth of the unrestricted fare on the same route—or about the same differential as in the United States. Monopoly and duopoly routes, and routes without *shinkansen* (bullet train) competition are more expensive than others. These pricing patterns suggest that airfares are determined by the market.

Petrazzini (1996) applied a similar methodology to estimate the impact of regulatory barriers in telecommunications. He estimated that deregulation of Japanese telecoms would generate $19 billion in cost reductions annually by 2010 and another $10 billion in quality benefits. Again, this is not an estimate of the pure efficiency gain, nor are any estimates of resulting additional international trade in telecoms products or services provided. (In common with the civil aviation case, most of this cost saving would presumably amount to a reduction of regulatory generated rents to the benefit of Japanese consumers.) As with the previous studies on merchandise trade, from today's vantage point, this estimate probably overstates the potential gains to telecoms deregulation to a certain degree—some deregulation has occurred since the study was undertaken, and the underlying growth rate of demand is probably overestimated. Using a conventional CGE model, Verikios and Zhang (2000) report that the pure welfare gain for deregulation of telecoms would be $1.6 billion, coming almost entirely from terms-of-trade effects and the enhancement of Japan as a location of investment. These studies ignore cross-industry spillovers, dynamic gains, and other effects that could be quite significant in this case.

The IMF (1998) reports several attempts to formulate comprehensive estimates of the gains to deregulation. Studies done by MITI, the EPA, and the OECD in 1997 all concluded that deregulation could raise Japanese GDP by 6 percent. The EPA found that half of the productivity increase experienced in telecoms and civil aviation during the period 1987-95 was associated with increased competition in each sector resulting from the permitted entry of a single new entrant into each sector, and that the transfer of theretofore monopoly rents to consumers was substantial. In another study, MITI found that deregulation could create 7.4 million jobs in medical care, information technology and telecoms, distribution, and new manufacturing technologies (Stokes 2000). The OECD (1997) concluded that the gains to deregulation could be bigger in Japan than in three large European countries.[70]

Unfortunately, equivalent studies to the ones done on Japan of the direct impact of these policies on US industrial composition and trade patterns are generally unavailable, though Richardson (1993) estimates that US regulations, mainly in the form of export regulations, reduce US exports by $30 billion annually. Most of this is due to regulations of the Coordinating Committee for Multilateral Export Controls, however, and would not be expected to significantly impede trade with Japan. The most obvious regulatory barrier to services trade is the Jones Act, which mandates that ships traveling between US ports must be built in US

---

70. These studies do not identify the gains to foreigners in general and Americans in particular associated with deregulation and opening in Japan. Perhaps the most ambitious estimate on this score comes from Lincoln (2001). He observes that if one takes a high-end (6 percent) estimate of the foreign firms' share of sales in Japan (i.e., one that accepts Weinstein's proposed adjustments to the data on foreign firm activities) and increases it to the level observed in the United States (12.4 percent—still below other industrial countries) this would imply a doubling of exports and FDI into Japan. For the United States, this might mean increasing exports by $70 billion, from roughly $66 billion in 1997 to $136 billion, and increasing accumulated investment from $36 billion in 1997 to $75 billion. If one did the same calculation using the unadjusted data (i.e., the foreign firm share of corporate sales in Japan was 2.4 percent) this would imply a quintupling of the foreign presence.

shipyards, owned by US citizens, and operated by US crews. Estimates of the annual efficiency loss caused by the Jones Act range from $556 million to $2.8 billion.[71] Again, although this is costly to the US economy, it is unlikely that the impact of this restriction falls significantly on Japan.

As noted above, Galloway, Blonigen, and Flynn (1999) estimate that the net welfare cost to the United States of antidumping actions is $4 billion annually, and this certainly underestimates the impact of these cases today, for the reasons given above. Nearly a fifth of these cases involve Japan. The impact on Japan, though surely negative, contains some ambiguity: Although antidumping cases restrain exports, Japanese exporters in what are predominant oligopolistic markets can exploit their ability to set prices in the US market and the process of administrative review to extract rents, so that some of the reduction in export volume is offset by higher prices. They can also invest in the United States and serve the US market from local facilities.

In summary, both Japan and the United States maintain a variety of barriers to economic exchange, both globally and bilaterally. On the whole, the United States appears to be somewhat more open than Japan. US barriers tend to be concentrated in textiles and apparel (and are now being revived in steel) and—with the exception of its antidumping cases— are largely irrelevant to bilateral trade. Japanese barriers are more ubiquitous, but have been declining over time. More and more, internal regulatory issues are the focus of bilateral discussion. The stakes are not trivial. The 1997 findings that comprehensive deregulation could increase Japan's GDP by 6 percent would be equivalent to all Japanese growth in the second half of the 1990s. Yet it is unclear whether the same modalities used to resolve trade disputes in earlier periods will be effective in dealing with this new agenda. It is to this topic that we now turn.

---

71. See Hufbauer and Elliott (1994), Hahn (1998), and US ITC (1999).

5

Resolving Trade Disputes

In some respects, the second half of the 19th century was a golden era of globalization, driven by technological advances and politically facilitated by the Pax Britannica and its associated institutions. It would take the better part of the 20th century for the world to once again attain the levels of cross-border movements of goods, capital, and people that it had seen at the end of the 19th.

Japan tried to opt out of this process, but was forcibly opened to trade by the "Black Ships" in 1854 and the conclusion of the "unequal treaties" with the United States and other Western powers afterward. Despite this initial reluctance to globalize, the 50 years that followed the Meiji Restoration in 1868 were a remarkable period of modernization, during which Japan adapted a myriad of foreign social and technological innovations to its own ends.[1]

This densely populated country with a relatively high level of education and social capacity quickly developed a comparative advantage in labor-intensive manufactures. Ironically, the "unequal treaties," which until 1911 severely limited the Japanese government's ability to impose import tariffs, may have actually fostered Japan's development by forcing the country to specialize along the lines of its comparative advantage. The limitation on tariffs also encouraged the use of other policy tools, such as low-interest loans and government procurement preferences for "strategic" industries, establishing a precedent that would continue for a cen-

---

1. See Allen (1946), Lockwood (1954), Hunsberger (1964), Morishima (1982), and Noguchi (1995) for informative economic histories.

tury. In the first instance of a recurrent pattern, Japanese exports were met by discriminatory trade restrictions imposed by trade partners fearing "import surges."[2]

The second half of the 20th century proved to be a second era of globalization, again driven by technological advance, this time enabled by the leadership of the United States. Reductions in trade barriers and transportation and communication costs has facilitated the globalization of the US economy during the past four decades, when the share of international trade (exports plus imports) in national income has nearly tripled from less than 10 percent in the late 1960s to nearly 30 percent in the late 1990s. As in the earlier period of globalization, Japan's initial response has been less than enthusiastic.

The expansion of international commerce, although contributing to prosperity, creates winners, losers, and political tensions. It is not surprising that the process of economic integration has been marked by intermittent periods of conflict. Moreover, Japan and the United States are dissimilar in history and political culture, and this dissimilarity itself has been a source of tension. The resolution of these conflicts has been strongly conditioned by the institutions of the international system. Central to this process has been the General Agreement on Tariffs and Trade (GATT) and its successor, the World Trade Organization.

Japan applied to join the GATT in 1952. Its application was initially opposed by a number of countries, but the United States strongly supported the application, and Japan was granted provisional membership in 1953 and full membership in 1955.[3] Once in the GATT, Japan participated in successive rounds of multilateral negotiations (including the Tokyo Round of the 1970s). In cases in which GATT panels found against Japan (e.g., in the case of some agricultural quotas), Japan had a good track record in complying with GATT panel decisions (though in some cases removal of trade restrictions was accompanied by the introduction of more direct forms of support). Adverse panel rulings were arguably a constructive form of *gaiatsu*, or foreign pressure, from a multilateral organization, which Japan had voluntarily joined and supported.

However, because of the GATT's ineffective dispute settlement procedure, many trade conflicts continued to be addressed bilaterally and often resolved in a discriminatory fashion. In addition to GATT-consistent forms of protection, such as antidumping measures, Japanese exports were subject to grey-area measures, such as Section 301 actions. The most extensive

---

2. See Saxonhouse (1996) for a history of charges of unfair trading practices against Japan.

3. At the time of Japan's admission to full membership in 1955, 14 countries, accounting for 34 percent of world imports, invoked Article 35 ("non-application") to limit their liberalization commitments. By 1960, Australia was the only industrialized country still invoking Article 35. It discontinued this practice in 1964 (Hunsberger 1964).

were the orderly marketing arrangements (OMAs) invented by Japan and the United States in the 1950s and applied to textile trade, the forerunner of the so-called voluntary restraint agreements (VRAs) or voluntary export restraints, which the United States and European Union applied to Japanese steel and automobile exports in the 1970s and 1980s.[4] In the 1990s, Japan and the United States would pioneer the use of voluntary import expansion agreements (VIEs) in an effort to expand foreign sales in the Japanese market.

Trade relations between the two countries reached a watershed in the mid-1990s. The formation in 1995 of the WTO and its improved dispute settlement mechanism severely circumscribed the ability of the United States to undertake unilateral policies against Japan. At roughly the same time, as described in chapters 2 and 3, it was becoming clear to policymakers in the United States that the two countries were likely to be entering a more than transitory period in which US macroeconomic performance was likely to be stronger than that of Japan, and that excessive weakness, not excessive strength, was the main risk to US prosperity emanating from Japan. Last, as will be discussed in chapter 6, developments on the security front encouraged a diminution of policy-driven economic conflict. These mutually reinforcing developments fostered a shift from the acrimonious trade relations of the first half of the decade to the era of relative quiescence that has continued through the present.

Bilateral Relations

For most of the postwar era, Japan-United States bilateral trade relations were marked by a gradual reduction of protection, which was achieved largely through the GATT system, with the imposition of GATT-inconsistent protection in particular sectors. In Japan these interventions were confined largely to the agricultural sector, whereas the United States imposed quantitative restrictions on Japanese exports of textiles, steel, color televisions, automobiles, and machine tools. Indeed, from the 1960s through the mid-1980s, bilateral trade relations in large part revolved around successive episodes of United States-imposed special protection against Japanese exports.

The Market-Oriented Sector-Specific Talks

In the United States, the system of Congressional acquiescence and oversight began to fray in the mid-1980s under the dual pressures of mounting

---

4. For those who think that there is anything new under the sun, see Hunsberger (1964), table 7-10, which lists Japanese goods subject to GATT-inconsistent price and/or quantitative restrictions in a number of markets in 1960. See de Melo and Tarr (1992, 1996) for estimates of the impact of more recent US quantitative restrictions.

US trade deficits and divided government.[5] The second presidential administration of Ronald Reagan essentially reversed field in trade policy and began a proactive attempt to redirect domestic political pressure from import protection to export expansion. The global manifestation of this policy shift was the launch in 1986 of the Uruguay Round of negotiations in the GATT; the Japan-specific initiative was the Market-Oriented Sector-Specific (MOSS) talks, begun in 1985, that covered telecoms equipment and services, other electronic products, wood products, and medical equipment and pharmaceuticals. Since this time, Japan and the United States have been in nearly constant parallel negotiations globally through the GATT-WTO, regionally through APEC, and bilaterally as well. The bilateral negotiations have been characterized by several constant themes: an intermittently shifting relative emphasis between broad issues of structural change in Japan versus the liberalization of specific priority sectors; the use of targets, benchmarks, or other quantitative indicators in sectoral negotiations; and the issue of potential discrimination against other trade partners.

The MOSS talks were not regarded as a great success by the US side. Although the electronics-sector negotiations were generally regarded as successful, achievement of improved market access in telecommunications, and medical equipment and pharmaceuticals, was hampered by regulatory barriers. The wood products negotiations, which threatened the interests of Japan's politically influential forestry and construction interests, were characterized by all-night negotiating sessions and brinkmanship, and in the end accomplished little.[6] The MOSS talks did not exhaust the universe of bilateral sectoral negotiations during this period, with the Semiconductor Trade Agreement of 1986 (STA) being the most prominent example of a sector-specific bilateral negotiation outside the MOSS framework.

The STA established a market share target for foreign semiconductor consumption in Japan, and, as such, was the first so-called VIE arrangement with a numerical target.[7] Unlike previous VERs, which accentuated the power of the government of Japan vis-à-vis its private firms by giving

---

5. See Kunkel (2001) for an excellent history of bilateral trade relations, focusing on the period from the second US presidential administration of Ronald Reagan through the second administration of Bill Clinton.

6. US negotiators dubbed the exercise the More of the Same Stuff (MOSS) negotiations. See Tyson (1992), Bergsten and Noland (1993), and ACCJ (2000) for evaluations of the MOSS talks.

7. See Bergsten and Noland (1993) and Flamm (1996) for more detailed analysis of the semiconductor trade agreement and quantitative estimates of its impact. Both studies conclude that the STA had the effect of boosting foreign firms' semiconductor sales in Japan. Alan Wolff, an active participant in representing the US semiconductor firms legally, concluded that the agreement was "entirely successful" and that now "there is peace in this product sector with no complaints on either side of the Pacific Ocean" (Wolff 1999, 4).

bureaucrats control over access to the lucrative US market, the Semiconductor Trade Agreement put the government of Japan in a very uncomfortable position. The Americans clearly regarded the market share target of 20 percent as a binding commitment subject to retaliation for noncompliance.[8] However, the government of Japan had no way of ensuring that the target would be met; and, in a stunning role reversal, was reduced to the position of supplicant to private firms.

In February 1987, Oki Electric salespeople were lured into documenting sales at less than fair market value in Hong Kong, violating the price floor provision of the STA. In an increasingly tense atmosphere, in which both houses of Congress voted to recommend retaliation, and the Defense Department issued an alarming report on the state of the US industry, the Reagan administration announced the imposition of $300 million in punitive tariffs on Japanese exports to the United States, which were to be removed only when the market share in Japan of foreign firm-produced semiconductors reached 20 percent.

Within Japan, some regarded the hapless Oki Electric salespeople as having been "framed," and the experience tilted political influence away from the "doves," who had argued for compromise with the United States, toward the "hawks," who advocated a firm if not confrontational posture. Although some Japanese negotiators claimed that the market-share figure was only a target and that sanctions would not be imposed while honest efforts were being undertaken, others criticized the agreement for sending Japan down the slippery slope of accepting market-distorting numerical targets.

In effect, the two countries came away from the negotiations having learned diametrically opposing "lessons." In Japan, the lesson was to forswear any future agreements containing numerical targets subject to penalties. In the United States, the market-share approach was seen as an effective way of opening markets in Japan. The following year, the Japan Task Force of the official Advisory Committee on Trade Negotiations, generalizing from the STA, recommended that the US government consider a policy of "temporary quantitative indicators" or market-share targets in its dealings with Japan. This divergence in views would echo through subsequent negotiations over autos and auto parts.

Within the United States, the MOSS and semiconductor talks coincided with a period of growing Congressional frustration over the trade deficit and a "do-nothing" Reagan administration. In 1986, legislation was introduced in the House and Senate that would have imposed an import surcharge on Japan, but the bills never came to a vote. The following year, Representative Richard Gephardt proposed the infamous "Gephardt

---

8. This target was included in a secret side letter to the original 1987 agreement. When the pact was renegotiated and revised in 1991, the target was made public and explicit.

Amendment," which would have authorized retaliation if countries with large bilateral surpluses (such as Japan) did not meet specified surplus reduction targets. The legislation passed the House, but never came to a vote in the Senate. In 1988, when Congress did pass trade legislation, it included a "Super 301" provision that authorized retaliation against countries that impeded US exports.[9]

The Structural Impediments Initiative

Faced with the task of implementing the 1988 Trade Law and both dubious and weary of negotiating sector by sector with uncertain effects, the incoming George Bush administration reevaluated US strategies and tactics. The result was the Structural Impediments Initiative (SII), a series of meetings held at the undersecretary level starting in September 1989, which was intended to address the underlying regulatory access barriers in Japan on a systemic basis. SII had the appearance of genuine two-way talks, in that both sides raised issues of concern, in part to assuage Japanese sensitivities after US unilateral retaliation in the semiconductor case.

For the United States, issues of concern included savings and investment behavior in Japan (in particular, the excess of Japanese savings over investment, which was thought to contribute to the bilateral surplus with the United States); land use policies, thought to contribute to high land and housing prices (and, inter alia, to high personal savings rates and the large current account surplus) and discourage foreign investment; exclusionary business practices and *keiretsu* relationships; the Japanese distribution system; and protection of intellectual property rights. Issues of Japanese concern included low US savings and investment, in particular public budget deficits; export controls and lack of export promotion; and inadequate research and development, education, and training, including adoption of the metric system. Despite the surface appearance of reciprocity, the United States played the role of the demandeur in these talks. The Japanese "demands" were pro forma, and no one seriously expected the Japanese government to significantly influence either US fiscal policy or the (non)adoption of the metric system.

---

9. The behavior of Japanese negotiators during this period inflamed matters further. ACCJ (2000) characterizes the attitudes of Japanese negotiators as "zero-sum," and, indeed, one senior Japanese official once characterized the point of trade negotiations as to "find your opponent's weak spot and prick it." Makoto Kuroda, a senior Japanese negotiator, caused an uproar in 1987 during the MOSS talks when he reportedly stated that US supercomputer firms would never be able to sell in Japan and that the United States might have to nationalize its producers to save them from the coming Japanese onslaught. Kuroda denied making this statement, which had been reported both in the press and US diplomatic cables. Manyin (2000) provides a nuanced assessment of more recent Japanese negotiating tactics, contrasting its "reactive" intransigence in agriculture with its proactive stance in antidumping.

Whether anyone seriously believed that the United States was going to change Japanese land use policies is debatable. To his credit, newly appointed US Ambassador to Japan Michael Armacost mobilized a public relations blitz in an attempt to convince the Japanese public that the negotiations were not a zero-sum game, and that, indeed, the US deregulation agenda would improve the living standard of the typical Japanese household.

The era of good feelings proved to be short-lived. In the end, SII proved to be largely an educational experience for high-level US policymakers, many of whom had had no personal experience with Japan. To the extent that progress was made, it tended to be on topics such as the distribution system, where a specific measure (the Large-Scale Retail Store Law) could be linked to a specific outcome (the ability of Toys 'R Us to successfully enter Japan). Japan undertook increases in public investment, strengthened its competition policy capability, and made modest changes in taxation and land use laws. SII appears to have had no impact on policy in the United States, though on at least one occasion the US side claimed that the Bush tax increase was undertaken as part of US SII commitments.[10] The Bush administration continued to negotiate sector-specific deals with Japan that embodied quantitative targets or indicators, most notably the second Semiconductor Trade Agreement (1991) and the auto and auto parts agreement of 1992.

The Framework Agreement

The incoming Bill Clinton administration placed an unprecedented emphasis on the US *economic* relationship with Japan when it took office in January 1993, reflecting the emphasis on economic issues ("It's the economy, stupid") in candidate Clinton's campaign. By this time, US enthusiasm for broad structural talks had burned out, and the new administration convened a series of high-level interagency meetings to formulate a new Japan strategy almost immediately upon taking office. The internal consensus that emerged from those meetings was that those earlier agreements that had most enhanced market access had included quantitative targets, such as the Semiconductor Trade Agreements (1986, 1991) and the auto and auto parts agreements (1987, 1992), all negotiated by the Republican Reagan or Bush administrations.[11] The vision that emerged from these deliberations was of a Framework Agreement—a multifaceted, bilateral negotiating framework that would cover macroeconomics, struc-

---

10. For more detailed assessments of SII, see Bergsten and Noland (1993), Schoppa (1997), Lincoln (1999), and ACCJ (2000).

11. As discussed in the following section, evidence exists that these agreements had been unusually effective.

Box 5.1 The Framework Agreement

The 1993 United States-Japan Framework for a New Economic Partnership called for Japan to make a significant reduction in its global current account surplus and then specified five "baskets" of sectoral and structural issues for negotiation. The first basket concerned "Government Procurement," including Japanese government procurement of telecoms and medical equipment. The second basket involved "Regulatory Reform and Competitiveness," including reforms in the financial and insurance sectors. The third basket was labeled "Other Major Sectors," although only one sector, autos and auto parts, was identified. The fourth basket, "Economic Harmonization," included subbaskets on FDI, buyer-supplier relationships (i.e., *keiretsu*), and intellectual property rights. The final basket was "Implementation of Existing Arrangements and Measures," which included discussion of the flat glass industry. The agreement then went on to mention areas of mutual cooperation in such fields as international environmental protection and international public health.

tural issues, and sectoral issues, in a series of "baskets" and "subbaskets" (see box 5.1). The new administration approached its Japanese counterparts about renewing negotiations under a new political framework.

When formal negotiations began in June 1993, the Japanese government was badly split. Having been burned by the Semiconductor Trade Agreement, MITI was dead set against any agreement that might contain numerical targets subject to penalties, while others, notably the Ministry of Foreign Affairs (MOFA), felt that it was important to reach some accommodation with the new administration.[12] In the end, lame-duck Prime Minister Kiichi Miyazawa instructed the Japanese negotiators to accept the possible use of quantitative indicators. The agreement to begin negotiations was signed by President Clinton and Prime Minister Miyazawa the following month.

The substantive issues of the Framework Agreement were not new—by this point, Japan and the United States had been negotiating over the same issues for the better part of a decade. The Clinton administration's treatment of these issues contained three innovations, however. First, economics was given new primacy. Historically, political and security affairs had received precedence in bilateral relations. Summit communiqués began with discussions of political and security issues, with economics shunted to the end. Bureaucratically, the US State and Defense departments typically weighed in against taking a confrontational line with Japan on trade issues.

In this regard, the Clinton policy marked a departure. The Framework Agreement contained no overarching statement about political or security

---

12. Following one presummit negotiating session in Tokyo, stunned US negotiators returning to their hotel witnessed a scuffle involving officials from MITI and MOFA in the lobby of the Okura Hotel.

relations, and the State Department-managed global cooperation issues (such as global environmental issues and international public health issues), which had figured prominently in the Bush-Miyazawa communiqué, were tacked on at the end. In subsequent speeches and testimony, Armacost's successor as ambassador to Tokyo, former Vice President Walter Mondale, led with economics. Mondale recruited a special economic advisor, Edward Lincoln of the Brookings Institution, to his embassy staff.

Internally, the bilateral economic relationship received unprecedented high-level political attention. The Clinton administration created a National Economic Council (NEC), analogous to the National Security Council (NSC), to demonstrate the importance of economics issues. The NEC's deputies group held long meetings on an at least a weekly basis, with participants at the undersecretary and assistant-secretary level of the NEC, the US Trade Representative (USTR), the Treasury, the State Department, the Commerce Department, and the Council of Economic Advisers normally in attendance. Representatives of the Department of Justice, the Department of Defense, the National Security Agency, the National Intelligence Council, and other agencies often participated.

Second, the new administration sought to regularize the use of quantitative targets or indicators, which had been used in an ad hoc, haphazard manner by the Reagan and Bush administrations. This was resolutely opposed by the Japanese side, which quite genuinely did not want to generalize the use of quantitative indicators with respect to market access in Japan. Although the imposition of VERs in the 1970s and 1980s had enhanced the power of the bureaucracy over the private sector by giving it direct administrative control over access to the lucrative US market, and effective control over the investment and expansion plans of Japanese firms, agreements to boost imports (VIEs) had the opposite effect—they put the bureaucracy at the mercy of private firms to fulfill its political commitments.[13] Moreover, most Japanese regarded VIEs as welfare-reducing, and regarded US claims as to their desirability with considerable skepticism.[14]

At the same time, in contrast to the skillful courting of Japanese public opinion by the Bush administration during the SII talks, the Clinton administration did a poor job of explaining exactly what it was after, other than to assert that it sought multiple quantitative benchmarks or indicators, with no single indicator dispositive of a failure to uphold the

---

13. For welfare analyses of VIEs, see Dinopoulos and Kreinin (1990), Greaney (1996, 1999), and Nagaoka (1997).

14. The typical argument was that if Japanese sourcing practices were so discriminatory, then why were they not obviously more self-defeating? If Japanese producers were not efficiently sourcing semiconductors or auto parts, then why were Japanese finished products using these goods—electronics and autos—globally competitive?

Box 5.2 Dueling letters

The Clinton administration's Japan policy during its first 2 years in office unleashed what one set of observers described as "a general wringing of hands." An early example of this was a 27 September 1993 open letter to President Clinton signed by 37 US economists, including four Nobel Prize winners, decrying US demands for "managed trade" and recommending that President Clinton "abandon" them. The letter set off a torrent of charges and countercharges made through private correspondence and the op-ed sections of leading newspapers. Japanese economists wrote a similar letter, and both the US and Japanese letters received extensive coverage in the Japanese press.

These missives were followed on 1 March 1994 by a letter to President Clinton and Prime Minister Hosokawa signed by 16 foreign policy luminaries, including a former US secretary of defense, which stated that the United States should "set aside demands for quantitative indicators." The administration had its defenders, however: on 14 February 1994, 78 US corporate chief executives, economists, and commentators, including a former secretary of labor, wrote the president expressing the view that a lasting, meaningful solution to the trade problem could only come through "innovative mechanisms geared toward results that can be measured in a number of ways."

Despite its reputation for degrading the multilateral trade system, the Clinton administration clearly understood that the Uruguay Round agreement under negotiation would effectively end the unilateral use of Section 301—and hence its ability to retaliate—a subtlety that its critics appear to have overlooked.

agreement, thereby absolving it of the charge that it was proposing VIEs.[15] In part, this reticence to publicly explain its goals was deliberate—the maintenance of ambiguity would frustrate the Japanese tactic of trying to drive wedges between different bureaucratic actors, as had successfully been done in the past, while enabling the lead US negotiator (at this time W. Bowman Cutter of the National Economic Council) the leeway to cut a deal in the end.

However, nature abhors no vacuum more than a political one, and in the absence of a convincing public articulation of its position, the Clinton administration's policy was effectively defined by its critics, who pilloried the United States for advocating "managed trade" (see box 5.2).[16] Although there is no real evidence that the Japanese negotiators shared the ideological predilections of some of the administration's critics, the Japanese side eagerly exploited the public relations problems of the Clin-

---

15. One could easily devise multiple indicators or indices of private- or public-sector efforts to improve market access short of market share targets, and devise responses short of trade retaliation. The Clinton administrations never did this, however.

16. Ironically, during the next presidential election, the Bob Dole campaign would lambaste the Clinton administration for being insufficiently resolute in its pursuit of numerical targets in trade with Japan.

ton administration. In contrast to the SII experience, the Japanese press was filled with editorials denouncing the Clinton line.[17]

The third innovation of the Clinton administration was the use of semi-annual meetings of the heads of government as action-forcing events. The notion, derived from past negotiating history, was that the two bureaucracies would negotiate, and then the Japanese Liberal Democratic Party (LDP) power brokers would be brought into the endgame to cut the deals and force the recalcitrant Japanese bureaucracy to accede to market-opening agreements.

This structured use of regular high-level political contact to reach agreement was probably not a bad approach to the Japan that had existed for the previous 40 years. Unfortunately for the Clinton administration, it came into office after the Japanese bubble had burst and just as Japan entered a period of political instability unprecedented in the postwar era, as the public disaffection with the LDP—which had been rising since a series of political scandals in the late 1980s—peaked. In February 1994, in the first heads of government meeting under the Framework Agreement, President Clinton did not meet with an LDP heavyweight capable of cutting a deal, but rather Prime Minister Morihiro Hosokawa, head of a weak, vaguely reformist, coalition government, and the first non-LDP prime minister since 1952.[18] Instead of being an action-forcing event, the Clinton-Hosokawa summit rebounded on the United States, forcing it to scale back its demands for fear of undercutting a nascent reformer and toppling the incumbent Japanese government. For the first time ever, Japan and the United States were unable to reach an economic agreement before a summit. Hosokawa's rejection of the US proposal on autos and parts was hailed by Japanese who regarded the semiconductor deal as a mistake, and lauded by some outside Japan as well.

The result, from the standpoint of the Clinton administration, was a disaster, though it gamely maintained the line that no agreement was better than a bad agreement and pledged to continue negotiations under the Framework Agreement umbrella. It had allocated a colossal amount of high-level political and bureaucratic resources to the bilateral economic relationship and had nothing to show for it. It had been unable to secure Japanese agreement on the use of quantitative indicators. The "managed-trade" charge, whatever its validity, was sticking, and the United States was losing the transpacific public relations campaign. The policy had alarmed third parties, such as Australia and the European Union, which feared being adversely affected by discriminatory deals.[19]

---

17. See Schoppa (1997).

18. As an indication of the unsettled state of Japanese politics, Clinton would go on to meet with seven more Japanese prime ministers during his two terms in office.

19. In contrast to the 1987 and 1992 auto agreements negotiated by the Reagan and Bush administrations, respectively, the Clinton administration was scrupulous about framing its demands in nondiscriminatory multilateral terms. Greaney (2000), in fact, finds evidence

In the aftermath of the Clinton-Hosokawa summit, the USTR reasserted its historic primacy in trade negotiations, and the focus of US attention shifted to more narrow, mercantilist sectoral concerns. This reached its apotheosis (or nadir, depending on one's perspective) in the 1995 confrontation over the hardy perennial, autos and auto parts.

Autos and auto parts featured prominently for a number of reasons. These were largely unionized industries with strong connections to Washington. Because of previous negotiations, a bureaucratic infrastructure had developed to handle auto issues and act as a point of contact for the US industry. Finally, when Clinton took office in January 1993, an overhaul of the US health care system led by First Lady Hillary Clinton was the highest political priority of the incoming administration. President Clinton concluded that he would need the support of Representative John Dingell, an auto industry ally and chair of the powerful House Commerce Committee, if he were to get health care reform legislation through Congress. For these reasons, the auto sector received a highly sympathetic hearing from the Clinton administration on trade matters, and alone was awarded its own "basket" in the Framework Agreement.

Yet despite the collapse of the Clinton healthcare initiative in March 1994, the USTR and the Commerce Department continued to press Japan on autos, demanding that it undertake measures that would make it easier for Japanese automobile dealers to handle foreign cars, increase the use of foreign auto parts in Japanese auto assembly (including by Japanese "transplant" factories in the United States), and ease the use of foreign parts in the aftersales market.[20] After failing to reach an agreement with Japan before a self-imposed 1 October 1994 deadline, the administration took the unusual step of self-initiating a Section 301 case against Japan. The subsequent negotiations made little progress, and in May 1995, President Clinton announced two actions: the filing of a WTO case, and the imposition of 100 percent punitive sanctions against Japanese luxury cars, effective immediately, but with actual duties not to be collected until a deadline at the end of June. This time, however, events did not follow the old script.

The dispute-resolution system of the GATT was dysfunctional: there were no time-bound procedures, and "defendants" could block negative

---

of possible trade diversion stemming from the earlier 1987 auto agreement, providing some justification for third-party concerns.

20. The first two issues directly involved competition policy issues and the third a regulatory matter. In principle, auto dealers in Japan are independent businesses and can handle cars produced by different manufacturers. It was alleged that, in reality, the dealers faced retribution from their dominant suppliers if they sold competitors' models, and the JFTC had never made an antitrust issue of this. As a consequence, only a minuscule share of dealers handled competing brands or foreign products. The second issue involved the vertical relationships between Japanese assemblers and their suppliers. The third issue involved regulations involving safety inspections and certification procedures that allegedly had the effect of encouraging garages to use original equipment parts in making repairs.

dispute panel reports. As a consequence, dispute settlement amounted to a protracted process of "shaming" an offending signatory into compliance, which was occasionally effective, for example, in the case of some agricultural trade disputes involving Japan. But a determined opponent could block the acceptance of a dispute panel report, and the GATT had never actually authorized retaliation for noncompliance with a panel ruling. Understandably, Japan was passive in its use of the GATT's admittedly weak dispute-settlement mechanism, seldom bringing complaints to the GATT.

The establishment of a new dispute-settlement mechanism was one of the crowning achievements of the Uruguay Round. It provided for time-bound procedures, and ended the practice of defendants vetoing unfavorable panel reports. Instead, panel reports were to be accepted unless overturned by consensus.

So when the United States unilaterally announced retaliation without the authorization of the WTO, Japan broke with its past passivity and responded by announcing that it would file a countercase against the United States, arguing that the imposition of punitive sanctions without WTO authorization amounted to a violation of the US tariff binding under the Uruguay Round agreement. For most Japanese, the auto dispute was puzzling. Japanese autos had a well-deserved reputation for excellence, and if US autos did not sell in Japan, it must be because their characteristics (size, low fuel efficiency, left-side steering) made them inappropriate for Japanese conditions. Most critically, there was no constituency in Japan in favor of compromise with the US demands for a VIE. Instead of the US appeals to enlightened Japanese self-interest under the SII, these demands were regarded more as a manifestation of the self-interested desires of particular US firms.

A series of tense negotiations ensued. One day before the retroactive collection of duties was to begin, the United States blinked. A toothless, face-saving compromise in which the United States achieved none of its core goals was announced. (On the critical issue of quantitative indicators, the joint announcement issued by Kantor and Hashimoto contained the amazing disavowal that "Minister Hashimoto said the Government of Japan has had no involvement in this calculation because it is beyond the scope and responsibility of the government. He said that USTR's estimates are solely its own.")[21] Both countries dropped their respective WTO cases.[22]

---

21. "Joint Announcement by Ryutaro Hashimoto, Minister of International Trade and Industry of Japan, and Michael Kantor, United States Trade Representative, Regarding the Japanese Auto Companies' Plans," 28 June 1995. http://www.mofa.go.jp/region/n-america/us/economy/date/archive/26_7.html.

22. Levinsohn (1997) concludes on the basis of an interesting econometric analysis that European, not US, producers would have been the primary beneficiaries had the sanctions been imposed. In comparison with this self-defeating imposition of protection, the actual

Politically, the Clinton administration was able to get away with this incredible climb-down in part because the appreciation of the yen over the previous two years had led to a surge in US exports to Japan (including in autos and parts) and a narrowing of the bilateral trade gap.

The confrontation over autos amounted to the death knell of US unilateralism. For reasons described in chapters 2 and 3, the failure on autos coincided with a period in which US policymakers more and more viewed the major threat to the US economy emanating from Japan to be one of weakness—not strength. There was concern that trade tensions could actually contribute to negative macroeconomic outcomes in Japan, for example, by contributing to exchange rate misalignment. Last, as will be discussed in chapter 6, the 1994 nuclear confrontation with North Korea and the brutal rape of a Japanese schoolgirl by US servicemen in Okinawa the following year contributed to a reemphasis on security issues in the bilateral relationship and a desire to diminish conflict in the trade realm.[23]

The result was a period of relative quiescence that continues to this day.[24] The locus of US attention reverted from sectoral issues back to structural issues with the 1997 Enhanced Initiative on Deregulation and Competition Policy, the successor to the Framework Agreement. Ironically, foreign penetration into the Japanese auto and auto parts sectors subsequently increased substantially in the late 1990s, primarily as a result of merger and acquisition activity associated with financial difficulties in Japan, not policy actions.

The Economic Partnership for Growth

The accession to power of the Junichiro Koizumi cabinet in Japan and the George W. Bush administration in the United States led to a reformulation of bilateral talks, which were announced at the Bush-Koizumi summit in June 2001. The two governments announced a United States-Japan Economic Partnership for Growth, which in significant respects was built on the 1997 Enhanced Initiative on Deregulation and Competition Policy

---

outcome—a weak trade-promotion pact—may not have been a bad outcome, despite its origin in a trade threat.

23. See Schoppa (1997) and Lincoln (1999) on the trade-security linkage during this period. See Noland (2000a, chap. 4) for an account of the North Korea confrontation.

24. It is interesting that the one case that followed the old threat and counterthreat script was a 1997 dispute involving harbor services. Maritime services were not covered under the General Agreement on Trade and Services (GATS), and the main protagonists were each country's respective maritime commissions, not the WTO-socialized USTR or MITI. The dispute was resolved after the US Federal Maritime Commission (FMC) threatened to block US ports to Japanese ships unless its Japanese counterpart reformed its discriminatory practices. It has been argued that the only reason that the US FMC was able to make such a credible threat was that it is an independent agency and outside the direct control of the White House (Creel 1997; Stokes 2000).

Box 5.3 The Economic Partnership for Growth

The 2001 Economic Partnership for Growth established a subcabinet group that would meet at least on an annual basis to oversee a multifaceted engagement process. The main innovation of the partnership was to formally involve private-sector representatives in the talks, through a "Private Sector/Government Commission," a body that would meet before the subcabinet group to provide input and include private-sector representatives selected by their respective governments.

At the working level, the partnership created four "initiatives." A Regulatory Reform and Competition Policy Initiative largely reaffirmed the existing efforts carried out under the Enhanced Initiative. Working groups would address cross-sectoral issues, such as competition policy and commercial code issues, whereas four sector-specific working groups would be devoted to telecommunications, information technologies, energy, and medical devices and pharmaceuticals. (The housing working group of the 1997 Enhanced Initiative was disbanded.) Each of these groups would incorporate private-sector input on an ad hoc basis.

Other initiatives established under the partnership included a Financial Dialogue on macroeconomic and financial-sector issues. An Investment Initiative on issues relating to FDI was created to address the issues of transparency, corporate governance, and factor markets, which have been identified as the main impediments to foreign investment in Japan. The Trade Forum was established to discuss trade issues and serve as an "early warning mechanism" for emerging problems. The desirability of private-sector participation in each of these initiatives was recognized, although the modalities of such involvement were left undefined.

(see box 5.3). It is not surprising that the partnership could be regarded as a continuation of previous bilateral initiatives. Like the Agreed Framework—the product of the Clinton administration's incoming attempt to set the agenda in its economic relationship with Japan—the partnership addresses the mix of macroeconomic, structural, and trade issues that the two governments have discussed bilaterally for years. Indeed, the working group on medical devices goes all the way back to the MOSS talks conducted by the Reagan administration and the Yasuhiro Nakasone cabinet during the mid-1980s.

The partnership does differ in several ways from the earlier Clinton policy. First, economic issues are once again clearly taking a back seat to traditional security concerns. Second, even within the economics sphere, the partnership is much looser than the Agreed Framework. Under the partnership, meetings are to be held on an "at least annual" basis, not more regularly as was the case of the Agreed Framework. Unlike the Agreed Framework, meetings of the heads of governments are not programmed into the package to be action-forcing events. Third, the partnership contains no language with respect to quantitative targets.

The partnership breaks with the past by formally involving the private sectors of each country. In some sense, this merely makes formal what has been informal practice all along. Moreover, this could be constructive, to the extent that private-sector participants may have a better grasp of more and more important technical issues raised by these discussions than their public-sector counterparts. However, private participation is circumscribed in notable ways under the agreement: each government gets to select its private-sector participants, and the discussion agenda is set ex ante by each government. Indeed, the handpicking of the private-sector representatives would appear to limit the usefulness of the exercise. The two governments could be predictably expected to select representatives whose corporate agendas mirror their respective government's negotiating positions. In effect, the private representatives could be expected to largely reproduce the zero-sum nature of the negotiations. It would be more constructive (though potentially more embarrassing for the officials involved) if the US (or Japanese) government were able to select some Japanese (or US) private participants. Each government then would be expected to select some foreign "allies," and thus more realistically reproduce the crosscutting cleavages that exist with respect to these issues.

WTO Dispute Settlement

Since the WTO's establishment, Japan has initiated complaints at a rate of slightly more than one per year (see appendix table A.1 at the back of the book). About half the cases involve the United States, and about half involve the automobile industry in some way. WTO panels have regularly upheld Japanese complaints.

At the same time, Japan's partners have taken it to the WTO at a rate of about two cases per year (appendix table A.2). As is often the case in the WTO, many of these disputes are settled bilaterally without going through the complete adjudication process. In the cases that have resulted in panel rulings, Japan has lost two (the complaint about discriminatory taxation on alcoholic beverages brought by Canada, the European Union, and the United States, and an agricultural quarantine case brought by the United States) and has won one, the (in)famous Kodak-Fuji case on photographic film. Japan has also used its third-party rights in 25 cases, mostly involving the United States and/or the European Union (appendix table A.3).

The United States, perhaps reflecting its relative abundance of lawyers and cultural compatibility with formal legal proceedings, has been the leading participant in the WTO dispute-settlement system, being involved as a complainant, defendant, or third party in more than half of WTO cases (appendix tables A.4-A.6). Likewise, it has prevailed in more than 60 percent of the cases that have been settled, in the sense that the WTO panel has ruled in its favor, or the issue has been settled bilaterally before the panel issued its report. Of the 27 cases in which the United States brought complaints to the WTO, the United States has prevailed in 24. In cases related to Japan, the United States has triumphed in cases involving discriminatory taxation of liquor, import restrictions on certain varieties of fruit (including apples and cherries), and protection of intellectual property rights with respect to sound recordings. Its sole loss came in the celebrated Kodak-Fuji film case.

The photographic paper and film industry is a classic oligopoly: increasing returns to scale in manufacturing and a heavy emphasis on new product development effectively deter new competitors from entering the market, and four firms—Kodak (United States), Fuji (Japan), Agfa (Germany), and Konica (Japan)—dominate the global marketplace. Kodak and Fuji alone account for nearly three-quarters of the photographic film market globally, with each maintaining a market share of roughly 70 percent in their respective home markets, and each accounting for roughly a third of third-market sales (with the remainder going to the competitive fringe manufacturers).

According to sophisticated econometric research by Goldberg and Knetter (2000), Fuji had been gaining in competitiveness relative to Kodak for 25 years. Some of the proximate causes are not hard to identify. After Polaroid introduced its revolutionary SX-70 instant color film camera in 1972, Kodak spent lavishly to develop its strikingly similar alternative, which it introduced in 1976. Polaroid sued for patent infringement, and in 1985 a federal judge ordered Kodak out of the market and levied a $925 million fine, the largest judgment ever in a patent infringement case. Kodak would dissipate more of its capital in a 1988 takeover of Sterling Drugs, which the company would sell off 6 years later.

In the meantime, Fuji introduced 400-speed film in 1976, at the time faster than any Kodak manufactured. And when Kodak declined to sponsor the 1984 Los Angeles Olympics, Fuji stepped in and used the opportunity as a springboard to expand its distribution capacity and market share in Kodak's home market. By the early 1990s, Fuji's sales per employee were nearly twice Kodak's.

In August 1993, reeling from the Fuji onslaught, Kodak filed an antidumping petition, alleging that Fuji and Konica were dumping color photographic paper components from Japan and Fuji's subsidiary in the Netherlands. In March 1994, a preliminary determination by the US Department of Commerce assessed dumping margins in excess of 300 percent. (The Commerce Department was able to assess a high margin even on the products coming from the Netherlands by using a loophole that was subsequently closed in the Uruguay Round agreement.) In August 1994, Fuji and Konica signed an agreement in which they agreed to raise their export prices in return for the suspension of the antidumping case. Exports of color photographic paper to the United States plunged. At little cost, Kodak had gained some temporary breathing room in its most important market, although in response to the dumping suit, Fuji accelerated its construction of a state-of-the-art facility in Greenwood,

South Carolina. The plant would come online in March 1996, and within a year, Fuji's color paper market share in the United States would exceed its presuit level (Komuro 1998).

George M.C. Fisher, the former chair and chief executive officer (CEO) of Motorola, became the CEO of Kodak in December 1993. Fisher had been a central figure in Motorola's struggle to open the Japanese cellular phone market, and he proceeded to apply the same strategy at Kodak. In May 1995, apparently without consulting the JFTC or the US Justice Department, the relevant competition policy authorities, Kodak filed a Section 301 petition with USTR, alleging that the Japanese government policies (or its inaction) had denied Kodak its rights under bilateral and multilateral agreements to which the United States and Japan were signatories.

The USTR accepted the petition, initiating an investigation in July and requesting bilateral consultations with the Japanese government. With USTR's assent, Kodak had in essence "privatized" trade policy, turning an antitrust case in which it was unlikely to prevail in either jurisdiction into an international trade dispute.[25] This time, however, emboldened by their victory in the auto case, the Japanese government refused to engage, repeating its oft-stated position that it would not negotiate under the threat of sanctions, and arguing that Kodak's allegations involved private-party behavior, so it would be improper to engage in government-to-government negotiations before an investigation by the JFTC. (The JFTC would subsequently self-initiate its own investigation and conclude that Fuji had remedied anticompetitive practices for which it had been cited in 1989, and that there was no evidence of ongoing anticompetitive behavior.)[26] The USTR proceeded with its investigation, and concluded in June 1996 that Japanese government policies had indeed placed an unreasonable burden on US commerce.

This finding alone would have justified retaliation under US domestic law. However, the USTR faced the same dilemma as it had a year earlier in the auto case: if it proceeded with unilateral retaliation, Japan would surely take it to the WTO for violating its Uruguay Round commitments. Moreover, in mid-1996, the Clinton administration wanted neither a visible confrontation with Japan nor an obvious failure—going to the WTO

---

25. According to one legal scholar, Merit Janow, Kodak could have taken up the case in the United States under the Sherman Act. However, evidentiary standards are typically more stringent in antitrust cases than in trade cases, and it is unlikely that Kodak would have won in the US courts (Greaney 1997). Kodak did eventually bring a complaint to the JFTC.

26. The JFTC did recommend changes in some Fuji business practices, however. E.g., it indicated that Fuji should revamp its system of security deposits that it required from primary wholesalers because the high interest that it paid on these deposits could act as a disincentive for the wholesalers to handle competitors' merchandise.

would permit the administration to kick the can down the road, past the looming November elections.

So, this time, instead of threatening unilateral retaliation, citing Articles 3 (national treatment), 10 (transparency), and 23 (nullification and impairment), the USTR filed its own WTO case, alleging that Japanese government "countermeasures" had denied the United States its benefits from Japan's liberalization commitments on photographic paper and film in the Kennedy (1967), Tokyo (1979), and Uruguay (1994) rounds. (In the Uruguay Round, Japan completely removed tariffs on photographic film and paper.) The government of Japan denied all US claims. The European Union exercised its third-party rights and formally endorsed the US complaint.

A dispute-settlement panel was established in September 1996, and in April 1997, the United States submitted to the panel a nearly 200-page brief, together with 20,000 pages of documentation. The panel then heard arguments, and it issued its preliminary ruling in December 1997 and its final report in January 1998. It makes interesting, if voluminous, reading.

On almost every single point of principle, the panel found in favor of the United States. Rejecting Japan's position, it found that administrative guidance and private actions could be considered "countermeasures." It rejected Japan's argument that the alleged nullification and impairment should be limited to Uruguay Round commitments, finding that alleged violations of prior GATT commitments could be a legitimate target of complaint. In most instances, it rejected Japanese claims that the United States should have been aware of the measures that Japan was undertaking at the time that the tariff agreements were negotiated, and hence the United States could not claim that these nullified or impaired expected benefits. This was not a "strict-constructionist" panel. On matters of principle, the panel interpreted its mandate broadly. Ironically, the sovereignty-obsessed United States had done more than any other WTO signatory to widen the scope of the nullification and impairment provision.

The problem, from a US perspective, was that it had a weak case in the particulars. It claimed that a broadly worded 1967 Cabinet decision on economic policy in the wake of Japan's capital account liberalization amounted to a liberalization countermeasure in the photographic paper and film market. The panel rejected this contention. It alleged that 1970 MITI guidelines on photographic film impaired the competitive strategies of foreign producers in the Japanese market (e.g., by setting uniform transaction terms with wholesalers) and encouraged the establishment of single-brand wholesalers. The panel rejected these claims, observing that the guidelines were "origin-neutral" (i.e., they did not discriminate between Japanese and foreign producers) and that single-brand wholesalers had been the norm in both Japan and the United States before 1970.[27]

---

27. By limiting the ability of potential entrants to discount prices and pursue other innovative strategies, this regulation could be thought of as inhibiting entry to the benefit of incumbent

Similarly, the United States claim that a 1971 Basic Plan for systematizing the distribution system amounted to a barrier was rejected on the grounds that this was a general government plan to improve efficiency in the distribution of all products, not just photographic products, and in any event was neutral with respect to the origin of the products. The panel report goes on to similarly reject the US allegations regarding a laundry list of other Japanese government measures, the most recent of which was undertaken in 1975.

Actions speak louder than words. Despite the feigned outrage at the panel report (USTR Charlene Barshefsky would describe the panel report as displaying "an instinct for the capillary"), the United States did not appeal the panel's report, which was accepted in April 1997. It was the first time in the WTO's brief history that a losing party had not appealed a panel decision.[28] Some reformers in Japan also expressed disappointment, hoping that an adverse ruling would have spurred further deregulation efforts.

To the extent that Kodak and other foreign producers are disadvantaged in the Japanese market, this seems to be more related to capital-market imperfections manifested in the apparent inability to purchase a Japanese wholesaler and thus crack the Fuji-dominated distribution system than market interventions of the Japanese government per se.[29] (Presumably, establishing a wholly new distribution system would be another, albeit highly costly, option.) The impression one gets is that Kodak and Fuji behave like two Cournot duopolists, which more or less control their respective domestic markets and compete in third-country markets. From a national standpoint, policy has two goals—assist your firm in exploiting the external market, while at the same time limiting its monopolistic tendencies in the domestic market. The textbook answer in this case is to subsidize production (to precommit to high output levels and force the foreign rival up its cost curve) and use taxes to make the domestic firm behave like a perfectly competitive industry.

Because we cannot subsidize production, barriers to entry in each of the (large) domestic markets could be a second-best precommitment

---

producers. The issue from the standpoint of the United States was that the incumbents were domestic producers and the potential entrants were foreigners.

28. During the early stages of the Vietnam War, Senator George Aiken advised that the United States should declare victory and withdraw. The US government's actions after the film case would have made the good senator proud: it announced that it would treat Japanese representations that it did not hamper foreign access in the film market nor tolerate anticompetitive behavior as formal commitments and established an interagency task force to monitor these "commitments." In its subsequent reports, the task force credited itself with improving market conditions in Japan.

29. The fact that Kodak had earlier severed its tie to its own exclusive distributor further reduced the credibility of its case.

mechanism. It appears that both Kodak and Fuji do a reasonable job of creating such barriers. In this setup, penetrating the rival's home market has a real zero-sum aspect to it and would be resisted accordingly. At the same time, it should be noted that firm and national interests are not identical, and neither country appears to do a good job at disciplining pricing internally. Although it might be in the US (or Japanese) interest to increase Kodak's (or Fuji's) monopoly power vis-à-vis the rest of the world, it is not in the US (or Japanese) interest to increase Kodak's (or Fuji's) monopoly power domestically.

In this light, Kodak's proposed remedy of a Section 301 case made sense: Two likely outcomes were either some increase in access to Japan or retaliation against Fuji in the US market, either of which would suit Kodak's purposes (although Kodak denied that it was interested in protection through retaliation). However, from a national standpoint, joint antitrust might be a preferable policy, to discourage monopolistic pricing in each domestic market, but the JFTC evinced no interest. Likewise, the use of taxes to discipline Kodak's behavior in the domestic market would seem unlikely. From a public-policy standpoint, the question then arises: would the United States be better off pursuing antitrust action against Kodak here in the United States? The issue would be whether the gains to US consumers through lower prices would offset the damage to Kodak's competitiveness abroad.

From Kodak's standpoint, the question is: Was it worth the gamble? It spent millions on private litigation, and indeed, the potential gains to the firm from a successful prosecution of its case were considerable, yet Fuji's demonstrated ability to successfully compete from US facilities raises the issue of just how large or permanent those private gains would have been.

With the notable exception of the Kodak-Fuji case, the United States has prevailed in the vast majority of cases that it has brought to the WTO. Perhaps it is not surprising that the United States has fared less well when it has been in the dock. WTO panels have ruled against it in 8 out of 17 cases. Most notably, Japan and others have successfully challenged the United States on aspects of its antidumping law.

The Future WTO Agenda

Although the new dispute-settlement system represents a noteworthy advance over the old GATT system, the WTO faces a number of challenges. The most immediate are what to do in the aftermath of the debacle at the Seattle trade ministerial, and how to integrate China into the organization. In the long run, issues of personnel and substantive agenda will reemerge.

The 1999 attempt to launch a new round of multilateral trade negotiations in Seattle was driven by a political compromise left over from the

Uruguay Round, rather than any global groundswell for trade liberalization.[30] To secure a conclusion to the last round of negotiations, the United States accepted less than complete reform of agricultural trade practices on the part of the European Union, in return for a commitment to revisit the issue in 1999. Services trade liberalization was left similarly incomplete. This is the origin of the so-called built-in agenda of talks on agriculture and services. A certain sense of urgency was attached to the negotiations over agriculture, inasmuch as the "peace clause," which prohibits WTO cases against certain practices (principally undertaken by the European Union and United States), is due to expire at the end of 2003.

This built-in agenda shaped participants' negotiating strategies heading into Seattle. From a Japanese negotiator's standpoint, the built-in agenda was a loser. In agriculture, Japan typically sides with the European Union against the United States and the Cairns Group of self-identified nonsubsidizing agricultural exporters. It originated the term "multifunctionality" as an excuse to maintain internal supports to agriculture. It prosaically observed that its current tariff levels "reflect particular domestic situations" and expressed an interest in strengthening disciplines on the use of export restrictions, reflecting its concerns about food security. In the area of trade in services, Japan is relatively uncompetitive in much of the services sector, and has not pushed as hard as the European Union or United States for liberalization in this area.

Instead, the European Union, Japan, and many other observers argued that a successful round would have to have three characteristics: it would have to be "comprehensive," it would have to be a single undertaking, and it would have to strengthen rules and disciplines as well as market access. The notion of a "comprehensive round" was motivated by the recognition that Japan needed to broaden the agenda to hide its inevitable concessions in agriculture, and use gains in other areas to make an agreement emerging from the new negotiations politically palatable at home.[31] Specifically, Japan made tightening the antidumping provisions a high

---

30. Just the opposite: The developing countries believed that they had been taken to the cleaners during the Uruguay Round, the previous round of negotiations, and were skeptical about taking on further trade liberalization commitments, and far better prepared to defend their interests in these negotiations. Similarly, Asia was still recovering from its financial crisis, and policymakers there believed they already had enough issues with which to grapple. Japan showed its lack of interest in further trade liberalization by blocking the Early Voluntary Sectoral Liberalization effort in the Asia-Pacific Economic Cooperation forum by opposing forestry and fisheries liberalization. And in the United States, President Clinton was unable to secure "fast-track" trade negotiating authority from the US Congress. See Schott (2000) for further details.

31. Japan could not expect major mercantilist gains from service liberalization (the other component of the built-in agenda) to balance its concessions in agriculture. Put crudely in the mercantilist terms of WTO negotiations, the built-in agenda offered the United States two winning issues and Japan two losing issues.

priority (i.e., strengthening "rules and disciplines"), and in the weeks leading up to the meeting, had stitched together a broad international coalition that clearly had the United States on the defensive.[32] On agriculture, Japan found an eager ally in the European Union, which jumped onto the multifunctionality bandwagon to distract attention from its more and more indefensible export subsidies.

In the run-up to the meeting, the Clinton administration—which had been refused the authority to negotiate on the customary "fast-track" basis by Congress and hence could not be confident of the approval of any concessions that it might make during the negotiations, showed little flexibility—largely trying to limit the agenda to agriculture and services, where the United States would not be expected to make major concessions. It simultaneously tried to force onto the agenda relatively new and controversial issues such as the relationship between trade and labor standards, and trade and environmental concerns (see box 5.4).[33] As MITI correctly observed, such an approach jeopardized progress on even the built-in agenda, because it left most participants with no incentive to move forward (MITI 1999a). Once in Seattle, officialdom was caught off-guard by the degree of public mobilization against the talks by a wild melange of protest groups, whose motivations and aspirations appeared at times only tenuously connected to the issue at hand. And despite police intelligence, the authorities in Seattle appeared unwilling or unable to comprehend the violent tendencies of some of these groups.[34]

Yet in the end, it was the traditional dispute between the European Union and the United States over agriculture—the same dispute that had nearly scuttled the launch of the earlier round of negotiations and nearly torpedoed those negotiations a half-dozen times—rather than the shenanigans of the Raging Grannies or the Ruckus Society that sank the Seattle negotiations. Japan appeared content to hold the European Union's coat

---

32. See Manyin (2000).

33. The United States also pushed for a number of "immediate deliverables," such as a second information technology agreement, government procurement transparency, and an e-commerce tariff moratorium.

34. The Clinton administration's behavior in Seattle was perplexing. It sought to promote the labor and environmental issues. But President Clinton's statement in Seattle that he would like to see economic sanctions used against countries not meeting labor standards took his Cabinet members in Seattle by surprise, and destroyed any possibility of making progress on the issue. Indeed, conversations with a number of developing-country negotiators indicated that the president's remark, together with the behavior of the demonstrators, strengthened their resolve to resist US demands—with some regarding the demonstrators as an officially sanctioned attempt to physically intimidate foreign negotiators. The Japanese delegation, led by its foreign minister, could not attend the opening ceremony or plenary session because the local police could not provide an escort from the hotel where the Japanese delegation was staying to the convention center.

Box 5.4 Trade and the environment

Both Japan and the United States favor the inclusion of environmental issues in the world trade system, and Japan floated a proposal in 1996 to allow WTO signatories to use trade sanctions to enforce multilateral environmental protection agreements, such as the Montreal Protocol on chlorofluorocarbon emissions. The Japanese proposal was unable to gain many adherents among either developing or industrial countries, and the issue of integrating environmental concerns into the world trade system continues to bedevil the WTO. The two countries have also come into conflict over US unwillingness to adhere to the Kyoto Protocol on global warming.

Bilaterally, the two countries have clashed on issues relating to endangered species, most prominently whales. By the mid-1980s, global whale populations were on the brink of collapse, and in 1985 the International Whaling Commission (IWC), of which both Japan and the United States are members, voted a moratorium on commercial whaling. Iceland, Japan, and Norway continued to hunt whales on a limited basis for scientific purposes, as is permitted under IWC rules. Whale populations began to recover, and in 1992, these three countries petitioned the IWC to rescind the moratorium on whaling. Their 1992 petition was rejected, as have been subsequent attempts to weaken the moratorium at each annual meeting of the IWC.

Japanese hunting for "scientific" purposes has been criticized by other IWC members, including the United States, which has restricted Japanese fishing activities in its waters, and at times has threatened to impose sanctions. In light of its failure to weaken the whaling moratorium, Tokyo indicated that it would use its foreign aid budget to encourage some small island nations to join the IWC to support Japan's position, and by the 2000 and 2001 meetings of the organization, Japan, in a coalition with six Caribbean countries, was able to block an Australia-New Zealand proposal to impose a total ban on whaling in the South Pacific. Indeed, at the 2001 meeting, Japanese official Masayuki Komatsu caused a furor when, in an interview with the Australian Broadcasting Corporation, he admitted that Japan actively sought to buy votes with its aid program. (Calling the minke whale "the cockroach of the ocean" did not help matters.)

In the end, the whale imbroglio may be solved by scientific research—although not of the kind Japan normally invokes. A study presented to the IWC by a Japanese academic found that whale meat sold in Japan contained high levels of dioxin and two other carcinogens. Health concerns may ultimately prove to be the savior of the whales.

on agriculture, and its sin was one of omission—passively allowing an opportunity to slip away—rather than one of commission.

In the aftermath of Seattle, the effort to launch a new round foundered. The European Union, and to a lesser extent Japan, moved to right the organization, restarting the agricultural and services negotiations (although the European Union initially blocked the consensus on selecting the chair of the agriculture talks) and undertook a series of "confidence-building" measures, including the extension of the 31 December 1999 deadline for developing countries to implement WTO agreements on intellectual property, investment measures, and customs valuation.[35] For its part, the United States pursued the quixotic agenda of relaunching the round before the Okinawa summit in June 2000, although some within the US government regarded a Japanese proposal to set up a distinguished-persons group to assess the most propitious path for future progress as a delaying tactic.

Prospects for a new WTO round improved following the inauguration of the George W. Bush administration in 2001. The United States dropped its insistence on a limited agenda and accepted the comprehensive agenda of the European Union and Japan (Lamy and Zoellick 2001). The G-7 leaders also gave the initiation of a new WTO round a push at their July 2001 summit in Genoa. Indeed, with the major trading countries agreeing on the broad outlines of an agenda, the major stumbling block to a successful launch of a new round of WTO negotiations at the ministerial in Doha, Qatar, would appear to be opposition by the developing countries.

In this respect, the Bush administration still has not secured fast-track negotiating authority (renamed trade promotion authority), and a domestic consensus on the problematic "social clause" issues remains unattained. It could well be the case that the difficulty of reaching an agreement with the developing countries and the lack of fast-track authority on the part of the United States will mean that the WTO membership will nominally launch a new round in Doha, but that this will, in effect, simply amount to an agreement to formally continue negotiating the agenda.

Beyond the built-in agenda of agriculture and services, the industrial-products trade agenda is dominated by traditional tariff cutting and the need to better integrate antidumping and competition-policy rules. Intellectually, the tariff-cutting exercise is a well-understood process, amenable to traditional WTO tariff-offer negotiations, and it is simply a matter of reaching international consensus on an acceptable formula. The problem here is political rather than conceptual—in the United States, the textile industry is already angling to get its products excluded from the tariff-cutting process, and in Japan, the government torpedoed the Early Voluntary Sectoral Liberalization (EVSL) in APEC over some minimal primary products tariffs. Yet even these obstacles are amenable to deal making—not a trivial task, but not one fraught with the conceptual problems of the other agenda items.

Reform of antidumping rules and the creation of a more coherent international competition-policy regime present a great challenge. Japan has led the international coalition demanding reform of antidumping proce-

---

35. The urgency of this effort seemed to be tied to the likelihood of China's accession to membership after the successful conclusion of the bilateral talks between China and the European Union, with Pascal Lamy, the EU commissioner for trade, publicly admitting that it would be easier to conclude the next round of WTO negotiations if China were not a full participant.

dures, which it regards, with significant justification, simply as process protectionism. Its major opponent has been the United States. Within the United States, there is little intellectual consensus as to what the goals of a desirable international competition policy might be, beyond prohibiting horizontal collusive practices such as cartels; politically, the issue has been captured by import-competing firms, which regard competition policy as prospectively a much less protection-friendly alternative to the existing, and WTO-consistent, antidumping laws. Within the US government, the bureaucracy is split: The Antitrust Division of the Justice Department fears that any multilateral accord would amount to a dumbing down of US law, weakening US antitrust practices; the USTR, stung by its defeat in the WTO in the Kodak-Fuji case, opposes narrowing antidumping laws in the interests of its import-competing clients.

The antidumping-competition policy issue is an inside-the-Beltway matter in comparison with the hot-button issues of the social clause. The US agenda on labor and environmental issues of recent years has found little support in Japan, which has not experienced the degree of public and nongovernmental-organization mobilization on these issues as have the European Union and United States, and has been on the defensive in a number of international disputes involving endangered species (see box 5.4).

In addition to the agenda issues, in the long run, the organization will have to deal with personnel issues as well. The last time around, Japan actively promoted Thailand's Supachai Panitchpakdi, while the United States backed New Zealand's Mike Moore in a protracted dispute over who would succeed Italy's Renato Ruggiero as the WTO director general. An eventual compromise was reached in which Moore and Supachai would split the term. This haggling did nothing to promote the institutional development of the organization. Another such brawl can be expected in 2005, when the Moore-Supachai term ends. The search for Supachai's successor could get entangled with personnel decisions made in other international organizations, as will be discussed in chapter 6.

Taken together, these observations suggest that the WTO may face some difficult times ahead. Although the system has served Japan well, it typically displays a lack of leadership, and on a series of issues on the horizon, its positions conflict with those of the United States, the organization's dominant member. We will return to these issues in chapter 7.

Regional Initiatives

Japan stands alone as the only large industrial country that does not participate in preferential regional trade arrangements. However, dissatisfaction with the WTO could encourage it and other countries in Asia to go their own way, creating regional preference arrangements similar to those that exist elsewhere.

The sole major existing regional initiative, the Asia Pacific Economic Cooperation forum, includes countries from outside Asia, most notably the United States. Indeed, APEC was originally an Australian initiative; some Asians wanted US involvement to counterbalance Japan, which had a similar proposal, and APEC's first meeting was held in Canberra in November 1989. The next big step was in November 1993 when, at the first APEC "leaders' meeting," the United States hosted history's first pan-Asian summit—held, ironically, outside Asia. APEC's membership accounts for more than 2 billion people, 40 percent of the world's population, and more than half of global output. An officially appointed Eminent Persons Group issued a report calling for free trade and investment in the region by 2010 for rich members and 2020 for poor ones, a goal that the governmental leaders adopted in their Bogor Declaration of 1994 (APEC Eminent Persons Group 1993, 1994).

Because of the great political and economic diversity among the APEC membership, no one anticipates "deep integration" along the lines of the European Union. Rather, much activity has been directed toward "business facilitation"—streamlining procedures and the like. Progress on trade and investment implementation has been uneven. Agriculture is a highly sensitive issue, and Japan attempted to carve out agriculture from the accelerated liberalization commitments at the Bogor (1994) and Osaka (1995) leaders' meetings. Later, in November 1998, Japan torpedoed the EVSL initiative, which would have required it to eliminate, during a 10-year period, its relatively low tariffs on forest and fishery products.[36] Japan is not unique in this regard: South Korea and one or two other members have been willing to let Japan take the lead in opposing agricultural trade liberalization within APEC, much the same way that Japan stands behind the European Union in the WTO. For its part, the Clinton administration lacked the statutory authority to implement early tariff cuts in several of the EVSL sectors (though it had residual authority from the Uruguay Round negotiations for others).

The growth of regionalism outside Asia and the failure of the WTO meeting in Seattle have encouraged Asian countries to take a second look at regional economic integration schemes. The old East Asian Economic Caucus idea has been revived as the Association of Southeast Asian Nations Plus Three (ASEAN + 3; the "three" being China, Japan, and South Korea) initiative. Official studies are under way on the possibilities of a Northeast Asia Free Trade Area involving China, Japan, and South Korea; a Japan-ASEAN FTA; and a free trade area for all of East Asia,

---

36. See Green (2001) for a detailed account of Japan's experience with APEC and the collapse of the EVSL initiative.

known to the cognoscenti as the "10 + 3." Negotiations on an FTA between Japan and Singapore are expected to be completed in 2001, and preliminary discussions are at various stages with Mexico, South Korea, and possibly others.[37]

Article 24 of the GATT and Article 5 of the General Agreement on Trade in Services (GATS) specify the conditions under which preferential trade arrangements are consistent with signatories' WTO obligations. The WTO must be notified of the intent to form an FTA. The FTA must not raise barriers to other parties. Tariffs within the FTA must be reduced to zero within "a reasonable time period," which was codified in the Uruguay Round agreement as 10 years. Trade restrictions must be abolished in "substantially all sectors." Finally, liberalization should target the services sector per the GATS.

For Japan and its potential partners, the problem is the "substantially all sectors" requirement. Because of the political influence of its inefficient agricultural sector, Japan is constrained to look to partners that either do not have an agricultural sector (Singapore) or have similarly inefficient agricultural sectors (South Korea), or run the risk of a WTO challenge if it attempts to exclude agriculture from an agreement (ASEAN or Mexico).[38] Indeed, because of the agriculture-sector problem, Japan has proposed an ersatz FTA with Canada that would exclude goods altogether, covering only services and investment. Japan's search for regional alternatives to the multilateral system is hamstrung by its own agricultural lobby.

Of the FTAs that Japan is considering, the one with Singapore, a city-state that pursues virtually free trade today, would be the easiest to complete, and perhaps unsurprisingly, convey the smallest direct trade benefits to Japan.[39] However, it is possible that provisions of the agreement relating to cross-national factor mobility (e.g., involving reforms of professional accreditation and financial markets) might serve as a constructive form of *gaiatsu*, whereby the need to conform to an external agreement could be used to leverage badly needed domestic reforms.[40]

Of more direct trade interest is the possibility of an FTA with South Korea. The two governments have commissioned studies of this possibility (Cheong 1999; Yamazawa 2000) and the idea has also been evaluated by Scollay and Gilbert (2001).[41] All three studies use static CGE models

---

37. Initial discussion of these possibilities preceded the fiasco in Seattle. Japan has maintained that it was approached by all of its potential partners, although in the South Korean case there is some disagreement on this point.

38. See JETRO (2000) for a discussion of a possible Japanese FTA with Mexico.

39. Scollay and Gilbert (2001), using a CGE model, find that the benefits to Japan would be virtually imperceptible.

40. For example, see Joint Study Group (2000).

41. Lee (2000) contains a wide-ranging discussion from the Korean perspective, while Cheong (1999) summarizes the underlying technical model.

to evaluate a prospective Japan-South Korea FTA. These models have significant limitations, notably their inability to capture dynamic economic effects and the absence of any reaction functions on the part of other trading nations.[42] Nevertheless, they are the obvious starting point for any serious analysis of a prospective FTA.

Yamazawa's conventional model generates the result that when Japan and South Korea enter into an FTA, Japan's bilateral surplus with South Korea increases. The United States is adversely affected by trade diversion.[43] As would be expected, the impact on the smaller economy is bigger than the impact on Japan: South Korea's real GDP increases 0.3-0.4 percent, while the effect on Japan is "marginal." The implicit message is that an FTA would have little impact on either economy and could well create problems with the United States.

In search of bigger numbers, Yamazawa then presents another variant, in which he assumes that large, sectorally nonuniform productivity increases accompany the formation of the FTA. In this variant, he obtains qualitatively similar results (e.g., Japan's bilateral surplus increases, and the United States is adversely affected by trade diversion), but both Japan and South Korea experience large real national income increases (on the order of 10 percent). This latter result, however, appears to be driven by the assumed productivity gains rather than anything intrinsic to the FTA.

Cheong's results are, if anything, even less supportive of the desirability of a Japan-South Korea FTA. In his model, not only does Japan's bilateral surplus with South Korea increase, but South Korean welfare actually declines—although, as in the case of Yamazawa's original model, these effects are quite small. Cheong then sets out to reverse the latter result, and comes up with two possibilities: unspecified "preferential rules of origin" and the inclusion of China in the FTA.

Like Cheong, Scollay and Gilbert obtain the result that a Japan-South Korea FTA would reduce welfare in South Korea, and like Yamazawa they find that it would also reduce welfare in the United States. They then model an FTA that excludes agriculture. This reduces, but does not

---

42. Yamazawa's model is a conventional Walrasian CGE embodying the assumption of constant returns to scale in production, with two alternative macro "closures." It has 11 sectors and 7 regions. The underlying data were taken from the Purdue University Global Trade Analysis Project. This means that quantitative restrictions, such as those existing in the agriculture or textile and apparel sectors, have been converted to tariff equivalents. Cheong provides even fewer details about his model. The Scollay-Gilbert model is similar to Yamazawa's, though far better documented. It contains 21 sectors and 22 regions. See Scollay and Gilbert (2001, appendix A) for further details.

43. Japan and other Asian countries have defended their interests in preferential schemes with reference to their trade-diversion losses resulting from the formation of the European Union and NAFTA. Krueger (1999) in an ex post assessment, finds little evidence of diversion. Noland (1995a), in an ex ante analysis, estimated that the long-run trade-diversion effects of NAFTA on South Korea could be substantial, as Mexico upgraded its export profile.

eliminate, the negative impact of the FTA on South Korea (and also presumably on the United States).[44]

Ultimately, these models may badly misspecify the workings of a Japan-South Korea FTA—for instance, not capturing the effects of enhanced investment flows. They do, however, point to something that could be problematic politically. Levels of protection are generally higher in South Korea than in Japan. Moreover, South Korea pursued a policy of actively discouraging imports from Japan through its "import diversification program," until this policy was terminated in June 1999 as part of the IMF's conditionality for its December 1997 standby package. When the policy ended, imports from Japan surged in a number of sectors, causing public protest in South Korea. Relations improved dramatically with South Korean President Kim Dae-jung's state visit in November 1998. But they subsequently took a turn for the worse in 2001, with controversies erupting over new Japanese school textbooks, which were regarded by the government of South Korea as whitewashing Japanese actions during the colonial period, and the visit by Prime Minister Koizumi to the Yasukuni Shrine, a Shinto shrine that includes among its honored dead a number of Japanese imperialists and war criminals. Any FTA with Japan will be a hard sell politically in South Korea.

From a US perspective, its major interest is in seeing that any preferential integration schemes in Asia are WTO-consistent. The requirements that an FTA cover "substantially all products" and include services creates a substantial hurdle for Japan to surmount. Any agreement that actually met these requirements would probably be beneficial to the United States, or involve only minimal trade-diversion losses.

The real risk, from a US perspective, would be WTO-inconsistent free trade areas involving the major economies of Northeast Asia. If China, Japan, and/or South Korea were able to carve out sectors (most likely agriculture) from such agreements, the risk of the United States suffering significant losses would increase. We will return to this issue in chapter 7, when we will specify some rules to ensure that preferential agreements would be "building blocks" to greater international trade liberalization and prosperity, rather than "stumbling blocs."

Assessment

Japan and the United States have engaged in an intense process of negotiation since the mid-1980s over access to the Japanese market. Given the

---

44. The FTA that excludes agriculture mitigates some of the negative impact on South Korea because it reduces the amount of inefficient trade-diverting agricultural exports from South Korea to Japan. That is, under an FTA, South Korea is encouraged to use resources that could be better deployed elsewhere in the economy to produce agricultural exports that are sent to the preferentially opened Japanese market. This hurts more efficient agricultural exporters, e.g., the United States.

time, resources, and political capital devoted to this endeavor, from a public-policy standpoint, the ultimate question is whether it has been worth it.

A statistical analysis by Noland (1997a) found evidence that US policymakers have devoted more attention to bilateral trade and investment issues than Japan's economic characteristics would appear to warrant. Moreover, this study was unable to detect any evidence that this activity had had an impact on aggregate trade and investment flows.

It could be that the econometric models used in that study were simply too crude to detect changes in discrete sectors. Greaney (2000) examined industry trade flows sector by sector, and with two exceptions she found little evidence that bilateral trade agreements had statistically significant effects on trade flows. The two exceptions were the semiconductor agreement and the 1987 auto agreement, although in the latter case, she also discovers evidence of trade diversion away from EU producers.[45] This suggests that Clinton administration policymakers may not have been deluded into believing that quantitative indicators might be a useful tool in increasing foreign market access, and that third parties might have had reasons for concern about such agreements.

Both of these studies used econometric models to evaluate the agreements, and both use exports from the United States as the basis for evaluating the effects of these agreements.[46] An alternative methodology has been pursued by the American Chamber of Commerce (ACCJ 2000), which surveyed knowledgeable observers about the impact of 63 major agreements concluded since 1980. Of these, 58 were subjected to evaluation, and 51 received subjective numerical scores for content, implementation, and results.[47] In comparison with earlier surveys, the ACCJ reports

45. "In most cases, the data suggest limited impacts on Japan's imports of targeted manufactured products, particularly from the US. In fact, in many sectors, growth in Japan's imports of targeted products from the US slowed after an agreement was signed. However, in two high profile cases involving autos and semiconductors, I do find some evidence that suggests positive impacts of the agreements on bilateral trade flows. In the auto case, I find evidence consistent with trade diversion, favoring imports from the US over those from the EU, rather than pure trade creation" (Greaney 2000, 127-28). Greaney's results for semiconductors would be consistent with the analyses of Bergsten and Noland (1993) and Flamm (1996), who concluded that the 1991 agreement had a significant positive impact on foreign sales in Japan. Stokes describes the agreement as "probably the single most successful American trade agreement with Japan" (Stokes 2000, 68).

46. One possibility is that the agreements generate increased sales by US multinational firms, but that these products are sourced from locations outside the United States. This is the famous "who is us?" conundrum; such agreements may benefit US capital, but may do little for US labor.

47. Some observations were dropped from the sample because they were considered subject to ongoing negotiation or were too recent to evaluate, whereas others, such as an agreement on science and technological cooperation, were regarded as too amorphous to be evaluated.

Figure 5.1 Trade agreement evaluation scores by sector

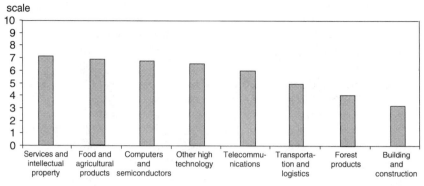

Source: ACCJ (2000).

that "in general, service industries reported significant improvements, while most manufacturing industries found little or no change" (ACCJ 2000, 17).

However, the sectoral averages reported in figure 5.1 suggest that a more nuanced interpretation is warranted. Although it is true that "services and intellectual property" received the highest average score (7.1 on a 10-point scale), the building and construction sector (also a service) received the lowest average score (3.2). Food and agricultural products received the second highest score (7.0), but another primary-products sector (forest products) received the second lowest score (4.1). A careful examination of the individual underlying cases suggests that the results are more idiosyncratic than consistent within sectors (the extreme cases of agreements that received ratings of above 8.5 or below 2.5 are shown in figure 5.2). Instead of broad sectoral characteristics, success appears to be more highly correlated with the existence of visible barriers and GATT-WTO norms and the absence of entrenched opposition by Japanese special-interest groups.[48] There is no statistical evidence in the scores of increasing

---

48. The relatively successful beef, sound recording, and tomato cases all reflect the existence of well-established GATT-WTO norms. The relatively unsuccessful cases of construction and paper reflect the power of entrenched special-interest groups and their allied ministries. The contrast between the cases of cellular telephones and government procurement of telecoms equipment is instructive in this regard. The cellular phone agreement essentially created the cellular phone market in Japan. Although there were significant disputes about the terms under which Japanese and foreign firms would compete, in contrast to government procurement, where NTT had a stable of traditional suppliers, the density of connections between the Ministry of Telecommunications and local service providers was lower.

Figure 5.2 Highly successful and unsuccessful trade agreements, scores by sector

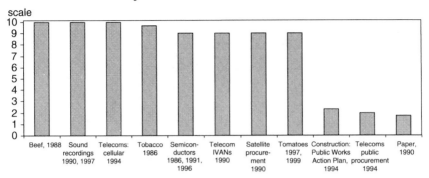

Source: ACCJ (2000).

or decreasing US negotiating effectiveness over time or across five presidential administrations.[49]

This suggests a conundrum created by two conclusions, one positive and one normative. The positive conclusion is that there is some evidence that past agreements embodying market-share targets have been unusually effective in stimulating import penetration into Japan. The normative conclusion is that, although they have stimulated imports, it is less clear that their impact enhanced welfare for either Japan or third parties that may have been disadvantaged by import diversion.

In any event, this is a moot point. The experience of the past 20 years has set the Japanese government against entering into any more agreements containing market-share targets backed by penalties. At the same time, the formation of the WTO has severely reduced the ability of the United States to demand such agreements. The bottom line is that, whatever their impact in the past, VIEs are not an option for the future. Instead, Japan and the United States need to develop alternative policy approaches to improving market access through the multilateral channels of the WTO. Specific recommendations will be detailed in chapter 7.

Conclusions

Japan is clearly changing. It is becoming less distinct in international terms than it was 10, or even 5, years ago. This is not to say that Japan is no longer distinct—its inward FDI is minuscule for a country its size; the role of foreign firms in its economy remains far smaller than their role in other major industrial economies; and its prices still appear to be

---

49. Noland (1997a) reaches a similar conclusion.

high, indicating less than complete integration between its markets and those elsewhere in the world. Nevertheless, these differences are diminishing.

At the same time, Japan's share of world output is shrinking. And, from a US perspective, Japan is becoming less important. This is not to say it is unimportant—Japan remains the world's largest importer of agricultural goods and the largest market for US farm products, and Japan and the United States will remain rivals in high-technology products and services for the foreseeable future. This is simply to say that in relative terms, the importance of Japan in US trade and investment is declining.

From a US perspective, this fall in relative importance, together with Japan's declining distinctiveness internationally, undercuts the justification for a Japan-specific US economic policy. Again, this is not to say that the United States should ignore Japan, or that the USTR Japan desk should close up shop. Indeed, in some regards, the changing agenda will require the focus of even more specific resources on Japan-related issues, as will be discussed below. It is simply to say that Japan-specific policies will more and more be undertaken in the context of US multilateral, plurilateral, and regional policies.

Forty years of tedious and at times corrosive bilateral negotiations have yielded a mixed bag of uncertain results. From the US standpoint, it is not from lack of trying: The United States has, at times, devoted extraordinarily high-level resources to Japan-related issues, which almost surely could have been better spent dealing with other problems. Nor is the United States solely responsible for this state of affairs: The lack of a credible opposition to governance by the LDP, in effect, has forced the US government to play the role of the opposition party in Japanese politics.

Ultimately, this is untenable: The US government is not the political opposition in Japan, and the US government will never play this role skillfully in Japanese domestic political terms. As the agenda shifts more and more toward domestic regulatory issues, the US government will be less and less able to usefully play its traditional role. The fact that the trade policy agenda is shifting more and more toward the services sector and regulatory issues implies that the principal beneficiaries of reform will be domestic residents (even more so than in the case of traditional traded-goods liberalization), and the justification for this traditional US role is even further weakened. Indeed, by becoming so embedded in Japanese domestic politics and playing a role for which it is fundamentally ill-suited, the United States risks compromising its ability to pursue its conventional and legitimate foreign policy interests or constructively intervening when it really counts—in real crises (see box 5.5).

Indeed, to most Japanese, the United States has lost its aura as a legitimate exerter of *gaiatsu*. Many commentators who hailed the United States as acting as an effective opposition party pushing deregulation against the

Box 5.5 The last gasp of *Gaiatsu*?

Gaiatsu, or foreign pressure, has a long history in Japan-United States trade relations—extending back to the Black Ships, some might say. When Japan and the
United States launched the Enhanced Initiative on Deregulation and Competition
Policy in 1997, one of the key sectors identified in the negotiations was telecommunications. NTT, the Japanese national telecommunications monopoly, was being
transformed into a holding company for a long-distance carrier, NTT Communications, and into two companies providing local telephone service, NTT East and
NTT West. The process of deregulating Japan's huge, complex telecoms market
created a vast array of issues for the Japanese government—and US negotiators.

US firms in the international telecoms services market feared that Japanese regulators would set the interconnection fees between the local and long-distance provider
in such a way as to facilitate NTT Communications' penetration of the international
services market, in effect using the captive local market to cross-subsidize the international subsidiary. Moreover, new entrants into the Japanese domestic market were
charging that the NTT group was using its unique access to the system to impede
competition—for example, by denying them physical access to relevant facilities,
charging a higher fee to foreign carriers to link a call into the NTT network than it
charged its own retail customers, or bundling different types of service lines together
and requiring that foreign service providers lease the whole bundle to gain access
to a specific asset. (The issue of access denial led to a JFTC investigation in October
2000.) A similar set of interconnection fee issues had arisen in the wireless market
with respect to the dominant carrier, NTT DoCoMo. Foreign equipment suppliers
claimed that NTT was using the establishment of unique technical standards to
frustrate those wishing to sell "off the shelf" into the Japanese market, in contraven-
tion to existing procurement agreements. The foreigners found an ally in METI,
representing the interests of the Japanese electronics firms that would see their
markets grow with the spread of information technology.

The US industry argued that the USTR would have substantial leverage in future
negotiations with Japan, insofar as NTT Communications, the new international
service provider, would have to apply for a license in the United States to provide
service between Japan and the United States. In March 1998, Deputy USTR Richard
W. Fisher began pressing his Japanese counterpart on a number of telecoms
issues, including the issue of interconnection fees. In June, the United States
extracted a commitment from the Japanese side to adopt a cost-based standard
at the end of 2000, while reducing fees in the interim. The action then shifted to
the issue of the interim rate cuts, which had been left undefined in the agreement.
The two sides continued to negotiate for another year, with the United States at
one point threatening a WTO case against Japan.

A broad agreement was reached in July 2000, a few days before the Japanese
government hosted the G-7 summit on Okinawa. The agreement included provisions to cut by about 35 percent the interconnection fees of greatest interest to
the US side (other fees, of greater interest to Japanese consumers, received smaller
cuts), to establish the rights for firms to provide high-speed Internet access and
build their own networks, and to open new points of access by "unbundling"
subscriber lines and special equipment.

The agreement should improve the competitiveness of the Japanese telecommunications market, bringing some benefits to Japanese consumers of telecommunications services (including Japanese businesses) and help US service providers.
Even so, METI made the need for additional liberalization of the telecoms market
the centerpiece of its 2001 White Paper. What is notable about this case is how it
harkens back to now-familiar themes: the US government uses denial of market
access to support one Japanese faction against another, for the ill-defined benefit
of a US producer lobby.

vested interest-ridden LDP became disillusioned after the semiconductor imbroglio, the auto and auto parts showdown, and the Kodak-Fuji dispute. From the Japanese perspective, the United States evolved from the promoter of an efficient market economy to a narrowly self-interested demandeur. Now, United States-initiated *gaiatsu* is almost a dirty word in Japan. To the extent that the United States is willing to insert itself into Japanese politics, it should do so only when the stakes are high, and preferably when pressure can be multilateralized through concerted action with others. We will return to this theme in chapter 7.

6

Global Issues

The interaction of Japan and the United States is not confined to the economic issues discussed in the previous chapters. These two largest and richest economies in the world have special responsibilities with respect to the provision of international public goods in the economic, political, and security realms. Because of their unique histories, however, the two countries have played very different roles in these fields, and these differences have at times created tensions in their bilateral relationship.

Of the many political and cultural differences between Japan and the United States, the key asymmetry that conditions their responses to the whole panoply of global issues has been Japan's defeat in the Second World War and the emergence of the United States as a global superpower. Following its defeat, Japan adopted, under US pressure, a Constitution that renounces war and narrowly circumscribes the role of the military in Japanese society.[1] Under the leadership of Prime Minister Shigeru Yoshida, Japan in effect became a military vassal of the United States: During the Cold War, Japan allied itself with the United States, and continues to permit the stationing of US forces on its soil to this day. Under Yoshida and his successors, Japanese foreign policy became, in effect, commercial policy.

The collapse of the Soviet Union and the end of the Cold War, however, undercut the primary public justification for this arrangement. More than

---

1. Article 9 of the Japanese Constitution states that "the Japanese people forever renounce war as a sovereign right of the nation and the threat or use of force as a means of settling international disputes . . . land, sea, and air forces, as well as other war potential, will never be maintained."

a decade later, the two governments continue to search for a security arrangement that is acceptable both to their respective publics and to the rest of Asia, which continues to harbor concerns about both Japanese military ambitions and the regional role of the United States.

During the Cold War, one response to Japan's atrophied role in international security affairs was to promote a larger Japanese role in development assistance, often under the rubric of "burden sharing," "comprehensive security," and the like.[2] However, as the Japanese economy developed and Japan became a more important commercial rival to the United States, some Americans began to criticize this arrangement—in which the United States played the difficult and costly role of security guarantor, while Japan acted as a regional benefactor, using its aid programs to promote its own national commercial interests—as "neomercantilist" (Pyle 1992) and "economic warfare" (Huntington 1993). Likewise, some in Japan began to question the country's lack of influence in international financial institutions (IFIs) when it was outspending the United States on development assistance in relative terms, and, from 1991 onward, in absolute terms as well.[3]

After the collapse of the Soviet Union, a rough foreign policy consensus embodying a number of elements began to emerge in Japan. The maintenance of the United States-Japan security alliance was deemed central. Ironically, the end of the Cold War coincided with increased perceptions of North Korean threats and uncertainty about the future aims and development of China. As Green (2001) observes, a poll conducted at the end of 1999 showed higher support for the United States-Japan alliance than at any time since 1984. Yet polling data also show considerable support for reducing the US military presence in Japan—this appears to be a combination simply of NIMBY (not in my backyard) objections and a recognition among the Japanese public that US forces on Okinawa are in large part deployed for potential missions well outside Japan's immediate security concerns (Hosokawa 1998).

In parallel to the rising level of security anxiety, there was a dissipation of some of the idealism that had marked Japanese security policy since the end of the Second World War, and a growing acceptance of the legitimacy of the Japan Self-Defense Forces (JSDF). Yet there was little consensus as to the appropriate mission of the JSDF, and a constitutional revision, which would be needed for the JSDF to play a more conventional national security role, remained highly controversial.

---

2. See Balassa and Noland (1988, chap. 7) for examples of such Cold War-era statements and rationalizations.

3. E.g., in 1980, Finance Minister Michio Watanabe stated at the joint World Bank-IMF annual meetings that "appropriate adjustments need to be made so that each member's quota share reflects its economic reality" (quoted in Green 2001, 233).

At the same time, there was a renewed interest in, and commitment to, Asia. However, Japan confronted a situation in which there was an absence of regional organizations such as the European Union or North Atlantic Treaty Organization (NATO) to mediate historical enmities. Moreover, despite the continued reliance on the United States, there was a desire for a more "independent" foreign policy stance. The desire for greater independence and a larger regional role, and the need for Asian institution building, created possibilities for conflict with the United States in the context of the continued US security guarantee and its quasi-hegemonic position in the post-Cold War world.

Put differently, since the late 1980s changing circumstances have rendered obsolete implicit arrangements that were in place for a half-century. It is not surprising that the ongoing process of reorienting the bilateral relationship to better reflect current reality has proven to be complicated, and at times painful. In this chapter, we examine the roles of Japan and the United States in the provision of several international public goods. The maintenance of a liberal, rules-based international trade system is one of these, and was discussed in chapter 5 in the context of trade policy. Here, we first consider the international financial arena, including issues involving the international financial architecture and development assistance. We then move on to a topic of great sensitivity, the security issue, which for both countries turns on issues of self-identity at home and legitimacy abroad. Finally, we take on other issues of global cooperation, such as public health and the environment. As decades of discussions of "burden sharing," and more recently of "responsibility sharing," have demonstrated, ultimately each country's roles in these areas are a product of its unique historical circumstances, and cannot be disentangled from the other's in any meaningful way.

International Finance

The US dollar has been the key currency of the international financial system since the Second World War. By necessity, US policy took foreign considerations into account, even if they conflicted with domestic objectives. In this respect, the US situation has been unique. The Bretton Woods system for financial capital established at the end of the war did not embody the presumption of the trade system, namely, that goods should flow freely across borders subject to limited government intervention in the form of tariffs. Instead, it was recognized that, to facilitate macroeconomic management, governments could restrict cross-border movements of capital and the overseas use of their currencies. Japan, like other countries in the immediate postwar period, maintained controls on capital flows, and the yen was not freely convertible in international markets.

In Japan, bank loans were the principal source of capital for industrial firms. To the extent that the industrial sector engaged in international trade, it did so by exporting from domestically located production facilities (i.e., Japanese firms were exporters, not multinationals with global production networks). The upshot was that both the banks and firms had a common interest in the maintenance of a stable, internationally competitive exchange rate, and had no particular interest in promoting the use of the yen outside Japan. Furthermore, the subordination of the Bank of Japan to the Ministry of Finance, and the high degree of access of the large banks to MOF officials, meant that these private preferences were readily transmitted to Japanese policymakers (Henning 1994).

Over time, changes in the external environment and the nascent globalization of the Japanese industrial sector contributed to shifts in the underlying preferences of the private sector. Controls on both the inflow and outflow of capital were kept in place until a process of liberalization was begun in 1979. However, beginning in the early 1980s, the "internationalization" of the yen became the subject of contentious negotiations between the US and Japanese governments, with the US side pressing Japan to undertake policies more rapidly to promote the international use of the Japanese currency, including lifting restrictions on the euro-yen market, encouraging the development of a short-term market in government securities and forward markets in the yen, and creating a market in bankers' acceptances (Frankel 1984).[4]

In fact, the use of the yen as an invoice currency and reserve currency did subsequently increase during the next decade, though not as rapidly as the increase in Japanese income or Japanese capital outflows. Japanese policy remained ambivalent, reflecting diverse private and bureaucratic preferences. Although parts of the private sector and parts of the Ministry of Finance pressed for a more prominent role for the yen, the highly regulated nature of Japan's domestic financial markets, and a lack of trust in Japanese authorities taking international considerations into account in setting policy, acted as a brake on this process.[5]

Nevertheless, the growth of intraregional trade and the increasing use of the yen as an invoice currency by Japanese multinational firms encour-

---

4. As Frankel (1984) makes clear, the US government had a variety of motivations in pursuing capital-market liberalization in Japan. At the time, the US government was running large budget deficits, and some officials were most interested in selling US government debt in Japan. They were interested in encouraging capital outflow to finance the US government deficit. Others wrongly believed that there would be a net inflow of capital into Japan, contributing to a yen appreciation and taking pressure off import-competing sectors in the United States.

5. See Ito (1993), Hamada (1994), and Moreno (1996) on the internationalization of the yen and Japanese policy. See Council on Foreign Exchange and Other Transactions (1999) for an example of pro-internationalization views from the Ministry of Finance.

aged the notion of a "yen bloc" in Asia, harkening back to the Greater East Asian Co-Prosperity Sphere of the 1930s. The alarmist tone of the popular discussion is captured by the cover headline on the 5 August 1991 international edition of *Newsweek*: "The Yen Bloc: Asia's Message to Washington: Sayonara, America."[6]

Rather than a discriminatory bloc, what in fact developed during the 1990s was a disjuncture between the real and financial sides of the economies in Asia. On the real side, Asian economies became more and more integrated with Japan, as Japanese multinational firms created production networks in Asia, with Japan supplying high-value-added components for assembly into finished products in lower-wage Asian locations. Japanese banks increased their presence in the Asian economies in parallel. At the same time, as the Asian economies developed, shifting their export profiles toward more sophisticated manufactures, they more and more competed with Japanese-based production in world markets, especially in the United States, and earned export receipts primarily in US dollars (Noland 1997c). The Asian economies were increasingly tied to Japan as a source of intermediate inputs and finance (with the loans sometimes denominated in yen), whereas the ultimate export destination was the United States, and the export receipts were in US dollars.

Most critically, rather than abandoning the dollar as the "yen bloc" paranoiacs expected, Asian countries implicitly or explicitly pegged their own currencies to the dollar, despite the importance of Japan to their economies. As Ito, Ogawa, and Sasaki (1998) demonstrate, the weight of the yen in an optimal currency basket for the Asian countries was higher than the actual weight accorded to the yen in exchange rate management; as a consequence, these economies were subject to external shocks when the yen-dollar exchange rate moved.[7] In the early 1990s, they encountered difficulties paying back yen-denominated loans as the yen appreciated

---

6. Plus ça change, plus c'est la même chose. The term "yen bloc" is often used rather loosely, conflating Japan's increasing intraregional trade during the period with the notion that the yen would play a predominant role in regional finance. See Maidment (1989), Frankel (1993), Melvin and Peiers (1993), Petri (1993), Kwan (1994), and Aggarwal and Mougoue (1996) for analyses of regional integration and the yen bloc idea.

7. During the 1990s, the Thai baht was fixed in the narrow range of 25.2-25.6 to the US dollar. The Malaysian ringgit was allowed a bit more flexibility, staying within a 10 percent band of 2.5-2.7 ringgit to the dollar. The Philippine peso moved within a 15 percent band of 24-28 to the dollar until 1995, when it was fixed at 26.2. Indonesia maintained a crawling peg, and the currency was allowed to depreciate in nominal terms from 1,900 rupiah to the dollar in 1990 to 2,400 rupiah to the dollar at the beginning of 1997. The South Korean won followed a controlled float, but was held within a narrow range of 770-800 won to the dollar from early 1993 to mid-1996, when it was allowed to depreciate about 10 percent.

against the US dollar, and in the mid-1990s they began to lose export competitiveness as the yen depreciated.[8]

Anecdotal evidence suggests that profit margins on much of this lending were extremely thin, and, according to Bank for International Settlements (BIS) figures, as the Japanese banks' financial situations deteriorated in the second half of 1995, they began to withdraw from Asia.[9] This capital outflow (along with a variety of other factors) contributed to the crisis that began in Thailand in July 1997 and quickly spread throughout the region.[10] It is precisely a replay of this scenario of financial-market shocks emanating from a weak Japanese economy that the United States and the rest of the world continue to face.

The crisis brought to the fore the issue of Japan's role, both institutionally and through the use of its currency. As in the previous discussion of trade policy, in the finance and development sphere there is a similar set of themes: disagreement over substantive and key leadership issues, and a possible Japanese and Asian desire to go their own way. The focal points have been Japanese and Asian dissatisfaction over the performance of the US government and the Washington-based International Monetary Fund during the Asian financial crisis, subsequent debates over reform of what has come to be known as the "international financial architecture," and proposals for regional initiatives that could run counter to policy emanating from "Washington."[11]

The Asian Financial Crisis

Tokyo and Washington clearly reacted differently to the Asian crisis, reflecting differences in ideology, national interests, and perhaps under-

---

8. After the crisis, Japanese authorities continued to promote basket-peg policies as a means of advocating the international, or at least regional, use of the yen. See Ueda (1998) and Noland et al. (1999) for further discussion of exchange rate shocks in the Asian financial crisis.

9. For overviews, see Ostrom (1998); Baily, Farrell, and Lund (2000); and Green (2001). According to BIS figures, Japanese banks reduced their exposure to the rest of Asia by an estimated $30 billion in 1998, accounting for roughly 30 percent of the net capital outflow the region experienced in 1998. By 1999, nearly half of the Japanese banks that had been operating in Asia in mid-1997 had pulled out, and according to Bank of Japan figures, Japanese bank lending to Asia was 40 percent below its 1997 level. The Japanese withdrawal was initially offset by increased European lending, but as the crisis exploded in the second half of 1997, the Europeans also pulled out.

10. See Noland et al. (1999) for an account of the crisis and its effects, and Kaminsky and Reinhart (2000) for a discussion of the role of Japanese bank lending in regional contagion.

11. Many in Asia regard the IMF as a front for the US government and do not distinguish between the actions and positions of the two entities. In part this reflects ignorance, but in part it is an understandable response to the predominant influence that the United States wields in the IMF, and the fact that in the case of South Korea, the IMF program conditionality

standings of the crisis. The US government initially underestimated the severity of the crisis, with President Clinton describing it as "a glitch in the road" at the APEC summit in November 1997.[12] Furthermore, relative to Japan, the United States was unsympathetic to the capital channeling and cronyism that had contributed to the crisis; and again relative to Japan, US banks and financial institutions had less at stake in the region. Crudely put, the US government initially regarded the crisis as a modest regional affair, largely of the Asians' own making. Thailand was stunned by the initial US refusal to come to its financial assistance at the onset of the crisis, in contrast to the United States' forthcoming stance vis-à-vis Mexico during its crisis of 1994-95.[13] It was only after the crisis spread to South Korea and threatened to spread to Brazil and Russia that the United States was shaken out of its complacency.

Asian disappointment with US reticence was compounded by what are widely regarded as fundamental mistakes in the IMF programs that actually exacerbated the crisis.[14] These perceptions—that the United States was an unreliable ally, and that the economic prescriptions being written by Washington were at best incompetent and at worst malevolent—created an opportunity for Japanese leadership on regional financial issues, despite the fact that the sluggish growth of the Japanese economy, the yen depreciation of 1995-97, and the weakness of the Japanese banking sector contributed to the crisis in the first place.[15] Taking advantage of this opportunity, in September 1997 Japan proposed an Asian Monetary Fund (AMF). The fund was reportedly to be capitalized at $100 billion.

---

included items of direct mercantilist interest to Japan and the United States but of questionable relevance to the financial crisis.

12. Like many of us, the president later changed his tune, in a 14 September 1998 speech to the Council on Foreign Relations describing the Asian crisis as "the biggest financial challenge facing the world in a half century." This also turned out to be wrong.

13. The United States participated in the "second line of defense" associated with the second IMF program in Thailand. However, even this participation was purely symbolic, inasmuch as the US Department of the Treasury fought the actual use of second-line funds and has never disbursed a dime.

14. Joseph E. Stiglitz, at the time the chief economist of the World Bank, contemporaneously put forward serious criticisms of the IMF programs (Stiglitz 1998, 1999). To cite another example, Masaru Yoshitomi, dean of the Asian Development Bank Institute, described the IMF's program in Indonesia as having made the situation "even worse" (Dow Jones, 25 June 2001). For a detailed analysis of one IMF program, see Noland (2000a, chap. 6).

15. In the interest of brevity, these statements blur distinctions among Asian countries. In Indonesia, in particular, some segments of the society actually welcomed the IMF, which was regarded as less cozy with the Suharto regime than the World Bank. At possibly the other extreme, there was a widespread view in South Korea that the IMF program was a deliberate attempt to subvert the South Korean economy, which was believed to pose a threat to the United States in sectors such as automobiles. Indeed, in South Korea, the crisis is commonly referred to as "the IMF crisis."

The idea was that the regional fund could quickly disburse funds without regard to quota limitations and policy conditionality, as was the case with IMF lending.

The proposal was blocked by Chinese, IMF, and US opposition, with "Washington" fearing that an AMF would degrade the *global* financial system by undercutting the IMF, whereas China opposed it out of geopolitical rivalry.[16] (It did have the effect of spurring the US Department of the Treasury to redouble its efforts to secure an IMF quota increase, as is discussed below.) The MOF then came back with the New Miyazawa Initiative (named for Finance Minister Kiichi Miyazawa), a $30 billion financial assistance plan for the region that consisted largely of sovereign debt guarantees, trade credits, and low-interest loans, which could be interpreted as an action comparable to the United States' support of Mexico in 1994-95[17] (see box 6.1). Cynics claimed that this was simply a backdoor means of providing public funds to Japanese banks and corporations through their Asian subsidiaries.[18] There is probably some truth to this, but whatever the motivation, Japan extended more official assistance to strapped economies in Asia than did the United States. At the same time, it should be noted that in 1998-99 exports from the most heavily affected Asian economies to the United States rose, while those to Japan fell. In essence, the United States enabled trade, while Japan provided aid.[19]

Asian Regionalism

In November 1997, the Southeast Asians invited the heads of government from China, Japan, and South Korea to attend the ASEAN summit in Kuala Lumpur.[20] The next year this "ASEAN + 3" group met again in Hanoi, and China took the lead in proposing that the group explore possibilities for financial cooperation. The following year in Manila, the

16. See Altbach (1997), Hamada (1999), and Green (2001) for further discussion. Green argues that beyond the international opposition to the plan, the AMF proposal was opposed by large parts of the MOF itself.

17. The "old" Miyazawa Initiative was a 1980s debt-crisis plan (see Green 2001 for details). The government of Japan subsequently announced that, beyond the "New Miyazawa Initiative," an additional ¥2 trillion would be made available for sovereign loan guarantees. This money, if disbursed, would offset the roughly $30 billion of net lending that Japanese banks withdrew from the region in 1998.

18. Green quotes an unnamed MOF official as saying that the Miyazawa Initiative was "one part of the overall measures to resolve the financial situation in Japan" (2001, 255). See also Goad (1998).

19. The two countries cooperated in 1998 in funding the Asian Growth and Recovery Initiative through the multilateral development institutions. Japan followed this up in 2000 with proposals for debt relief for the world's poorest countries, as is discussed below.

20. See Henning (forthcoming 2002) for a detailed history of Asian monetary cooperation.

Box 6.1 The New Miyazawa Initiative

After the AMF idea was rejected, at an APEC finance ministers' gathering in October 1998, Japanese Finance Minister Kiichi Miyazawa announced a new initiative to assist the five most heavily affected Asian crisis countries. Under the plan, dubbed the New Miyazawa Initiative (the first Miyazawa Plan was a 1980s debt-crisis plan), Japan pledged $30 billion, half for short-term trade finance and loans, and half for medium- to long-term lending. The modalities of these commitments included use of Export-Import Bank of Japan (JEXIM) loans, acquisition of sovereign bonds issued to Asian governments by JEXIM, and concessional loans through Japan's budget for official development assistance.

The actual disbursement of funds was done through a very bureaucratic process, and ironically, the long-term money was exhausted before the short-term money. Indeed, the convoluted nature of the process led to complaints by the supposed beneficiaries, and some skepticism about disbursement figures released by the Ministry of Foreign Affairs and the true magnitude of "additionality" (Castellano 1999a, 1999b, 2000b).

A second part of the plan aimed at increasing the use of the yen internationally, by encouraging other Asian countries to hold the yen as a reserve currency as part of basket-peg exchange rate policies, and to encourage greater use of the yen-denominated financial instruments such as "Samurai" bonds in private markets. Operationally, JEXIM would guarantee private bank loans to Asian countries, and guarantee sovereign bonds issued by Asian governments. In March 1999, the Board of the Asian Development Bank approved the establishment of an Asian Currency Crisis Support Facility underwritten by Japan.

group formally identified items for cooperation, and after 2 years of dormancy, Japan's Ministry of Finance resuscitated a watered-down version of the AMF proposal in the spring of 2000 (Kuroda 2000). The Japan-dominated Asian Development Bank (ADB) floated a report stressing the need to "seriously consider" an AMF—a position from which it subsequently backed away.[21] The problem was in some ways similar to the one that confronts Japan with respect to FTAs: it did not want to be perceived as originating the policy proposal, but rather as responding to the entreaties of others, a predilection that Rix (1993) described as "leadership from behind." In the case of the AMF, Japanese officials invariably described the AMF as an ASEAN and Japanese proposal. It is not surprising that Thailand has emerged as Japan's most reliable ally in this regard.

The ASEAN finance ministers did indeed consider the proposal in their meeting in Brunei in March 2000, but shelved it in favor of a less ambitious regional currency-swap arrangement involving China, Japan, and South

---

21. See Asian Development Bank (2000). ADB President Tadao Chino later tried to clarify, stating that there may be a role for an AMF, but that the IMF should remain the lead agency in handling future crises (IMF, Morning News, 12 April 2000). The ADB would later announce that improved regional conditions and the growth of the swap networks had lessened the urgency of establishing an AMF.

Korea, while agreeing to conduct a "study on the modalities and mechanisms for a regional financing arrangement to supplement the existing international facilities."[22]

At the ADB annual meeting held in Chiang Mai, Thailand, in May 2000, the ASEAN+3 agreed to what came to be known as the "Chiang Mai Initiative," a three-part cooperative framework instituting a network of bilateral medium-term (up to 1 year) foreign exchange credit arrangements among the central banks, undertaking regional macroeconomic surveillance, and committing to technical assistance. This time, the opposition from the United States and the IMF was muted. Although the amounts committed to the so-called Network of Bilateral Swap Arrangements to date are modest, in the future this arrangement could involve much larger mutual currency supports (Bergsten 2001a).[23] Unlike the precrisis swap arrangements, which were designed merely to provide liquidity against collateral (such as US Treasury bonds), the new system of extending hard currency loans in exchange for local currencies carries real exchange rate risk. In addition, the Asian countries are contemplating exchange rate stabilization schemes and new "early warning systems" to head off future crises.

To some, this appears to be the AMF by incremental means. Apart from the politics, such an organization could be justified on several grounds. First, it is clear that currency crises and their associated trade shocks have a strong regional component (Kaminsky and Reinhart 2000). This means that countries have a particular interest in the financial stability of their neighbors—which suggests that surveillance may be more effective on the regional, rather than global, level. Second, as a practical matter, recent bailouts have had a strongly regional flavor: the United States committed significant resources to the Mexican bailout of 1994-95, while Japan put forth most of the bilateral support in the Asian financial crisis. In financial terms, creating an Asian regional organization would not be difficult (the

---

22. Before the Asian crisis, a number of central banks had established currency swap and repurchase ("repo") agreements, but these were easily swamped by the crisis. Agreements among the members of the organization of East Asian and Pacific central banks and the organization of Southeast Asian central banks were deepened and expanded in January 2000, and once again in May 2000. Apart from emergency lending by the Asian Development Bank, preexisting regional institutions did not play major proactive roles in the crisis. APEC and ASEAN were largely developed by their members' foreign ministries; their finance ministries (in particular the US Treasury, in the case of APEC) have remained unenthusiastic, and neither organization has a highly developed financial component, although the Manila Framework Group, which was created by APEC, has had a modest role in the region since 1997. Rhetorically, at least, both organizations have continued to support liberalization, however, and they may have served to constrain backsliding.

23. Some specific new arrangements were announced at the ADB annual meeting in Honolulu in May 2001. See Kim, Ryou, and Wang (2000) and Henning (forthcoming 2002) for good overviews of these issues.

Asian countries possess nearly $1 trillion in official reserves), especially if China and Japan were to commit significant resources. Indeed, this last point may be the strongest reason for an Asian institution: It would provide a venue for building regional confidence and trust.

The great potential disadvantage of the organization would be the threat it could pose to the globally oriented IMF, and it is not surprising that this emerged as a point of contention as the details of the Chiang Mai Initiative were worked out. For an AMF to succeed, lending conditionality would have to be carefully worked out with the IMF. If it were to lend in the absence of conditionality, the existence of a large pool of public money would create moral hazard on a gargantuan scale and would in all likelihood lead to the eventual collapse of the IMF system, because the IMF would be overwhelmed by the moral hazard problems that such AMF lending would fuel.[24] This is, in the words of Rose (1999), "an argument for a *good* AMF, not an argument for *no* AMF" (emphasis in the original). In May 2001 it was confirmed that the new financial arrangements would be "complementary" or "supplementary" to the IMF, and that only 10 percent of the funds could be drawn before triggering IMF linkage.

Until the organization develops a credible surveillance mechanism, it will remain subservient to the IMF. However, if it does develop effective surveillance, this could put Japan in a very difficult bind: It will be caught between the United States and the rest of Asia, with the latter pressuring it to put its considerable financial resources squarely behind the regional organization.

Today, the Chiang Mai Initiative has wide support in Japan. However, should the initiative evolve toward a robust AMF, Japan's external bind would be manifested internally in a split between, on one hand, Asia-oriented regionalists and critics of the "Washington consensus," who would support Japan's taking an assertive posture in the regional organization; and, on the other hand, those who would regard Japan's economic and security interests as better served by a continued orientation toward the United States and the global institutions.[25]

The Global System

Parallel to this discussion of greater regional cooperation in Asia has been a more general discussion about what should be done to reform the financial architecture in general, and the IMF in particular. Again, the United States has led the international debate (although Japan, the Euro-

---

24. In a May 2001 speech, MOF Vice Minister Haruhiko Kuroda indicated that US concerns about moral hazard were well-founded and that crisis prevention should be the focus.

25. For the definition of the "Washington consensus," see Williamson (1990).

pean Union, and the United States did cooperate in the formation of the Group of Twenty (G-20), a group of systemically significant economies convened to consider international financial architectural reform. As was mentioned above, in the spring of 1998, the specter of an AMF spooked the US Treasury into pushing the US Congress to increase the US quota commitment to the IMF. It was argued that, although the existing set of institutions might be suboptimal, it was unwise to reorganize the fire department in the midst of a fire (e.g., Noland 1998b). The political quid pro quo for Congressional approval of the quota increase was the establishment of a panel of outside experts, the International Financial Institution Advisory Commission, charged with assessing the public-sector international financial institutions. This commission, chaired by longtime IMF foe Allan Meltzer (it came to be known as the Meltzer Commission), was time-bound to issue its report in March 2000.

The US Treasury Department—anticipating that the commission would issue a strongly market-oriented critique of the international financial institutions—attempted to preempt the commission by issuing its own reform recommendations, many of which had originally been proposed in a Council on Foreign Relations Task Force report (CFR 1999). The Clinton administration proposal, initially articulated in Summers (1999) and developed at length in US Treasury (2000), calls for the IMF to phase out long-term lending, and to take on a more narrow crisis-prevention mission than its current activities encompass. In particular, it calls for the IMF to serve as a quasi-lender of last resort, loaning significant amounts at "prices to encourage rapid repayment" (Summers 1999, 6). At the same time, it seems to support the same kind of intrusive conditionality that proved so controversial in the Asian crisis, arguing that "issues of social cohesion and inclusion . . . should be addressed as a condition for IMF support" (Summers 1999, 6).[26] Eventually the Treasury dropped its insistence on eliminating the long-term lending facility.

When the Meltzer Commission report was released in March (IFIAC 2000), as expected, the majority report reflected a near obsession with the notion of moral hazard and called for greatly restricting the IMF to functioning as a quasi lender of last resort to prequalified countries; a wholesale downsizing and reorganization of the system of multilateral development banks; and the abolition of such institutions as the Multilat-

---

26. The Treasury position is unclear on this point. Some have interpreted this ambiguity as reflecting a desire by the Clinton administration in general, and Treasury in particular, to preempt the Meltzer Commission report, while at the same time preserving support from Congressional members concerned about labor, human rights, etc. On this point, the Meltzer Commission report's majority statement would abolish policy conditionality ("the IMF would not be authorized to negotiate policy reform"), whereas the minority dissent defends this practice, without specifying the policies on which it is appropriate to condition IMF lending. See Goldstein (2001) for an evaluation of IMF conditionality.

eral Investment Guarantee Agency (traditionally headed by a Japanese national) and the multilateral development banks' private-sector arms, such as the World Bank Group's International Finance Corporation.

Japanese (and European) government reaction, as might be expected, has been sympathetic to neither the "less money with more conditions" thrust of the Summers proposal nor the "moral hazard über alles" stance of the Meltzer Commission. Japanese Finance Minister Kiichi Miyazawa described as "unrealistic" the idea of limiting the IMF's lending activities to short-term emergency credits.[27] In his address to the March 2000 meeting of the Manila Framework group, MOF Vice Minister Hirohiko Kuroda called for the IMF to limit the inclusion of structural reform conditionality in its assistance packages, despite the fact that Japan benefited from the abolition of South Korea's "import-diversification program" as part of South Korea's December 1997 standby agreement. This stand would be consistent with previous Japanese attempts to substantively influence the IFIs in the direction of greater sympathy to state intervention in economic life than that embodied in the "Washington consensus."

Japan and the United States found more agreement on a second issue, however. Influence within the IMF is largely a function of the weighted voting scheme in its Executive Board. These weights are determined by a country's quota, or the amount of foreign exchange it makes available to the IMF. For more than two decades, Japan has been signaling what it regards as its underweighting within the IMF Executive Board. In 1990, a general capital increase produced a realignment of relative quotas, and Japan moved up from fifth place to share second place with Germany, behind the United States. The Summers proposal recommends a recalculation of member quotas (the basis for weighted voting within the organization and, in principle, determining the amount of resources that a country can call upon in a crisis).[28] This could have important implications for Asia, inasmuch as most Asian countries (with the notable exception of China) would appear to be underweighted (and European countries similarly overweighted). In this respect, the United States and Japan appear to be on the same side.[29] Nevertheless, it proved difficult diplomatically

---

27. Quoted in Castellano (2000d).

28. The quota constraint on borrowing was bent for Mexico in 1994 under US pressure, and was broken dramatically during the Asian crisis, when South Korea was permitted to borrow nearly 20 times its quota.

29. In his speech to the Manila Framework Group, Kuroda argued that "a reassessment of the quota distribution to reflect the changes in the global economy is urgently needed" (*Financial Times*, 22 March 2000), a position reportedly reaffirmed by Minister of Finance Kiichi Miyazawa and Bank of Japan Governor Masaru Hayashi in the IMF's International Finance and Monetary Committee the following month.

The real problem appears to be the overweighting of Europe. Japan's economy is half as large as that of the United States or European Union, but its quota (6.2 percent) is one-third of the US quota (17.2) and only one-fifth of Europe's (33.8 percent). The problem with quota

to allocate to Japan the unambiguously second largest IMF national quota. South Korea is even further underweighted, and other Asian countries such as Thailand are arguably so, constraining their access to IMF resources, and limiting their influence in its Executive Board.

This issue came to a head in the struggle over who would succeed Michel Camdessus as managing director of the IMF. Despite Japan's rising financial contributions to the organization, no Japanese national has held this top leadership post.[30] Traditionally, the managing director job has gone to a European, while the presidency of the World Bank has gone to an American. A Japanese has traditionally led the Asian Development Bank. (The other regional development banks are also led by nationals from the region.) After protracted internal negotiations, the European Union nominated a German, Caio Koch-Weser, for the post. In the meantime, while the Europeans were negotiating, in a break from previous practice, Japan put forward its own candidate, Eisuke Sakakibara, a former MOF vice minister and a promoter of the Asian Monetary Fund. Some other Asian countries (though notably not China) were convinced to give token public support to his candidacy.[31] A disparate coalition of developing countries would eventually nominate a third candidate, the acting managing director, Stanley Fischer. After no consensus was achieved in the IMF Executive Board, in a second iteration of the process, the European Union nominated another German, Horst Köhler, the United States indicated his acceptability, and he received the endorsement of the Executive Board.

It is a bit hard to know what to make of the Japanese action. Sakakibara was well known for his nationalistic views, and under the circumstances was surely unacceptable to the United States (and many others). In 1990 he published a book, *Beyond Capitalism*, which touted the superiority of the Japanese noncapitalist market economy. Later, in a speech delivered during a 1996 visit to Washington directly addressing issues of financial

---

reallocation would not be giving Asia a greater share; it would be how to reduce the European share while preserving the historical prerogatives of individual countries. Simply treating the EU member countries (or, alternatively, the European Central Bank members) as a single member could result in the European quota exceeding that of the United States. This would not only be unacceptable to the United States on diplomatic grounds, but in theory it would require moving the IMF and World Bank headquarters to Brussels (which no one wants), because the charter states that the organizations' headquarters must be located in the capital of the largest member. See IMF (2000) for an extensive analysis of the quota issue.

30. Expectations of increased Japanese influence had been rising for some time. At the peak of the bubble economy, a September 1989 *Euromoney* cover story announced that "Japan Takes Over the IMF" and went on to predict that a Japanese national would succeed Managing Director Michel Camdessus. When the time came, Camdessus was reappointed.

31. In the end, only Thailand voted for Sakakibara, while China supported Koch-Weser, and the others, following the US example, abstained.

management and development, he dismissed the advisability of financial market liberalization, curtailment of government-led capital channeling, and reorientation of financial systems away from bank-centered indirect systems and toward market-centered direct finance (Sakakibara 1996). The following year he characterized the Thai crisis as demonstrating that "the Washington consensus [on the Bretton Woods institutions] was over" (quoted in Green 2001, 247) and led a ham-handed attempt to create an AMF. During the 1998 MOF financial scandal, he received a formal warning (see box 3.2). The fact that Japan promoted such a controversial figure could be interpreted as an indication of just how weak the Japanese pool of potential candidates for important international positions actually is.

It appears that the nomination was not meant to be taken at face value, but rather to signal Japan's unwillingness to accept the continued European stranglehold on the managing director job.[32] Sakakibara said as much himself, describing his candidacy as "symbolic" and stating that Japanese authorities had launched his candidacy despite knowing "that the chance of my getting the position was very low." Indeed, if a Japanese national did secure the managing director position, Japan would come under pressure to release its hold on the ADB presidency—to another Asian country (i.e., not to the European Union or United States).[33]

This fiasco, coming on the heels of the Moore-Supachai debacle at the WTO, vividly illustrated the fundamental bankruptcy of the national "reservation" system for selecting the senior leaders of the international institutions.[34] In this sense, the Japanese action should be regarded as a success, even if it did not yield short-run benefits. That said, it appears that Japan continues to punch below its weight in the IFIs, focusing on a narrow agenda of getting Japanese nationals into high-level appointments and engaging in an intellectually quixotic attempt to define a "new development paradigm," as described below.

Development Assistance

In large part, the international financial issues involve policy toward emerging markets. Explicitly concessional assistance toward less-developed countries has historically been an important part of the international economic policies of both Japan and the United States. This was particu-

---

32. See Reuters, 10 March 2000, and the *Financial Times*, 24 March 2000, for the quotes.

33. The problem for Japan is that, given the quota-weighted voting system, no other Asian country (with the possible exception of China) could provide major support for a Japanese candidacy at the IMF in exchange for Japanese support in the ADB.

34. See Kahler (2001) for recommendations for reforming the system of selecting senior leaders of international institutions.

larly important during the Cold War, when the developing world was an important venue for East-West rivalry. As with other parts of the Cold War legacy, Japan and the United States are engaged in an ongoing process of reorienting their policies to reflect the changing realities of the post-Cold War world.

From a US perspective, the United States is using its aid program in its multilateral and bilateral dimensions to support the globally desirable social aims of peace, democratization, and development, whereas Japan plays a far more narrowly targeted mercantilist game. The questionable programmatic nature of the Japanese program simply fuels this sense of grievance on the part of the United States, whether justified or not. This issue has lain dormant since the hysteria over a "yen bloc" reached its peak in the early 1990s. However, the issue of foreign assistance could be expected to emerge as another point of contention during the next flare-up in Japan-United States economic tensions. This could be particularly acute if aid issues became linked to security issues.

Multilateral Programs

Part of the Cold War policy pursued by the West was to support friendly regimes with concessional financial assistance, in large part through loans disbursed by national, regional, and global public-sector financial institutions. With the end of the Cold War, the justification for such lending and the fiction of repayment declined pari passu. Debt relief caught the public imagination (especially in the United Kingdom and United States), and by the late 1990s an international political consensus had emerged that some official debt forgiveness was in order—although considerable intellectual controversy remained as to whether debt relief was a particularly effective means of fostering economic development.

The Highly Indebted Poor Countries (HIPC) Initiative—begun under the auspices of the World Bank and IMF in 1996—became the centerpiece of the debt relief enterprise. Country eligibility was determined largely according to the debt-export ratio and per capita income, making only the poorest of countries eligible. If external debt was calculated to be unsustainable, multilateral official lenders—including the World Bank, regional development banks, and IMF—were to undertake a reduction in their claims, whereas provisions covered debts owed to bilateral official lenders and commercial lenders.[35] According to the World Bank, "the net-present value of public debt in the 33 countries likely to qualify (approximately $90 billion) would be reduced by about half after HIPC and tradi-

---

35. Multilateral and bilateral creditors are expected to each bear roughly 48 percent of HIPC's costs, with commercial creditors accounting for the rest (International Development Association and International Monetary Fund 2001, table 6).

tional debt relief" (World Bank 2001, 4). In return for debt forgiveness, HIPC countries must undertake poverty reduction measures under World Bank and IMF supervision. In fact, before debt relief, the participating countries on average spent more on debt service than on health and education combined. Since debt relief, spending on social services has increased markedly.

So who will pay for these good works? In the case of the multilateral creditors, which are financial intermediaries, funding for debt relief has come from a combination of national contributions to the HIPC Trust Fund and, secondarily, IMF gold sales. The European Union and Japan will bear the predominant costs of relief of official bilateral debt, whereas the United States will absorb relatively little cost through this channel, reflecting the high grant component of US official development assistance (ODA). Funding for the HIPC Trust Fund has come primarily from the European Union and the United States, with Japan contributing only about a third as much (International Development Association and International Monetary Fund 2001, tables 11 and 15).

Although it is not an exaggeration to argue that there is an international political consensus behind HIPC—support for the initiative appears to be the only position on which the US Treasury, the Meltzer Commission (in both its majority and minority reports), and the Japanese Ministry of Finance agree—there have been differing degrees of enthusiasm for the project. For understandable reasons, of the major creditor countries, the United Kingdom and United States, which have active public movements for debt relief and little official lending (and hence bear little of the burden of debt forgiveness), have been the most accepting; in contrast, the governments of France and Japan have been the least enthusiastic. Initially the Japanese Foreign Ministry stated that countries that asked for complete debt relief would not be eligible to receive fresh loans, and in at least one case, the Japanese ambassador to a country considering participating in the HIPC scheme stated that Japan would cut off aid if that country applied. In part, this can be attributed to Japan's historical emphasis on loans as a vehicle for development assistance and emphasis on the need to repay loans. More to the point, most HIPC participants are in sub-Saharan Africa—a region of little strategic interest to the Japanese government and little financial exposure to Japanese firms.

Differing attitudes toward the HIPC effort point to a broader problem, similar to that encountered with respect to the IMF: although Japan has increased its funding to the multilateral development organizations, its influence over policy remains limited. At the World Bank and its soft-loan window, the International Development Association, Japanese contributions have increased relative to the US contribution, although the United States remains the largest contributor. Influence within these organizations is largely determined by the extent of financial contributions, and the United States has maintained blocking power over major policy issues. Furthermore, by custom the president of the World Bank is an American, and, as discussed above, the managing director of the IMF, its sister institution, is a European. No high-ranking positions in either organization are traditionally reserved for a Japanese citizen. The one multilateral financial institution where the Japanese are dominant is the ADB. Although the United States and Japan hold equal capital shares, the president is customarily a Japanese national.

Japanese nationals make up less than 2 percent of IMF staff and less than 1 percent of World Bank staff—figures far below the shares of Japan's financial contributions. This disjuncture between Japanese financial contributions and staffing levels has resulted in at least one public threat to reduce funding for UN agencies (though not for the IFIs, per se) (Hamada 1999).[36] It is sometimes argued that a shortage of qualified Japanese personnel willing to enter the international civil service hampers attempts to increase Japanese influence in these organizations. Although this may have been true in the past, there is no reason for it to be true in the future. In the short run, the relatively early retirement age in the Japanese civil service means that there is a pool of former senior government officials who could undoubtedly be induced to enter into international civil service with the proper incentives. The problem is that they tend to be generalists, and few meet the professional standards and qualifications of the IFIs. In the long run, a support system of incentives and rewards for service in international organizations could be more fully integrated into career advancement ladders. International leadership requires the development and support of such a capacity.

This matter is not purely an issue of national representation, however; there also is an ideological component. Japan has a history of trying to push the IFIs toward more interventionist policies. In the late 1980s and early 1990s, Japanese officials expressed uneasiness with the ideological basis of staff work at the IFIs and the notion of policy conditionality, and undertook a number of actions aimed at reorienting the ideological basis of policy in the IFIs. For example, the MOF cosponsored seminars with the IMF in which Japanese representatives promoted the virtues of state-led capital channeling to developing-country policymakers. Japanese officials were highly critical of the World Bank's 1991 *World Development Report*, which emphasized the advisability of relying on market mechanisms to spur growth; it issued a rebuttal, "Issues Relating to the World

---

36. According to N. Tanaka, Japan provides "nearly 25 percent of the [OECD's] funding but only 5 percent of the administrative staff and virtually none of the initiatives in meetings" (1992, 27). In 1999, Japan's UN ambassador, Yukio Sato, indicated that funding for international organizations would be put at risk if Japan did not receive a proportionate number of positions for its nationals—although the real constraint is a lack of qualified Japanese applicants (Green 2001).

Bank's Approach to Structural Adjustment," which criticized what it regarded as the Bank's free-market orthodoxy and which pushed industrial policies and capital channeling as an alternative. The Overseas Economic Cooperation Fund (OECF) responded by underwriting World Bank research activities that yielded the controversial *East Asian Miracle* study (World Bank 1993).[37] (Later, it would finance a second World Bank project along these same lines in the wake of the Asian crisis, in an attempt to influence IFI policy and secure an intellectual imprimatur for Tokyo's policies.) The MOF then underwrote the establishment in Tokyo, not Manila, of the Asian Development Bank Institute, a think tank charged with developing an alternative development paradigm.

Bilateral Programs

In addition to these multilateral activities, both Japan and the United States have maintained extensive programs of bilateral engagement, ranging from trade and investment insurance and facilitation programs to pure grants. Historically, US aid has primarily gone to geostrategically important countries, without a great deal of weight placed either on relative need or programmatic effectiveness. For example, in 1999, the five largest recipients of US aid were Israel, Russia, Egypt, Ukraine, and Bosnia and Herzegovina (OECD 2001). Only about a sixth of US aid goes to the 48 least-developed countries. In recent years, in addition to the traditional goals of supporting security, economic development, and providing for humanitarian relief, US policymakers have taken on the additional tasks of supporting the economic and political transformation of formerly socialist countries, addressing transnational problems such as communicable diseases, and promoting democracy abroad (Lancaster 2000).

For Japan, a whole panoply of aid programs has been justified in terms of *keizai kyoryoku* ("economic cooperation"), without much regard for the degree of concessionality or their explicit mercantilist rationale. As one observer put it, "making the world safe for Japanese business is seen as a perfectly worthy goal of national policy" (Johnstone 1998, 91). Taken together, these programs are large; are focused on Asia; could be characterized by a high degree of bureaucratic fragmentation, rivalry, and questionable effectiveness; and have been continually questioned by outside observers, who have wondered if they are more about Japanese commercial interests than development.

Among the bureaucratic actors are the Japan Bank for International Cooperation (JBIC), created through the merger of the Export-Import

---

37. See Wade (1996) and Terry (2001) for detailed descriptions of the origins of the *East Asian Miracle* study and Japanese government involvement. The essays contained in Fishlow et al. (1994) are readable critiques of the study itself.

Bank of Japan (JEXIM), supplier of loans to support exports, imports, and overseas investment projects, and the Overseas Economic Cooperation Fund (OECF). In addition to providing concessional loans to developing-country governments, JBIC also provides limited lending, equity investments, and guarantees to Japanese private-sector-led projects in developing countries. The Japan External Trade Organization (JETRO), heavily subsidized by METI, promotes Japanese exports and, important in this context, technology transfer to developing countries. The Japan International Development Organization (JAIDO), established in 1989 by the Japanese government and the Japan Federation of Economic Organizations (Keidanren), provides equity support, loan guarantees, and consulting services for Japanese private-sector projects in developing countries. The Japan Overseas Development Corporation (JODC) promotes trade and investment in developing countries by Japanese small and medium-sized enterprises and supports personnel exchanges, mainly in the form of Japanese experts dispatched to developing countries. The Association for Overseas Technical Scholarship (AOTS) underwrites programs to bring trainees from developing countries to Japan (Johnstone 1998).

The JBIC, which supplies loans to support exports, imports, and overseas investment projects, is large—more than 13 times larger than the Export-Import Bank of the United States. According to Johnstone (1998), JBIC and METI programs support 36 percent of Japanese exports, whereas the comparable respective figures for France and the United States are 15 and 2 percent.

Most JBIC activity supports either Japanese exports or FDI by Japanese firms, with more than half of these funds disbursed in Asia. That said, the degree of "additionality" embodied in this activity is questionable, inasmuch as it reproduces financing undertaken by the private sector in other countries. Indeed, this could be regarded as yet another instance in which Japanese public-sector financial institutions squeeze out possibly more efficient and less socially risky activities by private-sector institutions.

Japan's foreign aid program is also quite large. The OECD definition of financial assistance is that grants or loans have economic development or welfare as their primary objective, and carry concessional financial terms (i.e., a grant element of at least 25 percent). For purposes of comparison, financial assistance to developing countries is often expressed in the donor's currency as a percentage of GNP. As Japan grew richer, the share of Japanese national income devoted to ODA rose over time, and by the 1990s exceeded the average of the G-7 (figure 6.1), though at roughly a third of 1 percent, it remained far below that of historically generous nations such as Denmark (1.0 percent), Norway (0.91 percent), and the Netherlands (0.85 percent), and the UN's target of 0.7 percent. Even so, the Japanese aid budget has been declining in recent years, a victim of

Figure 6.1 Official development assistance, 1975-98 (percent of GNP)

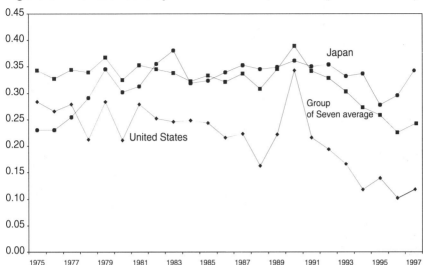

Sources: Organization for Economic Cooperation and Development, Development Assistance Committee; World Bank, *World Development Indicators*, February 2000; IMF, *International Financial Statistics*, March 2001.

poor Japanese economic performance and a lack of enthusiasm in the business community for the "softer" emphasis on social capacity building and environmentally oriented projects.[38] By comparison, the United States has historically been one of the least generous donor countries, and today it ranks dead last in its share of GDP devoted to ODA among the 22 members of the OECD's Development Assistance Committee, behind even poorer countries such as Portugal and Greece.

As the yen has appreciated since the 1970s, the Japanese contribution in dollar terms has grown substantially. Today, Japan is easily the largest aid donor in dollar terms, at more than $13 billion, despite reductions in its aid budget in the late 1990s (table 6.1). Most Japanese aid is in the form of yen-denominated loans, and at times countries have had trouble repaying these debts during periods of yen strength, through no fault of the Japanese official lenders.[39] Moreover, despite international calls to focus aid on the least-developed countries, Tokyo's most recent (1999) programmatic review reiterated its strategic emphasis on East Asia and intention to reemphasize aid flows to this region.

---

38. MOFA's "soft" agenda appears to lack the same domestic political support as METI's more commercially oriented program. Some Japanese corporate leaders have gone so far as to call for "re-tying" aid (cf. Altbach 1998), and in FY1999 the share of tied loans did in fact increase to its highest level in 10 years (Castellano 2000c).

39. During the early 1990s, Asian countries encountered difficulty in repaying such yen-denominated loans. China went so far as to request that Japanese official development assistance be denominated in US dollars; Japan refused.

Table 6.1 OECD Development Assistance Committee, members' official development assistance (ODA), 1998
(millions of dollars)

Country	ODA	Country rank by ODA	ODA as percent of GDP	Country rank by ODA as percent of GDP
Denmark	1,747	8	1.00	1
Norway	1,327	12	0.91	2
Netherlands	3,232	6	0.85	3
Sweden	1,580	10	0.70	4
Luxembourg	111	22	0.64	5
France	6,946	3	0.49	6
Belgium	908	14	0.37	7
Japan	13,175	1	0.35	8
Switzerland	897	15	0.34	9
Finland	407	17	0.33	10
Germany	6,653	4	0.31	11
United Kingdom	4,227	5	0.31	12
Canada	1,739	9	0.30	13
Spain	1,529	11	0.28	14
Australia	960	13	0.27	15
New Zealand	129	21	0.25	16
Austria	516	16	0.24	17
Portugal	259	18	0.24	18
Ireland	198	19	0.24	19
Italy	2,446	7	0.21	20
Greece	179	20	0.15	21
United States	9,580	2	0.12	22
All countries	44,770		0.24	

OECD = Organization for Economic Cooperation and Development.

Source: OECD data.

In fact, China has been the recipient of large aid flows from Japan. This is becoming more controversial in Japan in light of the rapid growth of Chinese military expenditures, the privatization of some public-sector projects supported by Japanese ODA, and the portrayal in China of this aid as being war reparations.[40] Aid to China was reduced in the FY2002 budget.

Although the scale of Japanese activities is large, observers both inside and outside Japan have expressed reservations about the lack of programmatic vision and the quality of the programs. For one thing, a much lower

---

40. Indeed, 1995 Chinese nuclear tests led to a temporary suspension of Japanese grants to China. Japanese aid to Burma has also been controversial, causing frictions with Western countries since the late 1980s.

percentage of Japanese assistance takes the form of grants (only about a half), relative to the OECD average (and more than 95 percent for the United States). Japanese officials have responded that there is not the same cultural tradition of charity in Japan, and it is felt that loans, for which repayment is expected, will be used more wisely than grants. Besides, in recent years Japanese grants to both multilateral and bilateral sources have at times exceeded the entire aid budget of France, the world's third largest donor.

A second concern involves programmatic implementation. The Japanese programs are administered by a plethora of bureaucratic organizations, variously under the auspices of the EPA, MOF, MITI, and MOFA, with considerable overlap in their missions and a history of bureaucratic rivalry in program implementation. The 2001 bureaucratic reorganization gave MOFA primary responsibility for coordinating aid programs.

Although the size of the Japanese ODA program grew rapidly, the number of staff remained roughly constant, and over the course of a decade, the amount of funding per staff increased fivefold, greatly exceeding that observed in other major donors. Add fragmented administration and the relative lack of experience or specialized skills among the Japanese staff, and the picture that emerges is of an overwhelmed bureaucracy experiencing difficulty discharging its duties to disburse funds and oversee project implementation. Indeed, employees of private-sector ODA contractors have been known to work full time in government aid offices (Craib 1994). These conditions have contributed to slow disbursement of funds, allegations of de facto aid tying, and periodic revelations of money wasted due to corruption, mismanagement, and poor project implementation in recipient countries (Johnstone 1998).

Finally, there are suspicions among many observers that the Japanese foreign aid program is undertaken primarily to support Japanese commercial interests—as is arguably the case elsewhere. Indeed, the Japanese aid program did have its origins in early postwar programs largely aimed at securing raw materials for the Japanese economy in exchange for Japanese-produced manufactures. Despite recent emphases on social capacity and institution building, and environmentally oriented projects, lending activities remain significantly concentrated on large, capital-intensive infrastructure projects, more so than in the case of other major donors.[41]

Japanese firms arguably have a comparative advantage in these projects, and throughout the 1970s, aid was explicitly tied to the purchase of Japanese products. Although the share of explicitly tied aid has fallen in recent years (the share of explicitly tied aid fell from 100 percent in the

---

41. Ironically, among the most prominent manifestations of "greener" aid has been Japan's effort to encourage atmospheric pollution abatement in China, in response to acid rain in Japan generated by dirty power plants in China, many of which were built with Japanese official assistance (Green 2001).

early 1970s to less than 5 percent in the early 1990s, and despite its recent increase, remains well below the US figure), it is often argued that this understates the effective degree of tying that occurs.[42] Indeed, the government of Japan has given skeptics ample ammunition on this point—for example, MITI's promotion in the late 1980s of the New Asian Industrial Plan (or "Asian Brain") proposal, which explicitly envisioned an aid-supported MITI coordination of Asian countries' industrial policies to promote Japanese commercial interests, or its late-1990s plans to use ODA as a "pump primer" for FDI by Japanese firms. As former Prime Minister (and future Finance Minister) Kiichi Miyazawa stated in 1997, "Development assistance should be linked to private sector money. Because our aid was untied, it didn't show a Japanese face. We should reduce aid while coming up with more effective ways of dispensing it."[43]

What this does is create another potential flashpoint in Japan-United States relations. From the standpoint of Japan, it is a major contributor to development assistance at both the multilateral and bilateral levels, yet has virtually no influence over the policy of the multilateral institutions or even initiatives such as HIPC. It is, in effect, getting little political return on its investment, and domestic support for international assistance is fading as the Japanese economy remains in the doldrums.

Security Issues

Although Japan emphasized the economic dimension of its foreign policy, traditional military security has remained the core concern of the United States. During the Cold War, this division of roles suited Japan well. But even Japan's Shigeru Yoshida, who became Prime Minister in 1948, recognized that Japan would eventually outgrow the "Yoshida Doctrine" of minimal rearmament, close association with the United States, and focus on economic recovery.[44] In the security sphere, successive Japanese governments interpreted Article 9 of the Constitution as affirming the constitutionality of maintaining standing armed forces to deter aggression,

---

42. On implicit and explicit aid tying, see Doherty (1987), Ensign (1992), Arase (1995), Hatch and Yamamura (1996), and Evans and Oye (2001). In May 2001, members of the OECD Development Assistance Committee reached an agreement on circumscribing aid-tying after 3 years of negotiations. However, Japan was successful in getting consultancy services excluded from the agreement, claiming that its consultancy sector was too weak to compete internationally. This loophole may allow Japan to continue to effectively tie large infrastructural projects, inasmuch as it is alleged that in the past project feasibility studies have been used to write specifications to advantage particular providers and to keep such providers abreast of preproject developments.

43. The *Nikkei Weekly*, 9 June 1997.

44. Pyle (1992) argues that the Yoshida Doctrine was a "cynical" foreign policy that even Yoshida came to regret. See also Ozawa (1994) on this point.

but strictly limiting their role to the defense of the home islands. The constitutional prohibition against collective self-defense effectively prevented Japan from joining military alliances such as the Southeast Asia Treaty Organization or the Security Treaty between Australia, New Zealand, and the United States. And as a matter of policy, during the Cold War, the Japanese government declined to participate in UN peacekeeping activities—a restriction that Japan would gradually loosen in the 1990s.

Given the circumscribed role of the military, Japan relied heavily on the United States for military protection and for defense of its vital strategic interests abroad, taking shade, as some Japanese politicians put it, under the largest tree (Green 2001). The centerpiece of this relationship is the 1960 Treaty of Mutual Cooperation and Security, which lays out a set of reciprocal obligations. Under the treaty, the United States promised to defend Japan in case of attack. In turn, Japan agreed to consult with the United States about regional security problems, maintain forces to deter aggression (subject to the constitutional limitation), and come to the assistance of US forces if attacked in Japan. The treaty does not obligate Japan to participate in regional security schemes, nor come to the aid of the United States if US forces are attacked outside Japan.

The modus operandi of security cooperation is operationalized in the Guidelines for Japan-US Security Cooperation and the Status of Forces Agreement (SOFA). These documents spell out the division of labor between the two countries' armed forces under various contingencies and set forth Japan's obligation to furnish, without cost, areas and facilities for US forces in Japan. In the 1960 agreement, the United States, in turn, agreed to bear "without cost to Japan" the remaining expenses associated with maintaining the troops. Pursuant to these agreements, the United States provides a conventional and nuclear security umbrella over Japan, and maintains a presence of about 47,000 troops, mostly garrisoned on the far southerly island of Okinawa.

By the late 1980s, before the end of the Cold War, the United States-Japan security relationship was coming under noticeable stress. Japan imports roughly 70 percent of its oil from the Middle East, and this oil dependency encouraged a diplomatically solicitous posture vis-à-vis the producing nations. In the cases of the boycott of Iranian oil after the seizure of the 1979 US embassy and sanctions against alleged state-sponsored terrorism, Japan acceded to the US position only after substantial prodding.[45] Similarly, Japan made substantial efforts to placate Iran during the 1987 hostilities in the Persian Gulf, refusing to support the proposed

---

45. Yet, it should be recognized that, unlike some NATO allies, Japan did eventually support United States-initiated sanctions after the seizure of the US embassy in Tehran and the Soviet invasion of Afghanistan. As one observer put it, Japan participated in the United States-led Olympic boycott and economic sanctions, "while less principled Western allies rushed in to accept Soviet contracts that would have otherwise gone to Japan" (Reed 1983, 57).

trade embargo, or send minesweepers. Eventually, after months of deliberations on the constitutionality of support for the Gulf minesweeping effort, Japan agreed to provide about $10 million worth of electronic navigation equipment to the naval forces involved.

These events coincided with Japan's emergence during the latter part of the Cold War as a commercial rival of the United States. It was not lost on many observers that Japanese defense expenditures were low by international standards (Balassa and Noland 1988, table 7.1). In effect, Japanese defense expenditures have been politically fixed at 1 percent of GDP—meaning that, in relative terms, during this period Japanese expenditures lagged behind not only major European countries such as France (3.9 percent), Germany (3.1 percent), Italy (2.2 percent), and the United Kingdom (5.1 percent), but even small or neutral countries such as Sweden (2.8 percent), the Netherlands (3.1 percent), and Norway (3.1 percent).[46] In some quarters, this was taken as evidence that Japan was getting a "free ride"—using its aid budget to promote its commercial interests while sheltering under the US security umbrella.[47]

These stresses mutated, but did not disappear, with the end of the Cold War and a decade of subpar Japanese economic performance. Indeed, the outbreak of the Gulf War in 1990 amounted to a significant shock to the system (see box 6.2). As A. Tanaka put it, "Japan appeared totally unprepared to make timely and meaningful responses to this first international crisis of the post-Cold War era" (1995, 92). Green describes a situation in which "Japanese officials failed to predict the onset of the war, failed to predict the overwhelming victory of the United States, and then failed to send personnel to the conflict in spite of unprecedented international pressure to do so" (2001, 17). Instead, Japan's contribution was limited to financial support, leading one Japanese observer to liken the United States to samurai of the Tokugawa period who, although allowed to bear arms, were poor, whereas Japan is like the *chonin* (merchants) who, although without formal political authority, were rich (Hamada 1994). An American observer quipped, "Now we know the meaning of collective leadership: the United States leads, and the United States collects" (Bergsten 1991, 1).[48]

---

46. The 1 percent figure for Japan is a bit of a fudge; if broader NATO accounting conventions were used, Japanese expenditures would rise several tenths of a percent. The main reason is that the NATO definition includes pension costs, and 40 percent of JSDF personnel are officers with sizable pensions. Indeed, the Japanese figure would rise by another two-tenths of a percent if pre-JSDF (i.e., Imperial Army) pensions were included. In absolute terms, Japanese military expenditures are the fourth highest in the world, behind the United States, France, and the United Kingdom.

47. For contemporaneous examples, see Sullivan (1981) and comments contained in MacIntosh (1987).

48. See Pyle (1992), Lincoln (1993), and Funabashi (1999) for more details.

Box 6.2 The Gulf War

Japanese officials initially downplayed the Iraqi invasion of Kuwait, indicating that there was no reason to send troops and opining "the whole thing may be a ploy by the U.S. to sell arms to Saudi Arabia and Israel to bolster the sluggish U.S. defense industries" (quoted in Lincoln 1993, 221). Once the United Nations moved toward an embargo of Iraq, Japan got in line, and Tokyo attempted to identify nonmilitary ways to contribute to the allied effort, while providing modest financial assistance.

The results were dreadful. As allied troops gathered in the Persian Gulf region, Prime Minister Toshiki Kaifu publicly promised a medical team of 100 specialists, but only 26 could be found, and even these quickly returned home before hostilities commenced. The idea of using Japanese aircraft to airlift home third-country refugees (mainly from South Asia and the Philippines) who had fled Kuwait was floated by the foreign ministry, but opposed by the transport ministry. Tokyo then pledged to transport food, water, and medical supplies, but negotiations between the foreign ministry, the transport ministry, and Japan Airlines resulted in a "convoluted plan," which eventually was scrapped (Ozawa 1994, 37). The possibility of using ships was mooted, but withdrawn when the longshoremen's union objected. The possibility of using JSDF aircraft was raised, but this too was eventually rejected. In the end, the government of Japan chartered a US airline to transport the supplies.

As Japan dithered, international pressure to contribute to the effort increased, and eventually the Ministry of Finance effectively took control of the Gulf War policy. Japan boosted its financial contribution to the war effort to $13 billion (financed by a tax increase), though not before a Japanese government spokesperson had announced that Japan would not be "a cash dispensing machine" and the US House of Representatives had overwhelmingly voted to begin removing US troops from Japan unless the Japanese paid all basing costs, despite the fact that Japan already provided the most generous host support of any security partner, at a cost of roughly $5 billion annually.

In the context of its abysmal failure to formulate any meaningful nonfinancial policy, Japan's contribution was derided as "checkbook diplomacy," both at home and abroad. Legislation was introduced to allow JSDF personnel to participate in UN peacekeeping operations after hostilities had ended, but the government was unwilling to push it through political opposition in the Diet, and it was not passed until 1992—well after the war had ended.

Perhaps the diplomatic fallout from the war is best conveyed by the following anecdote: "After the war, a JSDF official had a conversation with an American officer who had actually fought at the front. When the talk turned to the role that Japan had played in the war, the JSDF officer strongly defended Japan's contribution: 'Japan sent no personnel but each citizen gave more than $100 to the effort.' His calculation was based on Japan's $13 billion total contribution, including aid given to Gulf region nations. The American officer answered, 'Fine, I'll give you $100 and you go fight in my place'" (Ozawa 1994, 38-39). Never had $13 billion bought so little goodwill.

Box 6.3 The North Korean nuclear crisis

In March 1993, North Korea announced its intention to withdraw from the Nuclear Non-Proliferation Treaty, and in May it test-fired a Nodong missile capable of hitting population centers in Western Japan. In December 1993, a leaked US National Intelligence Estimate concluded that North Korea had developed one or two nuclear weapons. In May 1994, North Korea began unloading spent fuel rods from its nuclear reactor at Yongbyon, a possible precursor to the manufacture of nuclear weapons. North Korea and the United States were headed toward a possible military confrontation over the North Korean nuclear program.

Despite the obvious threat that a combination of nuclear weapons and missile-delivery systems would present to Japan, US officials were stunned by the reactions of their Japanese counterparts when they began serious contingency planning in the spring of 1994. Although any large-scale US military action on the Korean peninsula would require the use of US bases in Japan, prospects for Japanese assistance beyond this passive role were highly uncertain. Prosaic requests such as simplified customs procedures at Narita Airport, or the use of tugboat services if damaged US ships broke down, were refused. Japan Maritime Self-Defense Force officials indicated that they would be unable to provide ships for minesweeping or surveillance unless directly attacked or provided legal cover by a UN mandate. Embassy sources privately reported that it was even unclear whether damaged US planes, unable to return to their bases in Japan, would be permitted to land at Japanese civilian airports, or whether Japanese civilian hospitals could be used to treat evacuees should the military medical system be overwhelmed. To the exasperated Americans' dismay, this was the Gulf War redux. As one former MOFA official observed, "Japan has been a genius at disappointing its allies" (Okazaki 2001).

The following year, the alliance received another wake-up call in the form of a military confrontation between the United States and North Korea (see box 6.3).[49] At the same time that Japan and the United States were fumbling to deal with the North Korean threat, the two countries were embroiled in an increasingly acrimonious trade dispute on autos and parts, which would culminate in Japan calling the US sanctions bluff in the WTO (as was detailed in chapter 5). The possibility of a nuclear war was defused by former President Jimmy Carter's June 1994 visit to Pyongyang, while the prospects for its paler trade variant were obviated by President Clinton's climb-down on sanctions the following year. Nevertheless, it was apparent to many that there had to be a better way.

A combination of substantive problems and a sense that increased effort had to be made on security concerns to offset the corrosive trade relationship contributed to a bilateral security review, which came to be known as the Nye Initiative (after US Assistant Secretary of Defense Joseph Nye). This effort culminated in the April 1996 Clinton-Hashimoto

---

49. See Ozawa (1994), Funabashi (1999), Noland (2000a), and Green (2001) for additional details.

Joint Security Declaration, which reaffirmed the importance of the alliance to regional security and stability and the US commitment to a 100,000-troop, forward-deployed presence in Asia; initiated a review (completed the following year) of the Guidelines for US-Japan Security Cooperation to focus on regional cooperation in response to regional contingencies; agreed to a new Acquisition and Cross-Servicing Agreement; agreed to return key US military installations on Okinawa in the context of a continuing US presence; and promised to work together to induce China to play a constructive regional role.

The revised 1997 guidelines refocused the alliance on regional contingencies, and addressed some of the problems encountered in the Gulf War and Korean crises. The revisions provided for 40 areas of cooperation, including Japanese minesweeping of sea lanes; intelligence gathering; Japanese rear-area support for the United States in regional crises, including search and rescue missions; logistics support, including round-the-clock US use of Japanese hospitals, ports, and airfields, and the provision of fuel and equipment; and the use of Japanese vessels to evacuate Japanese citizens from conflict areas. However, for all the plethora of detail, the document leaves key terms, such as "surrounding areas" and "rear area," undefined. The Chinese immediately criticized Tokyo for failing to carve out Taiwan from potential areas of conflict covered under the agreement.

Japan and the United States were able to reach a new accommodation—despite Japanese public outrage over the horrific rape of an Okinawan schoolgirl by three US servicemen in September 1995—in part because of increasing Japanese unease over North Korean and Chinese ambitions (in March 1996, China fired missiles into the Taiwan Strait) and the absence of any real multilateral security structures in Asia.[50] In the words of one observer, "Japan has no place else to go" (Green 2001, 22).

The political leadership in Japan, possibly motivated by that recognition, has devoted increasing resources to rearmament. In the words of one analysis, "the wall that separates Japan's armed forces from being a potent military force is paper thin," with the JSDF representing a large, modern force backed by considerable technological and industrial might.[51] In particular, in recent years Japan has greatly increased its force projection

---

50. The rape affected the substantive negotiations by increasing pressure on the United States for base consolidation. It was followed by additional sexual assaults and further regrettable incidents involving US personnel on Okinawa in subsequent years. See Wanner (1997a, 2000), Bandow (1998), Funabashi (1999), and Howell (1999) for discussion. See Dixon (1999) and Rozman (2000) on the absence of effective regional security arrangements. Pyle (1992) traces this lacuna back to Yoshida's reluctance to involve Japan in integration efforts, as occurred in Western Europe.

51. "Will Japan Re-Arm?," Stratfor, 28 May 2001, http://www.stratfor.com/home/promo/0105282155.

capabilities. It has acquired Airborne Warning and Control System aircraft; is in the process of increasing its aerial refueling capacity; and has concluded an agreement with Singapore to use bases there during a crisis.

In 1997, the Defense White Paper first publicly addressed regional security issues rather than focusing on areas immediately around Japan. That said, the constraints on Japan taking on a greater regional security role seem to be more political than technological. The United States-Japan alliance is still not a fully functioning military alliance, and the hope that Japan and the United States can develop a special relationship along the lines of that between the United Kingdom and United States contained in the "Armitage Report" (IISS 2000) would seem to be wishful thinking, at least in the medium run, as the report's authors acknowledge. Although one day Japan may become the "UK of the East" or Prime Minister Nakasone's "unsinkable aircraft carrier," that day is a long way off.

Looking Toward the Future

Japan's postwar foreign policy has been marked by the centrality of economics and financial contributions. Today, Japan maintains the largest official reserves in the world of nearly $400 billion, and these resources convey a potentially huge role to influence global financial developments. Yet paradoxically, the country's slowing growth and worsening fiscal position have contributed to a national malaise.

The limits of *keizai kyoryoku*—the primary tool for promoting Japan's vision of a regional order—have become clear. The two principal beneficiaries have been China and Indonesia, and one is disintegrating and the other is emerging as Japan's principal security challenge. Concerns over the Japanese government budget have already begun to affect this core aspect of its foreign policy, as evidenced by recent cutbacks in foreign assistance, to cite one example.[52] Continued subpar economic performance could lead to cutbacks in host-nation support for US military bases in Japan. More generally, dwindling resources and the vision of receding influence could fuel more insistent demands to rectify the status quo, for example, for increased Japanese influence in the IFIs, or for political quid pro quos for Japanese financial contributions in other venues. As Green observes,

> The debate in Tokyo is about how to maintain Japan's diplomatic "weight" in the world at a time of declining relative power. The domestic pressure will almost

---

52. In discussions about the 2001 budget, some senior policymakers in the LDP floated the notion of cutting the aid budget by 30 percent and terminating assistance to China. In the end, the budget was cut by only 3 percent. Another 10 percent cut was adopted for FY2002, and aid to China has been considerably reduced.

certainly increase for the Japanese government to get more influence for its money. Phrases like "no taxation without representation" and prioritizing "national interest" are now far more common in the halls of the Diet and the government than the phrases "international contribution" and "obligation" that characterized spending on international affairs in the late 1980s and early 1990s. (2000, 2)

At the same time, while the more shrill calls for burden sharing have diminished, the fact remains that Japan spends considerably less than the other industrial countries on responsibility sharing, and this issue is unlikely to disappear (table 6.2). The world is confronted by a Japan that possesses huge financial resources, self-doubt about its economic future, and a highly uncertain political will to use resources to influence external events.

A key variable in how this tension is resolved will be the outcome of Japan's ongoing process of self-definition and internal political realignment. Mochizuki (1998) identifies the two dominant strains in the internal Japanese debate as those wishing to see Japan become a more "normal country" and those espousing the notion of a "civilian power."[53] The normal-country perspective, which was greatly strengthened by Japan's politically traumatic experience in the Gulf War, emphasizes the need for constitutional revision to permit Japan to play a more reciprocal role in the United States-Japan military alliance. Supporters of this perspective envision Japan cooperating with the United States and South Korea in the case of military action on the Korean peninsula, and strengthening Japanese capabilities to play a more effective balancing role vis-à-vis China.[54]

Some who take this position also emphasize the importance of reinvigorating multilateral security institutions (including the United Nations). Japan made a push for a permanent seat on the UN Security Council in the early 1990s, but the initiative did not come to fruition, owing to the reluctance of the other members to grant a permanent seat to a country that did not commit combat troops to peacekeeping operations (PKOs),

---

53. The "normal-country" position is frequently associated with Ozawa (1994), but many others support variants of this position; the notion of a "civilian power" was first proposed by Maull (1990) and subsequently popularized by Funabashi (1991, 1992). Mochizuki (1998) also identifies two weaker tendencies: those who support a "pacifistic state" and those supporting the notion of Japan as "a great autonomous power." To be clear, when we advocate treating Japan as a "normal country," we mean it in the generic sense—not in the special sense of the phrase invoked here.

54. Both Ozawa (1994) and the editors of the *Yomiuri Shimbun* have proposed draft constitutional revisions. *Yomiuri* polling showed that in 1993 for the first time a majority of respondents favored constitutional revision, mostly in the context of clarifying the constitutionality of JSDF participation in collective security (in the form of UN missions) and collective defense (providing reciprocal military support to the United States). Green (2000) notes that 90 percent of Diet members under the age of 50 support constitutional revision. Prime Minister Koizumi has raised the possibility of constitutional revision.

Table 6.2 Responsibility sharing among the major industrial nations, 1998 (dollars)

Country	Millions of dollars			As percent of GDP			Per capita		
	Defense spending	ODA	Total	Defense spending	ODA	Total	Defense spending	ODA	Total
France	40,241	6,947	47,188	2.8	0.5	3.3	684	118	802
Germany	32,867	6,654	39,521	1.5	0.3	1.9	401	81	482
Italy	22,969	2,447	25,416	2.0	0.2	2.2	399	42	441
Japan	36,695	13,176	49,871	1.0	0.3	1.3	290	104	395
Netherlands	6,873	3,232	10,105	1.8	0.8	2.6	438	206	644
Norway	3,122	1,328	4,450	2.1	0.9	3.0	704	300	1,004
United Kingdom	36,780	4,228	41,008	2.7	0.3	3.0	623	72	694
United States	263,373	9,580	272,953	3.2	0.1	3.3	974	35	1,010

ODA = official development assistance.

Sources: http://www.defenselink.mil/pubs/allied_contrib99/chartill-3.html; World Bank, World Development Indicators, February 2000.

and, if the number of seats were to be expanded, the desire of some developing countries for any expansion of permanent seats to include some of them. (Current policy permits deployment of JSDF personnel only with the unambiguous permission of countries receiving the forces—even in the case of UN-mandated peacekeeping, humanitarian relief, or emergency evacuation.)[55] China opposed the bid, declaring Japan "unfit" to sit on the Security Council, though it is unclear to what extent this reflected genuine Chinese animosity toward Japan, and how much was motivated by rivalry for regional leadership and political expedience. In South Korea, the Japanese textbook controversy led the National Assembly in July 2001 to adopt unanimously a resolution calling on the government to oppose any Japanese attempt to secure a seat on the Security Council.

The "civilian power" view regards the ideals embodied in the constitution as worth preserving and supports an increasingly "independent stance" and the reduction of the US military presence in Japan, especially on Okinawa. Yet Japan has made little progress proactively on a long agenda of nonmilitary international activities, for which Japan has substantial technical capacity, though evidently not the political will (Lincoln 1993).

Underlying this debate is a considerable ambivalence among the Japanese elite about Japan's relationship with the United States and the nature of Japanese democracy. As Berger eloquently puts it,

> The decisive element behind Japanese security behavior has been the emergence of a peculiar culture of antimilitarism. This culture is based on lingering doubts in the Japanese general public as well as in considerable segments of the nation's elite regarding the strength of Japanese democracy and its ability to control the armed forces. In a very real way, the Japanese defense debate has been more a debate regarding the strength of Japanese democracy than a discourse on how to best meet external military threats. (1999, 191)

He is not alone in this assessment. Both Katzenstein (1996) and Hook (1996) concur that the cultural politics of the Yoshida Doctrine are so deeply embedded that domestic political realignment, not Japan's external security situation, will drive changes in Japanese security policy.

---

55. A Japan Maritime Self-Defense Force minesweeping flotilla was dispatched to the Persian Gulf in 1991, and a Japan Ground Self-Defense Force construction battalion was sent to Cambodia in 1992-93 as part of UN peacekeeping efforts. Japanese personnel subsequently participated in PKOs in Mozambique and the Golan Heights, and the humanitarian relief effort in Zaire. Japan notably did not provide personnel for peacekeeping efforts in East Timor (although it did provide money), claiming that Japanese participation in the East Timor PKO would violate the 1992 law's requirement that peacekeepers have to be invited by the receiving country—despite the Indonesian government's acceptance of a multinational peacekeeping force under UN auspices.

This is not to say that external developments will have no impact on Japan. With regard to the United States, there appear to be two obvious variables that could affect the internal debate within Japan. First, if, as is likely, Japan's emergent foreign policy takes on a more multilateral, legalistic, United Nations-centric character, this could bring it into conflict with the increasingly unilateralist character of US foreign policy. In 1999, the US Senate rejected the Comprehensive Test Ban Treaty (CTBT). And the United States has failed to ratify the Land Mine Treaty; is considering legislation that would undercut its commitment to the Rome Statute on war crimes to the International Criminal Court; has rejected a draft agreement to enforce an international ban on biological weapons; is demanding that an agreement on international trafficking in small arms be watered down; and has stated its unwillingness to ratify the Kyoto Protocol on global warming, which is engendering a particularly negative reaction in Japan, given its role in the negotiation of the protocol.[56] Moreover, the United States is likely to abrogate the Anti-Ballistic Missile (ABM) Treaty, and its proposal for national missile defense (NMD) was harshly criticized at the 2000 Nuclear Non-Proliferation Treaty Review conference. Moreover, although UN PKOs are a focal point of the Japanese debate over its security role, the United States has shown little enthusiasm for participation in these activities in recent years. In each case, opponents of the international agreements could cite weaknesses in the agreements or special circumstances that could justify derogation by the United States, and in the specific case of the Kyoto Protocol the United States has indicated its willingness to search for new mutually acceptable options. Nevertheless, taken as a whole, it would appear that the United States is out of step with the rest of the international community, and it is this assessment that could fuel tensions with Japan.

These tendencies are likely to be accentuated by the Bush administration, which has evinced skepticism about international cooperation. The 2001 failure of the United States to secure seats on the UN Human Rights Commission and International Narcotics Control Board has called into question the US commitment to pay its UN arrears. Indeed, given the ambivalent Japanese attitudes toward the United States, US unilateralism could encourage the strengthening of both the extreme "pacifistic state" and "autonomous great power" tendencies, which are at present marginalized in the Japanese internal debate. Conversely, the perception of significant diminution of the US security commitment to Asia (e.g., a sudden reduction in forward-deployed US forces) could unsettle Japan and have a similar effect of radicalizing its internal debate on security issues.

---

56. Regarding the Kyoto Protocol, Prime Minister Koizumi took a conciliatory line during the June 2001 summit, but later agreed with the Europeans to move forward with the treaty, despite US objections.

The most obvious, foreseeable points of tension in this regard are the interrelated debates over the ABM Treaty, theater missile defense (TMD), and NMD. Japan is a self-declared nonnuclear power, which, after some hesitation, signed and ratified the CTBT. The United States-Japan discussions over TMD began in earnest in 1993, in the wake of the North Korean Nodong missile test. Progress was slow, however, due to concerns about cost, effectiveness, and Chinese objections, but received another boost in 1998 when, without warning, the North Koreans test-fired a long-range Taepodong missile over the main Japanese island of Honshu. One of the Japanese government's responses was to formally announce the country's participation in the United States-led TMD research and development program (though it has not committed to production and deployment).[57] The subsequent US push for the larger NMD program has raised similar issues on the Japanese side (cost, effectiveness, Chinese objections), and thus far the Japanese government has remained noncommittal.

The second obvious potential source of tension is economic. It is taken as axiomatic that tensions in the trade arena make cooperation in other areas more difficult, and it would be difficult to argue that bad economic relations make for good security relations.[58] At the same time, there is little evidence to support the contention that trade conflict inevitably erodes security cooperation.[59] The Nye Initiative, which resulted in the joint declaration and the guidelines revisions, was undertaken in part to compensate for problems on the trade side, and was part of a conscious ratcheting down of trade tensions by the Clinton administration. This is simply to say that there is a degree of endogeneity in response and a role for political leadership in alliance management.

As the preceding discussion has made clear, there is ample room for rivalry and tension between Japan and the United States in the economic and security spheres. As a consequence, in the interests of alliance manage-

---

57. See Cronin, Giarra, and Green (1999), Green and Dalton (2000), Harris and Cooper (2000), and Green (2001) for more discussion of ballistic missile defense issues in the context of the Japan-United States relationship. It is interesting to note that, although the North Korean missile launch boosted Japanese interest in TMD, in the context of Japan's ambivalence about the United States and interest in greater self-reliance, it also helped increase Japanese public support for its indigenous spy satellite program (Wanner 1999a, 1999d).

58. For example, Mochizuki writes: "Current trade imbalances, both bilateral and regional, between Japan and the United States can have a corrosive effect on American domestic support for the bilateral security relationship. . . . An aggressive U.S. trade policy will inevitably strain political relations with Japan and may make Japanese leaders somewhat more reluctant to work with the United States on security-related issues" (1999, 244).

59. An analytically distinct, though related, issue involves military procurement. Japan and the United States have a history of tension in this area, often related to the aerospace sector, e.g., Japan's desire to develop and build its own fighter plane, the FSX. See Samuels (1994), Alexander (1995), Green (1995), Stone (1999), Rubenstein (1999), and Chinworth (1999) for more on this issue.

ment, there have been compensatory efforts to promote cooperation in other, less contentious areas. So, for example, the 1993 Framework Agreement contained a section on "A Common Agenda for Cooperation in Global Perspective." This agenda sought to identify avenues for bilateral cooperation in the global arenas of environmental protection, new technology, human resources, population control, and AIDS.

It is hard not to be a little cynical about this effort. On the Japanese side, subsequent Japanese leaders did not evince the same degree of diplomatic commitment to these issues as they did to the more traditional economic and security concerns. (In this respect, they differ from their European counterparts, who at times have given high prominence to these sorts of global issues in their diplomacy with the United States.) On the US side, the Clinton move was seen to some as a fillip to the recently installed Assistant Secretary of State Global Affairs Timothy Wirth, a political ally of the president's. Seven years later, in August 2000 at the Republican Party convention, eventual Bush administration Deputy Secretary of State Richard Armitage cleared the air, stating:

> The United States is not solely responsible for the resolution of problems which we have not caused. Our priorities would be first the well-being and security of our nation and our allies and our friends. But if we attempt to be all things to all people, we'll end up doing very little for anyone. It is the height of insincerity to suggest that AIDS is at the top of our national security list. To suggest that it's at the height of our national security agenda is cynical.[60]

The June 2001 joint statement by President Bush and Prime Minister Koizumi, having addressed first security and then economics, concluded with the traditional invocation of the two countries' shared commitment to tackle the global threat of AIDS and to seek to find common ground on the vexing issue of global warming.

Besides the United States, there are at least two other countries that could have a significant role in how Japanese foreign policy and the United States-Japan security alliance evolve: North Korea and China.[61] The 2001 Defense White Paper identifies North Korea as Japan's primary security concern (JDA 2001). Its nuclear and missile programs and naval incidents in the Japan Sea are the most immediate source of discomfort for Japan, and have facilitated closer Japanese security cooperation with both the United States and South Korea. In December 1998, a North Korean submarine, presumably sent into South Korean waters to land

---

60. See http://www.foreignpolicy2000.org/convention/archives/t_armitage.html.

61. Japan has significant national interests beyond these two countries, most notably its unresolved territorial dispute with Russia over four southern Kurile islands (the Northern Territories, in Japanese discourse). For overviews focusing on China and North Korea, see Wanner (1999b, 1999c), Harris and Cooper (2000), and Green (2001). On the Japan-Russia territorial dispute, see Wanner (1997b).

saboteurs, was discovered by South Korean air reconnaissance. Rather than killing the crew, scuttling the sub, and committing suicide, the North Korean commander fled south toward Japan with South Korean air and sea vessels in pursuit. The sub sank 30 miles outside Japanese territorial waters, obviating the need for a Japanese response. Things went differently 4 months later, when Japanese Maritime Safety Agency coast guard vessels discovered and fired upon two antennae-laden vessels thought to be North Korean spy ships. The incident sparked an emergency midnight cabinet meeting that authorized Japan Maritime Self-Defense Force ships to give chase under Article 82 of the Self-Defense Force Law. The North Koreans got away.[62]

In the long run, however, China may play a more important role. Wariness of China is on the rise in Japan, stemming from a number of factors. First has been China's generally harsh rhetoric toward Japan. This rhetorical antagonism, together with Japanese perceptions of relative decline via-a-vis China and unease with globalization, has stimulated the rise of a new, reactionary, inward-looking identity politics, as evidenced by Prime Minister Koizumi's August 2001 visit to the Yasukuni Shrine. This domestic political development is likely to contribute to more conflictual Sino-Japanese relations. Second, concern about China was given a significant boost by China's 1996 firing of missiles into the Taiwan Strait. Historically, Japan has had better political relations with Taiwan than either North or South Korea, and the Japanese were shocked by what they regarded as Beijing's bellicosity.[63] A third factor has been repeated Chinese naval incursions into Japan's exclusive economic zone, though unlike the North Korean incursions into Japan's territorial waters, these are permitted under the Law of the Sea, and might be likened to US aerial surveillance of China. These concerns have been heightened by the rapid increase in Chinese military expenditures, the new Chinese emphasis on high-technology warfare, and China's alleged role in proliferation of weapons of mass destruction and their delivery systems (JDA 2001).

Enhanced cooperation between Japan and the United States has not been welcomed by either Pyongyang or Beijing. The Chinese criticized both the 1996 United States-Japan Joint Security Declaration and the 1997 Security Guidelines revision, and have objected vociferously to bilateral cooperation on TMD and the possibility of cooperation on NMD. The Chinese believe that these missile defense schemes are aimed at them. They see TMD as fostering Taiwanese independence by rendering ineffective their ballistic missile threat against the island, and NMD as negating their nuclear forces and promoting US hegemony and Japanese remilitari-

---

62. See Cossa (1999), Wanner (1999b), and Hughes (2000) for further details.

63. See Green (2001) for evaluations of contemporary China-Japan relations, and Arase et al. (2001) for polling data indicating growing mistrust between China and Japan.

zation. Their likely response is to accelerate the modernization and deployment of their nuclear-armed missiles (to preserve their deterrent against these presumably imperfectly effective systems), while exploring the possibility of developing their own antimissile system, possibly in collaboration with Russia.[64] In the extreme case, China might attempt preemptive military action against Taiwan before the deployment of an extended deterrence-enhancing US NMD system.

Of course, the impact of TMD and NMD on security affairs in Northeast Asia is ambiguous, owing to uncertainties about the effectiveness of the technologies and the reactions of the state actors. Japanese analysts understand that the missile defense programs potentially enhance Japanese security by reducing terrorist or blackmail threats and increasing the credibility of US extended deterrence (Ogawa 2000). At the same time, the deployment of missile defenses could spark a regional arms race. As one commentary put it, Japan at present "is like a poker player who keeps anteing up and waiting to see the next card before deciding to stay in the game or fold" (Medeiros 2001, i).

How the future relationship between China and Japan plays out will depend on Chinese behavior, both internally and externally. Greater transparency in military affairs, restraint with respect to Taiwan, and evolution toward greater political liberalization internally would likely assuage Tokyo's concerns and contribute to greater Japanese independence vis-à-vis the United States.[65] (Conversely, if the United States were to behave harshly toward China, Tokyo would distance itself from Washington.) However, if China were to use force against Taiwan, the result would be to deepen Japan's wariness of China, and provoke the same sort of reactions as did the North Korean missile tests. Increases in internal repression could have a similar, though less dramatic, effect on Japanese perceptions of China.

Even trade relations are becoming an irritant, with one analyst going so far as to argue that bilateral trade frictions could have a similar effect on Sino-Japanese relations (Silver 2000). In April 2001 Japan placed safeguard restrictions on Chinese exports of shiitake mushrooms, leeks, hand trowels, and tatami rushes used to make mats. China responded by imposing 100 percent tariffs on Japanese cars, mobile phones, and air conditioners. Regardless of the merit, the Japanese should not have been surprised; China had engaged in similarly disproportionate retaliation against South Korea in a comparable dispute over trade in garlic a year earlier.

The dispute could be interpreted as revealing as much or more about the political capture of trade policy in Japan as about Sino-Japan relations. Nevertheless, the ease with which such economically negligible sectors

---

64. For examples of such Chinese views, see Gu (2000), Chu (2000), and Medeiros (2001).

65. See Kato (1999) for suggestions for China-Japan military confidence-building measures.

were able to obtain protection and put significant Japanese economic interests at risk may say something about the general unease in Japan with respect to China. Yet, as in the case of Japan-United States relations, we are skeptical that trade relations are likely to have such a direct impact on national security issues. Indeed, if the two countries could surmount their political differences, their natural economic complementarity could be the basis of highly mutually beneficial economic relations (Xie 2001). China's prospective entry into the WTO should curb its tendency toward disproportionate retaliation, calming this aspect of Sino-Japanese relations.

A potential Chinese challenge for regional leadership is yet another source of prospective tension. Although there is lingering unease with Japan in much of Asia, Japan is, after all, a relatively stable, predictable, bourgeois democracy. Presumably, this contributes to greater legitimacy and acceptance, at least in comparison with authoritarian, and possibly expansionist, China. Regional apprehension toward a more assertive China could be sparked by territorial disputes (e.g., Taiwan, the Spratly Islands) between China and its neighbors. The presence of ethnic Chinese minorities in many neighboring Asian countries could further complicate a Chinese bid for regional leadership. If nothing else, however, China has shown that it is willing to play its cards—something that Japan seems reluctant to do.

Conclusions

The Second World War and its aftermath still hang heavily over Asia more than a half-century after the end of the war and of Japan's empire. It turned the United States into the predominant regional power that it remains today. It poisoned Japan's relations with its neighbors, which remain awkward and ambivalent.

This legacy remains unresolved within Japan as well. The Cold War provided a convenient rationale for the Yoshida Doctrine of minimal rearmament, close association with the United States, and a focus on commercial policy. With the end of the Cold War, Japan—and, by extension, the United States and Japan's neighbors—have been forced to reassess Japan's place in the world.

Japan is confronted with a slew of global and regional issues in the areas of trade, finance, development, and security. It has enormous financial resources and considerable institutional capacity that potentially could be brought to bear on these problems. The effective exercise of Japanese power is constrained, however, by its internal politics, and its ongoing process of national self-definition.

The rise of China is likely to force the issue. China's ascendancy poses challenges for Japan in the economic, diplomatic, and security fields. The degree of interdependence and cooperation between Japan and the United States is such that the emergence of China will inevitably have significant repercussions for the bilateral relationship, affecting, for example, how the United States might regard the development of regional economic institutions in Asia. Specific policy recommendations for enhanced bilateral cooperation in managing China's integration into the international system, as well as other bilateral economic and security issues, are taken up in chapter 7.

7

Building a New Japan-United States Economic Relationship

The Case for Normalcy

Japan represents an anomaly for the United States: It is the only country toward which the United States, more or less consistently, has adopted a country-specific foreign economic policy. The rest of US international economic relationships—even with larger economies, such as the European Union or its larger trading partners, such as Canada and Mexico—are conducted primarily as elements of its global economic strategy.[1] But the strong US economic performance throughout the 1990s, led by sectors where Japan had been regarded as a major threat less than a decade earlier, demonstrates that it can succeed quite nicely without much accommodation from Japan. Japan's "decade of decline" makes clear that it was never the threat that some Americans perceived it to be—and, indeed, that Japanese economic weakness may be a greater risk for the United States than Japanese economic strength ever was. The revisionists were simply wrong to argue that Japan was so "different" and so important that Japan-specific policies were required for the United States to restore its economic progress.

---

1. Canada and Mexico are of course members of NAFTA but all of its institutional arrangements are trilateral and, even with them, the intensity of US interchange is far less than it has been with Japan.

The whole case that Japan is unique has weakened substantially in recent years. As was observed in chapter 3, internal institutions regarded as uniquely Japanese, such as lifetime employment and the *keiretsu* system, are eroding. An ongoing process of deregulation is creating a Japanese economy that looks more and more like those of other major industrial economies. Changes include complete privatization of Japan Airlines (unlike Air France, which remains under government control) and partial privatization of NTT (just as in Germany) and Japan Rail (which is de jure more private than Amtrak). Airfares have been deregulated as much as in the United States. Store hours have been lengthened, and stores are open as much as US stores (and much more than those in continental European countries). Most automakers in Japan are controlled by foreigners. Large banks, insurance companies, and securities firms are being bought up by foreigners. The unthinkable of just 15 years ago is occurring virtually every day.

Moreover, recent research by Porter and two Japanese colleagues (Porter, M. Sakakibara, and Takeuchi 2000) concludes persuasively that Japan's hypercompetitiveness in the earlier period was based primarily on management practices that could be, and were, readily emulated by non-Japanese firms rather than by government supports that demanded governmental counteraction abroad. In any event, governmental industrial policy clearly plays a much smaller role in Japan today than in the past. Deregulation and privatization are occurring at a faster pace than in some European countries. This justification for Japan-specific policies by the United States, one of the most important in the traditional lexicon, has also waned substantially.

The analysis of trade and investment relations in chapter 4 indicates that Japan's relative global economic importance is eroding as well. European unification and the creation of the euro mean that the European Union is now the largest economic unit in the world, far larger than Japan. The yen is now a distant third among global currencies, far behind the new euro as well as the dollar. The rise of China may mean that Japan will even lose its status as the key economy in the Asia-Pacific region. The anomaly of the past would be even greater in the future if the United States were to continue to pursue a unique "Japan policy."

Even in its bilateral relations with the United States, Japan's salience is falling. As was shown in chapter 4, Japan accounts for a declining share of US trade and investment (and the difference in the modalities of trade and investment with Japan—e.g., US investment in subsidiaries as distinct from joint ventures—is declining as well). Even with respect to the traditional lightning-rod issue of the US trade deficit, the share accounted for by Japan is down to about a fifth, as opposed to more than half during the 1980s, even as the total size of the US imbalance has soared. It is in fact clear that the current account deficit is a global problem for the United

States, reflecting factors that apply across all of its international economic relationships, and that it must find a global solution—as was also the case at the previous peak of the deficit, in the middle 1980s, when the United States had to engineer a steep depreciation of the dollar against all the other major currencies but when it particularly sought correction against the yen. Even the issue of macroeconomic imbalances can no longer be viewed as a "Japan problem" and the efforts of American industry to promote a weaker dollar in 2001 were, unlike the past, not directed primarily at the yen.

Closely related is the issue of Japan's "unfair" treatment of foreign competition. This charge of course continues to be heard and—because it is based so much on motivations as well as observed results—will never disappear. However, after substantial foreign takeovers of Japanese financial institutions, the sale of Nissan to Renault, and the widespread penetration of foreign brand-name retailers—such as Starbucks Coffee, Toys 'R Us, and Amazon.com—the specter of unfair treatment has become largely obsolete.

Moreover, concerns about Japan do not loom large in the backlash against globalization in the United States, the major threat to continued openness of US policy. The backlash focuses primarily on developing countries that allegedly pose threats of "low-wage competition" and "races to the bottom" with respect to the environment, labor, and other standards. Hence, Japan does not represent a threat to the maintenance of an open US trade policy, as it did in the 1970s (when it prompted the Nixon import surcharge) and the 1980s (when it, along with the massive dollar overvaluation and "benign neglect" of the first Reagan administration, led Congress to seriously consider sweeping protectionist legislation).

For all these reasons, the time has come for the United States to start treating Japan as a "normal country" and to address it henceforth primarily in the same multilateral context that largely determines the US stance toward the rest of the world. This does *not* constitute a proposal for "benign neglect" or for "bypassing" Japan. It does *not* mean ignoring continuing US economic problems with Japan nor Japan's continuing economic problems with the United States. It does not rule out bilateral, or even unilateral, initiatives that are consistent with the multilateral rules, or even that go beyond them in extreme and unusual cases. It certainly does not preclude active bilateral cooperation between Japan and the United States, especially where they can work together to provide leadership in the global institutions, as they have on occasion done in the past.

It does suggest, however, that the United States no longer needs to treat Japan separately as a special, unique target of a country-specific foreign economic policy. It is not clear, in fact, that it made sense to do so in the past. Japan's macroeconomic impact on the United States has always been rather modest. Moreover, as was demonstrated in chapter 5, the tangible results of the frequently intense US pressures on Japan during the past 30 years have been exceedingly modest, despite an enormous variety of approaches and huge expenditures of political capital. Some of the wide array of Japan-specific policies pursued by the United States during this extended period—such as the campaign to achieve abolition of the Large-Scale Retail Store Law—were met largely by accommodation, whereas some others did not produce any tangible results, at least from the viewpoint of the "results-oriented" camp. Changes and reforms have tended to happen in Japan when US demands have made economic sense and have won allies within Japan itself, but results have not been delivered when US demands have lacked a coherent rationale and domestic supporters.

The final element in the equation is the reduction in the US ability to prompt changes in economic policy in Japan, as revealed so clearly by the failure of the last major US trade initiatives in the middle 1990s and of the equally aggressive US efforts to change Japanese macroeconomic and financial policies in the late 1990s. This is partly the natural result of the maturation of Japan to a point where it no longer feels such an acute need for US patronage and approval. It is partly due to the idiosyncratic twists and turns in the policy of the United States itself, which have left Japan successively feeling betrayed (as in the Asian financial crisis) and beleaguered (as in so many of the trade disputes). It is partly due to the end of the Cold War, with the consequent sharp reduction in Japan's need for protection by an external superpower. It is partly due to Japan's persisting economic weakness and the new found strength of the United States, which suggests to many Japanese both that the United States no longer needs their help and that they can no longer afford to give it. And it is particularly due to the creation of the World Trade Organization, with its dispute-settlement mechanism that protects Japan against US unilateralism.

There is considerable evidence that Japanese resistance to *gaiatsu* has risen substantially and that future efforts to deploy it will be more likely to jeopardize the overall relationship than to win Japanese acceptance of US objectives. As was discussed in chapter 6, this effect could be compounded by the inevitable fiscal pressures of Japan's huge budget deficit and national debt, and the subsequent rapid aging of the population. These pressures have already led to modest cuts in Japan's aid budget and calls to reduce "support costs" for the US military, and they could pose an increasing threat to the security relationship, especially if the overall ties between the countries were to sour. One traditional element in the security debate, emanating from the foreign policy and national security community, has always been that the economic tensions should be ignored or at least downplayed to avoid jeopardizing the broader relationship. As the relative importance of security issues has again risen in the US calculus, with the ascent of China replacing the decline and demise of the Soviet Union, that concept clearly takes on added weight. For the future, the prospects of US "success" for any Japan-specific policy are thus even slimmer. Indeed, one should be careful in measuring "success" in Japan-United States negotiations. If it is measured in terms of a "level playing field," by harmonizing regulation, there is a chance that further negotiations can succeed. However, if it is measured by limiting the amount of Japanese exports to the United States or artificially increasing the amount of US exports to Japan, then its chances are slim.

In his extensive analysis of the prospects for change in Japan, Lincoln concludes that "actual job loss and bankruptcy have not been sufficiently widespread to produce a strong political movement in favor of more radical or thorough reform" (2001, 203). Moreover, the tight interlocking of the various parts of the Japanese economic system means that even successful reforms of individual elements do not produce much actual change. Lincoln estimates that the sum of Japan's "vested interests" in portions of the status quo add up to a majority of the population (2001, 8), confirming a remark once made to one of the authors by reform advocate Ichiro Ozawa that the Japanese public *likes* its web of extensive governmental regulation and that it would take a very strong government in Japan to carry out an extensive restructuring program.[2]

Perhaps the Koizumi cabinet will turn out to be such a government. But even if it does, Japan is unlikely to respond quickly in the future to even aggressive US reform urgings. Indeed, such forcefulness is more likely to lead to US frustration (and perhaps Japanese backlash) than to Japanese action. This combination of probable outcomes adds further to the case for a much more measured US policy approach toward Japan. This outlook suggests that future US administrations and Congresses would be well advised to eschew Japan-specific economic policies, even if one believes that their predecessors were correct to pursue them.

The most important factor underlying this prescription is the revival of the US economy in the 1990s, as was traced in chapter 2. Indeed, in a previous work, two of the present authors argued that the "restoration of satisfactory economic growth and international competitiveness in the United States itself would go far to defuse tension with Japan, as much of the hostility toward that country reflects America's own performance and the resulting tendency to look for scapegoats abroad" (Bergsten and Noland 1993, 4). We added that a successful implementation of US economic reforms would "noticeably reduce the intensity of US-Japan economic conflict" (18). In particular, we advocated a sharp reduction in the

---

2. Two other leading foreign observers of Japan, Abegglen (2001) and Dore (2001), agree with Lincoln's conclusions—though they approve of the outcome, whereas Lincoln deplores it.

public-sector deficit; adoption by the private sector of competitiveness-enhancing Japanese practices, where applicable; and a willingness to share leadership with Japan in managing the world economy.

The record in the intervening years has been largely positive. In the private sector, US firms have indeed raised their productivity sharply, in part by adopting innovative management techniques developed by their Japanese rivals. In the public sector, the United States has made enormous progress in improving its finances. It has made less progress in other areas (e.g., public education) that we identified in our earlier work, and which remain sources of significant concern. Nevertheless, the future for the US economy looks considerably brighter than it did a decade ago. A confident United States should be well positioned to engage Japan cooperatively in resolving bilateral issues and managing the world economy more generally.

Indeed, it now appears that the quarter-century of acute US economic hostility toward Japan, from the early 1970s through the middle 1990s, was the result of a unique historical coincidence. The United States encountered substantial economic difficulties in the early 1970s—just as Japan was emerging into global economic prominence. The United States restored satisfactory levels of economic expansion and stability, with sound underlying government policies, only in the middle 1990s—just as Japan was slipping into its "decade of decline." In retrospect, it seems clear that this coincidental juxtaposition of Japanese rise and US (temporary, if prolonged) fall goes far to explain the decisions by successive US administrations to adopt the unique Japan-specific policy that prevailed for about 25 years.

As viewed from the middle of 2001, the next half-decade or so looks most likely to witness a continuation of the late 1990s: a reverse combination of US economic strength and Japanese weakness. We must be careful, however, not to assume that this state of affairs will last indefinitely, any more than did the opposite juxtaposition of 1970-95. Indeed, the weaknesses revealed in the US economy in 2000-01 could turn out to be lasting. And Japan, under the Koizumi government, could adopt far-reaching reforms and even enjoy a period of catch-up growth that would recoup some of the huge output gap that opened up during its decade of stagnation. Our proposals for Japan-United States economic relations in the period ahead must nevertheless rest on the best judgments we can reach about the outlook for the two economies, tempered of course by the history and realities of the direct relationship between them.

Restoring Japanese Economic Vitality

Unfortunately, in contrast to the United States, Japan's macroeconomic performance for the past decade has been disappointing. Following the bubble period of the late 1980s and early 1990s, officials made a series of macroeconomic policy mistakes that left the economy limping for a decade. Monetary policy remained tight for too long after the bubble burst. Fiscal policy was opaque, and the imposition of a tax increase in 1997—though understandable in terms of Japan's long-term health—was premature and pushed a weak economy into first recession and then a liquidity trap.

Unwise lending by the banks and reckless commitments by the insurance sector—along with poor prudential regulation on the part of the authorities, in the context of the excesses of the bubble period and the weakness of the economy in its aftermath—have left the financial sector burdened with huge nonperforming loans and Japan as a country with vastly underfunded public and private liabilities. The weakness of the banks impairs their ability to act as efficient financial intermediaries, undermining the confidence of both consumers and investors, and thereby weakening the economy at its core. Public concern about the future boosts precautionary savings, reducing both consumption and investment. The result is a vicious circle, in which slow growth creates more NPLs, which further undermine confidence and impair the ability of the banks to finance recovery.

The government has made progress in financial-sector reform ("the Big Bang" and the establishment of the independent Financial Services Agency, to name two), but the political consensus necessary to resolve the problems of the banking sector has been absent. The weakness of the MOF-led regulatory system, and the historically clubby relationship between MOF officials and the financiers that they regulate, has meant that there has been no serious accounting of the incompetence (and at times outright corruption) that allowed the system to deteriorate. Without accountability, voters have been understandably unwilling to countenance using the large sums of public money that are necessary to recapitalize the banking system. And the politicians—caught between their own unwillingness to act decisively with respect to the financial establishment, and the public's unwillingness to fund a massive bailout—have temporized.

This delay has been extremely costly. It has plunged the economy into a vicious circle of slow growth and financial distress. Most importantly, the authorities must address the NPL issue far more aggressively. The stance thus far has been to recognize and write down NPLs at a rate that was consistent with bank profitability (i.e., banks have only classified loans as nonperforming and written them down as they had profits to do so). In addition, the financiers who have been subject to legal proceedings have all come from failed institutions. The lesson that the government has inadvertently conveyed, that one can avoid investigation by keeping one's institution afloat, has reinforced the private sector's incentive to evergreen NPLs.

This approach was consistent with the interests of the banks, which did not want to admit to an erosion of their capital bases and voluntarily apply for an injection of funds. It was in the interest of their NPL borrowers that wanted to avoid foreclosure. It was in the interest of the FSA, which did not want to admit that it had made a mistake in 1999 when it erroneously indicated that the capital injection at that time had fixed the problem. It was in the interest of incumbent politicians who did not want to go back to the public for more money to fix the banking system. Given this coincidence of interests, it is perhaps not surprising that the policy has amounted to a stable equilibrium in both economic and political terms—but one that has permitted the continued deterioration of the economy and, even more important, has made the ultimate resolution of the problem ever more costly and ever more disruptive.

The crucial issue is that, as the costs mount, deferring the resolution of the problem is not in the interest of the country as a whole. The formation of the Koizumi government gives the FSA the political support it needs to address the problems more forcefully. First, it can broaden the definition of problem loans to encompass all financial institution loans—not just those of the major banks.[3] Second, it can encourage weak banks to "voluntarily" accept a capital injection. (The preferable alternative would be new legislation that would permit the direct nationalization of the banks and their closure or recapitalization under new managements.) Third, the government needs to clearly signal that malfeasance at existing institutions will be dealt with firmly to discourage the socially harmful evergreening of NPLs.

Aggressive action toward the banks would act as a further drag on growth in the short run. It has been estimated that the Yanagisawa Plan to force the major banks to clear their NPLs in 3 years could lead to 20,000 corporate bankruptcies and the elimination of 200,000 jobs. Resolution of the extensive problems beyond the major banks could ultimately lead to more than 1 million people losing their jobs.

Although repairing the banks might slow the economy in the short run, however, it is necessary to restore long-run growth. In addition, decisive action by the government should actually restore public confidence. Forward-looking equity markets would rise, strengthening bank balance sheets. Decisive action would also encourage capital inflow, further reinforcing the rise in asset prices (and the exchange rate). Most important, decisive action by the government and increases in equity prices would help both to reduce precautionary savings and to generate a positive wealth effect to encourage private consumption. The result

---

3. The FSA has defined the problem in an excessively narrow way. Such a strategy has a certain bureaucratic logic—the "problem" is sufficiently small that it can be dealt with largely using resources already allocated for financial-sector cleanup—but it does not begin to address the totality of the *real* problem.

would be a virtuous circle that could help offset some of the short-run frictional slowdown due to financial-sector disruption.

The most critical reason for forceful action, however, is the unpalatable alternative faced by Japan. At best, it could experience another decade of lost growth. At worst, it could face a major crisis at almost any time as the increased transparency of the accounting system reveals the depth of the problems facing the financial and corporate sectors: a renewed Japan premium in world financial markets, bank runs as in late 1997, and capital flight from the yen. The case for definitive action is overwhelming.

In addition, the short-run depressive effect of decisive action to deal with financial-sector troubles could be partly offset by macroeconomic policy. The case for more aggressive monetary policy is straightforward: Japan is in a liquidity trap, and the Bank of Japan should adopt an inflation-targeting approach to extricate the economy. More expansionary monetary policy can be supported by more expansionary fiscal policy— although, in the case of fiscal policy, greater nuance is required because of legitimate long-term concerns regarding the high level of existing budget deficits and national debt, and the society's prospective aging and thus early need for substantial increases in welfare spending.

In the long run, Japan needs to address the problem of its fiscal health with respect to both the accumulation of excessive government debt in recent years and the likely needs of an aging population in the near future. Prime Minister Koizumi has announced his intention to limit the issuance of bonds in fiscal 2002 to ¥30 trillion. Such fiscal consolidation should be pursued, but in a flexible manner.

In particular, the termination of substantial wasteful expenditures on public investments of dubious merit will free up resources in the budget. Some of these resources should be redirected to expanded safety-net and worker-retraining programs to address the problems of those left unemployed by the reduction of public investments and the essential restructuring of the financial system.[4] Some can be used to fund tax breaks targeted at residential housing; housing construction is 30 percent below its 1991 peak, and it would be far better to use the construction industry to build suitable housing (as recommended in chapter 3) than to build roads to nowhere. This would offset some of the loss of aggregate demand and help cushion the blow for the construction sector.

The remainder of the budget savings can be devoted to financial-sector cleanup (although loans to the financial sector do not technically count as current budgetary expenditures under existing Japanese accounting conventions). This would help square the circle of the desire to consolidate fiscal policy while recognizing that public money will be required to

---

4. These new programs might usefully include a component for wage insurance as proposed for the United States in Kletzer (2001).

finance recapitalization of the financial system. At the same time, it should be recognized that tax revenues expected at the time the bond-issuance pledge was made by Koizumi are unlikely to be realized, given the weakness of the economy. The government should not be dogmatic on the timing of its adherence to the bond-issuance ceiling; indeed, it needs to interpret the pledge as relating to the budget on a full-employment basis.

More aggressive financial-sector cleanup policies, undertaken in the context of supportive monetary and fiscal policies, should help return Japan to a stable growth path in the medium run. Indeed, in light of the huge output gap that has developed during the past decade, Japan might even experience several years of supernormal "catch-up growth." The restoration of sustainable domestic demand-led economic growth in Japan would be not only in Japanese interests, but in the interests of the United States and the entire world as well. A growing Japan would contribute to the world economy rather than threaten it. It would be far more likely to act in concert with the United States to address global issues, such as development and security. Moreover, it would be a more attractive destination for US exports and investment.

Nevertheless, no matter how desirable such outcomes might be from a US as well as Japanese perspective, the United States can do little to ensure their realization, beyond providing hortatory encouragement and peer pressure through groups such as the G-7, the IMF, and the OECD. Although the United States may have expertise for Japan to draw upon, it has little leverage through which to encourage Japan to adopt the desired prescriptions. In contrast, the United States has a greater capacity to influence outcomes in the areas of trade and investment, where the linkages between the two economies are much more direct. It is to these bilateral trade and investment links that we now turn.

Reorienting the Trade Relationship

Japan and the United States should continue to shift the resolution of their trade and investment conflicts away from bilateral channels and toward multilateral forums, such as the WTO and the OECD. As was noted above, as Japan becomes less distinct, the "less" is the justification for addressing these issues bilaterally. Moreover, to the extent that Japanese political institutions remain weak, and Japan continues to rely on external pressures to stimulate its own reform process, it is better that this pressure come from multilateral organizations (e.g., the WTO) or agreements that Japan has entered into voluntarily (e.g., the Japan-Singapore FTA) than ad hoc from the United States. Better yet, of course, would be a domestic political force capable of self-initiating reform without foreign pressure; the Koizumi government, which has publicly put structural reform at the center of its domestic agenda, would appear to be the best bet to achieve this since the Hosokawa cabinet collapsed in 1994.

The Role of the WTO

The changes in global trading rules, embodied in the creation of the World Trade Organization, bear emphasis, as was described in chapter 5. The new Dispute Settlement Mechanism (DSM) essentially precludes the United States from using unilateral devices, such as Section 301, either against alleged violations in sectors covered by the WTO or as a basis for retaliation in those sectors—which amount to the vast bulk of world trade.[5] Japan would simply threaten to take the United States to the WTO, where it would almost surely be granted authority to retaliate against such US practices. Indeed, the United States retreated quickly when Japan threatened WTO action if the United States acted on its threat to retaliate in the auto parts dispute in 1995. (By contrast, Japan was unable to get the GATT even to convene a panel when it sought to counter the US retaliation in the semiconductor case in 1987.) In this sense, the establishment of the WTO forces the Japan-United States trade relationship into a more "normal" pattern, which we regard as desirable.

At the same time, the new DSM presents a powerful new tool for the United States to pursue its trade objectives toward Japan. The United States won 23 of the first 25 cases it brought under the new arrangements, achieving liberalization of the target country's trade regime in each instance. Japan has a good record of adhering to judgments against it in the GATT and now the WTO. Indeed, an important reason for the United States to emphasize normal multilateral channels in its trade efforts with Japan is its need to win Japanese agreement to bring competition policy and other important but uncovered issues into the WTO so that the DSM also may apply to them. Even when the United States loses, as in the Kodak-Fuji case, the WTO can resolve a complaint brought by the United States that would have been much messier if the WTO had not had the power of the DSM.

The antidumping issue is a difficult one. From a pure economics standpoint, it would be better to abandon antidumping cases altogether and adopt a competition-policy standard, but this would be difficult from a political or negotiating standpoint. Given these realities, the WTO is also extremely useful, because it both legitimates and constrains the United

---

5. Technically, the United States could still use Section 301 (or simply apply unilateral increases in its import barriers) if it were willing to pay compensation to other countries or accept retaliation from them. There would be little point in doing so, however, and the domestic politics of such a sequence of steps would almost surely be damaging for any presidential administration that took them—as is intended to be the case.

States and its partners in the application of the few remaining tools in their unilateral arsenals.

Both antidumping duties, and countervailing duties against government subsidies, are permitted under current WTO codes. Japan (and many other countries) will clearly try to negotiate changes in these rules in future multilateral trade negotiations, and the United States may decide to accept some modifications in their implementation to constrain their use by its partners and to obtain concessions by Japan (and other countries) on other issues. Again, the WTO provides major benefits for US trade policy.

It is difficult to imagine the two countries making much bilateral progress on the two outstanding issues of border protection that now confront them: agriculture in Japan, and antidumping in the United States. These issues must be addressed multilaterally, to reach solutions that are both coherent economically and sustainable politically. Japan is not going to undertake discriminatory agricultural liberalization with the United States, and the United States is not going to create a Japan-specific waiver in its antidumping laws. To secure its goals, the United States needs METI and Japanese manufacturing interests on its side to overcome opposition by the Ministry of Agriculture, Forestry, and Fisheries and rural interest groups. Conversely, Japan needs to offer the United States something big to induce change in antidumping practices, because Congress regards the antidumping law as the last line of defense against hidden protection in Japan (and "low-wage" imports from poor countries).

For any government, exploiting these cross-issue trade-offs and creating the internal political clout to overcome entrenched domestic issues is less difficult in "big-package" multilateral negotiations (Bergsten 2001). Japan and the United States are no exceptions. In particular, the built-in agenda of agriculture and services coming out of the Uruguay Round offers Japan little in the mercantilist terms of domestic politics. The US position in Seattle—of simultaneously trying to limit the conventional trade agenda to these topics while adding the new "social clause" issues of trade and the environment and trade and labor—encouraged Japan (and the European Union) to play an obstructionist role. If progress is to be made, the agenda must be broad enough to allow all participants to point to "victories" or "achievements" when selling it at home.

Extending the Agenda: Competition Policy

So what should Japan and the United States be pushing in the WTO (and APEC) to realize their respective interests in a more constructive way? One can imagine three significant additions to the built-in WTO agenda on which the two countries could usefully cooperate, and that would increase the likelihood of the United States achieving its goals in agriculture and services: a multilateral accord on competition policy that would embrace antidumping measures, stronger WTO rules to govern bilateral or plurilateral free trade agreements, and new procedures for selecting the future leaders of the key multilateral economic institutions.

The first and most important would be a multilateral accord on competition policy. This would have to involve the European Union and could most naturally be done in the WTO. As a fallback, one could possibly imagine an Asia-specific initiative in APEC or, more likely, a plurilateral agreement in the OECD (which would exclude the developing countries, which might act in an obstructionist manner in the WTO).[6]

The issues of competition policy and antidumping are related. Antidumping laws were originally an attempt by national authorities to deter predatory behavior by foreign firms with respect to domestic producers for which the "reach" of national competition policies was inadequate. Today in practice, however, the application of antidumping laws has little to do with deterring predation and instead serves largely as a mechanism for shielding inefficient local producers from foreign competition, in effect transferring rents from domestic consumers to domestic and foreign producers. As the practice has proliferated around the globe, the United States has emerged as the second leading *target* of new antidumping actions in recent years, following China, as well as a leading initiator of antidumping cases.

In the United States, there is an understandable wariness about "surrendering" antidumping policy for an international accord on competition policy. To start, there is no single international competition-policy standard, and what constitutes unacceptable or illegal behavior varies enormously across countries.[7] Even where laws do exist, there may be significant differences in content, sectoral scope, and entities covered.[8] Many, though not all, countries, for example, prohibit horizontal cartels but not vertical exclusive dealerships. These differences even extend to core competition-policy rules in major industrial countries, including Japan.[9]

---

6. The competition-policy issues are not of great relevance for most developing countries, which would probably be wary of taking on new obligations in an area of policy in which their own domestic competence remains rudimentary in most cases and nonexistent in others. Another approach would be to have a plurilateral competition-policy code in the WTO from which developing countries could opt out, as proposed by the European Union.

7. See OECD (1996) and Graham and Richardson (1997) for excellent overviews of industrial-country competition policies.

8. See OECD (1996) for an elaboration of these issues.

9. For example, under the Japanese Anti-Monopoly Law (AML), a private monopolization or cartel is illegal only if it restricts competition "contrary to the public interest," a phrase that is subject to multiple (and contradictory) interpretations (Matsushita 1997). However, at least one former US official intimately familiar with the issue regards enforcement, not the law itself, as the problem.

These cross-national differences in legal standards are compounded by differences in enforcement procedures and the severity of penalties for illegal behavior. In Japan, for instance, alleged lax enforcement of competition policies has been a source of trade and investment friction with both the United States and the European Union. Many observers in the United States, with reason, are quite skeptical about Japan's (or China's, or South Korea's) seriousness about competition policy, as least as generally understood in the European Union or United States.[10]

Japan and the United States have been in continual negotiation over competition-policy issues since the Carter administration, and the key bureaucratic actor in this regard is the Japan Fair Trade Commission. In part because of US pressure, in the past decade the JFTC received a bigger budget, bigger staff, and more statutory independence. Although the JFTC has historically been regarded as the lapdog of the interventionist MITI, the incompatibility between the goals of the two organizations seems to have declined as METI (as it has now become) has reinvented itself as the champion of deregulation.

In recent years, the JFTC's scrapes have been with other ministries (e.g., construction and transportation) over JFTC actions toward their client industries. Indeed, from an international perspective, the JFTC appears to be fairly large and active, at least as measured by budget or staff. In addition, Japan and the United States have signed a positive comity agreement, so that if one competition-policy authority suspects anticompetitive behavior in the other's market it can request an investigation by its counterpart agency. US courts and the Department of Justice have no way to compel foreign firms to produce evidence for their own investigations, however.[11]

The issue (beyond some possible inadequacies in Japanese law) is the JFTC's willingness to vigorously pursue and prosecute potential violations. Outside Japan, there is considerable skepticism about the JFTC as a watchdog. A survey done by the International Institute for Management

---

10. See Bergsten and Noland (1993) and MITI (1996) for examples of such friction with Japan involving the European Union and United States. In an attempt to address this issue, the European Union and the United States have spearheaded the establishment of a Global Competition Forum, which is intended to be a think tank that brings together competition-policy professionals from public, business, academic, and consumer bodies (Monti 2001). See Morici (2000) for a comparison of EU, Japanese, and US approaches to competition policy.

11. During the presidential primaries in 1992, when incumbent President George Bush was taking a drubbing from both his Republican challenger and Democratic opponents for being soft on trade in general, and soft on Japan in particular, the Justice Department revived the notion of the extraterritorial application of US antitrust laws, which had been abandoned during the Reagan administration. This was immediately denounced in Japan, which threatened to enact blocking statutes prohibiting its firms from complying with US court rulings (as other countries had done in similar episodes of this type). Internal opposition within the Bush administration and foreign blocking threats effectively killed this initiative.

Development found that the United States had the 5th best competition policies in the world (following Australia, Germany, Canada, and the Netherlands), whereas Japan ranked 17th (following Mexico, India, and Brazil).[12] Stokes (2000) notes that only one survey by the economics section of the JFTC has ever led to an investigation. Despite enhanced legal penalties, no one has ever gone to jail in a Japanese antitrust case. In cases in which offending executives were subject to criminal sanctions, they received suspended sentences. Instead, most cases end up in formal injunctions (corrective actions) but with consent (*kankoku shinketsu*) rather than going through a court procedure to a verdict (*shinketsu*) with a penalty.[13] Ariga, Ohkusa, and Nishimura (1999) find that monitoring activities by the JFTC appear to be more effective in disciplining market power than formal actions.[14] Although chapter 4 documented a number of specific actions undertaken by the JFTC, one gets the impression that the behavior exposed represents little more than the tip of the iceberg.

No one would claim that the JFTC is as effective as it could be, and one can easily identify areas in which it needs to articulate coherent competition policies. For example, with new entrants and the complete deregulation of airfares, competition policy must be applied to questions such as whether incumbent airlines have pursued anticompetitive pricing policies to discourage new entrants on particular routes; how landing slots should be allocated between established carriers and new entrants; and what rights should be accorded to passengers bumped from overbooked flights. After more than 20 years of air travel deregulation, the United States has considerable experience in dealing with these sorts of issues.

Another example is telecommunications. What is the appropriate policy toward the dominant NTT group, when Internet access can also be achieved through a cable television provider, and the Internet may permit the long-distance telephone communication to bypass the long-distance telephone service provider? A third area is the impact of foreign mergers on Japanese consumers, as in the proposed merger of General Electric

---

12. *The Economist*, 16 May 1998.

13. Penalties are imposed, however. For example, in 2000, the JFTC imposed $62 million in fines on firms for violating the AML. See Morici (2000) for a description of the JFTC's enforcement options and procedures.

14. Using an econometric model, they find that the JFTC can influence profit margins by listing firms on a suspicious-pricing and anticompetitive-behavior "watch list" (involving monitoring and compulsory reporting). Industries on the list tend to have higher concentration ratios, as measured by the market shares of the top three firms. In contrast, industries subject to formal injunctions do not have higher than average concentration ratios, and the injunctions do not affect profit margins. Of course, as the authors admit, their result merely establishes the relative effectiveness of monitoring—not the optimality or desirability of the underlying profit margins.

and Honeywell, where the JFTC has issued regulations, though it remains to be seen how these will be applied and to what end.

Beyond the issue of its legal mandate, the JFTC seems to suffer from a lack of intellectual vitality. To the extent that it embodies any particular concept of competition policy, it is the traditional antitrust mantra: A large market share is bad, collusion is bad, and price fixing is bad. It does not appear to have incorporated modern concepts from industrial organization (e.g., the theory of contestable markets or notions of dynamic pricing) into its policy framework, despite their obvious relevance to a raft of issues that Japan confronts (Graham and Lawrence 1996). It would be desirable for the JFTC to increase its analytical capability; this could be accomplished by creating a chief economist position with significant staff resources and hiring a highly regarded applied microeconomist from outside the government to fill it.

From a US perspective, despite the JFTC's uneven record of accomplishment, there are reasons not to dismiss the competition-policy approach out of hand. Ultimately, this is where the action is, and the United States eventually will have to reach mutually acceptable accommodations on competition-policy issues, not only with Japan but with China and South Korea as well. The question is one of tactics. The United States is more likely to reach agreements that it regards as satisfactory, and that would be politically sustainable in these countries, if it worked multilaterally in concert with Australia, the European Union, New Zealand, and other countries with similar competition-policy traditions, than if it were to try to do so bilaterally.[15] Japan would seem to be the obvious first "non-Western" candidate for possible integration into a multilateral competition-policy scheme.[16]

The appointment of a strong independent chief economist to modernize the JFTC's economic analysis and serve as an improved basis for policy-making would be a start. But in the end, to achieve results, improved analysis will need to be combined with effective enforcement. This could be particularly important with respect to public works and construction, where the problems are large and the government's responsibility direct. Only when the JFTC is revamped will Japanese competition policy be credible, and cooperative competition policy be in a position to replace antidumping.

Likewise, it may prove advantageous to reemphasize the process of strengthening international norms with respect to regulation and corporate governance through the OECD. Skeptics will counter that agreements

---

15. This is not to say that bilateral international cooperation agreements with like-minded countries might not be steppingstones to multilateral accords. See Graham (2000).

16. See Graham (2000), Morici (2000), and Monti (2001) for alternative conceptions of what such a regime might entail.

reached in the OECD lack an enforcement mechanism. This is true but, although the formal dispute-settlement process of the GATT was ineffective, the establishment of international norms in the context of a consensual process was useful in achieving trade liberalization in Japan, despite the absence of credible sanctions. If an external anchor is needed to spur Japanese reform, it would be both more effective and less damaging to bilateral relations if it were to come through a multilateral consensual process in which Japan was a voluntary participant.[17]

Moreover, even accepting the mercantilist logic of trade negotiations, the value of the negotiating concession that the United States would have to make—acquiescence in tightening disciplines on the use of antidumping laws—is falling. Although the United States is by far the major user of this form of protection, US firms are increasingly the targets of antidumping actions as more and more countries adopt this trade-policy instrument. And, as maddening as the US government's application of its antidumping law is to others, the degree of transparency and economic rationality in other countries' application of their own antidumping laws is even lower. The United States should quit while it is still ahead.[18]

The acceptance of tightened disciplines on antidumping laws, in return for a strengthened international standard on competition policy, would be a hard sell from the domestic political perspective of the United States. However, US trade negotiators have faced similar "sacred cows" before: The absence of an injury test in the US countervailing duty statute was viewed as sacrosanct by Congress before the Tokyo Round in the 1970s, and the quotas on textile and apparel imports enjoyed similar status in the 1980s and 1990s before the Uruguay Round. In both cases, however, US negotiators were ultimately able to win approval to liberalize the objectionable practices by combining two elements: concessions by the other major countries on both the key issue itself (respectively, commitments to limit export and other subsidies, and liberalization of their own imports of textiles and apparel) and on other issues of compelling national interest to the United States (including, respectively, bringing services trade into the GATT and a strong agreement to protect intellectual property rights).

In addition to an agreement on competition policy itself, the United States is thus likely to need significant concessions from its major trading partners to win domestic political support for the deal. The main areas

---

17. Some argue that market pressure alone, mainly in the form of increased foreign investment and the increased role of foreign financial intermediaries in the economy, will be sufficient to achieve improvements in Japanese corporate governance. Although foreigners may play a constructive role in this regard, we remain skeptical that market forces alone will generate a fundamental transformation of Japanese corporate governance.

18. Messerlin (2000) recommends a number of changes in WTO rules to impede the abuse of antidumping laws.

where such concessions could convince Congress to accept some tightening of international disciplines for the use of antidumping measures are the modern perennials of US export interest: agriculture and services. Japan, in particular, will have to agree to substantial reductions in its agricultural and services protection to enable US negotiators to win domestic support for any eventual WTO package. (The European Union also will have to liberalize substantially on agriculture but in mercantilist terms, like the United States, it will generally *benefit* from liberalization in the services sector.)

Shaping the New Free Trade Agreements

Another potential element of a new WTO negotiation that could help "sell" the eventual package in the United States, as well as make sense on its merits, could be a strengthening of the WTO rules that cover bilateral and plurilateral free trade agreements. As was discussed above, Japan is in the process of exploring FTAs with a variety of countries. It alone among the major industrial countries does not now participate in regional preference schemes, and can rightly argue that it has been adversely affected by trade diversion stemming from the formation of the European Union and NAFTA. That said, both Japan and the United States (and indeed the whole world) stand to lose if the locus of international trade policy shifts from the WTO to a crazy quilt of preference schemes. Indeed, the United States could be disadvantaged by trade diversion arising from Japan's FTAs—just as Japan can argue that it may be further harmed by the Free Trade Area of the Americas (FTAA).

Since about 1998, Japan has begun cautiously exploring—and also receiving approaches from other countries concerning—the possibility of a series of bilateral free trade agreements. A high-profile discussion was launched with South Korea by the countries' heads of government. Bilateral talks were initiated with both Mexico and Singapore—the latter reportedly intended as an initial sally into ASEAN that Japan would hope to extend eventually into similar bilateral talks with Malaysia, the Philippines, Thailand, and ultimately Indonesia (although many in those countries would prefer that any such discussions with Japan be conducted by ASEAN as a group rather than bilaterally, and Japan in fact proposed a Japan-ASEAN FTA in early 2001).

At the time of this writing, the Japan-Singapore agreement seems likely to be concluded in 2001, but it is unclear whether any of the numerous other regional and subregional initiatives in East Asia, including those launched by Japan, will succeed (Scollay and Gilbert 2001). It is clear, however, that there has been a debate for some time in Tokyo over whether Japan should continue to place priority on its relationship with the United States or whether it should shift to an "Asia-first" strategy. The new regional initiatives (which are taking place in the monetary area as well, initially via the Network of Bilateral Swap Arrangements under the so-called Chiang Mai Initiative) that were described in chapter 6 represent an initial, perhaps tentative and experimental, step in the latter direction.

These initiatives clearly represent a possible new course for Japanese foreign economic policy, with which the United States must reckon as it considers its own policy for the future. Knee-jerk US opposition to such groupings in Asia, including Japan, could of course invite considerable resentment; if the European Union, NAFTA, Mercosur, and other regional agreements are viewed as building blocks for multilateral economic integration, so should regional agreements in Asia (Lawrence, Bressand, and Ito 1996). Construction of a free trade agreement or two by Japan is nothing but a move toward more normal-country status.

We believe that this new Japanese gambit strengthens the case for the United States to move beyond a Japan-specific economic policy in favor of treating Japan as a very important but normal part of US foreign economic policy—including a heavy reliance on multilateralism to pursue most US priority objectives. Strengthening the existing multilateral institutions in both trade and finance, and their "democratization" to include an increased role for Japan and other Asian countries, would lessen the desire (or excuse) for Japan (or other countries in East Asia) to opt for regionalism as an alternative strategy. The Asians, including Japan, could of course still develop regional arrangements—just as the United States has done with NAFTA and the Europeans have done much more extensively. But their doing so *within* the framework of an effective, appealing multilateral system would obviate most of the risks that might otherwise result for global economic cooperation, and in particular the risks for Japan-United States relations that could evolve from a Japanese movement away from the global institutions.[19]

As a consequence, a strengthening of GATT Article 24 concerning preferential schemes, and the WTO process of reviewing preferential agreements for compliance, could be another new item of mutual cooperation. Japan and the United States could do several things to ensure that their own preferential agreements do not undermine the global system. First, they could push for reform on this issue within the WTO. One change would be to clearly define the key term "substantially all sectors," which is required to make FTAs legal under the WTO, to eliminate the possibility of sectoral carve-outs. A second change would be to rule out the use of grey-area measures, such as VERs in preferential arrangements, *without* grandfathering the existing soft FTAs.[20] Third, rules of origin are some-

---

19. In their report to the G-7 heads of government in July 2000, the G-7 finance ministers endorsed the pursuit of Asian regional financial arrangements that are "supportive of the IMF's objectives and responsibilities in the global economy" (G-7 Finance Ministers 2000).

20. In theory, the Uruguay Round agreement foreclosed the use of VERs in the context of preferential arrangements. However, this practice has yet to be challenged. Similarly, there

times written to frustrate liberalization in particular sectors, effectively undermining the "substantially all sectors" requirement; this problem could be addressed through strengthened "rules on rules," such as requiring that rules of origin be the same for all sectors (Lawrence 1995).

Other reforms could seek to limit the likelihood of injury to third parties through trade diversion. Conceptually, the most straightforward approach would be to require FTA participants to reduce their external tariffs to compensate disadvantaged outsiders. The problem, of course, is that this requires economic, not legal, analysis, and it is difficult to imagine WTO signatories ever agreeing to submit their trade policy to this kind of constraint. A plausible alternative would be to adopt a rule that external tariffs must be reduced to the tariff of the lowest member (in effect converting FTAs into relatively liberal customs unions) or, less daunting, that external tariffs be reduced to the average of the FTA participants' tariffs.[21] Although such schemes would not eliminate the possibility of trade-diverting FTAs, they would in effect raise the "reservation price" of entering an FTA and thus reduce the likelihood of a proliferation of welfare-reducing agreements.

Last, WTO members also could be required to submit their preferential arrangements to annual WTO reviews. The objective would be to generate peer pressure and moral suasion to ensure that FTAs expand world trade by producing more trade creation than diversion. The existing Trade Policy Review Mechanism could be used for this purpose (Keesing 1998). Having staked out such a position in the WTO, Japan and the United States could voluntarily submit their own FTAs for review before the procedure was even formally adopted by the organization.

Some will object that what is good for the goose is good for the gander, and that it would be hypocritical for the United States—having entered into NAFTA and proposed an FTAA (along with possible bilateral FTAs with Chile, Jordan, and Singapore)—to try to deny others the joys of regionalism. But this line of argument fails on three grounds. First, NAFTA is largely, if not completely, consistent with Article 24, and innovative aspects of NAFTA (e.g., liberalization of investment and services) in fact became a model for the Uruguay Round. Second, all countries stand to lose if regional agreements proliferate unchecked. Third, Japan, given its problems in agriculture and services, cannot realistically expect to achieve major benefits through WTO-consistent FTAs.

Japan may of course counter that the rush to conclude preferential arrangements has been led by the European Union and United States, and that Asian schemes are reactive and defensive. But the real issue is whether the prospective Asian agreements will be WTO-consistent. Rather

---

was some attempt to strengthen Article 24 in the Uruguay Round, but this effort foundered on how to treat existing EU deals.

21. See Frankel (1997) for further discussion along these lines.

than criticizing such explorations a priori, the United States should emphasize the need for any such agreements to be consistent with Article 24. For Japan, it may be desirable to give the United States something on Article 24 (as part of a bigger package) in return for something much more important—strengthened disciplines on antidumping.

Another potential area of Japan-United States cooperation in the WTO, indeed in this case in the multilateral economic organizations more broadly, is leadership selection. Japan and the United States backed opposing candidates in the struggle to succeed Renato Ruggiero as director general of the WTO in 1999. This, in and of itself, is unremarkable and should not be subject for concern. However, what the struggle itself signaled (as was reaffirmed in a similar fight soon thereafter over the managing directorship of the IMF) is that the "national reservation" system of filling the top spots at international institutions is fundamentally bankrupt. Reform of the leadership-appointment process is another area of potential mutual cooperation—in this case spanning trade, finance, and development (Kahler 2001).

Recalibrating US Trade Policy

What would be the tactical implications for the United States of this proposed new approach to Japan? It is traditional for area specialists to complain that the United States does not "do enough" with respect to their area of concern and to recommend an increase of resources—whether that area be Japan, Africa, or anywhere else. But advocates of "doing more" with respect to Japan must face the reality that exports to Japan account for less than 1 percent of US national income. Even if one accepts the high-end estimates of the potential mercantilist gains from enhanced access to Japan, the experiences of the Bush administration (SII negotiations undertaken at the undersecretary level) and the Clinton administration (undersecretary-level negotiations, plus semiannual meetings of heads of government) do not support the view that the United States has not devoted enough high-level attention to the problem. The reality is just the opposite: Those resources would surely have been better spent addressing other problems that confront the United States internally or strengthening the multilateral system externally.[22]

---

22. One exception to this notion would be in the area of compliance, where the United States is notoriously weak. According to Stokes (2000, 73), "the Commerce Department's Market Access and Compliance Unit, which monitors the implementation of US trade agreements, had seventeen people working on Japan issues in 1992. It 2000, it had nine." See also Lincoln (1999). But even with respect to monitoring, it should be recognized that the relative amount of resources devoted to Japan-specific activities should probably decline as Japan's relative importance in US economic life lessens.

Rather, the United States needs to strengthen some skill-specific areas in its dealings with Japan. The first area for improvement would be Japanese language skills. At times, the USTR has had only one person on the Japan desk who actually spoke Japanese. A second area of improvement would be competition policy. Trade negotiators and antitrust lawyers do not see the world in exactly the same terms. If competition policy is going to become more and more central to the bilateral agenda, then it behooves the US government to strengthen the degree of cooperation between the USTR and the Department of Justice (DOJ). One possibility would be to begin a permanent program of cross-secondments between the two organizations.[23] Another would be to initiate a cross-recognition policy that DOJ has the right to participate in any discussion of competition-policy issues with Japan, and the USTR has the right to participate in antitrust activities that DOJ pursues in conjunction with the JFTC.

The issue of competition policy, the need to strengthen the skill set embodied in the bureaucracy, and the need to better integrate activities across the bureaucracy are simply leading indicators of a more general phenomenon that the United States will face more and more in the future. As the Japan-United States trade agenda shifts away from traditional border measures and toward domestic regulatory issues, the necessary professional backgrounds and skills of US negotiators will have to change as well. Again, this may require improving the human capital of the bureaucracy (e.g., improving expertise in technical issues relating to information technology), while at the same time improving the coordination and integration of activities between the USTR and a growing number of agencies within the US government. This is particularly important in the context of the US system of complainant-driven trade-policy formation. Without the capacity to evaluate competing industry and firm claims on attention and resources, the US system can easily degenerate into an orgy of rent seeking in which the squeaky wheel gets the grease.

These personnel and organizational improvements will not be easy, either in terms of recruitment or coordination. The skills that will be needed to conduct Japan policy will more and more correspond to skills in demand outside the government. Compensation will have to be adjusted accordingly to recruit and retain staff.[24] Bureaucratically, coordination will have to be genuine. Today, the US government maintains an extensive

---

23. Along with cross-agency secondments, the two governments could usefully consider expanding cross-government secondments, e.g., those currently carried out through the Mansfield Center for Pacific Affairs.

24. Political realities mean that it will be very difficult to pay civil servants with marketable skills salaries comparable to what they can earn in the private sector. Intangible compensation is not limited by the Constitution, however. High government officials could make a start by forswearing the practice of scoring cheap political points by bad-mouthing the federal bureaucracy, as has been the case for well over two decades.

network of interagency groups, including several devoted to Japan policy. In large part, these serve as mechanisms for defining turf. In the future, no single agency will embody the skill set necessary to successfully and effectively integrate the skills and perspectives needed to achieve US national interests.

These staffing and coordination issues are genuine challenges for the successful implementation of public policy. They will be difficult to surmount for global issues. They will be even more difficult to overcome for a series of country-specific or regional policies. These considerations underscore the notion that the United States would be better served if it were to deemphasize Japan-specific policies, and to root its dealings with Japan more firmly in multilateral forums. Indeed, given the increasing informational complexity of the issues that the multilateral forums will be called upon to resolve, Japan and the United States would do well to increase expenditures on the WTO, strengthen its secretariat, and professionalize the treatment of its dispute panel members.[25]

Rebasing the Monetary Relationship

The international monetary system carries no deterrents to unilateral action similar to those for the trading system that are now imbedded in the WTO. The United States can unilaterally stimulate (sometimes with jawboning alone) appreciation of the yen, as it arguably did in 1993-95 in pursuit of its trade-policy (as well as trade-balance) goals, without running afoul of any rules that would authorize Japanese "retaliation." The current regime of unilaterally managed floats leaves each major country with enormous discretion. Moreover, Japan's huge trade surpluses and massive foreign exchange reserves enable it to deflect virtually any conceivable external financial pressure.

In an earlier book on this topic, two of the authors proposed the restoration of the yen-dollar target zone that had been implemented for a year or so in the middle 1980s as a "reference range" under the Baker-Miyazawa initiative (Bergsten and Noland 1993, especially 208-10). That bilateral accord preceded the Louvre Agreement that broadened the agreement to adopt reference ranges for the full G-7. Our third author has endorsed similar proposals in his own writings on the topic (Takatoshi Ito 1989).

We continue to believe that the sharp gyrations in the yen-dollar rate, which have been the most marked of the fluctuations among any of the major currencies throughout the three decades of generalized floating of exchange rates, have significantly exacerbated Japan-United States trade and broader economic tensions. They have done so by producing prolonged misalignments, generally dollar overvaluations, that have

---

25. See Schott (1998) for further discussion.

increased the external imbalance between the two countries and intensified protectionist pressure in the United States. They have also produced significant financial disruptions and risks, including for Japan, when the yen also has become misaligned—in both directions, as with its excessive appreciation to 80:1 against the dollar in 1995 and its subsequent excessive depreciation to 150:1 in 1998.

Both countries would thus benefit from the installation of a more stable monetary regime, either bilaterally or more broadly among the G-7. We recognize, however, that the present positions of these countries reject such a system as either undesirable or infeasible, or both.[26] Hence, there is no practical prospect for the adoption of such reforms in the near future, and we will not make a major point of recommending them in this volume.

There is another potential area for multilateralizing the monetary relationship that offers more immediate prospects, however. As stressed in chapter 3, and earlier in this chapter, the weaknesses of Japan's banking system lie at the heart of its economic difficulties over the past decade and continue to cast a dark shadow over its outlook. Hence the United States has increasingly emphasized the need for fundamental banking reform in its entreaties toward Japan over the past couple of years.

The opportunity for multilateralization lies with the decision of the International Monetary Fund in early 1999, largely in the wake of the Asian monetary crisis (and similar earlier crises), to launch a Financial Sector Assessment Program. That program monitors financial sectors in member countries, developed and emerging alike, in an effort to promote preventive actions and thereby head off future disruptions. In August 2001, the IMF asked Japan to agree to an assessment of the country's financial system, including the state of nonperforming loans at the banks, under the new program. Japan's initial reaction was hesitant but the program offers an excellent opportunity to replace traditional American *gaiatsu* with a multilateral approach in a critical policy area that should be much more acceptable to Japan.

In the meanwhile, and partly because of US unwillingness to consider substantial changes in the global financial architecture, Japan appears to be actively considering a new policy alternative that could be important for its relationship with the United States: the creation of regional financial arrangements in East Asia that could reduce Japan's dependence on US markets and the fluctuations of the dollar. We have already noted that Japan is promoting these arrangements in the trade area, but it is doing so in the monetary area as well.

On finance, Japan has bounced back from the rebuff (mainly by China and the United States) of its proposal for an Asian Monetary Fund in

---

26. The reasons for those views are explained and countered to in Bergsten and Henning (1996).

1997. As was described in chapter 6, the ASEAN + 3 group (in which the "3" consists of China and South Korea, along with Japan) announced in May 2000 their agreement to create a regionwide network of currency swaps (really medium-run credits) to help them respond to future crises without relying so heavily on Washington. The group announced the first bilateral credit lines under this so-called Chiang Mai Initiative in May 2001. More broadly, the ASEAN + 3 group has held annual summit meetings since 1997, and its finance ministers now meet when opportunities arise.

This process can be compared with the initial series of regional agreements among European countries in the early 1950s and the first steps toward the creation of the worldwide G-10 swap network and General Arrangements to Borrow in the early 1960s. The embryonic Asian initiatives could evolve over time into a true Asian Monetary Fund and even— as was already proposed by the respected head of the Hong Kong Monetary Authority, Joseph Yam—into an Asian currency unit à la euro (though the Japanese Ministry of Finance quickly indicated that such a development could only be realized in the distant future, if at all). A central motive for all these monetary initiatives is greater regional autonomy and self-determination, more and more independent of the United States and the Washington-based international financial institutions (Bergsten 2001a).

Although some Americans may reflexively see such efforts as threatening US interests, this need not be the case. The integration of China into the institutions and norms of the liberal global order is likely to be one of the greatest strategic challenges of the next generation. Indeed, an ideologically hostile and territorially expansionist China is probably the only threat sufficiently large to fuel the kind of "deep integration" between Japan and the United States that some advocate. Rather than be forced down this difficult and dangerous road, it would be far better to integrate China into the international system in a way that would not only facilitate more harmonious relations between it and the rest of the world but would avoid the need for the United States and Japan to pursue the dubious chimera of deep integration. To the extent that regional institutions act as another thread in the web drawing China into the international system, the United States should be supportive of Japanese efforts to construct regional arrangements in Asia—as long as those institutions do not detract from the global institutions.

In the same way, a multilateral focus for US policy *toward* Japan would also improve the prospect for conducting at least some parts of US policy *with* Japan. Despite its weakness, Japanese agreement is essential for pursuit of key global initiatives, such as a new trade round in the WTO and convincing reform of the international financial architecture. In addition, Japan's new flirtation with regionalism needs to be firmly anchored in a multilateral context (as has been indicated so far). These extremely important US goals would be served by renewed emphasis on multilateral channels in handling the economic problems between the two countries themselves.

On the central issue of macroeconomic and monetary policy, the United States has at least three significant institutional levers vis-à-vis Japan: the "finance G-7" of finance ministers and central bank governors of the seven leading industrial democracies (Canada, France, Germany, Italy, Japan, the United Kingdom, and the United States), the IMF, and the Manila Framework Group (MFG). A further institution, an Asian Monetary Fund, may be developing albeit without US membership.

The MFG was created by virtually all the APEC countries in late 1997, partly as an alternative to the AMF proposal. Its chief goal was to institute a process of multilateral surveillance over the (mainly emerging) Asian economies, and it has met annually since that time. It has not produced tangible results beyond what the IMF would do in any case. But it might be useful for multilateralizing constructive pressure on Japanese economic policy, because it brings together all of Japan's Asian neighbors—the countries that are both most dependent on Japan's economic health and most important to it politically—along with the United States.

With skillful multilateral diplomacy, the United States could mobilize considerable international pressure in support of policy reforms in Japan. It could use the G-7 to coordinate the efforts of the largest industrial countries, and the regional organizations to involve Japan's neighbors. This would undoubtedly require greater effort and more creativity than simply pursuing Japan bilaterally, as in the past. It would almost certainly be both more effective and more appropriate for the circumstances of the period ahead, however, and thus clearly worth the effort. Similarly, with skillful multilateral efforts, Japan could counter-argue its case to the United States.

Reconfiguring Japan's Foreign Economic Policy

Japan may well be the prime beneficiary of the liberal postwar order, yet its ability to influence that order has been constrained by US dominance, lingering suspicion of Japan in the rest of Asia, and Japan's own internal politics.

Japan's external environment began to change radically with the collapse of the Soviet Union, and with it the comfortable verities of the Yoshida Doctrine. Paradoxically, the period following the end of the Cold War has seen increased tensions in Northeast Asia and reaffirmed the importance to Japan of the Japan-United States security alliance. At the same time, Japan has groped for a strategic framework that would reflect its increasing attention toward Asia as a region, and its desire to differentiate its foreign policy from that of the United States.

In this respect, the Asian financial crisis was a critical event for Japan. Asia has been shaken by its experience during the financial crisis, and this has led to a reappraisal of its relationship with the United States and the Washington-based multilateral economic institutions. There is a sense of disappointment with both aspects of "Washington," and this—together with US initiatives that are likely to encounter opposition in Asia—has created an unprecedented opportunity for Japanese diplomacy. This opening could be widened by an economic slowdown and any accompanying rise in US protectionism (Noland 2000b).

In such an environment, it would be understandable if the Asians intensified their efforts at regional cooperation, either as a complement to or a substitute for multilateral cooperation. Yet Japan's ability to lead such an effort is uncertain. Ironically, one of the reasons that the United States is so influential in setting the agenda in Asia is that the Asian economies remain dependent on the US market as the ultimate destination of a significant part of their output (even if this dependence has lessened over time; Noland 1994). If Japan wants to wield more influence in the region, it must develop a strategic approach to the panoply of international issues it faces. It will have to import more, and establish better political and economic relations throughout the region, especially with China, the region's second largest economy (Ikenberry 2000).

Reform of Japan's internal policymaking process is essential to permit such changes to occur. To start, strong leadership on the part of the prime minister's office, to coordinate the actions of ministries that are used to pursuing their own narrow bureaucratic interests, is necessary to effectively pursue the national interest. To date, Japan has been too defensive in trade negotiations, allowing internationally uncompetitive sectors to determine its stance. There has been no high-level political commitment to overcome domestic lobbies that, for example, effectively vetoed the Early Voluntary Sectoral Liberalization program in APEC in 1998 and support perpetuation of the extraordinarily tight import regime in rice.[27] A more assertive and responsible policy, emphasizing the importance of open markets for Japan's internationally competitive sectors, is highly desirable and in fact necessary if Japan is to become an active player, including an active partner with the United States, in pursuing an effective multilateral economic strategy.

If narrow sectoral interests continue to exert a disproportionate impact on policy, Japan will put its economic standing and international influence

---

27. As one long-time foreign observer put it, "APEC will fail without effective leadership from Japan. Japan placed at risk major national interests by granting excessive influence to sectors now of minor importance to its national performance. Effective leadership requires the Japanese polity to assert national over minor sectoral interests" (Garnaut 1999, 2).

at risk. It could find itself isolated in a sea of regionalism—surrounded by the FTAA, the European Union, and a new China-ASEAN Free Trade Area linkage—sinking under the weight of its highly protected rice farmers and construction workers.

A far preferable alternative would be for Japan to assert constructive leadership in world forums such as the IMF, the World Bank, and the WTO, and regional ones such as APEC, ASEAN + 3, and the bilateral FTAs. For this to happen, Japan must make an internal decision to reorganize its agriculture and construction industries while acting on a strategic vision at the international level. In this regard, *gaiatsu* is no guide. Leadership is necessary.

The most important challenge for Japan is to find a political mechanism to make decisions without *gaiatsu*. Otherwise, it will be under constant pressure from the United States, the WTO, the IMF, and other international organizations to reform and change. But simply responding to the demands of others is hardly a recipe for advancing national interests. Regional organizations, such as the prospective FTAs and a nascent Asian Monetary Fund, could be a good training ground for the Japanese bureaucracy in forming its own policy without *gaiatsu*. Peer pressure in these groups may operate in a quite different way from the past frustrating experience of the Japan-United States bilateral relationship or Japan's seemingly reluctant participation in the multilateral trade negotiation process.

Other countries, especially the United States, tend to be skeptical of the will and skill of Japan's politicians and bureaucracy to reform themselves. Japan therefore must show the world that, for example, its competition policy can be strengthened and its protectionism can be curtailed without *gaiatsu*. In this regard, there are encouraging signs: the initial directions of the Bush administration in toning down public criticism of Japan, and of the Koizumi government in declaring its intention to pursue structural reform without respect for sacred cows.

Suppose that Japan were to reform its internal policymaking process successfully and seek a greater role in international affairs? Such an effort would still be impeded by lingering distrust of Japan in the region, especially in China. For example, despite South Korean President Kim Dae-jung's proactive policy of improving relations with Japan, bilateral relations have deteriorated due to such emotive issues as Japanese sexual enslavement of foreign women during the Second World War and the approval of public school textbooks that appear to whitewash Japan's behavior. Kim went so far as to cancel joint military exercises, cancel a scheduled opening of the South Korean market to some Japanese cultural products, recall Seoul's ambassador to Tokyo, and refuse to meet with a visiting Japanese political delegation in protest of the textbook issue. And South Korean reaction has been mild compared with that in China, where the Chinese Communist Party has made Japan bashing a staple. Both countries reacted angrily to Prime Minister Koizumi's August 2001 visit to the Yasukuni Shrine. Australia, which has called for Japan to play a more active role in regional military affairs (e.g., the peacekeeping mission in East Timor), and Singapore, which signed a base agreement with Japan, would appear to be exceptions to this trend.

For its part, Japan remains understandably wary of China, particularly in light of its authoritarian political system. The kind of political exigencies that fueled the rapprochement between France and Germany in Europe after the Second World War appear to be missing in Asia, and will continue to hamper regional cooperation, at least in the medium run.

Surmounting these obstacles is a hard task. From a Japanese perspective, the path of less resistance is to remain under the US security umbrella, continue to export to the United States, and maintain a focus on the WTO-centered global trade system. But there is no guarantee that Japan will continue in this manner, because such a policy would require a continual rebalancing of Japanese interests. Japanese economic performance would determine the resources available for such an economics-centered foreign policy, whereas its relative performance would condition both Japanese demands for influence in global and regional policymaking bodies, and the receptiveness to those demands by the United States and other participants.

The balancing act on the security side is just as delicate. Although there is widespread support for the Japan-United States security alliance in both countries, within Japan there is also considerable unease about the US military presence and the prospective missions of Okinawa-based US forces. The Government of Japan's low-profile stance in the wake of the April 2001 emergency landing on the Chinese island of Hainan by an Okinawa-based US surveillance plane, and its reaction in July 2001 to another sexual assault involving a US serviceman on Okinawa, are illustrative of Tokyo's ambivalence.

The alternative—a significant rupture in the Japan-United States alliance, perhaps as the culmination of a conflict between growing Japanese desires for policy autonomy and increasing US unilateralism—would pose very difficult issues for Japan and the region. No such rupture is conceivable from the US side, though some observers continue to believe that the United States has leverage in its economic relationship with Japan due to its contribution to the military protection of Japan. This is simply not credible now—if it ever was. As a practical matter, the United States cannot reconfigure its security relationships around the world in response to trade disputes that occur on a fairly regular basis, or in response to the even less frequent disagreements over macroeconomic or financial policy. Moreover, even if there were some viable way of operationalizing the linkage between US security and economic interests, it is hard to imagine economic disputes of such a magnitude that the United States, after 50 years of the security alliance, would reduce its security support for Japan in response to economic tensions—especially in light of the declining salience of those tensions as emphasized throughout this book.

In Japan, such a break, were it to occur, could be traumatic, forcing the country to confront heretofore unresolved issues of its politics and history that it has avoided thus far. A rupture in security relations with the United States could prompt Japan to remilitarize, possibly calling into question its renunciation of nuclear weapons and destabilizing Asia. Alternatively, such a rupture could encourage a Japanese accommodation with China—both nightmare scenarios for the United States.[28]

For Japan and the United States, this implies two options. The first is the status quo policy of trying to make the alliance between the two countries work against some ill-defined security threat. Rather than attempting to use the presence of its troops as leverage over Japan on economic issues, the United States would need to address issues of mutual interest between the two countries that cut across the economic and security spheres. Politically, this means that both governments must proactively build domestic constituencies for bilateral engagement. On the economics side, this is done naturally through private-sector contacts—especially if there is a continued surge in foreign direct investment by US-based companies in Japan—though there is always room for improvement.

On the security side, it means greatly expanding participation in dialogue beyond the mid-level bureaucrats who primarily manage bilateral security matters. This requires a much more intensive effort to bring high-level officials, legislators, and private-sector opinion leaders into the mix. Such a process would be greatly facilitated by improved relations between Seoul and Tokyo, because any US presence for an explicitly regional role would require a reconfiguration of US forces in Northeast Asia, as well as new political understandings about their potential missions.[29] It is important that policymakers not become captive to shibboleths, such as the commitment of 100,000 US troops to Asia, which may well be unrelated to actual expected missions—especially because the presence of US troops is not costless in terms of political relationships. For example, the United

---

28. See McNaugher (1994) and Halperin (1999).

29. For example, bureaucratically, US forces in Japan and South Korea are under separate commands that report to the Commander in Chief, Pacific Area Command in Hawaii, and the forces based in South Korea are not configured for missions off the peninsula. The structure of the Combined Forces Command, under the UN mandate in Korea, integrates US and Korean troops and officers. If US forces in Northeast Asia were to be reoriented toward a regional role, it would require reconfiguration of the forces, reorganization of the command structure, and political agreements with Japan and Korea about their potential activities—in the Taiwan Strait, for example.

States may be able to fulfill its regional missions without the US Marine contingent on Okinawa.[30]

Programmatically, making the alliance work is less a matter of bold new initiatives that of achieving improved consultation between Tokyo and Washington on the whole panoply of international issues that they face. This includes both economic and security issues, as well as each country's positions in the international institutions. The Armitage Report (IISS 2000) contains numerous specific recommendations along these lines. For example, Washington must accept a greater political role for Japan and understand that there is a difference between genuine consultation and mere forewarning.[31] At the same time, Tokyo should be reminded that global and regional policy initiatives undertaken without prior consultation with Washington—such as the AMF proposal in 1997, and the FTAs that it has launched unilaterally in recent years—are unlikely to succeed.

The alternative to making the alliance work would be for Japan to become an autonomous great power. Under current circumstances, without significant regional organizations to mediate festering historical animosities, this would run the risk of destabilizing Asia. Its huge costs, to Japan itself and to the United States as well as to regional and global stability, add strongly to the case for making every effort to restore the Japan-United States relationship—including in the economics sphere—in a modern and normal direction.

Toward Normalcy and Partnership

The United States and Japan are the world's two largest and richest national economies. Their policies and performance have significant implications not only for their bilateral relationship but for the world as a whole. Continuing Japanese economic weakness poses a far greater threat to the United States than Japan's previous strength ever was. As we have argued, Japan can recover in the coming years and resume expanding at a sufficient pace to avoid a "worst-case" scenario—albeit perhaps after

---

30. There are two sorts of operations in Northeast Asia in which US forces could be expected to participate. First would be the defense of South Korea. The key roles for Japan-based US forces would be naval and air combat support, and transportation. The lightly equipped Marines on Okinawa would not be particularly useful in a Korean invasion scenario. More heavily equipped US ground forces could be airlifted from bases in the United States. A second sort of operation would be in the Taiwan Strait. Again, the Japan-based forces that would be most relevant would be the naval and air units—not the Marines on Okinawa.

31. For example, there is no evidence that President Bush gave the Japanese forewarning before announcing in April 2001 that the United States would do "whatever it took" (presumably involving US military assets stationed in Japan) to defend Taiwan.

a further period of difficulty that could accompany the additional reforms that are needed to provide a foundation for sustained future growth.

The most likely prospect for the initial decade or so of the 21st century is in fact relatively optimistic for both Japan and the United States. In the 1970s and much of the 1980s, Japan was the most dynamic economy in the world, while the United States lagged behind badly. In the 1990s, these roles were dramatically reversed; the United States was clearly up, and Japan was clearly down. But an important source of the recent US resurgence was its earlier troubles and the catalyst for reform they represented; Japan is quite likely now going through a similar challenge-and-response cycle, though perhaps it will last for a longer period, in light of the lesser flexibility of both its economic and political systems.

This outcome will be of critical, probably decisive, importance for the economic relationship *between* Japan and the United States. Their prolonged economic conflict correlates almost perfectly with the quarter-century, from the early 1970s through the middle 1990s, when US economic performance lagged and Japan was achieving global prominence. The reversal of these conditions in the latter half of the 1990s has already led to a dramatic change in the relationship, in the direction of ending the unique Japan-specific policy that the United States had maintained for so long.

As has been noted, we hope and believe that Japan will recover and again become a positive contributor to the world economy. We also believe that the United States will resume most, if not necessarily all, of the dynamism that it exhibited in the second half of the 1990s and thus eschew any return to the Japan bashing of the previous generation. Indeed, steady and stable growth in the two largest national economies would be optimal for the world as a whole, as well as for their bilateral relationship.

Beyond these likely paths of national economic performance, we conclude that a large number of structural conditions argue strongly for a restoration of normalcy in that relationship. Japan, in the wake of recent global developments—the completion of the European Union, the creation of the euro, and the rapid rise of China to prominence in East Asia—has simply become a smaller factor in the world economy, world trade, and international finance. Japan's share of US trade and investment have fallen sharply, and Japan's share of the US external imbalance has dropped from half to less than a quarter.

Even more important, many of the factors that seemed unique about Japan's dramatic economic ascendancy in the earlier period, and seemed to justify a unique US policy in response, turn out not to have been so unique after all (e.g., lean manufacturing techniques) or are rapidly eroding (e.g., lifetime employment). In particular, government industrial policy, the basis for the so-called strategic trade theory rationale for special US approaches to Japan, has virtually disappeared (and the infamous MITI has even become reform-minded METI).

Perhaps most important, US ability to influence policy in Japan has dropped precipitously. Our analysis in fact suggests that the results of past US efforts, even when US leverage was considerably greater, were exceedingly modest in terms of the expenditure of US effort and political capital. More recently, more US efforts have wound up in utter failure: the auto talks in 1995 on the trade side, the pleas to head off the disastrous tax increases in 1997 on the macroeconomic side, and the repeated calls to act decisively to resolve the problem of the nonperforming bank loans on the financial front.

In theory, there remain the traditional three sources of US leverage on Japan: closing the domestic market, stimulating appreciation of the yen, and withdrawing US security protection—or, much more likely, threats of all three. But all three are even less credible now than in the past. The "new WTO" precludes virtually any unilateral market closure by the United States. Sharp yen appreciation can significantly hurt a US economy at or near full employment, by generating inflation and higher interest rates. The rise of China requires maintenance of the security alliance with Japan at least as much as the Cold War did. More broadly, the sharp increase in US economic openness and the decline in Japan's openness tilt the impact of any distortions in the economic relationship—whether new trade barriers in the United States or sharp currency swings—against the United States much more than against Japan.

We return, at the end of this volume, to the theme that has permeated its pages. Japan and the United States experienced a number of years of economic conflict during a historical period when, for reasons unrelated to their relationship, the United States suffered substantial, sustained economic travail while Japan performed exceedingly well. It is now clear that this juxtaposition, although prolonged, was temporary—indeed, a historical accident that turned out to have had far-reaching implications for both countries (and for the world as a whole). At a minimum, we can project with some degree of confidence that such a juxtaposition is highly unlikely in the years ahead—for it would require a re-reversal of the pattern of the past decade.

In the years immediately ahead, the most plausible scenario is in fact that both countries will do reasonably well. The United States is likely to do better in some years, and Japan may do better in others. Such a return to "economic normalcy" counsels an adoption of "policy normalcy" along the lines proposed here. This normalcy will lay the foundation for a relationship of true partnership rather than the patron-client norms that, for all the rhetoric to the contrary, have largely prevailed to date.

Such a partnership could not come at a better time for the world economy as a whole, as well as for the national interests of both Japan and the United States. The global economic system is clearly at risk, less from the demonstrations of antiglobalization protesters than from the erosion of the perceived effectiveness of the traditional multilateral institutions. Both the International Monetary Fund and the World Trade Organization are viewed with suspicion if not downright hostility in a growing number of quarters, and are blamed by normally responsible people (and even governments) for such alleged failures as "worsening the Asian financial crisis" and "exposing the world to Frankenfoods." The new regional initiatives, on both the trade and financial fronts, represent both reactions to these developments and potentially an accelerated erosion of the global system—and could decisively cripple this system if they were to evolve into such far-ranging ventures as the East Asia Free Trade Area and Asian Monetary Fund that are already on some drawing boards, including in Tokyo.

There is thus an urgent need for Japan and the United States, along with the European Union, to start cooperating to restore the legitimacy and effectiveness of the multilateral order. They have clearly failed to do so in recent years: Japan-United States (as well as European Union-United States) conflicts were at the heart of the failure in Seattle to launch a new trade round that would revive the WTO, Japan's rejection of the EVSL program in APEC effectively scuttled the entire trade program of an initiative that had been launched to bolster transpacific security as well as economic ties, and Japan's initiative to create a new Asian Monetary Fund in the teeth of the financial crisis of 1997 represented a frontal attack on the United States and "its" Washington-based international institutions. Japan-United States cooperation to repair all this damage, and to initiate a new period of constructive cooperation in the multilateral context, is imperative.

Hence, a termination of the unique Japan policy maintained by the United States for almost three decades could have extremely positive effects. It would eliminate a major irritant, and the high degree of uncertainty, in the relationship between the two countries. US policy has already been moving in this direction, as has been shown throughout the book. The time has come for the United States to clearly enunciate this new approach. By doing so, it could herald a new era in Japan-United States relations, along with far better prospects for the world economy in the period ahead.

Appendix

Table A.1 Cases brought by Japan under the WTO

Case	Case number	Date	Resolution
Brazil: Certain Automotive Investment Measures	WT/DS51	30 July 1996	Pending consultation.
Canada: Certain Measures Affecting the Automotive Industry	WT/DS139/1	3 July 1998	Appellate body reversed aspects of panel ruling in favor of Japan.
Indonesia: Certain Measures Affecting the Automobile Industry	WT/DS55, WT/DS64	4 October 1996	Panel ruled in favor of Japan. Indonesia revised contested measure.
United States: Antidumping Act of 1916	WT/DS162/1	10 February 1999	Appellate body upheld panel ruling in favor of Japan
Antidumping Measures on Certain Hot-Rolled Steel Products from Japan	WT/DS184/1	18 November 1999	Under panel consideration.
Continued Dumping and Subsidy Offset Act of 2000	WT/DS217/1	21 December 2000	Pending consultation.
Imposition of Import Duties on Automobiles from Japan under Sections 301 and 304 of the Trade Act of 1974	WT/DS6	19 July 1995	Settled bilaterally.
Measures Affecting Government Procurement	WT/DS95/1	18 July 1997	Panel suspended. Authority for reestablishment of panel expired.

Sources: Ministry of International Trade and Industry, Japan; World Trade Organization.

Table A.2 Cases brought against Japan under the WTO

Case	Complainant	Case number	Date	Resolution
Tariff Quotas and Subsidies Affecting Leather	EC	WT/DS147/1	8 October 1998	Pending consultation.
Procurement of a Navigation Satellite	EC	WT/DS73/1	26 March 1997	Settled bilaterally.
Measures Affecting Imports of Pork	EC	WT/DS66	15 January 1997	Pending consultation.
Measures Concerning Sound Recordings	EC	WT/DS42	24 May 1996	Settled bilaterally.
Measures Affecting the Purchase of Telecommunications Equipment	EC	WT/DS15	18 August 1995	Settled bilaterally.
Tax on Alcoholic Beverages	EC, United States, Canada	WT/DS8, 10, 11	27 September 1995	Appellate body upheld panel ruling against Japan. Measures implemented.
Measures Affecting Agricultural Products	United States	WT/DS76/1	7 April 1997	Appellate body upheld panel ruling against Japan. Bilateral agreement expected.
Measures Affecting Consumer Photographic Film and Paper	United States	WT/DS44	13 June 1996	Panel ruled in favor of Japan.
Measures Affecting Distribution Services	United States	WT/DS45	13 June 1996	Pending consultation.
Measures Concerning Sound Recordings	United States	WT/DS28	9 February 1996	Settled bilaterally.

EC = European Community.

Sources: Ministry of International Trade and Industry, Japan; World Trade Organization.

Table A.3 Cases in which Japan participates as a third party

Case	Complainant	Case number	Date	Resolution
Argentina: Definitive Antidumping Measures on Imports of Ceramic Floor Tiles from Italy	EC	WT/DS189/1	26 January 2000	Under panel consideration.
Belgium: Administration of Measures Establishing Customs Duties for Rice	United States	WT/DS210/1	12 October 2000	Under panel consideration.
Brazil: Measures Affecting Patent Protection	United States	WT/DS/199/1	30 May 2000	Under panel consideration.
Measures Affecting Payment Terms for Imports	EC	WT/DS116/1	9 January 1998	Pending consultation.
Canada: Measures Affecting the Importation of Milk and the Exportation of Dairy Products	United States	WT/DS103/1	8 October 1997	Appellate body largely upheld panel ruling in favor of complainant. Dispute referred to original panel.
Patent Protection of Pharmaceutical Products	EC	WT/DS/114/1	19 December 1997	Panel ruled in favor of complainant.
Chile: Price Band System and Safeguard Measures Relating to Certain Agricultural Products	Argentina	WT/DS207/1	5 October 2000	Under panel consideration.
European Community: Antidumping Duties on Imports of Cotton-Type Bed-Linen from India	India	WT/DS141/1	3 August 1998	Appellate body largely upheld panel ruling in favor of complainant.

Measure	Respondent	Document	Date	Status
Measures Affecting the Exportation of Processed Cheese	United States	WT/DS104/1	8 October 1997	Pending consultation.
United Kingdom and Ireland: Customs Classification of Certain Computer Equipment	United States	WT/DS62, 67, 68)	11 February 1997	Appellate body reversed panel ruling in favor of complainants.
Hungary: Export Subsidies in Respect of Agricultural Products	Argentina, Australia, Canada, New Zealand, Thailand, United States	WT/DS35	27 March 1996	Settled, pending grant of waiver.
India:				
Import Restrictions	EC	WT/DS149	29 October 1998	Pending consultation.
Measures Affecting Customs Measures	EC	WT/DS150/1	30 October 1998	Pending consultation.
Measures Affecting the Automotive Sector	EC	WT/DS146/1	6 October 1998	Under panel consideration.
Measures Relating to Trade and Investment in the Motor Vehicles Sector	United States	WT/DS175/1	1 May 1999	Under panel consideration.
South Korea: Measures Affecting Government Procurement	United States	WT/DS163/1	16 February 1999	Panel ruled against complainant.
Philippines: Measures Affecting Trade and Investment in the Motor Vehicles Sector	United States	WT/DS195/1	23 May 2000	Under panel consideration.

(table continues next page)

Table A.3 Cases in which Japan participates as a third party *(continued)*

Case	Complainant	Case number	Date	Resolution
Thailand: Antidumping Duties on Angles, Shapes, and Sections of Iron or Non-Alloy Steel; H-Beams from Poland	Poland	WT/DS122/1	6 April 1998	Appellate body upheld panel ruling in favor of complainant.
Turkey: Restrictions on Imports of Textiles and Clothing Products	India	WT/DS34	21 March 1996	Appellate body upheld ruling in favor of complainant.
United States: Antidumping Act of 1916	EC	WT/DS136	9 June 1998	Appellate body upheld panel ruling in favor of complainant.
Antidumping Measures on Stainless Steel Plate in Coils and Stainless Steel Sheet and Strip from Korea	South Korea	WT/DS179	30 July 1999	Panel ruled in favor of complainant.
Definitive Safeguard Measures on Imports of Circular Welded Carbon Quality Pipeline from Korea	Korea	WT/DS202/1	13 June 2000	Under panel consideration.
Harbor Maintenance Tax	EC	WT/DS118/1	6 February 1998	Pending consultation.
Import Measures on Certain Products from the European Communities	EC	WT/DS165/1	4 March 1999	Appellate body ruled that satisfactory measures were implemented.
Import Prohibition of Certain Shrimp and Shrimp Products	India, Malaysia, Pakistan, Thailand	WT/DS58	8 October 1996	Appellate panel upheld ruling in favor of complainants. Dispute referred to original panel.

Measures Affecting Government Procurement	EC	WT/DS88/1	20 June 1997	Panel suspended at the request of the complainant.
Measures Affecting Textiles and Apparel Products	EC	WT/DS151/1	19 November 1998	Settled bilaterally.
Safeguard Measure on Imports of Lamb Meat from Australia	Australia	WT/DS178/1	23 July 1999	Panel ruling in favor of complainant under appeal.
Safeguard Measure on Imports of Fresh, Chilled, or Frozen Lamb from New Zealand	New Zealand	WT/DS177/1	16 July 1999	Panel ruling in favor of complainant under appeal.
Section 110(5) of the US Copyright Act	EC	WT/DS160/1	26 January 1999	Panel ruled in favor of complainant.
Section 211 Omnibus Appropriations Act	EC	WT/DS176/1	8 July 2000	Under panel consideration.
Sections 301-310 of the Trade Act of 1974	EC	WT/DS152/1	25 November 1998	Appellate body upheld ruling in favor of complainant.
Tax Treatment for "Foreign Sales Corporations"	EC	WT/DS108/1	18 November 1997	Appellate body upheld panel ruling in favor of complainant.

EC = European Community.

Sources: Ministry of International Trade and Industry, Japan; World Trade Organization.

Table A.4 Cases brought by the United States under the WTO

Case	Case number	Date	Resolution
Argentina—Certain Measures Affecting Imports of Footwear, Textiles, Apparel, and Other Items	WT/DS56	4 October 1996	Appellate body upheld panel decision in favor of the United States. Settled bilaterally.
Argentina—Certain Measures on the Protection of Patents and Test Data	WT/DS196/1	30 May 2000	Pending consultation.
Argentina—Measures Affecting Imports of Footwear	WT/DS164/1	1 March 1999	Under panel consideration.
Argentina—Patent Protection for Pharmaceuticals and Test Data Protection for Agricultural Chemicals	WT/DS171/1	6 May 1999	Pending consultation.
Australia—Measures Affecting the Importation of Salmonids	WT/DS21	17 November 1995	Settled bilaterally.
Australia—Subsidies Provided to Products and Exporters of Automotive Leather	WT/DS57, WT/DS126/1	4 May 1998	Panel ruled in favor of the United States.
Australia—Subsidies Provided to Products and Exporters of Automotive Leather	WT/DS106/1	10 November 1997	Panel withdrawn by the request of the United States. Settled bilaterally.
Australia—Textiles, Clothing, and Footwear Import Credit Scheme	WT/DS57	7 October 1996	Settled bilaterally.
Belgium—Administration of Measures Establishing Customs Duties for Rice	WT/DS210/1	12 October 2000	Under panel consideration.

Case	Document	Date	Status
Belgium—Certain Income Tax Measures Constituting Subsidies	WT/DS127/1	5 May 1998	Pending consultation.
Belgium—Measures Affecting Commercial Telephone Directory Services	WT/DS80/1	2 May 1997	Pending consultation.
Brazil—Certain Measures Affecting Trade and Investment in the Automotive Sector	WT/DS65	10 January 1997	Pending consultation.
Brazil—Certain Measures Affecting Trade and Investment in the Automotive Sector	WT/DS52	9 August 1996	Pending consultation.
Brazil—Measure on Minimum Import Prices	WT/DS197/1	30 May 2000	Pending consultation.
Brazil—Measures Affecting Patent Protection	WT/DS199/1	30 May 2000	Under panel consideration.
Canada—Certain Measures Concerning Periodicals	WT/DS31	11 March 1996	Appellate panel ruled in favor of the United States. Canada withdrew contested measure.
Canada—Measures Affecting the Importation of Milk and the Exportation of Dairy Products	WT/DS103/1	8 October 1997	Panel ruled in favor of the United States. Matter referred for further arbitration.
Canada—Patent Protection Term	WT/DS170/1	6 May 1999	Panel ruled in favor of the United States.
Chile—Taxes on Alcoholic Beverages	WT/DS109/1	11 December 1997	Pending consultation.
Denmark—Measures Affecting the Enforcement of Intellectual Property Rights	WT/DS83/1	14 May 1997	Pending consultation.

(table continues next page)

Table A.4 Cases brought by the United States under the WTO *(continued)*

Case	Case number	Date	Resolution
EC—Duties on Imports of Grains	WT/DS13	19 July 1995	Panel withdrawn at the request of the United States.
EC—Enforcement of Intellectual Property Rights for Motion Pictures and Television Programs	WT/DS124/1	30 April 1998	Pending consultation.
EC—Measures Affecting Meat and Meat Products (hormones)	WT/DS26	25 April 1996	Panel ruled in favor of the United States; arbitrators authorized retaliation.
EC—Measures Affecting the Exportation of Processed Cheese	WT/DS104/1	8 October 1997	Pending consultation.
EC—Measures Affecting the Grant of Copyright and Neighboring Rights	WT/DS115/1	6 January 1998	Pending consultation.
EC—Measures Relating to the Development of a Flight Management System	WT/DS172/1	21 May 1999	Pending consultation.
EC—Protection of Trademarks and Geographical Indicators for Agricultural Products and Foodstuffs	WT/DS174/1	1 June 1999	Pending consultation.
EC—Regime for the Importation, Sale, and Distribution of Bananas	WT/DS27	5 February 1996	Appellate panel ruled in favor of the United States. Tariff quotas must not discriminate by origin.
EC—Regime for the Importation, Sale, and Distribution of Bananas II	WT/DS158/1	20 January 1999	Pending consultation.
EC—Tariff Rate Quota on Corn Gluten Feed from the United States	WT/DS223/1	25 January 2001	Pending consultation.

Case	Number	Date	Status
EC, United Kingdom, and Ireland—Customs Classification of Certain Computer Equipment	WT/DS62,67,68	11 February 1997	Appellate body reversed panel ruling in favor of the United States.
France—Certain Income Tax Measures Constituting Subsidies	WT/DS131/1	5 May 1998	Pending consultation.
France—Measures Relating to the Development of a Flight Management System	WT/DS173/1	21 May 1999	Pending consultation.
Greece—Certain Income Tax Measures Constituting Subsidies	WT/DS129/1	5 May 1998	Pending consultation.
Greece—Enforcement of Intellectual Property Rights for Motion Pictures and Television Programs	WT/DS125/1	30 April 1998	Pending consultation.
Hungary—Export Subsidies in Respect of Agricultural Products	WT/DS35	27 March 1996	Settled, pending grant of waiver.
India—Measures Relating to Trade and Investment in the Motor Vehicle Sector	WT/DS175/1	1 May 1999	Under panel consideration.
India—Patent Protection for Pharmaceutical and Agricultural Chemical Products	WT/DS50	2 July 1996	Panel ruled in favor of the United States. India revised contested measure.
India—Quantitative Restrictions on Imports of Agricultural, Textile, and Industrial Products	WT/DS90/1	15 July 1997	Appellate body upheld panel decision in favor of the United States.
Indonesia—Certain Measures Affecting the Automobile Industry	WT/DS54,59	4 October 1996	Panel ruled in favor of the United States; Indonesia revised contested measure.

(table continues next page)

Table A.4 Cases brought by the United States under the WTO *(continued)*

Case	Case number	Date	Resolution
Ireland—Certain Income Tax Measures Constituting Subsidies	WT/DS130/1	5 May 1998	Pending consultation.
Ireland—Measures Affecting the Grant of Copyright and Neighboring Rights	WT/DS82/1	14 May 1997	Pending consultation.
Japan—Measures Affecting Agricultural Products	WT/DS76/1	7 April 1997	Appellate panel ruled in favor of the United States; modalities for implementation under consultation.
Japan—Measures Affecting Consumer Photographic Film and Paper	WT/DS44	13 June 1996	Panel ruled in favor of Japan.
Japan—Measures Affecting Distribution Services	WT/DS45	13 June 1996	Pending consultation.
Japan—Measures Concerning Sound Recordings	WT/DS28	9 February 1996	Settled bilaterally.
Japan—Taxes on Alcoholic Beverages	WT/DS11	27 September 1995	Appellate panel ruled in favor of the United States; Japan revised contested measure.
South Korea—Measures Affecting Government Procurement	WT/DS163/1	16 February 1999	Panel ruled against the United States.
South Korea—Measures Affecting Imports of Fresh, Chilled, and Frozen Beef	WT/DS161/1	1 February 1999	Panel ruled in favor of the United States. Measures implemented.
South Korea—Measures Concerning Inspection of Agricultural Products	WT/DS41	24 May 1996	Pending consultation.

South Korea—Measures Concerning the Shelf-life of Products	WT/DS5	3 May 1995	Settled bilaterally.
South Korea—Measures Concerning the Testing and Inspection of Agricultural Products	WT/DS3	6 April 1995	Pending consultation.
South Korea—Taxes on Alcoholic Beverages	DS 84/1	23 May 1997	Appellate panel ruled in favor of the United States. South Korea revised contested measure.
Mexico—Antidumping Investigation of High-Fructose Corn Syrup from the United States	WT/DS132/1	8 May 1998	Panel ruled in favor of the United States. Agreement under discussion.
Mexico—Antidumping Investigation of High-Fructose Corn Syrup from the United States	WT/DS101/1	4 September 1997	Pending consultation.
Mexico—Measures Affecting Telecommunications Services	WT/DS204/1	17 August 2000	Panel establishment deferred.
Mexico—Measures Affecting Trade in Live Swine	WT/DS203/1	10 July 2000	Pending consultation.
Netherlands—Certain Income Tax Measures Constituting Subsidies	WT/DS128/1	5 May 1998	Pending consultation.
Pakistan—Patent Protection for Pharmaceutical and Agricultural Chemical Products	WT/DS36	30 April 1996	Settled bilaterally.
Philippines—Measures Affecting Pork and Poultry	WT/DS102/1	7 October 1997	Settled bilaterally.

(table continues next page)

Table A.4 Cases brought by the United States under the WTO *(continued)*

Case	Case number	Date	Resolution
Philippines—Measures Affecting Trade and Investment in the Motor Vehicles Sector	WT/DS195/1	23 May 2000	Under panel consideration.
Portugal—Patent Protection under the Industrial Property Act	WT/DS37	30 April 1996	Settled bilaterally.
Romania—Measures on Minimum Import Prices	WT/DS198/1	30 May 2000	Pending consultation.
Sweden—Measures Affecting the Enforcement of Intellectual Property Rights	WT/DS86/1	28 May 1997	Settled bilaterally.
Turkey—Taxation of Foreign Film Revenues	WT/DS43	12 June 1996	Settled bilaterally.

EC = European Community.

Sources: World Trade Organization; US Trade Representative.

Table A.5 Cases brought against the United States under the WTO

Case	Complainant	Case number	Date	Resolution
Tariff Rate Quota for Imports of Groundnuts	Argentina	WT/DS111/1	19 December 1997	Pending consultation.
Safeguard Measure on Imports of Lamb Meat from Australia	Australia	WT/DS178/1	23 July 1999	Panel ruling against the United States under appeal.
US Patents Code	Brazil	WT/DS224/1	1 January 2001	Pending consultation.
Countervailing Duties on Certain Carbon Steel Products from Brazil	Brazil	WT/DS218/1	21 December 2000	Pending consultation.
Standards for Reformulated and Conventional Gasoline	Brazil	WT/DS4	19 May 1995	Panel ruled against the United States. Measures implemented.
Section 129(c)(1) of the Uruguay Round Agreements Act	Canada	WT/DS221/1	17 January 2001	Pending consultation.
Measures Treating Export Restraints as Subsidies	Canada	WT/DS194/1	19 May 2000	Under panel consideration.
Reclassification on Certain Sugar Syrups	Canada	WT/DS180/1	6 September 1999	Pending consultation.
Countervailing Duty Investigation with Respect to Live Cattle from Canada	Canada	WT/DS167/1	19 March 1999	Pending consultation.
Certain Measures Affecting the Import of Cattle, Swine, and Grain from Canada	Canada	WT/DS144/1	25 September 1998	Pending consultation.

(table continues next page)

Table A.5 Cases brought against the United States under the WTO *(continued)*

Case	Complainant	Case number	Date	Resolution
Countervailing Duty Investigation of Imports of Salmon from Chile	Chile	WT/DS97/1	5 August 1997	Pending consultation.
Safeguard Measure Against Imports of Broom Corn Brooms	Colombia	WT/DS78/1	28 April 1997	Pending consultation.
Restrictions on Imports of Cotton and Man-Made Fiber Underwear	Costa Rica	WT/DS24	22 December 1995	Measure at issue expired.
Definitive Safeguard Measures on Imports of Steel Wire Rod and Circular Welded Carbon Quality Line Pipe	EC	WT/DS214/1	30 November 2000	Pending consultation.
Countervailing Duties on Certain Corrosion-Resistant Carbon Steel Flat Products from Germany	EC	WT/DS213/1	10 November 2000	Pending consultation.
Countervailing Measures Concerning Certain Products from the European Communities	EC	WT/DS212/1	10 November 2000	Pending consultation.
Antidumping Duties on Seamless Pipe from Italy	EC	WT/DS225/1	7 November 2000	Pending consultation.
Section 306 of the Trade Act of 1974 and Amendments Thereto	EC	WT/DS200/1	5 June 2000	Pending consultation.

Measure	Complainant	Document	Date	Status
Section 337 of the Tariff Act of 1930 and Amendments Thereto	EC	WT/DS186/1	12 January 2000	Pending consultation.
Section 211 Omnibus Appropriations Act	EC	WT/DS176/1	8 July 1999	Under panel consideration.
Definitive Safeguard Measures on Imports of Wheat Gluten from the European Communities	EC	WT/DS166/1	17 March 1999	Appellate body upheld ruling against the United States, finding some measures still inconsistent.
Import Measures on Certain Products from the European Communities	EC	WT/DS165/1	4 March 1999	Appellate body upheld ruling against the United States, finding implemented measures acceptable.
Section 110(5) of the US Copyright Act	EC	WT/DS160/1	26 January 1999	Panel ruled against the United States.
Sections 301-310 of the Trade Act of 1974	EC	WT/DS152/1	25 November 1998	Appellate body upheld panel ruling in favor of the United States.
Measures Affecting Textiles and Apparel Products	EC	WT/DS151/1	19 November 1998	Settled bilaterally.
Imposition of Countervailing Duties on Certain Hot-Rolled Lead and Bismuth Carbon Steel Products Originating in the United Kingdom	EC	WT/DS138/1	30 June 1998	Appellate body upheld panel ruling against the United States. Measures implemented.
Antidumping Act of 1916 (I)	EC	WT/DS136	9 June 1998	Appellate body upheld panel ruling against the United States.
Harbor Maintenance Tax	EC	WT/DS118/1	6 February 1998	Pending consultation.
Tax Treatment for "Foreign Sales Corporations"	EC	WT/DS108/1	18 November 1997	Panel ruled against the United States. Arbitration suspended.

(table continues next page)

Table A.5 Cases brought against the United States under the WTO *(continued)*

Case	Complainant	Case number	Date	Resolution
Measures Affecting Imports of Poultry Products	EC	WT/DS100/1	18 August 1997	Pending consultation.
Measures Affecting Government Procurement	EC	WT/DS88/1	20 June 1997	Panel suspended. Authority to reestablish panel expired.
Measures Affecting Textiles and Apparel Products	EC	WT/DS85/1	23 May 1997	Settled bilaterally.
Antidumping Measures on Imports of Solid Urea from the Former German Democratic Republic	EC	WT/DS63	28 November 1996	Pending consultation.
The Cuban Liberty and Democratic Solidarity Act	EC	WT/DS38	3 May 1996	Panel suspended at the request of the complainant.
Tariff Increases on Products from the European Communities	EC	WT/DS39	17 April 1996	Panel withdrawn at the request of the complainant.
Continued Dumping and Subsidy Offset Act of 2000	EC, Japan, others	WT/DS217/1	21 December 2000	Pending consultation.
Antidumping and Countervailing Measures on Steel Plate from India	India	WT/DS206/1	4 October 2000	Pending consultation.
Measures Affecting Imports of Woven Wool Shirts and Blouses	India	WT/DS33	17 April 1996	Appellate body upheld panel ruling against the United States; measure at issue withdrawn.

Measures Affecting Imports of Women's and Girls' Wool Coats	India	WT/DS32	14 March 1996	Panel withdrawn at the request of the complainant.
Import Prohibition of Certain Shrimp and Shrimp Products	India, Malaysia, Pakistan, and Thailand	WT/DS58	8 October 1996	Appellate panel ruled in favor of complainants. Referred to original panel.
Antidumping Measures on Certain Hot-Rolled Steel Products from Japan	Japan	DS184/1	18 November 1999	Under panel consideration.
Antidumping Act of 1916 (II)	Japan	WT/DS162/1	10 February 1999	Appellate body upheld panel ruling against the United States.
Measures Affecting Government Procurement	Japan	WT/DS95/1	18 July 1997	Panel suspended. Authority to reestablish panel expired.
Imposition of Import Duties on Automobiles from Japan under Sections 301 and 304 of the Trade Act of 1974	Japan	WT/DS6	19 July 1995	Settled bilaterally.
Definitive Safeguard Measures on Imports of Circular Welded Carbon Quality Line Pipe from South Korea	Korea	WT/DS202/1	13 June 2000	Under panel consideration.
Antidumping Measures on Stainless Steel Plate in Coils and Stainless Steel Sheet and Strip from South Korea	Korea	WT/DS179	30 July 1999	Panel ruled against the United States.

(table continues next page)

Table A.5 Cases brought against the United States under the WTO (continued)

Case	Complainant	Case number	Date	Resolution
Antidumping Duty on Dynamic Random Access Memory Semiconductors of One Megabit or Above from South Korea	Korea	WT/DS99/1	14 August 1997	Panel ruled against the United States. Settled bilaterally.
Antidumping Duties on Imports of Colour Television Receivers from South Korea	Korea	WT/DS89/1	10 July 1997	Panel withdrawn at the request of the complainant.
Antidumping Investigation Regarding Imports of Fresh and Chilled Tomatoes from Mexico	Mexico	WT/DS49	1 July 1996	Settled bilaterally.
Safeguard Measure on Imports of Fresh, Chilled, or Frozen Lamb from New Zealand	New Zealand	WT/DS177/1	16 July 1999	Panel ruling against the United States under appeal.
Transitional Safeguard Measure on Combed Cotton Yarn from Pakistan	Pakistan	DS192/1	3 April 2000	Under panel consideration.
Import Prohibition of Certain Shrimp and Shrimp Products	Philippines	WT/DS61	25 October 1996	Pending consultation.
Standards for Reformulated and Conventional Gasoline	Venezuela, Brazil	WT/DS2, WT/DS4	25 March 1995	Panel ruled against the United States. Measures implemented.

EC = European Community.

Sources: World Trade Organization; US Trade Representative.

Table A.6 Cases in which the US participates as a third party

Case	Complainant	Case number	Date	Resolution
Argentina—Definitive Antidumping Measures on Imports of Ceramic Floor Tiles from Italy	EC	WT/DS189/1	26 January 2000	Pending consultation.
Argentina—Measures Affecting the Export of Bovine Hides and the Import of Finished Leather	EC	WT/DS155	23 December 1998	Panel ruled in favor of complainant.
Argentina—Safeguard Measures on Imports of Footwear	EC	WT/DS121/1	3 April 1998	Appellate body largely upheld panel ruling in favor of complainant.
Argentina—Transitional Safeguard Measures on Certain Imports of Woven Fabrics of Cotton and Cotton Mixtures Originating in Brazil	Brazil	WT/DS190/1	11 February 2000	Settled bilaterally.
Australia—Measures Affecting the Importation of Salmon	Canada	WT/DS18	5 October 1995	Appellate body reversed aspects of panel ruling in favor of complainant.
Brazil—Export Financing Program for Aircraft	Canada	WT/DS46	19 June 1996	Appellate body largely upheld panel ruling in favor of complainant.
Brazil—Measures on Import Licensing and Minimum Import Prices	EC	WT/DS183	14 October 1999	Pending consultation.
Canada—Certain Measures Affecting the Automotive Industry	Japan	WT/DS139/1	3 July 1998	Appellate body reversed aspects of panel ruling in favor of complainant.
Canada—Measures Affecting the Export of Civilian Aircraft	Brazil	WT/DS70	10 March 1997	Appellate body upheld panel ruling in favor of complainant.
Canada—Export Credits and Loan Guarantees for Regional Aircraft	Brazil	WT/DS22/1	22 January 2001	Under panel consideration.

(table continues next page)

Table A.6 Cases in which the US participates as a third party *(continued)*

Case	Complainant	Case number	Date	Resolution
Canada—Patent Protection of Pharmaceutical Products	EC	WT/DS114	19 December 1997	Panel ruled in favor of complainant.
Chile—Measures Affecting the Transit and Importation of Swordfish	EC	WT/DS193/1	19 April 2000	Under panel consideration.
Chile—Price Band System and Safeguard Measures Relating to Certain Agricultural Products	Argentina	WT/DS207/1	5 October 2000	Under panel consideration.
Chile—Taxes on Alcoholic Beverages	EC	WT/DS110/1	15 December 1997	Appellate body largely upheld panel ruling in favor of complainant.
Chile—Taxes on Alcoholic Beverages	EC	WT/DS87/1	4 June 1997	Appellate body largely upheld panel ruling in favor of complainant.
EC—Antidumping Duties on Imports of Cotton-Type Bed-Linen from India	India	WT/DS141/1	3 August 1998	Appellate body largely upheld panel ruling in favor of complainant.
EC—Measures Affecting Butter Products	New Zealand	WT/DS72	24 March 1997	Panel suspended at request of complainant.
EC—Measures Affecting Importation of Certain Poultry Products	Brazil	WT/DS69	24 February 1997	Appellate body largely upheld panel ruling in favor of complainant.
EC—Measures Affecting the Prohibition of Asbestos and Asbestos Products	Canada	WT/DS135	28 May 1998	Appellate body largely reversed panel ruling in favor of complainant.
EC—Patent Protection of Pharmaceutical Products	Canada	WT/DS153	2 December 1998	Pending consultation.

Guatemala—Antidumping Investigation Regarding Imports of Portland Cement from Mexico	Mexico	WT/DS60	15 October 1996	Appellate body ruled dispute had not been properly before the panel.
Guatemala—Definitive Antidumping Measure Regarding Grey Portland Cement from Mexico	Mexico	WT/DS156	5 January 1999	Panel ruled in favor of complainant.
India—Patent Protection for Pharmaceutical and Agricultural Chemical Products	EC	WT/DS79/1	28 April 1997	Panel ruled in favor of complainant.
South Korea—Measures Affecting Imports of Fresh, Chilled, and Frozen Beef	Australia	WT/DS169/1	13 April 1999	Appellate body upheld panel ruling in favor of complainant.
Nicaragua—Measures Affecting Imports from Honduras and Colombia	Colombia	WT/DS188/1	17 January 2000	Under panel consideration.
Turkey—Restrictions on Imports of Textile and Clothing Products	India	WT/DS34	21 March 1996	Appellate body upheld panel ruling in favor of complainant.
Thailand—Antidumping Duties on Angles, Shapes, and Sections of Iron or Non-Alloy Steel; H-Beams from Poland	Poland	WT/DS122/1	6 April 1998	Appellate body upheld panel ruling in favor of complainant.

EC = European Community.

Sources: World Trade Organization; US Trade Representative.

References

Abegglen, James C. 2001. Japan's Industries and Companies: Economic Dynamism and Social Continuity. In *Reform in Japan—Can Japan Change?* ed. Craig Freedman. Cheltenham, UK: Edward Elgar.

ACCJ (American Chamber of Commerce in Japan). 2000. *Making Trade Talks Work*. Tokyo: ACCJ.

Aggarwal, Raj, and Mbodja Mougoue. 1996. Cointegration among Asian Currencies: Evidence of the Increasing Influence of the Japanese Yen. *Japan and the World Economy* 8: 291-308.

Alexander, Arthur. 1995. *Japan's Potential Role in a Military-Technical Revolution*. JEI Report 1A. Washington: Japan Economic Institute.

Alexander, Arthur J. 1997a. *Japanese Direct Investment in the United States: Revising and Updating Perceptions*. JEI Report 42A. Washington: Japan Economic Institute.

Alexander, Arthur J. 1997b. U.S. Direct Investment in Japan: Another Dimension of the Economic Relationship. JEI Report 17A. Washington: Japan Economic Institute.

Allen, G.C. 1946. *A Short History of Modern Japan, 1867-1937*. London: Allen & Unwin.

Altbach, Eric. 1997. *The Asian Monetary Fund Proposal*. JEI Report 47A. Washington: Japan Economic Institute.

Altbach, Eric. 1998. *Tokyo Slashes Foreign Aid*. JEI Report 1B. Washington: Japan Economic Institute.

Aoki, Masahiko. 1984. Shareholders' Non-unanimity on Investment Financing: Banks vs. Individual Investors. In *The Economic Analysis of the Japanese Firm*, ed. Masahiko Aoki. New York: North-Holland.

Aoki, Masahiko. 1988. *Information, Incentives, and Bargaining in the Japanese Economy*. Cambridge: Cambridge University Press.

APEC Eminent Persons Group. 1993. A Vision for APEC. Singapore: APEC Secretariat.

APEC Eminent Persons Group. 1994. Achieving the APEC Vision. Singapore: APEC Secretariat.

Arase, David. 1995. *Buying Power: the Political Economy of Japan's Foreign Aid*. Boulder, CO: Lynne Rienner.

Arase, David, Joshua Fogel, Mike Mochizuki, and Quansheng Zhao. 2001. *China-Japan Relations: Old Animosities, New Possibilities*. Special Report, Asia Program. Washington: Woodrow Wilson International Center for Scholars.

Ariga, Kenn, Yasushi Ohkusa, and Hisashi Namikawa. 1991. The Japanese Distribution System. *Ricerche Economiche* 45, no. 2-3: 167-84.

Ariga, Kenn, Yasushi Ohkusa, and Kiyohiko G. Nishimura. 1999. Determinations of Individual Firm Mark-up in Japan: Market Concentration, Market Share, and JFTC Regulation. *Journal of the Japanese and International Economies* 13n, no. 4: 424-50.

Arize, Augustine C., and Jan Walker. 1992. A Reexamination of Japan's Aggregate Import Demand Function: An Application of the Engle and Granger Two-Step Procedure. *International Economic Journal* 6, no. 2: 41-56.

Asano, Masakazu. 1997. *The Retail Revolution in Japan*. Fuji Research Paper 4. Tokyo: Fuji Research Institute.

Asano, Masakazu. 1998. *The Japanese Consumer Market After Price Destruction*. Fuji Research Paper 8. Tokyo: Fuji Research Institute.

Asher, David L., and Robert H. Dugger. 2000. *Could Japan's Financial Mount Fuji Blow Its Top?* Working Paper Series 00-01. Cambridge, MA: MIT Japan Program.

Asian Development Bank. 2000. *ADB Clarifies Position on Recent Report*. News Release 26/00. Manila: Asian Development Bank.

Bacchetta, Philippe, and Eric van Wincoop. 2000. Does Exchange Rate Stability Increase Trade and Welfare? *American Economic Review* 90, no. 5: 1093-1109.

Baily, Martin. 2001. Macroeconomic Implications of the New Economy. Paper prepared for a symposium on economic policy for the information economy, sponsored by the Federal Reserve Bank, Kansas City (30 August-1 September).

Baily, Martin, Diana Farrell, and Susan Lund. 2000. The Color of Hot Money. *Foreign Affairs* 79: 2.

Balassa, Bela, and Marcus Noland. 1988. *Japan in the World Economy*. Washington: Institute for International Economics.

Bandow, Doug. 1998. *Okinawa: Liberating Washington's East Asian Military Colony*. Policy Analysis 314. Washington: Cato Institute.

Bank of Japan, ed. 2001. *The Role of Monetary Policy under Low Inflation: Deflationary Shocks and Policy Responses*. Monetary and Economic Studies (Special Edition), vol. 19, no. S-1. Tokyo.

Barrell, Ray, and Nigel Pain. 1999. Trade Restraints and Japanese Direct Investment Flows. *European Economic Review* 43, no. 1: 29-45.

Basu, Susanto, John G. Fernald, and Matthew D. Shapiro. 2001. *Productivity Growth in the 1990s: Technology, Utilization or Adjustment?* NBER Working Paper 8359. Cambridge, MA: National Bureau of Economic Research.

Bayoumi, Tamin. 2000a. The Morning After: Explaining the Slowdown in Japanese Growth in the 1990s. In *Post-Bubble Blues*, eds. Tamin Bayoumi and Charles Collyns. Washington: International Monetary Fund.

Bayoumi, Tamin. 2000b. Where Are We Going? The Output Gap and Potential Growth. In *Post-Bubble Blues*, eds. Tamin Bayoumi and Charles Collyns. Washington: International Monetary Fund.

Bayoumi, Tamin, and Gabrielle Lipworth. 1998. Japanese Foreign Direct Investment and Regional Trade. In *Structural Change in Japan*, eds. Bijan B. Aghevli, Tamin Bayoumi, and Guy Meredith. Washington: International Monetary Fund.

Beason, Richard, and David E. Weinstein. 1996. Growth, Economies of Scale, and Targeting in Japan (1955-1990). *Review of Economics and Statistics* 78, no. 2: 286-95.

Berg, Claes, and Lars Jonung. 1999. Pioneering Price Level Targeting: The Swedish Experience, 1931-1937. *Journal of Monetary Economics* 43: 525-51.

Berger, Thomas U. 1999. Alliance Politics and Japan's Post-War Culture of Antimilitarism. In *The U.S.-Japan Alliance*, eds. Michael J. Green and Patrick M. Cronin. New York: Council on Foreign Relations.

Bergsten, C. Fred. 1991. Burdensharing in the Gulf and Beyond. Statement before the Committee on Ways and Means, US House of Representatives, 13 March.

Bergsten, C. Fred. 1996. The Competitive Depreciation of the Yen. *Economist*, 2 November.

Bergsten, C. Fred. 2000. East Asian Regionalism: Towards a Tripartite World. *Economist*.

Bergsten, C. Fred. 2001a. America's Two-Front Economic Conflict. *Foreign Affairs* 80, no. 2 (March/April): 16-27.

Bergsten, C. Fred. 2001b. Strong Dollar, Weak Policy. *The International Economy,* July/August: 8-10.

Bergsten, C. Fred. 2001c. Fifty Years of Trade Policy. *The World Economy* 24, no. 1 (January): 1-13.

Bergsten, C. Fred, and C. Randall Henning. 1996. *Global Economic Leadership and the Group of Seven*. Washington: Institute for International Economics.

Bergsten, C. Fred, and Marcus Noland. 1993. *Reconcilable Differences? United States-Japan Economic Conflict*. Washington: Institute for International Economics.

Bernanke, Ben, Thomas Laubach, Frederic S. Mishkin, and Adam S. Posen. 1999. *Inflation Targeting: Lessons from International Experience*. Princeton, NJ: Princeton University Press.

BIS (Bank for International Settlements). 2000. *Annual Report*. Basel.

Blonigen, Bruce A. 1997. Firm Specific Assets and the Link Between Exchange Rates and Foreign Direct Investment. *American Economic Review* 87, no. 3: 447-65.

Blonigen, Bruce A. 2000. *Tariff-Jumping Antidumping Duties*. NBER Working Paper 7776. Cambridge, MA: National Bureau of Economic Research.

Blonigen, Bruce A., and Robert C. Feenstra. 1997. Protectionist Threats and Foreign Direct Investment. In *Effects of US Protection and Promotion Policies*, ed. Robert C. Feenstra. Chicago: University of Chicago Press.

Blonigen, Bruce A., and Stephen E. Hayes. 1999. *Antidumping Investigations and the Pass-Through of Exchange Rates and Antidumping Duties*. NBER Working Paper 7378. Cambridge, MA: National Bureau of Economic Research.

Bork, Robert H. 1966. The Rule of Reason and the Per Se Concept. *Yale Law Journal* 75, no. 3: 373-475.

Bork, Robert H. 1978. *The Antitrust Paradox: A Policy at War with Itself*. New York: Basic Books.

BPEA (Brookings Papers on Economic Activity). 2000. Gordon, Robert, Comments and Discussion, 212-22, on Jorgeson, Dale W., and Kevin J. Stiroh, Raising the Speed Limit: U.S. Economic Growth in the Information Age. BPEA 1:2000, 125-235.

Brander, James, and Paul R. Krugman. 1983. A "Reciprocal Dumping" Model of International Trade. *Journal of International Economics* 15: 313-21.

Brunner, Allan D., and Steven B. Kamin. 1996. Determinants of the 1991-1993 Japanese Recession. *Japan and the World Economy* 8: 363-99.

Burgess, Simon M., and Michael Knetter. 1998. An International Comparison of Employment Adjustment to Exchange Rate Fluctuations. *Review of International Economics* 6, no. 1: 151-63.

Calvin, Linda, and Barry Krissoff. 1998. Technical Barriers to Trade: A Case Study of Phytosanitary Barriers and U.S.-Japanese Apple Trade. *Journal of Agricultural and Resource Economics* 23, no. 2: 351-66.

Cargill, Thomas, Michael Hutchison, and Takatoshi Ito. 1997. *The Political Economy of Japanese Monetary Policy*. Cambridge, MA: MIT Press.

Cargill, Thomas, Michael Hutchison, and Takatoshi Ito. 2000. *Financial Policy and Central Banking in Japan*. Cambridge, MA: MIT Press.

Castellano, Marc. 1999a. *Japanese Foreign Aid: A Lifesaver for East Asia*. JEI Report 6A. Washington: Japan Economic Institute.

Castellano, Marc. 1999b. *Two Years On: Evaluating Tokyo's Response to the East Asian Financial Crisis*. JEI Report 30A. Washington: Japan Economic Institute.

Castellano, Marc. 2000a. *Forgiving Poor-Country Debt: Will Japan Lead the Way?* JEI Report 18A. Washington: Japan Economic Institute.

Castellano, Marc. 2000b. *Japan's Foreign Aid Program in the New Millennium: Rethinking Development*. JEI Report 6A. Washington: Japan Economic Institute.

Castellano, Marc. 2000c. *More of Japan's Aid Has Strings Attached*. JEI Report 24B. Washington: Japan Economic Institute.

Castellano, Marc. 2000d. *Tokyo, Washington Clash Over Reshaping IMF's Role*. JEI Report 1B. Washington: Japan Economic Institute.

Catte, P., G. Galli, and S. Rebecchini. 1994. Concerted Interventions and the Dollar: An Analysis of Daily Data. In *The International Monetary System in Crisis and Reform: Essays in Honor of Rinaldo Ossola*, eds. P. Kenen, F. Papadia, and F. Saccomini. Cambridge: Cambridge University Press.

CBO (Congressional Budget Office). 2001. *An Analysis of the President's Budgetary Proposals for Fiscal Year 2002*. Washington: CBO.

CEA (Council of Economic Advisers). 2000. *Economic Report of the President*. Washington.

CEA (Council of Economic Advisers). 2001. *Economic Report of the President*. Washington.

Ceglowski, Janet. 1996. The Recent Behavior of Japanese Imports: A Disaggregated Analysis. *Japan and the World Economy* 8: 443-57.

Ceglowski, Janet. 1997. On the Structural Stability of Trade Equations: The Case of Japan. *Journal of International Money and Finance* 16, no. 3: 491-512.

CFR (Council on Foreign Relations). 1999. *Safeguarding Prosperity in a Global Financial System*. New York.

Cheng Leonard K.H., and Mordechai Kreinin. 1996. Supplier Preference and Dumping: An Analysis of Japanese Corporate Groups. *Southern Economic Journal* 63: 51-59.

Cheong, Inkyo. 1999. *Economic Integration in Northeast Asia: Searching for a Feasible Approach*. Working Paper 99-25. Seoul: Korea Institute for International Economic Policy.

Chinworth, Michael. 1999. The Technology Factor in U.S.-Japan Security Relations. In *The U.S.-Japan Alliance*, ed. Michael J. Green and Patrick M. Cronin. New York: Council on Foreign Relations.

Choy, Jon. 1998. *Japan's Construction Industry: The Economic Engine That Can't*. JEI Report 34A. Washington: Japan Economic Institute.

Chu, Shulong. 2000. *TMD and East Asian Security*. Special Report. Berkeley, CA: Nautilus Institute.

Competitiveness Policy Council. 1992. *Building a Competitive America*. First Report to the President and Congress. Washington.

Cossa, Ralph A. 1999. *Beyond the Defense Guidelines*. NAPSNET Special Report, 22 April.

Council on Foreign Exchange and Other Transactions. 1999. Internationalization of the Yen for the 21st Century, Tokyo. Photocopy (20 April).

Craib, B. Anne. *Prospects for Japan's Foreign Aid Program: Quality Versus Quantity?* JEI Report 44A. Washington: Japan Economic Institute.

Creel, Harold J. 1997. *Squall over the Pacific*. ESI Series in American Competitiveness Issue 97-7. Washington: Economic Strategy Institute.

Cronin, Patrick M., Paul S. Giarra, and Michael J. Green. 1999. The Alliance Implications of Theatre Missile Defense. In *The U.S.-Japan Alliance*, eds. Michael J. Green and Patrick M. Cronin. New York: Council on Foreign Relations.

Davis, Bob, and David Wessel. 1998. *Prosperity: The Coming Twenty-Year Boom and What It Means to You*. New York: Random House.

Davis, Morris A., and Michael G. Palumbo. 2001. A Primer on the Economics and Time Series Econometrics of Wealth Effects. Federal Reserve Bank of New York. Photocopy.

Dekle, Robert. 1996. *Endaka and Japanese Employment Adjustment*. Working Paper 113. New York: Center on Japanese Economy and Business, Columbia Business School.

Dekle, Robert. 2000. Demography Destiny, Per Capita Consumption, and the Japanese Saving-Investment Balance. University of Southern California, Los Angeles. Photocopy (June).

de Melo, Jaime, and David Tarr. 1992. *A General Equilibrium Analysis of US Trade Policy.* Cambridge, MA: MIT Press.

de Melo, Jaime, and David Tarr. 1996. VERs under Imperfect Competition and Foreign Direct Investment: A Case Study of the US-Japan Auto VER. *Japan and the World Economy* 8: 11-33.

Destler, I.M. 1995. *American Trade Politics,* 3d ed. Washington: Institute for International Economics.

Dick, Andrew R. 1991. Learning-By-Doing and Dumping in the Semiconductor Industry. *Journal of Law and Economics* 14: 133-60.

Dick, Andrew R. 1994. Accounting for Semiconductor Industry Dynamics. *International Journal of Industrial Organization* 12: 35-51.

Dinopoulos, Elias, and Mordechai Kreinin. 1990. An Analysis of Import Expansion Policies. *Economic Inquiry* 28: 99-108.

Dixon, Anne M. 1999. Can Eagles and Cranes Flock Together? U.S. and Japanese Approaches to Multilateral Security After the Cold War. In *The U.S.-Japan Alliance,* eds. Michael J. Green and Patrick M. Cronin. New York: Council on Foreign Relations.

Dobson, Paul W., and Michael Waterson. 1996. *Vertical Restraints and Competition Policy.* Office of Fair Trading Research Paper 12. East Molesey, UK.

Dobson, Wendy, and A.E. Safarian, eds. 1995. *Benchmarking the Canadian Business Presence in East Asia.* Toronto: University of Toronto Press.

Dobson, Wendy, and A.E. Safarian, eds. 1996. *East Asian Capitalism: Diversity and Dynamism.* Toronto: University of Toronto Press.

Dodwell Marketing Consultants. 1997. *Industrial Groupings in Japan.* Tokyo: Dodwell.

Doherty, Eileen. 1987. *Japan's Aid Program Criticized.* JEI Report 46B. Washington: Japan Economic Institute.

Dore, Ronald. 2001. Reform? The Dubious Benefits of Marketization. In *Economic Reform in Japan—Can the Japanese Change?* ed. Craig Freedman. Cheltenham, UK: Edward Elgar.

Drysdale, Peter. 1995. The Question of Access to the Japanese Market. *Economic Record* 71, no. 214: 271-83.

Eaton, Jonathan, and Samuel Kortum. 1997. Engines of Growth: Domestic and Foreign Sources of Innovation. *Japan and the World Economy* 9: 235-59.

Economic Planning Agency. 1989. *Commodity Price Report.* Tokyo.

Encarnation, Dennis. 1992. *Rivals Beyond Trade.* Ithaca, NY: Cornell University Press.

Ensign, Margee M. 1992. *Doing Good or Doing Well?: Japan's Foreign Aid Program.* New York: Columbia University Press.

Evans, Peter C., and Kenneth A. Oye. 2001. International Competition: Conflict and Cooperation in Government Export Financing. In *The Ex-Im Bank in the 21st Century,* eds. Gary Clyde Hufbauer and Rita M. Rodriguez. Washington: Institute for International Economics.

Fallows, James. 1989. Containing Japan. *Atlantic Monthly,* May.

Fallows, James. 1994. *Looking at the Sun.* New York: Pantheon Books.

Faruqee, Hamid, and Martin Mühleisen. 2001. *Population Aging in Japan: Demographic Shock and Fiscal Sustainability.* IMF Working Paper WP/01/40. Washington: International Monetary Fund.

Findlay, Christopher, Gary Clyde Hufbauer, and Gautam Jaggi. 1996. Aviation Reform in the Asia Pacific. In *Flying High: Liberalizing Civil Aviation in the Asia Pacific,* eds. Gary Clyde Hufbauer and Christopher Findlay. Washington: Institute for International Economics.

Fishlow, Albert, Catherine Gwin, Stephan Haggard, Dani Rodrik, and Robert Wade. 1994. *Miracle or Design? Lessons from the East Asian Experience.* Policy Essay 11. Washington: Overseas Development Council.

Flamm, Kenneth. 1996. *Mismanaged Trade?* Washington: Brookings Institution.

Flath, David. 1989. Vertical Restraints in Japan. *Japan in the World Economy* 1, no. 2: 187-203.

Frankel, Jeffrey A. 1984. *The Yen-Dollar Agreement: Liberalizing Japanese Capital Markets*. Policy Analyses in International Economics 9. Washington: Institute for International Economics.

Frankel, Jeffrey A. 1993. Is Japan Creating A Yen Bloc in East Asia and the Pacific? In *Regionalism and Rivalry: Japan and the United States in Pacific Asia*, eds. Jeffrey A. Frankel and Miles Kahler. Chicago: University of Chicago Press.

Frankel, Jeffrey A. 1997. *Regional Trading Blocs in the World Economic System*. Washington: Institute for International Economics.

Frankel, Jeffrey A., and Kathryn M. Dominguez. 1993. *Does Foreign Exchange Intervention Work?* Washington: Institute for International Economics.

Friedman, Benjamin M. 2000. Japan Now and the United States Then: Lessons from the Parallels. In *Japan's Financial Crisis and Its Parallels to the U.S. Experience*, Special Report 13, eds. Ryoichi Mikitani and Adam S. Posen. Washington: Institute for International Economics.

Fujiki, Hiroshi, Kunio Okina, and Shigenori Shiratsuka. 2001. Monetary Policy under Zero Interest Rate: Viewpoints of Central Bank Economists. *Monetary and Economic Studies* 19, no. 2: 89-130.

Fukao, Kyoji. 2001. The Status of Foreign Investment in Japan. *Japan Economic Currents*, no. 8, May.

Fukao, Kyoji, and Keiko Ito. 2000. Foreign Direct Investment and Service Trade: The Case of Japan. Discussion Paper Series / Institute of Economic Research, Hitotsubashi University, Japan. Photocopy.

Fukao, Mitsuhiro. 1998. Japanese Financial Instability and Weaknesses in the Corporate Governance Structure. Keio University, Tokyo. Photocopy (7 March).

Funabashi, Yoichi. 1988. *Managing the Dollar: From the Plaza to the Louvre*. Washington: Institute for International Economics.

Funabashi, Yoichi. 1991. Japan and the New World Order. *Foreign Affairs* 70, no. 5: 58-74.

Funabashi, Yoichi. 1992. Japan and America: Global Partners. *Foreign Policy* 86 (Spring): 24-39.

Funabashi, Yoichi. 1995. *Asia-Pacific Fusion: Japan's Role in APEC*. Washington: Institute for International Economics.

Funabashi, Yoichi. 1999. *Alliance Adrift*. New York: Council on Foreign Relations.

Galloway, Michael P., Bruce A. Blonigen, and Joseph E. Flynn. 1999. Welfare Costs of US Antidumping and Countervailing Duty Laws. *Journal of International Economics* 49: 211-44.

Garnaut, Ross. 1999. The Future of APEC. *APEC Economies Newsletter* 3, no. 7 (July): 1-2. Asia Pacific School of Economics and Management. http://apsem.anu.edu.au.

Goad, Pierre G. 1998. Inflation Data from Asia Show Continued Financial Instability. *Wall Street Journal*, 3 March.

Godley, Wynne, and Alex Izurieta. 2001. As the Implosion Begins . . .? Prospects and Policies for the US Economy: A Strategic View. Jerome Levy Economics Institute, New York. Photocopy (June).

Goldberg, Pinelopi K., and Michael M. Knetter. 1996. *Goods Prices and Exchange Rates: What Have We Learned?* NBER Working Paper 5862. Cambridge, MA: National Bureau of Economic Research.

Goldberg, Pinelopi K., and Michael M. Knetter. 2000. International Rivalry in the Film Industry: Kodak v. Fuji. Department of Economics, Columbia University, New York. Photocopy (28 June).

Goldstein, Morris. 2001. *IMF Structural Conditionality: How Much Is Too Much?* Working Paper 01-4. Washington: Institute for International Economics.

Gordon, Robert J. 2000. Does the New Economy Measure Up to the Great Inventions of the Past? *Journal of Economic Perspectives*, Fall.

Gower, Luke, and Kali Kalirajan. 1998. Did Japanese Main Banks Improve the Technical Efficiencies of Their Non-Financial Client Firms in the 1980s? *Japan and the World Economy* 10: 455-66.

Graham, Edward M. 2000. Trade, Competition, and the WTO Agenda. In *The WTO after Seattle*, ed. Jeffrey Schott. Washington: Institute for International Economics.

Graham, Edward M., and Robert Z. Lawrence. 1996. Measuring the International Contestability of Markets. *Journal of World Trade* 30, no. 5: 5-20.

Graham, Edward M., and J. David Richardson. 1997. *Global Competition Policy*. Washington: Institute for International Economics.

Greaney, Theresa M. 1996. Import Now! An Analysis of Market-Share Voluntary Import Expansions (VIEs). *Journal of International Economics* 40, no. 1-2: 149-63.

Greaney, Theresa M. 1997. *US-Japan Bilateral Trade Disputes: End of an Era?* CGP-SSRC Seminar Series. New York: Center for Global Partnership.

Greaney, Theresa M. 1999. Manipulating Market Shares: The Indirect Effects of Voluntary Import Expansions. *Japan and the World Economy* 11: 95-113.

Greaney, Theresa M. 2000. Assessing the Impacts of US-Japan Bilateral Trade Agreements, 1980-1995. *World Economy* 24, no. 2: 127-57.

Greaney, Theresa M. 2001. Promoting Imports to Appease Trade Partners: Japan's New Trade Policies. Syracuse University, Syracuse, NY. Photocopy (19 January).

Green, Michael J. 1995. *Arming Japan*. New York: Columbia University Press.

Green, Michael. 2000. *Why Tokyo Will Be a Larger Player in Asia*. E-Notes. Philadelphia: Foreign Policy Research Institute.

Green, Michael Jonathan. 2001. *Japan's Reluctant Realism*. New York: St. Martin's Press.

Green, Michael J., and Toby F. Dalton. 2000. *Asian Reactions to U.S. Missile Defenses*. NBAR Analysis 11:3. Seattle: National Bureau of Asian Research.

Greenspan, Alan. 2000. Challenges for Economic Policymakers. Remarks at the 18th Annual Monetary Conference, sponsored by the Cato Institute, Washington (19 October).

Greenwald, Joseph. 1996. Binational Dispute Settlement Mechanisms. In *Managing US-Japanese Trade Disputes: Are There Better Ways?* eds. Wendy Dobson and Hideo Sato. Ottawa: Centre for Trade Policy and Law.

G-7 Finance Ministers. 2000. Report from G7 Finance Ministers to the Heads of Government, Fukuoka, Japan, 8 July. http://www.g7.utoronto.ca/g7/finance/fm20000708-st.html.

Gu, Guoliang. 2000. *TMD, NMD, and Arms Control*. Missile Defense Initiative Special Report. Berkeley, CA: Nautilus Institute.

Gust, Christopher, and Jaime Marquez. 2000. Productivity Developments Abroad. *Federal Reserve Bulletin*, October.

Hahn, Robert W. 1998. Government Analysis of the Benefits and Costs of Regulation. *Journal of Economic Perspectives* 12, no. 4: 201-10.

Hall, Brian J., and David E. Weinstein. 1996. *The Myth of the Patient Japanese: Corporate Myopia and Financial Distress in Japan and the US*. NBER Working Paper No. W5818. Cambridge, MA: National Bureau of Economic Research.

Halperin, Morton H. 1999. *The Nuclear Dimension of the U.S.-Japan Alliance*. http://www.nautilus.org/nukepolicy/Halperin/index.html.

Hamada, Koichi. 1994. Japan's Prospective Role in the International Monetary Regime. In *Japan: A New Kind of Superpower?* eds. Craig C. Garby and Mary Brown Bullock. Washington: Woodrow Wilson Center Press.

Hamada, Koichi. 1996. *Consumers, the Legal System and Product Liability Reform: A Comparative Perspective between Japan and the United States*. Working Paper 120. New York: Center for Japanese Economy and Business, Columbia Business School.

Hamada, Koichi. 1999. From the AMF to the Miyazawa Initiative: Observations on Japan's Currency Diplomacy. *Journal of East Asian Affairs* 13, no. 1 (Spring/Summer): 33-50.

Harris, Stuart, and Richard N. Cooper. 2000. The U.S.-Japan Alliance. In *America's Asian Alliances*, eds. Robert D. Blackwell and Paul Dibb. Cambridge, MA: MIT Press.

Hart, Oliver, and Jean Tirole. 1990. Vertical Integration and Market Foreclosure. *Brookings Paper on Economic Activity*, 205-76.

Hartcher, Peter. 1998. *The Ministry: How Japan's Most Powerful Institution Endangers World Markets*. Boston: Harvard Business School Press.

Hashimoto, Motomi. 1999. Recent Developments in Corporate Restructuring Legislation. *Capital Research Journal* 2, no. 4: 21-38.

Hatch, Walter, and Kozo Yamamura. 1996. *Asia in Japan's Embrace: Building a Regional Production Alliance*. New York: Cambridge University Press.

Helliwell, John F. 1998. *How Much Do National Borders Matter (Integrating National Economies)?* Washington: Brookings Institution.

Henning, C. Randall. 1994. *Currencies and Politics in the United States, Germany, and Japan*. Washington: Institute for International Economics.

Henning, C. Randall. Forthcoming 2002. *East Asian Financial Cooperation*. Washington: Institute for International Economics.

Hoetker, Glenn. 2001. Strong Institutions? Weak Institutions? 'Japanese-style' supplier relationships as a source of competitive *dis*advantage in the notebook computer industry. College of Commerce and Business Administration, University of Illinois at Urbana-Champaign. Photocopy.

Hook, Glenn D. 1996. *Militarization and Demilitarization in Contemporary Japan*. London: Routledge.

Hoshi, Takeo, and Anil Kashyap. N.d. *Keiretsu Financing*. MIT Press, Cambridge. Photocopy.

Hoshi, Takeo, and Sadao Nagaoka, eds. 2000. Monetary Policy under Low Inflation Environment. *Journal of the Japanese and International Economies* 14, no. 4 (December; Special Issue).

Hosokawa, Morihiro. 1998. Are U.S. Troops in Japan Needed? *Foreign Affairs* 77, no. 4: 2-5.

Howell, W. Lee. 1999. The Alliance and Post-Cold War Political Realignment in Japan. In *The U.S.-Japan Alliance*, ed. Michael J. Green and Patrick M. Cronin. New York: Council on Foreign Relations.

Hufbauer, Gary Clyde, and Kimberly Ann Elliott. 1994. *Measuring the Costs of Protection in the United States*. Washington: Institute for International Economics.

Hufbauer, Gary Clyde, and Ben Goodrich. 2001. *Steel: Big Problems, Better Solutions*. International Economics Policy Brief 01-9. Washington: Institute for International Economics.

Hufbauer, Gary Clyde, and Daniel H. Rosen. 2000. *American Access to China's Market: The Congressional Vote on PNTR*. International Economics Policy Brief 00-3. Washington: Institute for International Economics.

Hufbauer, Gary Clyde, and Erika Wada. 1999. *Steel Quotas: A Rigged Lottery*. International Economics Policy Brief 99-5. Washington: Institute for International Economics.

Hughes, Christopher W. 2000. Japan's Strategy-less North Korea Strategy. *Korean Journal of Defense Analyses* 12, no. 2 (Winter): 153-81.

Hunsberger, Warren S. 1964. *Japan and the United States in World Trade*. New York: Council on Foreign Relations.

Huntington, Samuel P. 1993. Why International Primacy Matters. *International Security* 17, no. 4: 68-83.

Hutchison, Michael. 1997. Financial Crises and Bank Supervision: New Directions for Japan? *FRBSF Economic Letter* 97-37 (12 December).

Hutchison, Michael, and Kathleen McDill. 1998. Determinants, Costs, and Duration of Banking Sector Distress. Department of Economics, University of California, Santa Cruz. Photocopy (8 October).

IFIAC (International Financial Institution Advisory Commission). 2000. *Report of the International Financial Institution Advisory Commission*. Washington.

IISS (Institute for International Strategic Studies). 2000. *The United States and Japan: Advancing Toward a Mature Partnership* (Armitage Report). IISS Special Report. Washington: National Defense University.

Ikenberry, G. John. 2000. The Political Economy of Asia-Pacific Regionalism. *East Asian Economic Perspectives* 11 (March): 35-61.

IMF (International Monetary Fund). 1998. *Japan: Selected Issues*. IMF Staff Country Report 98/113. Washington.

IMF (International Monetary Fund). 1999. *Japan: Staff Report for the Article IV Consultation.* IMF Staff Country Report 99/83. Washington.

IMF (International Monetary Fund). 2000. *Japan: Economic and Policy Developments.* IMF Staff Country Report 00/13. Washington.

International Development Association and International Monetary Fund. 2001. Heavily Indebted Poor Countries (HIPC) Initiative: Status of Implementation. Washington. Photocopy (18 April).

Ito, Osamu. N.d. The Japanese Way of Solving Financial Institution Failures. Kanagawa University, Yokohama. Photocopy.

Ito, Tadaaki. 1996. *Japan's Fiscal Crisis: Its Reality and Corrective Action.* Fuji Research Paper 2. Tokyo: Fuji Research Institute.

Ito, Takatoshi. 1989. *Was There a Target Zone?* Policy Studies Series 14. Tokyo: Japan Center for International Finance (June).

Ito, Takatoshi. 1992. *The Japanese Economy.* Cambridge, MA: MIT Press.

Ito, Takatoshi. 1993. The Yen and the International Monetary System. In *Pacific Dynamism and the International System,* eds. C. Fred Bergsten and Marcus Noland. Washington: Institute for International Economics.

Ito, Takatoshi. 1999. Why the Bank of Japan Needs an Inflation Target. *Financial Times,* 19 October.

Ito, Takatoshi. 2000. The Stagnant Japanese Economy in the 1990s: The Need for Financial Supervision to Restore Sustained Growth. In *Crisis and Change in the Japanese Financial System,* ed. T. Hoshi and H. Patrick. Boston: Kluwer Academic Publishers.

Ito, Takatoshi, and Kenneth A. Froot. 1989. On the Consistency of Short-Run and Long-Run Exchange Rate Expectations. *Journal of International Finance and Money* 3 (December): 487-510.

Ito, Takatoshi, and Anne O. Krueger. 2000. Introduction. In *The Role of Foreign Direct Investment in East Asian Economic Development,* eds. Takatoshi Ito and Anne O. Krueger. Chicago: University of Chicago Press.

Ito. Takatoshi, and Masayoshi Maruyama. 1991. Is the Japanese Distribution System Really Inefficient? In *Trade with Japan,* ed. Paul R. Krugman. Chicago: University of Chicago Press.

Ito, Takatoshi, Eiji Ogawa, and Yuri Nagataki Sasaki. 1998. How Did the Dollar Peg Fail in Asia? *Journal of the Japanese and International Economies* 12: 256-304.

Itoh, Motoshige. 1991. The Japanese Distribution System and Access to the Japanese Market. In *Trade with Japan,* ed. Paul R. Krugman. Chicago: University of Chicago Press.

Iwata, Kazumasa. 1997. *Industrial and Trade Policy in Japan.* Working Paper 70. Tokyo: University of Tokyo, Komaba, Graduate School of Arts and Sciences, Department of Advanced Social and International Studies.

Jaggi, Gautam, and Gena Morgan. 1996. Recent Civil Aviation Experience. In *Flying High: Liberalizing Civil Aviation in the Asia Pacific,* eds. Gary Clyde Hufbauer and Christopher Findlay. Washington: Institute for International Economics.

James, Harold. 2001. *The End of Globalization: Lessons from the Great Depression.* Cambridge, MA: Harvard University Press.

JDA (Japan Defense Agency). 2001. *Defense of Japan 2001.* Tokyo.

JERI (Japan Economic Research Institute). 2001. *The 21st Century World Economy and the Challenge for Japan.* Tokyo.

JETRO (Japan External Trade Organization). 2000. *Report on Closer Economic Relations Between Japan and Mexico.* http://www.jetro.go.jp/ec/e/report/fta_mexico/index.html (April).

Jinushi, Toshiki, Yoshihiro Kuroki, and Ryuzo Miyao. 2000. Monetary Policy in Japan Since the Late 1980s: Delayed Policy Actions and Some Explanations. In *Japan's Financial Crisis and Its Parallels to the U.S. Experience,* Special Report 13, eds. Ryoichi Mikitani and Adam S. Posen. Washington: Institute for International Economics.

Johnson, Chalmers. 1982. *MITI and the Japanese Miracle*. Stanford, CA: Stanford University Press.

Johnson, Chalmers, ed. 1995. *Japan: Who Governs?* New York: W.W. Norton.

Johnstone, Christopher B. 1995. *Japanese Foreign Aid Contractors Fined for Bid-Rigging*. JEI Report 41B 10-12. Washington: Japan Economic Institute.

Johnstone, Christopher B. 1998. How Much Bang for the Buck? Japan's Commercial Diplomacy in Asia. In *U.S. Commercial Diplomacy*, eds. Raymond J. Albright and others. New York: Council on Foreign Relations.

Joint Study Group. 2000. Japan-Singapore Economic Agreement for a NEW Age Partnership. Photocopy (28 September).

Jorgensen, Dale W., and Kevin J. Stiroh. 2000. Raising the Speed Limit: US Economic Growth in the Information Age. *Brookings Papers on Economic Activity* 2000:1. Washington: Brookings Institution.

Kahler, Miles. 2001. *Leadership Selection in the Major Multilaterals*. Washington: Institute for International Economics.

Kako, Toshiyuki, Masahiko Gemma, and Shoichi Ito. 1997. Implications of the Minimum Access Rice Import on Supply and Demand Balance of Rice in Japan. *Agricultural Economics* 16, no. 3: 193-204.

Kaminsky, Graciela L., and Carmen M. Reinhart. 2000. On Crises, Contagion, and Confusion. *Journal of International Economics* 51, no. 1: 145-67.

Kang, Jun-Koo, and Anil Shivadasani. 1999. Alternative Mechanisms for Corporate Governance in Japan. *Pacific-Basin Finance Journal* 7, no. 1: 1-22.

Kang, Jun-Koo, and René M. Stulz. 1997. *Is Bank-Centered Corporate Governance Worth It?* NBER Working Paper 6238. Cambridge, MA: National Bureau of Economic Research.

Kasa, Kenneth. 1997. Japanese Trade Deficits? *FRBSF Economic Letter* 97-28. Federal Reserve Bank of San Francisco.

Kashyap, Anil K. 2000. Discussions of the Financial Crisis. In *Japan's Financial Crisis and Its Parallels to the U.S. Experience*, Special Report 13, eds. Ryoichi Mikitani and Adam S. Posen. Washington: Institute for International Economics.

Kato, Hisanori. 1999. *China's Military Modernization and Japan-China Relations*. IIPS Policy Paper 209E. Tokyo: Institute for International Policy Studies.

Kato, Takao. 2001. The End of Lifetime Employment in Japan? Colgate University, Hamilton, NY. Photocopy (31 January).

Katzenstein, Peter. 1996. *Cultural Norms and National Security: Police and Military in Postwar Japan*. Ithaca, NY: Cornell University Press.

Kawai, Masahiro, Juro Hashimoto, and Shigemi Izumida. 1996. Japanese Firms in Financial Distress and Main Banks. *Japan and the World Economy* 8: 175-94.

Kawai, Masahiro, and Shujiro Urata. 1995. *Are Trade and Investment Substitutes or Compliments?* Institute of Social Science Discussion Paper Series F-50. Tokyo: University of Tokyo.

Keesing, Donald. 1998. *Improving Trade Policy Reviews in the World Trade Organization*. Policy Analyses in International Economics Series. Washington: Institute for International Economics.

Kim, Tae-Jun, Jai-Won Ryou, and Yunjong Wang. 2000. *Regional Arrangements to Borrow: A Scheme for Preventing Future Asian Liquidity Crises*. Seoul: Korea Institute for International Economic Policy.

Kletzer, Lori G. 2001. *Job Loss from Imports: Measuring the Costs*. Washington: Institute for International Economics.

Knetter, Michael M. 1997. Why Are Retail Prices in Japan So High? *International Journal of Industrial Organization* 15: 549-72.

Kojima, Kiyoshi. 1978. *Direct Foreign Investment*. Guildford, UK: Billings.

Komuro, Norio. 1998. *Kodak-Fuji Film* Dispute and the WTO Panel Ruling. *Journal of World Trade* 32, no. 5: 161-217.

Kotabe, Masaaki, and Kent W. Wheiler. 1996. *Anticompetitive Practices in Japan*. New York: Praeger.

Koyanagi, Masayuki. 2001. The Patent System in the Pro-Patent Age. *Inside/Outside Japan* 10, no. 4: 4-5.

Krause, Lawrence B. 1995. Graduate School of International Relations and Pacific Studies. University of California, San Diego. Personal communication (13 October).

Krueger, Anne O. 1999. *Trade Creation and Diversion under NAFTA*. NBER Working Paper 7429. Cambridge, MA: National Bureau of Economic Research.

Krueger, Anne O., and Takatoshi Ito. 2000. Introduction. In *Regional and Global Capital Flows: Macroeconomic Causes and Consequences*, eds. Anne O. Krueger and Takatoshi Ito. Chicago: University of Chicago Press.

Krugman, Paul, 1998. It's Baaack: Japan's Slump and the Return of the Liquidity Trap. *Brookings Paper on Economic Activity* 2: 137-205.

Kunkel, John H. 2001. Demanding Results: US Market Access Policies Toward Japan. Doctoral thesis, Australian National University, Canberra (May).

Kuroda, Makoto. 1989. Strengthening Japan-US Cooperation and the Concept of Japan-US Free Trade Arrangements. In *Free Trade Areas and U.S. Trade Policy*, ed. Jeffrey J. Schott. Washington: Institute for International Economics.

Kuroda, Haruhiko. 2000. Speech, Australian National University, Canberra (17 February).

Kwan, C.H. 1994. Economic Interdependence in the Asia-Pacific Region: Towards A Yen Bloc. *Nomura Asian Perspectives* 11, no. 2 (April).

Kwon, Eunkyong. 1998. Monetary Policy, Land Prices, and Collateral Effects on Economic Fluctuations. *Journal of Japanese and International Economies* 12: 175-203.

Lake, Charles D. II. 1998. An Evaluation of Structural Deregulation Talks in Promoting U.S. Market Access in Japan. Council on Foreign Relations Study Group, Washington. Photocopy (November).

Lamy, Pascal, and Robert B. Zoellick. 2001. In the Next Round. *Washington Post* (17 July).

Lancaster, Carol. 2000. *Transforming Foreign Aid*. Washington: Institute for International Economics.

Lardy, Nicholas. 1994. *China in the World Economy*. Washington: Institute for International Economics.

Lawrence, Robert Z. 1991. How Open Is Japan? In *Trade with Japan*, ed. Paul R. Krugman. Chicago: University of Chicago Press.

Lawrence, Robert Z. 1995. *Regionalism, Multilateralism, and Deeper Integration*. Integrating National Economies Series. Washington: Brookings Institution.

Lawrence, Robert Z., Albert Bressand, and Takatoshi Ito. 1996. *A Vision for the World Economy: Openness, Diversity, and Cohesion*. Integrating National Economies Series. Washington: Brookings Institution.

Lee, Jong-Wha, and Philip Swagel. 1997. Trade Barriers and Trade Flows Across Countries and Industries. *Review of Economics and Statistics* 74, no. 3: 372-81.

Lee, Kyung Tae. 2000. Economic Effects of and Policy Directions for a Korea-Japan FTA. Paper presented at a conference toward a Korea-Japan FTA: Assessments and prospects, Seoul (24 May).

Lettau, Martin, Sydney Ludvigson, and Nathan Barczi. 2001. A Primer on the Economics and Time Series Econometrics of Wealth Effects: A Comment. Federal Reserve Bank of New York. Photocopy (23 May).

Levinsohn, James. 1997. Carwars: Trying to Make Sense of U.S.-Japan Trade Frictions in the Automobile and Automobile Parts Markets. In *Effects of US Trade Protection and Promotion Policies*, ed. Robert Feenstra. Chicago: University of Chicago Press.

Lichtenberg, F., and G. Pushner. 1992. *Ownership Structure and Corporate Performance in Japan*. NBER Working Paper 4092. Cambridge, MA: National Bureau of Economic Research.

Lincoln, Edward J. 1990. *Japan's Unequal Trade*. Washington: Brookings Institution.

Lincoln, Edward J. 1993. *Japan's New Global Role*. Washington: Brookings Institution.

Lincoln, Edward J. 1999. *Troubled Times: U.S.-Japan Trade Relations in the 1990s.* Washington: Brookings Institution.

Lincoln, Edward J. 2000. Japan: A Continuing Dilemma for Open Trade Ideals, http://www.ustdrc.gov/research/japan.pdf

Lincoln, Edward J. 2001. *Arthritic Japan: Explaining the Slow Pace of Economic Reform.* Washington: Brookings Institution.

Lindsey, Brink, and Dan Ikenson. 2001. *Coming Home to Roost: Proliferating Antidumping Laws and the Growing Threat to U.S. Exports.* Center for Trade Policy Studies 14. Washington: Cato Institute.

Lindsey, Lawrence B. 2000. America's 17-Year Boom. *Wall Street Journal,* 28 January.

Lockwood, William W. 1954. *The Economic Development of Japan: Growth and Structural Change, 1868-1938.* Princeton, NJ: Princeton University Press.

Ludvigson, Sydney, and Charles Steindel. 1999. How Important Is the Stock Market Effect on Consumption? *Federal Reserve Bank of New York Policy Review,* July.

Lusardi, Annamaria, Jonathan Skinner, and Steven Venti. 2001. Saving Puzzles and Saving Policies in the United States. *Oxford Review of Economic Policy* 17, no. 1.

MacIntosh, Malcolm. 1987. *Japan Re-armed.* New York: St. Martin's Press.

McKenzie, Colin R. 1998. Japanese Foreign Direct Investment: The Role of Technology and *Keiretsu.* In *Japanese Economic Policy Reconsidered,* ed. Craig Freedman. Cheltenham, UK: Edward Elgar.

McKibbin, Warwick J. 1997. *The Macroeconomic Experience of Japan Since 1990.* Brookings Discussion Papers in International Economics 131. Washington: Brookings Institution.

McKinnon, Ronald I. 1998. The Foreign Exchange Origins of Japan's Liquidity Trap. Department of Economics, Stanford University, Stanford, CA. Photocopy (June).

McKinnon, Ronald I., and Kenichi Ohno. 1997. *Resolving Economic Conflict Between the United States and Japan.* Cambridge, MA: MIT Press.

McKinnon, Ronald I., and Kenichi Ohno. 1998. The Exchange Rate Origins of Japan's Economic Slump in the 1990s. Economics Department, Stanford University, Stanford, CA. Photocopy (September).

McMillan, John. 1991. *Dango:* Japan's Price Fixing Conspiracies. *Economics and Politics* 3, no. 3: 201-18.

McMillan, John. 1996. Why Does Japan Resist Foreign Market-Opening Pressure? In *Fair Trade and Harmonization,* vol. 1, eds. Jagdish Bhagwati and Robert E. Hudec. Cambridge, MA: MIT Press.

McNaugher, Thomas L. 1994. U.S. Military Forces in East Asia: The Case for Long-Term Engagement. In *The United States, Japan, and Asia,* ed. Gerald Curtis. New York: W.W. Norton.

Maidment, Paul. 1989. The Yen Bloc. *The Economist,* 15 July.

Maki, Atsushi. 1998. How High Consumer Prices Are in Japan! *Japan and the World Economy* 10: 173-86.

Makin, John H. 1996. *Japan's Disastrous Keynesian Experiment.* Washington: American Enterprise Institute.

Makin, John H. 2001. *Forget the Second-Half Recovery.* Washington: American Enterprise Institute.

Mann, Catherine L. 1999. *Is the US Trade Deficit Sustainable?* Washington: Institute for International Economics.

Mann, Catherine L. (Forthcoming 2002). The Current Account Deficit: Causes and Implications. *Journal of Economic Perspectives.*

Manyin, Mark. 2000. Revisiting Japanese Behavior in the Uruguay Round: Japan's Anti-Dumping Campaign. Library of Congress, Washington. Photocopy.

Marcus, Michael J. 2001. Regulatory Transparency in Japan. *Asian Perspectives* 20-22 (March).

Mason, Mark. 1992. *American Multinationals and Japan.* Cambridge, MA: Harvard University Press.

Matsunaga, Yusuke. 1997. Preparing for Old Age: The Challenge of Japan's Aging Society. *NRI Quarterly* 06-1: 22-35.

Matsushita, Mitsuo. 1997. The Antimonopoly Law of Japan. In *Global Competition Policy*, eds. Edward E. Graham and J. David Richardson. Washington: Institute for International Economics.

Maull, Hans W. 1990. Germany and Japan: The New Civilian Powers. *Foreign Affairs* 69, no. 5: 91-106.

Medeiros, Evan S. 2001. Ballistic Missile Defense and Northeast Asian Security: Views from Washington. Stanley Foundation, Beijing and Tokyo. Photocopy (April).

Meerschwam, David M. 1991. The Japanese Financial System and the Cost of Capital. In *Trade With Japan: Has The Door Opened Wider?* ed. Paul R. Krugman. Chicago: University of Chicago Press.

Melvin, Michael, and Bettina Peiers. 1993. On the Possibility of a Yen Currency Bloc for Pacific Basin Countries: A Stochastic Dominance Approach. *Pacific-Basin Finance Journal* 1, no. 4: 309-33.

Menon, Jayant. 1997. Japan's Intraindustry Trade Dynamics. *Journal of the Japanese and International Economies* 11, no. 2 (June).

Messerlin, Patrick A. 2000. Antidumping and Safeguards. In *The WTO After Seattle*, ed. Jeffrey J. Schott. Washington: Institute for International Economics.

METI (Ministry of Economy, Trade, and Industry). 2001. *White Paper on International Trade 2001*. Tokyo.

MITI (Ministry of International Trade and Industry). 1996. *1996 Report on the WTO Consistency of Trade Policies by Major Trading Partners*. Tokyo.

MITI (Ministry of International Trade and Industry). 1999a. *Is the Comprehensive Approach a Road to Success in Seattle?* http://www.miti.go.jp/info-e/cw99113e.html (November).

MITI (Ministry of International Trade and Industry). 1999b. Survey of Foreign and Domestic Price Differentials for Industrial Intermediate Input. http://www.miti.go.jp/english/report/data/gIP9907e.html (6 June).

MITI (Ministry of International Trade and Industry). 2000. *2000 Report on the WTO Consistency of Trade Policies by Major Trade Partners*. http://www.miti.go.jp/report-e/gCT0-0coe.html.

Mitsugi, Yoshihito, Masaki Takamoto, and Masatsugu Yamazaki. 1998. Information Technology and New Retail Strategies in Japan, *NRI Quarterly* 07-3 14-23.

Mizuno, Takanori. 1996. New York Hatsu, Daiwa Ginko Jiken. *From New York, the Daiwa Bank Incident* [in Japanese]. Tokyo: Diamond Publishing.

Mochizuki, Mike M. 1998. Japanese Security Policy. In *The U.S.-Japan Security Alliance in the 21st Century*. New York: Council on Foreign Relations.

Mochizuki, Mike M. 1999. Economics and Security: A Conceptual Framework. In *The U.S.-Japan Alliance*, eds. Michael J. Green and Patrick M. Cronin. New York: Council on Foreign Relations.

Monti, Mario. 2001. *Prospects for Transatlantic Competition Policy*. International Economics Policy Brief PB01-6. Washington: Institute for International Economics.

Moreno, Ramon. 1996. Will the Yen Replace the Dollar? *FRBSF Economic Letter* 96-30, 18 October.

Morici, Peter. 2000. *Antitrust in the Global Trading System*. Washington: Economic Strategy Institute.

Morishima, Michio. 1982. *Why Has Japan Succeeded? Western Technology and the Japanese Ethos*. Cambridge: Cambridge University Press.

Morsink, James, and Tamin Bayoumi. 2000. Monetary Policy Transmission in Japan. In *Post-Bubble Blues*, eds. Tamin Bayoumi and Charles Collyns. Washington: International Monetary Fund.

Mühleisen, Martin. 2000. Too Much of a Good Thing? The Effectiveness of Fiscal Stimulus. In *Post-Bubble Blues*, eds. Tamin Bayoumi and Charles Collyns. Washington: International Monetary Fund.

Mulgan, Aurelia George. 2000. Japan: A Setting Sun? *Foreign Affairs* 79, no. 4: 40-52.

Murakami, Takeshi. 1998. The Development of the ITC Industries and Their Impact on the Macroeconomy. *NRI Quarterly* 7, no. 1: 54-75.

Nagaoka, Sadao. 1997. Economic Consequences of VIE when Consumers Are Constrained. *Japan and the World Economy* 9: 557-65.

Nagaoka, Sadao, and Fukunari Kimura. 1999. The Competitive Impact of International Trade: The Case of Import Liberalization of the Japanese Oil Product Market. *Journal of the Japanese and International Economies* 13, no. 4: 397-423.

Nakamae, Tadashi. 2001. Reforming Japan's Banks. *Financial Times*, 16 May.

Nakatani, Iwao. 1984. The Economic Role of Financial Corporate Grouping. In *The Economic Analysis of the Japanese Firm*, ed. Masahiko Aoki. Amsterdam: North-Holland.

Nishimura, Kiyohiko G. 1993. The Distribution System of Japan and the United States. *Japan and the World Economy* 5: 265-88.

Nishimura, Yoshimasa, and Kin-yu Gyosei no Haiin. 1999. *Reasons of the Defeat in Banking Administration* [in Japanese]. Tokyo: Bungeishiju.

Noguchi, Yukio. 1995. *1940 Nen-taisei* [The 1940 System; in Japanese]. Tokyo: Toyo Keizai Shimposha.

Noland, Marcus. 1989a. Causality and the Japanese Current Account. *Asian Economic Journal* 3, no. 2: 116-37.

Noland, Marcus. 1989b. Japanese Trade Elasticities and the J-Curve. *Review of Economics and Statistics* 71, no. 1 (December 1989): 175-79.

Noland, Marcus. 1993. Industrial Policy and Japan's Pattern of Trade. *Review of Economics and Statistics* 75, no. 2: 241-48.

Noland, Marcus. 1994. *Implications of Asian Economic Growth*. Working Paper 94-5. Washington: Institute for International Economics.

Noland, Marcus. 1995a. Asia and the NAFTA. In *The US-Korea Economic Partnership*, eds. Youn-suk Kim and Kap-soo Oh. Burlington, VT: Ashgate Publishers.

Noland, Marcus. 1995b. Why Are Prices in Japan So High? *Japan and the World Economy* 7: 255-61.

Noland, Marcus. 1996a. Research and Development Activities and Trade Specialization in Japan. *Journal of the Japanese and International Economies* 10, no. 2: 150-68.

Noland, Marcus. 1996b. Trade, Investment, and Economic Conflict Between the US and Asia. *Journal of Asian Economics* 7, no. 3: 435-58.

Noland, Marcus. 1997a. Chasing Phantoms: The Political Economy of USTR. *International Organization* 51, no. 3: 365-87.

Noland, Marcus. 1997b. Competition Policy and Foreign Direct Investment. *Japanese Economy* 25, no. 5: 45-69.

Noland, Marcus. 1997c. Has Asian Export Performance Been Unique? *Journal of International Economics* 43: 79-101.

Noland, Marcus. 1997d. Public Policy, Private Preferences, and the Japanese Trade Pattern. *Review of Economics and Statistics* 79, no. 2: 259-66.

Noland, Marcus. 1998. Statement. *US House of Representatives International Relations Committee Hearings on the Financial Crisis in Asia*. http://www.iie.com/TESTMONY/jmn2-3.htm (4 February).

Noland, Marcus. 2000a. *Avoiding the Apocalypse: The Future of the Two Koreas*. Washington: Institute for International Economics.

Noland, Marcus. 2000b. Economic Interests, Values, and Policies. Paper presented to the National Intelligence Council-Federal Research Division, Library of Congress conference on East Asia and the United States, current status and 5-year outlook, Washington. http://www.iie.com/TESTMONY/nic2000.htm (17 February).

Noland, Marcus, Sherman Robinson, Li-Gang Liu, and Zhi Wang. 1999. *Global Effects of the Asian Currency Devaluations*. POLICY ANALYSES IN INTERNATIONAL ECONOMICS 56. Washington: Institute for International Economics.

OECD (Organization for Economic Cooperation and Development). 1996. *Antitrust and Market Access*. Paris.

OECD (Organization for Economic Cooperation and Development). 1997. *Report on Regulatory Reform*, vol. II. Paris.

OECD (Organization for Economic Cooperation and Development). 1999a. *Economic Survey of Japan*. Paris.

OECD (Organization for Economic Cooperation and Development). 1999b. *Regulatory Reform in Japan*. Paris.

OECD (Organization for Economic Cooperation and Development). 2000a. *Agricultural Policy Reform: Developments and Prospects*. Policy Brief. Paris.

OECD (Organization for Economic Cooperation and Development). 2000b. *Economic Survey of Japan*. Paris.

OECD (Organization for Economic Cooperation and Development). 2001. *Development Cooperation 2000 Report*. Paris.

Ogawa, Shinichi. 2000. *TMD and Northeast Asian Security*. Missile Defense Initiative Special Report. Berkeley, CA: Nautilus Institute.

Okazaki, Hisahiko. 2001. Statement at a forum on US-Japan strategic dialogue sponsored by the Center for Strategic and International Studies, Washington (11 May).

Okazaki, Tetsuji. 1993. Corporate Systems. In *Sources of Current Japanese Economic Systems* [in Japanese], eds. Tetsuji Okazaki and Masahiro Okuno-Fujiwara. Tokyo: Nihon Keizai Shimbun Press.

Okina, Kunio. 1999. Monetary Policy under Zero Inflation: A Response to Criticisms and Questions Regarding Monetary Policy. *Monetary and Economic Studies* 17, no. 3: 157-182.

Oliner, Stephen D., and Sichel, Daniel E. 2000. The Resurgence of Growth in the 1990s: Is Information Technology the Story? *Journal of Economic Perspectives*, 14(4): 3-32.

Ostrom, Douglas. 1998. *Japan and the Asian Economic Crisis: Part of the Solution or Part of the Problem?* JEI Report 8A. Washington: Japan Economic Institute.

Ozawa, Ichiro. 1994. *Blueprint for a New Japan: The Rethinking of a Nation*. Tokyo: Kodansha International.

Packer, Frank. 1999. Disposal of Bad Loans: The Case of the CCPC. Capital Markets Department, Federal Reserve Bank of New York. Photocopy (September).

Peach, Richard, and Charles Steindel. 2000. A Nation of Spendthrifts? An Analysis of Trends in Personal and Gross Saving. *Current Trends in Economics and Finance* 6, no. 10 (September). Federal Reserve Bank of New York.

Peek, Joe, and Eric S. Rosengren. 1997. The International Transmission of Financial Shocks: The Case of Japan. *American Economic Review* 87, no. 4: 495-505.

Peek, Joe, and Eric S. Rosengren. 1999. Determinants of the Japan Premium. NBER Working Paper 7251. Cambridge, MA: National Bureau of Economic Research.

Peek, Joe, and Eric S. Rosengren. 2000. Collateral Damage: Effects of the Japanese Banking Crisis on Real Activity in the United States. *American Economic Review* 90, no. 1: 30-45.

Petrazzini, Ben. 1996. *Global Telecom Talks: A Trillion Dollar Deal*. Policy Analyses in International Economics 44. Washington: Institute for International Economics.

Petri, Peter A. 1993. The Greater East Asian Trading Bloc: An Analytical History. In *Regionalism and Rivalry: Japan and the United States in Pacific Asia*, eds. Jeffrey A. Frankel and Miles Kahler. Chicago: University of Chicago Press.

Porter, Michael E., Mariko Sakakibara, and Hirotaka Takeuchi. 2000. *Can Japan Compete?* New York: Basic Books.

Posen, Adam S. 1998. *Restoring Japan's Economic Growth*. Washington: Institute for International Economics.

Posen, Adam S. 2000. The Political Economy of Deflationary Monetary Policy. In *Japan's Financial Crisis and Its Parallels to the U.S. Experience*, Special Report 13, eds. Ryoichi Mikitani and Adam S. Posen. Washington: Institute for International Economics.

Posen, Adam S. 2001. *Japan 2001—Decisive Action or Financial Panic*. International Economics Policy Briefs 01-4. Washington: Institute for International Economics.

Preeg, Ernest H. 1970. *Traders and Diplomats*. Washington: Brookings Institution.

Prestowitz, Clyde. 1988. *Trading Places: How We Allowed Japan to Take the Lead*. New York: Basic Books.

Prusa, Thomas J. 1997. The Trade Effects of U.S. Antidumping Actions. In *Effects of US Trade Protection and Promotion Policies*, ed. Robert Feenstra. Chicago: University of Chicago Press.

Pyle, Kenneth B. 1992. *The Japanese Question*. Washington: American Enterprise Institute.

Ramaswamy, Ramana, and Christel Rendu. 2000. Japan's Stagnant Nineties: A Vector Autoregression Retrospective. In *Post-Bubble Blues*, eds. Tamin Bayoumi and Charles Collyns. Washington: International Monetary Fund.

Reed, Robert F. 1983. *The U.S.-Japan Alliance: Sharing the Burden of Defense*. Washington: National Defense University Press.

Richardson, David J. 1993. *Sizing Up U.S. Export Distinctiveness*. Washington: Institute for International Economics.

Richardson, David J., and Howard Lewis. 2001. *Why Global Commitment Matters Most*. Washington: Institute for International Economics.

Rix, Alan. 1993. Leadership From Behind. In *Pacific Cooperation in the 1990s*, eds. R. Higgot et al. Canberra: Australian Fulbright Commission.

Roach, Stephen. 2001. *This Time Is Different*. New York: Morgan Stanley Dean Witter.

Rose, Andrew. 1999. Is There a Case for an Asian Monetary Fund? *FRBSF Economic Letter* 99-37, 17 December.

Rozman, Gilbert. 2000. *Restarting Regionalism in Northeast Asia*. North Pacific Policy Papers 1. Vancouver: Institute of Asian Research, Univerity of British Columbia.

Rubenstein, Gregg A. 1999. U.S.-Japan Armaments Cooperation. In *The U.S.-Japan Alliance*. eds. Michael J. Green and Patrick M. Cronin. New York: Council on Foreign Relations.

Rubin, Robert E. 2000. Ex-Im Bank and International Economic Policy Leadership. In *The Ex-Im Bank in the 21st Century: A New Approach*, eds. Gary Clyde Hufbauer and Rita M. Rodriguez. Washington: Institute for International Economics.

Ryan, Daniel J. 1997. Trends in Market Power and Productivity Growth Rates in US and Japanese Manufacturing. *Economics Letters* 57: 183-87.

Saeki, Naomi. 1997. *Jusen to Nokyo* [in Japanese; trans., Jusen and Agricultural Cooperatives]. Tokyo: Nogyo Tokei Kyokai.

Sakakibara, Eisuke. 1993. *Beyond Capitalism*. Lanham, MD: University Press of America.

Sakakibara, Eisuke. 1996. Globalization and diversity. In *Economic and Social Development into the XXI Century*, ed. Louis Emmerij. Washington: Inter-American Development Bank, 1997.

Sakakibara, Eisuke. 2000. U.S.-Japanese Economic Policy Conflicts and Coordination during the 1990s. In *Japan's Financial Crisis and Its Parallels to US Experience*, Special Report 13, eds. Ryoichi Mikitani and Adam S. Posen. Washington: Institute for International Economics.

Sakakibara, Mariko, and Michael E. Porter. 2001. Competing at Home to Win Abroad: Evidence from Japanese Industry. *Review of Economics and Statistics* 83, no. 3 (May): 310-22.

Salop, Steven C., and David T. Scheffman. 1983. Raising Rivals' Costs. *American Economic Review* 73, no. 2: 267-71.

Salop, Steven C., and David T. Scheffman. 1987. Cost Raising Strategies. *Journal of Industrial Economics* 36: 19-34.

Samuels, Richard J. 1994. *Rich Nation, Strong Army*. Ithaca, NY: Cornell University Press.

Samuelson, Robert J. 1995. Daiwa's Deeper Lesson. *Washington Post*, 8 November.

Sasaki-Smith, Mineko. 1999. Survey and Critique of the Japanese Financial Crisis. Paper presented to the Japan Economic Seminar, Washington (24 April).

Saxonhouse, Gary R. 1996. A Short Summary of the Long History of Unfair Trade Allegations Against Japan. In *Fair Trade and Harmonization*, vol. 1, eds. Jagdish Bhagwati and Robert E. Hudec. Cambridge, MA: MIT Press.

Sazanami, Yoko, Shujiro Urata, and Hiroki Kawai. 1995. *Measuring the Costs of Protection in Japan*. Washington: Institute for International Economics.

Schaede, Ulrike. 1999. Self-Regulation and the Sanctuary Strategy: Competitive Advantage through Cooperation by Japanese Firms. Graduate School of International Relations and Pacific Studies, University of California, San Diego. Photocopy (August).

Scher, Mark J. 1997. *Japanese Interfirm Networks and Their Main Banks*. New York: St. Martin's Press.

Scher, Mark J. 1999. Recent Developments in Bank-Firm Cross-Shareholding in Japan. Paper presented to the Japan Economic Seminar, Washington (13 November).

Scheve, Kenneth F., and Matthew J. Slaughter. 2001. *Globalization and the Perceptions of American Workers*. Washington: Institute for International Economics.

Schoppa, Leonard J. 1997. *Bargaining with Japan*. New York: Columbia University Press.

Schott, Jeffrey J. 1998. The World Trade Organization: Progress to Date and the Road Ahead. In *Launching New Global Trade Talks: An Action Agenda*, Special Report 12, ed. Jeffrey J. Schott. Washington: Institute for International Economics.

Schott, Jeffrey J. 2000. The WTO After Seattle. In *The WTO after Seattle*, ed. Jeffrey J. Schott. Washington: Institute for International Economics.

Scollay, Robert, and John P. Gilbert. 2001. *New Trading Arrangements in the Asia Pacific?* POLICY ANALYSES IN INTERNATIONAL ECONOMICS 63. Washington: Institute for International Economics.

Seike, Atsushi. 2001. The Changing Labor Market in Japan. *Japan Economic Currents*, 7 April.

Shafer, Jeffrey R. 2000. International Aspects of Japanese Monetary Policy. In *Japan's Financial Crisis and Its Parallels to U.S. Experience*, Special Report 13, eds. Ryoichi Mikitani and Adam S. Posen. Washington: Institute for International Economics.

Sheard, Paul. 1997. *Keiretsu*, Competition, and Market Access. In *Global Competition Policy*, eds. Edward M. Graham and J. David Richardson. Washington: Institute for International Economics.

Shikano, Yoshiaki. 2001. Japanese Non-performing Loans Represent the Latest Losses Due to the Collapse of the Asset-Price Bubble. *Japan Economic Currents*, 4 April.

Shiller, Robert J. 2000. *Irrational Exuberance*. Princeton, NJ: Princeton University Press.

Shimizu, Yoshinori. 2000. Convoy Regulation, Bank Management, and the Financial Crisis in Japan. In *Japan's Financial Crisis and Its Parallels to the U.S. Experience*, Special Report 13, eds. Ryoichi Mikitani and Adam S. Posen. Washington: Institute for International Economics.

Shinn, James. 1999. Corporate Governance Reform and Trade Friction. Council on Foreign Relations Study Group on U.S.-Japan Economic Relations, Washington. Photocopy (March).

Shinohara, Miyohei. 1982. *Industrial Growth, Trade, and Dynamic Patterns in the Japanese Economy*. Tokyo: Tokyo University Press.

Silver, Neil E. 2000. *The United States, Japan, and China*. New York: Council on Foreign Relations.

Southwick, Jim. 1998. A Review of U.S. Efforts to Address Market Access Barriers in Japan. Council on Foreign Relations Japan Study Group, New York. Photocopy (October).

Spencer, Barbara J., and Larry D. Qiu. 2000. *Keiretsu* and Relation-Specific Investment: A Barrier to Trade. NBER Working Paper 7572. Cambridge, MA: National Bureau of Economic Research.

Spiegel, Mark. 2001. The Return of the Japan Premium. *FRBSF Economic Letter* 01-06, 6 March.

Spiegel, Mark M., and Nobuyoshi Yamori. 2000. *The Evolution of Too-Big-to-Fail Policy in Japan*. Pacific Basin Working Paper Series Working Paper PB00-01. San Francisco: Center for Pacific Basin Monetary and Economic Studies, Economic Research Department, Federal Reserve Bank of San Francisco.

Staiger, Robert W., and Frank A. Wolak. 1994. Measuring Industry-Specific Protection: Antidumping in the United States. *Brookings Papers on Economic Activity: Microeconomics*: 51-103.

Steindel, Charles, and Kevin J. Stiroh. 2001. Productivity: What Is It and Why Do We Care About It? Federal Reserve Bank of New York. Photocopy (12 April).

Stiglitz, Joseph E. 1998. *More Instruments and Broader Goals: Moving Toward a Post-Washington Consensus*. WIDER Annual Lectures 2, Helsinki: WIDER.

Stiglitz, Joseph E. 1999. The Korean Miracle: Growth, Crisis, and Recovery. Paper presented to the International Conference on Economic Crisis and Restructuring in Korea, Seoul (3 December).

Stokes, Bruce. 2000. *A New Beginning: Recasting the U.S.-Japan Economic Relationship*. New York: Council on Foreign Relations.

Stone, Laura. 1999. Whither Trade and Security? A Historical Perspective. In *The U.S.-Japan Alliance*, eds. Michael J. Green and Patrick M. Cronin. New York: Council on Foreign Relations.

Sullivan, Leonard, Jr. 1981. The Real Long-Range Defense Dilemma: Burden Sharing. *Armed Forces Journal International* (October): 56-68.

Summers, Lawrence. 1999. The Right Kind of IMF for a Stable Global Financial System. http://www.ustreas.gov/press/releases/ps294.htm.

Summers, Robert, and Alan Heston. 1991. The Penn-World Table (Mark V). *Quarterly Journal of Economics* 106, no. 2: 327-68.

Suzuki, Yukio. 1997. Deregulation in Japan: The Nonmanufacturing Sectors. *NRI Quarterly* 06-3: 2-27.

Takahashi, Hiroyuki. 2001. Reforming Japan's Elderly Health Insurance. *Japan Economic Currents*, 6 March.

Tanaka, Akihiko. 1995. The Domestic Context: Japanese Politics and U.N. Peacekeeping. In *UN Peacekeeping: US and Japanese Perspectives*, eds. Selig S. Harrison and Masashi Nishihara. Washington: Carnegie Endowment for International Peace.

Tanaka, Nobuo. 1992. International Leadership. *Journal of Japanese Trade and Industry* 6: 26-28.

Terry, Edith. 2001. *How Asia Got Rich: Japan and the East Asian Miracle*. Armonk, NY: ME Sharpe.

Tyson, Laura D'Andrea. 1992. *Who's Bashing Whom? Trade Conflict in High-Technology Industries*. Washington: Institute for International Economics.

Ueda, Kazuo. 1998. The East Asian Economic Crisis: A Japanese Perspective. *International Finance* 1, no. 2: 327-38.

Ueda, Kazuo, and Yuri Nagataki Sasaki. 1998. The Import Behavior of Japanese Corporate Groups. *Japan and the World Economy* 10: 1-11.

Union Bank of Switzerland. 1991. *Prices and Earnings Around the Globe*. Zurich: Union Bank of Switzerland.

Urata, Shujiro. 1998. Explaining the Poor Performance of Japanese Direct Investment in the United States. *Japan and the World Economy* 10: 49-62.

US Department of Commerce. 1989. *Joint DOC/MITI Price Survey: Methodology and Results*. Washington.

US Department of Commerce. 1991. Results of the 1991 DOC/MITI Price Survey. *U.S. Department of Commerce News*, ITA 91-32, 20 May.

US ITC (US International Trade Commission). 1999. *The Economic Effects of Significant US Import Restraints: Second Update 1999, Investigation No. 332-325*. Publication 3201. Washington.

USTR (US Trade Representative). 2000. *National Trade Estimates*. Washington.

US Treasury. 2000. *Response to the Report of the International Financial Institution Advisory Commission.* Washington.

Van Wolferen, Karel. 1989. *The Enigma of Japanese Power: People and Politics in a Stateless Nation.* New York: Alfred A. Knopf.

Van Wolferen, Karel. 1990. The Japan Problem Revisited. *Foreign Affairs* 69, no. 4: 42-55 (Fall).

Verikios, George, and Xiao-gunag Zhang. 2000. Sectoral Impacts of Liberalizing Trade in Services. Paper presented to the Third Annual Conference on Global Economic Analysis, Melbourne (27-30 June).

Vogel, Erza F. 1979. *Japan as Number One: Lessons for America.* Boston: Harvard University Press.

Vogel, Erza F. 1985. *Comeback: Case by Case: Building the Resurgence of American Business.* New York: Simon and Schuster.

Wade, Robert. 1996. Japan, the World Bank, and the Art of Paradigm Maintenance. *New Left Review* 217 (May/June): 3-36.

Wanner, Barbara. 1997a. *Okinawan Base Controversy Dominates U.S.-Japan Security Discussions.* JEI Report 14A. Washington: Japan Economic Institute.

Wanner, Barbara. 1997b. *Tokyo and Moscow Strive to Move Beyond Northern Territories Impasse.* JEI Report 20A. Washington: Japan Economic Institute.

Wanner, Barbara. 1998a. *Financial Scandals Renew Focus on Bureaucratic Power.* JEI Report 9A. Washington: Japan Economic Institute.

Wanner, Barbara. 1998b. *Sokaiya Scandals, Economic Woes, Spotlight Japanese Corporate Governance.* JEI Report No. 3A. Washington: Japan Economic Institute.

Wanner, Barbara. 1999a. *Japan's Push to Develop Spy Satellites Presents New Challenges to Bilateral Armaments Cooperation. JEI Report 21A.* 28 May. Washington: Japan Economic Institute.

Wanner, Barbara. 1999b. *Mounting Anxiety Over North Korean Security Threat Fuels Defense Debate in Japan.* JEI Report 33A. Washington: Japan Economic Institute.

Wanner, Barbara. 1999c. *North Korean Wild Card Focuses Attention on Japan's Northeast Asian Diplomacy.* JEI Report 3A. Washington: Japan Economic Institute.

Wanner, Barbara. 1999d. *Uproar Over JDA Official's Remarks Raises Questions About Japanese Attitudes Toward National Security.* JEI Report 45A. Washington: Japan Economic Institute.

Wanner, Barbara. 2000. *Okinawan Base Relocation Continues to Test Relations with Naha, Washington.* JEI Report 4A. Washington: Japan Economic Institute.

Warner, Mark. 1996. Private and Public Impediments to Market Presence: Exploring the Investment/Competition Nexus. In *Investment Rules for the Global Economy,* eds. Pierre Sauve and Daniel Schwanen. Ottawa: CD Howe Institute.

Weinstein, David E. 1992. Competition and Unilateral Dumping. *Journal of International Economics* 32, no. 3/4: 379-88.

Weinstein, David E. 1996. Structural Impediments to Investment in Japan. In *Foreign Direct Investment in Japan,* eds. Masaru Yoshitomi and Edward M. Graham. Cheltenham, UK: Edward Elgar.

Weinstein, David E. 1997. FDI and *Keiretsu:* Rethinking US and Japanese Policy. In *Effects of US Trade Protection and Promotion Policies,* ed. Robert Feenstra. Chicago: University of Chicago Press.

Weinstein, David E., and Yishay Yafeh. 1995. Japan's Corporate Groups: Collusive or Competitive? *Journal of Industrial Economics* 43, no. 4: 359-76 (December).

Williamson, John. 1990. What Washington Means by Policy Reform. In *Latin American Adjustment,* ed. John Williamson. Washington: Institute for International Economics.

Wolff, Alan. 1999. The Japan Problem. Solved? Notes from a Close Friend and Battle-Scarred Critic of Japan. Remarks prepared for the Congressional Economic Leadership Institute-Economic Strategy Institute Forum, Washington (5 March).

World Bank. 1993. *The East Asian Miracle: Economic Growth and Public Policy.* New York: Oxford University Press.

World Bank. 2001. The HIPC Debt Initiative. http://www.worldbank.org/hipc/about/hipcbr/hipcbr.htm.

Wren-Lewis, Simon, and Rebecca Driver. 1998. *Real Exchange Rates for the Year 2000.* Policy Analysis 54. Washington: Institute for International Economics.

Wren-Lewis, Simon. 2000. How Much Is the Euro Undervalued? Paper prepared for the workshop on Euro-Dollar Relations, Brussels (25 January).

WTO (World Trade Organization). 1995. *Japan: Trade Policy Review.* Geneva.

Xie, Andy. 2001. Asia's Natural Partners. *Financial Times,* 6 June.

Yamauchi, Hirotaka, and Takatoshi Ito. 1996. Air Transport Policy in Japan. In *Flying High: Liberalizing Civil Aviation in the Asia Pacific,* eds. Gary Clyde Hufbauer and Christopher Findlay. Washington: Institute for International Economics.

Yamazawa, Ippei. 2000. Toward Closer Japan-Korea Economic Relations in the 21st Century. Paper presented at a conference, Toward a Korea-Japan FTA: Assessments and prospects, Seoul (24 May).

Yano, Makoto. 2001. Trade Imbalance and Domestic Market Competition Policy. *International Economic Review,* forthcoming.

Index

and "normal Japan" US economic
policy, 236, 237-38, 264
overview of factors, 38-40
productivity growth as factor, 39-44,
41*b*, 42*t*
savings and investment as factor, 39-
40, 46-48, 46*f*, 47*f*
trade dispute resolution overview, 158,
159
education system, US, deficiencies in, 8,
59
electronics sector, Japanese, 104*b*, 149*n*,
191*b*. *See also specific companies*
energy sector, Japanese, trade and
investment relations overview, 138,
144
Enhanced Initiative on Deregulation and
Competition Policy, 170, 191*b*
environmental issues
global issues overview, 215*n*, 226, 228
trade dispute resolution overview, 179,
180*b*, 182
equipment and software, nonresidential,
US investment in, 46, 47*f*
equity markets
and "normal Japan" US economic
policy, 240
US economic resurgence overview, 51-
52, 54, 56
euro, global economic rankings, 12*n*, 234
European Union
and "deep integration" US economic
policy, 19
HIPC Initiative, 209
IMF reform debate, 205-06*n*, 206-07
Japanese economic policy overview, 27
and Japan-specific US economic policy,
26
and "normal Japan" US economic
policy, 234, 246, 250, 252, 266
trade and investment relations
overview, 137*n*
trade dispute resolution overview, 175,
178-82, 187
evergreening, Japanese economic malaise
overview, 78
Export-Import Bank of Japan (JEXIM),
201*b*, 211-12
exports, Japanese. *See also specific trade
headings*
antidumping measures, 128-29, 128*b*
bilateral, as share of total exports, 115*f*
capital outflow statistics, 4, 4*f*, 56

composition of trade, 117*t*
and development assistance, 212
global issues overview, 196, 230
Japanese share of world exports, 4, 5*f*
and "normal Japan" US economic
policy, 237, 261
as percent of GDP, 12*f*
trade and investment relations
overview, 116, 154, 156
trade dispute resolution overview, 158-
62, 186
exports, US. *See also specific trade headings*
bilateral, as share of total exports, 115*f*
capital outflow statistics, 4, 4*f*, 56
composition of trade, 117*t*
and "normal Japan" US economic
policy, 237, 253
as percent of GDP, 12*f*
trade and investment relations
overview, 116, 119, 120-21, 153
trade dispute resolution overview, 158,
162, 187
US share of world exports, 4, 5*f*
external deficits. *See* trade and current
account deficits, Japanese; trade and
current account deficits, US

Federal Maritime Commission (FMC),
170*n*
Federal Reserve, US economic resurgence
overview, 35, 40, 48, 51, 57, 69
fertility rate, Japanese, 65*n*
Financial Recovery Commission, 142*n*
Financial Sector Assessment Program,
256
financial sector, Japanese. *See also specific
sectors*
Japanese economic malaise overview,
69-85, 71-72*b*, 73*b*, 74*b*, 105, 111
and "normal Japan" US economic
policy, 239-42, 256
trade and investment relations
overview, 132, 140-43
Financial Services Agency (FSA), 71-72*b*,
77-84, 240
fiscal deficits. *See* budget deficit,
Japanese; budget deficit, US
Fiscal Investment and Loan Program
(FILP), 131, 142
fiscal policy, Japanese. *See also* tax policy,
Japanese; *specific policy areas and
organizations*

and "normal Japan" US economic
policy, 259
as percent of GDP, 12f
trade and investment relations
overview, 116-19, 130b, 153-54
trade dispute resolution overview,
187n, 189-90
imports, US. *See also specific trade headings*
antidumping measures, 128, 128b,
130b, 173
bilateral, as share of total imports, 115f
capital inflow statistics, 4, 56
composition of trade, 117t
global issues overview, 200
as percent of GDP, 12f
trade and investment relations
overview, 121
trade dispute resolution overview, 158
income, per capita, Japan-US
comparisons, 2, 3t, 4n
Indonesia, global issues overview, 197n,
199n, 222, 225n
Industrial Bank of Japan, 69n
industries, Japanese. *See also specific*
industries and companies
corporate housing, 109
and development assistance, 215-16
global issues overview, 196-97
Japanese economic malaise overview,
102n
Japan-US comparisons, 5, 7
keiretsu, 82, 103, 104b, 105-06, 144, 146-
51, 153
and "normal Japan" US economic
policy, 234, 264
trade and investment relations
overview
economic context, 120-23
government policies, 124, 125, 128-34
private barriers, 144-50
regulatory issues, 134-44
US economic resurgence overview, 36,
38
industries, US. *See also* businesses, US;
specific industries and companies
Japan-US comparisons, 5, 7
trade and investment relations
overview, 120-22, 124, 126-29, 132-
33
trade dispute resolution overview, 161
US economic resurgence overview, 33,
38, 43, 45, 238
US trade policy formation, 17-18

inflation rate, Japanese, economic
malaise overview, 86t, 87
inflation targeting, 91-96, 241
inflows, capital. *See specific imports*
headings
information-technology sector. *See* high-
technology sector
ING-Barings, 80
insurance sector, Japanese. *See also*
financial sector, Japanese
Japanese economic malaise overview,
77
trade and investment relations
overview, 138, 140
interest rates, Japanese
and financial-sector problems, 74b, 75,
78, 80n, 84
and monetary policy, 85n, 86t, 87-89,
91-92, 94, 95, 95n
trade conflict and yen depreciation,
101n
interest rates, US, economic resurgence
overview, 32, 35, 46, 52, 57, 69
international affairs. *See* global issues;
specific policy areas
International Development Association,
209
international economic institutions. *See*
multilateral economic institutions
International Financial Institution
Advisory Commission, 204-05, 209
international financial system. *See also*
multilateral economic institutions;
specific institutions
global issues overview, 195-207, 201b
and "normal Japan" US economic
policy, 255-58
International Monetary Fund (IMF)
global issues overview, 198-200, 201n,
202-03
HIPC Initiative, 208-09
managing director position, 206-07,
210, 251
and "normal Japan" US economic
policy, 251n, 256, 258, 260, 266
reform debate, 203-07
trade dispute resolution overview, 186
and US economic policy alternatives,
24, 26
International Whaling Commission, 180b
investment, foreign. *See* foreign
investment, Japan; foreign

investment, US; trade and investment relations
investment, US private, and economic resurgence, 39-40, 46-48, 46*f*, 47*f*, 51-52, 55, 56, 57-59
Iran, security issues, 217-18
Iraq, security issues, 219*b*
Ishihara, Shintaro, 145-46

Japan Airlines, 139*b*, 219, 234
Japan Bank for International Cooperation (JBIC), 211-12
Japanese Maritime Safety Agency, 229
Japan External Trade Organization (JETRO), 212
Japan Fair Trade Commission (JFTC)
and "normal Japan" US economic policy, 246-48, 254
trade and investment relations overview, 137, 146, 149*n*
trade dispute resolution overview, 174, 177
Japan Federation of Economic Organizations, 212
Japan Ground Self-Defense Force, 225*n*
Japan International Development Organization (JAIDO), 212
Japan Maritime Self-Defense Forces, 220*b*, 225*n*, 229
Japan Overseas Development Corporation (JODC), 212
"Japan premium", 74*b*, 75, 84. *See also* interest rates, Japanese
Japan Rail, 234
Japan Self-Defense Forces (JSDF), 193-94, 218*n*, 219*b*, 221, 223*n*, 225
Japan-specific US economic policy
bilateral relationship overview, 14-18
described, 22-23
historical overview, 1, 2, 6, 27, 28*t*
normalcy policy overview, 233-38, 251, 255, 264, 266
trade dispute resolution overview, 190
US economic resurgence overview, 31-38, 60
Joint Security Declaration, 221, 229
Jones Act, 156
jusen companies, 72-73, 73*b*, 84*n*
Justice Department, US
and "normal Japan" US economic policy, 246, 254
trade and investment relations overview, 145

trade dispute resolution overview, 174, 182

Kaifu, Toshiki, 219*b*
Kajiyama, Seiroku, 77
Kantor, Michael, 169
keiretsu system
Japanese economic malaise overview, 82, 103, 104*b*, 105-06
trade and investment relations overview, 144, 146-51, 153
Kennedy administration, trade liberalization, 35-36
Kim Dae-jung, 186, 260
Koch-Weser, Caio, 206
Kodak-Fuji film case, 172, 173-77, 182, 243
Köhler, Horst, 206
Koizumi, Junichiro
bilateral relationship overview, 15
environmental issues, 226*n*
global issues overview, 10
Japanese economic malaise overview, 64*b*, 65*b*, 92, 99, 105*n*
and "normal Japan" US economic policy, 237, 238, 240-42, 260
security issues, 229, 261
trade dispute resolution overview, 170, 186
Komatsu, Masayuki, 180*b*
Konica, 173
Kumagai Gumi, 79
Kuroda, Haruhiko, 203*n*, 205
Kuroda, Makoto, 162*n*
Kyoto Protocol, 180*b*, 226

labor force, Japanese
declines and economic malaise, 65, 111
and housing problems, 107
Japan-US comparisons, 6
and structural reforms, 104-06
women's participation rates, 65*n*, 107, 111
labor force, US
growth and US economic resurgence, 37*t*, 40, 41*b*, 58
Japan-US comparisons, 6
labor productivity growth. *See* productivity growth, Japanese; productivity growth, US
land prices, Japanese
and bubble economy, 67-69
and financial-sector problems, 72, 81*n*

lost decade, 63
land use issues, Japanese
Japanese economic malaise overview, 107-10
trade and investment relations overview, 140
trade dispute resolution overview, 162-63
Large-Scale Retail Store Law, 137, 144, 163, 236
Law of the Sea, 229
legal proceedings, WTO. *See* World Trade Organization
legal system, Japanese. *See also specific organizations*
Japanese economic malaise overview, 107-10
and "normal Japan" US economic policy, 245-47
trade and investment relations overview, 133, 135n, 143-44
Liberal Democratic Party (LDP)
government spending, 64b
security issues, 222n
trade dispute resolution overview, 167, 190, 192
life insurance companies, Japanese, 77. *See also* financial sector, Japanese
lifetime employment, 105-06
Lincoln, Edward, 165
liquidity trap, 63, 88-91, 239, 241
Long-Term Credit Bank of Japan (LTCB), 76-77, 79

Maekawa Commission, 107
Malaysia, international financial issues, 197n
Manila Framework Group (MFG), 24, 202n, 258
Mansfield Center for Pacific Affairs, 254n
manufacturing, Japanese. *See also specific companies and sectors*
and development assistance, 215
Japanese economic malaise overview, 65, 66-67n
and "normal Japan" US economic policy, 244
trade and investment relations overview, 116-18, 147-50, 154
trade dispute resolution overview, 157
manufacturing, US. *See also specific companies and sectors*

trade and investment relations overview, 114, 116, 124
US economic resurgence overview, 38, 41
Market-Oriented Sector-Specific talks, 15, 159-62
mark-to-market accounting, 82, 85, 106, 150
Matsushita, 104b, 149n
Meltzer, Allan, 204
Meltzer Commission, 204-05, 209
mergers and acquisitions
Japanese economic malaise overview, 70, 79-80, 84
and "normal Japan" US economic policy, 235, 247-48
trade and investment relations overview, 121-23, 141, 142n, 149-50
trade dispute resolution overview, 170
military, Japanese
procurement issues, 227n
security issues, 2n, 193-94, 216-25, 219b, 220b
military, US, security issues, 170, 194, 217, 219b, 220-26, 220b, 236, 261-63
Ministry of Agriculture, Forestry, and Fisheries, 73b, 244
Ministry of Economics, Trade, and Industry (METI). *See also* Ministry of International Trade and Industry
and development assistance, 212, 213n
and "normal Japan" US economic policy, 244, 246, 264
trade and investment relations overview, 137, 191b
Ministry of Finance (MOF)
and development assistance, 209, 211, 215
international financial issues, 196, 200, 201
Japanese economic malaise overview
financial-sector problems, 70, 71b, 73-75, 73b, 74b, 77, 78, 78n, 207, 239
government spending issues, 64b
monetary policy, 93
security issues, 219b
trade and investment relations overview, 131
Ministry of Foreign Affairs (MOFA)
and development assistance, 201b, 209, 213n, 215
security issues, 220b

Other Publications from the Institute for International Economics

* = out of print

BOOKS

IMF Conditionality*   John Williamson, editor
1983   ISBN 0-88132-006-4
Trade Policy in the 1980s*   William R. Cline, editor
1983   ISBN 0-88132-031-5
Subsidies in International Trade*
Gary Clyde Hufbauer and Joanna Shelton Erb
1984   ISBN 0-88132-004-8
International Debt: Systemic Risk and Policy
Response*   William R. Cline
1984   ISBN 0-88132-015-3
Trade Protection in the United States: 31 Case
Studies*   Gary Clyde Hufbauer, Diane E. Berliner,
and Kimberly Ann Elliott
1986   ISBN 0-88132-040-4
Toward Renewed Economic Growth in Latin
America*   Bela Balassa, Gerardo M. Bueno, Pedro-
Pablo Kuczynski, and Mario Henrique Simonsen
1986   ISBN 0-88132-045-5
Capital Flight and Third World Debt*
Donald R. Lessard and John Williamson, editors
1987   ISBN 0-88132-053-6
The Canada-United States Free Trade Agreement:
The Global Impact*
Jeffrey J. Schott and Murray G. Smith, editors
1988   ISBN 0-88132-073-0
World Agricultural Trade: Building a Consensus*
William M. Miner and Dale E. Hathaway, editors
1988   ISBN 0-88132-071-3
Japan in the World Economy*
Bela Balassa and Marcus Noland
1988   ISBN 0-88132-041-2
America in the World Economy: A Strategy for
the 1990s*   C. Fred Bergsten
1988   ISBN 0-88132-089-7
Managing the Dollar: From the Plaza to the
Louvre*   Yoichi Funabashi
1988, 2d ed. 1989   ISBN 0-88132-097-8
United States External Adjustment and the World
Economy*   William R. Cline
May 1989   ISBN 0-88132-048-X
Free Trade Areas and U.S. Trade Policy*
Jeffrey J. Schott, editor
May 1989   ISBN 0-88132-094-3
Dollar Politics: Exchange Rate Policymaking in
the United States*
I.M. Destler and C. Randall Henning
September 1989   ISBN 0-88132-079-X
Latin American Adjustment: How Much Has
Happened?*   John Williamson, editor
April 1990   ISBN 0-88132-125-7
The Future of World Trade in Textiles and
Apparel*   William R. Cline
1987, 2d ed. June 1990   ISBN 0-88132-110-9

Completing the Uruguay Round: A Results-
Oriented Approach to the GATT Trade
Negotiations*   Jeffrey J. Schott, editor
September 1990   ISBN 0-88132-130-3
Economic Sanctions Reconsidered (2 volumes)
Economic Sanctions Reconsidered: Supplemental
Case Histories
Gary Clyde Hufbauer, Jeffrey J. Schott, and
Kimberly Ann Elliott
1985, 2d ed. Dec. 1990   ISBN cloth 0-88132-115-X
                        ISBN paper 0-88132-105-2
Economic Sanctions Reconsidered: History and
Current Policy
Gary Clyde Hufbauer, Jeffrey J. Schott, and
Kimberly Ann Elliott
December 1990   ISBN cloth 0-88132-140-0
                        ISBN paper 0-88132-136-2
Pacific Basin Developing Countries: Prospects for
the Future*   Marcus Noland
January 1991   ISBN cloth 0-88132-141-9
                        ISBN 0-88132-081-1
Currency Convertibility in Eastern Europe*
John Williamson, editor
October 1991   ISBN 0-88132-128-1
International Adjustment and Financing: The
Lessons of 1985-1991*   C. Fred Bergsten, editor
January 1992   ISBN 0-88132-112-5
North American Free Trade: Issues and
Recommendations*
Gary Clyde Hufbauer and Jeffrey J. Schott
April 1992   ISBN 0-88132-120-6
Narrowing the U.S. Current Account Deficit*
Allen J. Lenz
June 1992   ISBN 0-88132-103-6
The Economics of Global Warming
William R. Cline/*June 1992*   ISBN 0-88132-132-X
U.S. Taxation of International Income: Blueprint
for Reform*   Gary Clyde Hufbauer, assisted by
Joanna M. van Rooij
October 1992   ISBN 0-88132-134-6
Who's Bashing Whom? Trade Conflict in High-
Technology Industries   Laura D'Andrea Tyson
November 1992   ISBN 0-88132-106-0
Korea in the World Economy*   Il SaKong
January 1993   ISBN 0-88132-183-4
Pacific Dynamism and the International Economic
System*
C. Fred Bergsten and Marcus Noland, editors
May 1993   ISBN 0-88132-196-6
Economic Consequences of Soviet Disintegration*
John Williamson, editor
May 1993   ISBN 0-88132-190-7
Reconcilable Differences? United States-Japan
Economic Conflict*
C. Fred Bergsten and Marcus Noland
June 1993   ISBN 0-88132-129-X

Corruption and the Global Economy
Kimberly Ann Elliott
June 1997   ISBN 0-88132-233-4
Regional Trading Blocs in the World Economic
System   Jeffrey A. Frankel
October 1997   ISBN 0-88132-202-4
Sustaining the Asia Pacific Miracle:
Environmental Protection and Economic
Integration   André Dua and Daniel C. Esty
October 1997   ISBN 0-88132-250-4
Trade and Income Distribution   William R. Cline
November 1997   ISBN 0-88132-216-4
Global Competition Policy
Edward M. Graham and J. David Richardson
December 1997   ISBN 0-88132-166-4
Unfinished Business: Telecommunications after
the Uruguay Round
Gary Clyde Hufbauer and Erika Wada
December 1997   ISBN 0-88132-257-1
Financial Services Liberalization in the WTO
Wendy Dobson and Pierre Jacquet
June 1998   ISBN 0-88132-254-7
Restoring Japan's Economic Growth
Adam S. Posen
September 1998   ISBN 0-88132-262-8
Measuring the Costs of Protection in China
Zhang Shuguang, Zhang Yansheng, and Wan
Zhongxin
November 1998   ISBN 0-88132-247-4
Foreign Direct Investment and Development: The
New Policy Agenda for Developing Countries and
Economies in Transition
Theodore H. Moran
December 1998   ISBN 0-88132-258-X
Behind the Open Door: Foreign Enterprises in the
Chinese Marketplace   Daniel H. Rosen
January 1999   ISBN 0-88132-263-6
Toward A New International Financial
Architecture: A Practical Post-Asia Agenda
Barry Eichengreen
February 1999   ISBN 0-88132-270-9
Is the U.S. Trade Deficit Sustainable?
Catherine L. Mann/September 1999
ISBN 0-88132-265-2
Safeguarding Prosperity in a Global Financial
System: The Future International Financial
Architecture, Independent Task Force Report
Sponsored by the Council on Foreign Relations
Morris Goldstein, Project Director
October 1999   ISBN 0-88132-287-3
Avoiding the Apocalypse: The Future of the Two
Koreas   Marcus Noland
June 2000   ISBN 0-88132-278-4
Assessing Financial Vulnerability: An Early
Warning System for Emerging Markets
Morris Goldstein, Graciela Kaminsky, and Carmen
Reinhart
June 2000   ISBN 0-88132-237-7

Global Electronic Commerce: A Policy Primer
Catherine L. Mann, Sue E. Eckert, and Sarah
Cleeland Knight
July 2000   ISBN 0-88132-274-1
The WTO after Seattle
Jeffrey J. Schott, editor
July 2000   ISBN 0-88132-290-3
Intellectual Property Rights in the Global
Economy   Keith E. Maskus
August 2000   ISBN 0-88132-282-2
The Political Economy of the Asian Financial
Crisis   Stephan Haggard
August 2000   ISBN 0-88132-283-0
Transforming Foreign Aid: United States
Assistance in the 21st Century   Carol Lancaster
August 2000   ISBN 0-88132-291-1
Fighting the Wrong Enemy: Antiglobal Activists
and Multinational Enterprises
Edward M. Graham
September 2000   ISBN 0-88132-272-5
Globalization and the Perceptions of American
Workers
Kenneth F. Scheve and Matthew J. Slaughter
March 2001   ISBN 0-88132-295-4
World Capital Markets: Challenge to the G-10
Wendy Dobson and Gary C. Hufbauer,
assisted by Hyun Koo Cho
May 2001   ISBN 0-88132-301-2
Prospects for Free Trade in the Americas
Jeffrey J. Schott
August 2001   ISBN 0-88132-275-X
Lessons from the Old World for the New:
Constructing a North American Community
Robert A. Pastor
August 2001   ISBN 0-88132-328-4
Measuring the Costs of Protection in Europe:
European Commercial Policy in the 2000s
Patrick A. Messerlin
September2001   ISBN 0-88132-273-3
Job Loss from Imports: Measuring the Costs
Lori G. Kletzer
September 2001   ISBN 0-88132-296-2
The International Financial Architecture:
What's New? What's Missing?
Peter Kenen
September 2001   ISBN 0-88132-297-0
No More Bashing: Building a New Japan-United
States Economic Relationship
C. Fred Bergsten, Takatoshi Ito, and Marc Noland
October 2001   ISBN 0-88132-286-5

SPECIAL REPORTS

1   Promoting World Recovery: A Statement on
     Global Economic Strategy*
     by Twenty-six Economists from Fourteen
     Countries
     December 1982   ISBN 0-88132-013-7

WORKS IN PROGRESS

DISTRIBUTORS OUTSIDE THE UNITED STATES

**Australia, New Zealand, and
Papua New Guinea**
D.A. Information Services
648 Whitehorse Road
Mitcham, Victoria 3132, Australia
tel: 61-3-9210-7777
fax: 61-3-9210-7788
e-mail: service@dadirect.com.au
http://www.dadirect.com.au

Canada
Renouf Bookstore
5369 Canotek Road, Unit 1
Ottawa, Ontario K1J 9J3, Canada
tel: 613-745-2665
fax: 613-745-7660
http://www.renoufbooks.com

United Kingdom and Europe
(including Russia and Turkey)
The Eurospan Group
3 Henrietta Street, Covent Garden
London WC2E 8LU England
tel: 44-20-7240-0856
fax: 44-20-7379-0609
http://www.eurospan.co.uk

India, Bangladesh, Nepal, and Sri Lanka
Viva Books Pvt.
Mr. Vinod Vasishtha
4325/3, Ansari Rd.
Daryaganj, New Delhi-110002
India
tel: 91-11-327-9280
fax: 91-11-326-7224
e-mail: vinod.viva@gndel.globalnet.
ems.vsnl.net.in

Japan and the Republic of Korea
United Publishers Services, Ltd.
Kenkyu-Sha Bldg.
9, Kanda Surugadai 2-Chome
Chiyoda-Ku, Tokyo 101
Japan
tel: 81-3-3291-4541
fax: 81-3-3292-8610
e-mail: saito@ups.co.jp
**For trade accounts only.
Individuals will find IIE books in
leading Tokyo bookstores.**

Southeast Asia (Brunei, Cambodia,
China, Malaysia, Hong Kong, Indonesia,
Laos, Myanmar, the Philippines, Singapore,
Taiwan, and Vietnam)
Hemisphere Publication Services
1 Kallang Pudding Rd. #04-03
Golden Wheel Building
Singapore 349316
tel: 65-741-5166
fax: 65-742-9356

Thailand
Asia Books
5 Sukhumvit Rd. Soi 61
Bangkok 10110 Thailand
tel: 662-714-0740-2 Ext: 221, 222, 223
fax: 662-391-2277
e-mail: purchase@asiabooks.co.th
http://www/asiabooksonline.com

Visit our Web site at:
http://www.iie.com
E-mail orders to:
orders@iie.com